17.50
12-0

WITHDRAWN BY THE
UNIVERSITY OF MICHIGAN

# JOSEPH PULITZER
*Liberator of Journalism*

# JOSEPH PULITZER

*His Life & Letters*

*by*

DON C. SEITZ

"I have sworn upon the altar of God, eternal hostility against every form of tyranny over the mind of man."
                    THOMAS JEFFERSON.

AMS PRESS
NEW YORK

COPYRIGHT, 1924, BY
SIMON AND SCHUSTER, INC.

*Published, November, 1924*
*Second Printing, November, 1924*

Reprinted by arrangement with the original publishers.

Reprinted from the edition of 1924, New York
First AMS EDITION published 1970
Manufactured in the United States of America

International Standard Book Number: 0-404-05699-7

Library of Congress Card Catalog Number: 74-126692

AMS PRESS, INC.
New York, N.Y. 10003

## To the Memory of

JOHN A. DILLON, JOHN A. COCKERILL, J. B. McGUFFIN, WILLIAM H. MERRILL, GEORGE W. TURNER, BALLARD SMITH, JAMES F. GRAHAM, ERNEST O. CHAMBERLIN, JAMES W. CLARKE, JOSEPH D. JACKSON, WILLIAM VAN BENTHUYSEN, WILLIAM J. WARD, FREDERICK A. DUNEKA, HENRY LOOMIS NELSON, DAVID GRAHAM PHILLIPS, FOSTER COATES, GEORGE CARY EGGLESTON, JOSEPH A. ALTSHELER, ROBERT H. DEERY, GUS C. ROEDER, JOSEPH J. EAKINS, SAMUEL E. MOFFETT, JERE J. WOGAN, SYLVESTER J. E. RAWLING, JOHN NORRIS, CHARLES G. BUSH, CALEB M. VAN HAMM, ARTHUR H. BILLING, STEPHEN J. RICHARDSON, LOUIS V. DEFOE, HORATIO W. SEYMOUR, AND FRANK IRVING COBB

## Men of the World

# CONTENTS

| CHAPTER | | PAGE |
|---|---|---|
| | FOREWORD | xi |
| I. | CHARACTERISTICS | 1 |
| II. | BIRTH AND BEGINNINGS | 40 |
| III. | ST. LOUIS | 58 |
| IV. | THE POST-DISPATCH | 87 |
| V. | THE OLD "WORLD" | 115 |
| VI. | THE NEW "WORLD" | 129 |
| VII. | THE DAY'S WORK | 155 |
| VIII. | THE VENEZUELA AFFAIR | 189 |
| IX. | BRYANISM | 210 |
| X. | THE WAR WITH SPAIN | 237 |
| XI. | THE PARKER-ROOSEVELT CAMPAIGN | 256 |
| XII. | INSURANCE REFORM | 267 |
| XIII. | ROOSEVELTISM | 294 |
| XIV. | THE LAST CAMPAIGN | 323 |
| XV. | THE PANAMA PROSECUTION | 352 |
| XVI. | LAST YEARS | 386 |
| XVII. | METHODS | 416 |
| XVIII. | BENEFACTIONS | 435 |
| | GENEALOGICAL TABLE | 467 |
| | INDEX | 468 |

# ILLUSTRATIONS

|  | OPPOSITE PAGE |
|---|---|
| JOSEPH PULITZER | Frontispiece |
| ONE OF MR. PULITZER'S LAST WRITTEN MESSAGES | 21 |
| MR. PULITZER, ARTHUR H. BILLING AND EUGENE STEWART, ON THE BRIDLE PATH, CENTRAL PARK | 31 |
| RODIN, THE SCULPTOR, MODELING BUST OF MR. PULITZER | 38 |
| LOUISE BERGER | 40 |
| UDO BRACHVOGEL AND JOSEPH PULITZER | 53 |
| JOSEPH PULITZER AT TWENTY-ONE | 55 |
| MR. PULITZER AT A SUABIAN CHURCH FESTIVAL | 61 |
| MR. PULITZER AS A LEADER OF LIBERAL REPUBLICANISM | 74 |
| MR. PULITZER AT A ST. LOUIS BALL | 78 |
| MRS. KATE PULITZER AT THE TIME OF HER MARRIAGE | 90 |
| CARTOON FROM DIE LANTERNE ON BUYING THE ST. LOUIS DISPATCH | 100 |
| MR. PULITZER WELCOMING BEN BUTLER TO DEMOCRACY | 106 |
| ST. LOUIS POST-DISPATCH BUILDING | 112 |
| JOSEPH PULITZER AT FORTY | 159 |
| SITE OF THE PULITZER BUILDING, 1854 | 168 |
| THE PULITZER BUILDING, 53 TO 63 PARK ROW | 175 |
| STEAM YACHT LIBERTY | 289 |
| THE AUTHOR, MR. PULITZER AND JOSEPH PULITZER, JR. ON THE LIBERTY | 354 |
| MISS EDITH PULITZER, MR. PULITZER AND H. S. POLLARD AT MONTE CARLO | 391 |
| MR. PULITZER AND RALPH PULITZER ON FIFTH AVENUE | 405 |
| SCHOOL OF JOURNALISM | 445 |
| INNER COURT, SCHOOL OF JOURNALISM BUILDING | 453 |

# FOREWORD

SOME material for this volume was collected by the late George W. Hosmer, M.D., long Mr. Pulitzer's companion and physician, to whom was given an intimacy denied all others. In 1909, after twenty years of constant relationship, Dr. Hosmer, having passed his eightieth year, retired from active duty, took up his residence at Summit, N. J., and there began the work of writing a biography. He broke the news of his purpose to his subject in the autumn of 1910, apprising him of the fact that he had already compiled some twenty-five thousand words. This evoked the following characteristic reply:

VILLA CYNTHIA
Cap-Martin, Cabbe-Roquebrune
FRANCE (A.M.)
November 23, 1910

DEAR DOCTOR:

Just read your letter and nearly fainted when I came to the "25,000 words and still at it"!!! Why, you will beat Moneypenny. Hope you get the book (Disraeli's Life) and also Lord Acton's Essays on the French Revolution, likewise, Lord Rosebery's "Chatham." Don't fail to read Acton. It is really a wonderful work, so ought to give you a great deal of pleasure.

But returning to the 25,000 words, I wish you could write 2500 words of synopsis, or epitome, or summary, summing up as to what it is and as to what it is to conclude with.

Now for God's sake don't do this unless it gives

## Foreword

you pleasure, and don't do it then unless you are quite well.

All I can wish is that you should know how often and, in fact, how constantly I think of you and how delighted I was when your very recent letters indicated so plainly that both your health and spirits must have greatly improved.

In usual haste,
With affectionate regards,
JOSEPH PULITZER

DR. G. W. HOSMER,
SUMMIT, N. J.

Incidental with the coming of cool weather, Mr. Pulitzer had sent the Doctor a fur-lined overcoat as a remembrance and in reply to his acknowledgment, wrote, with further reference to the proposed life:

VILLA CYNTHIA,
Cap-Martin, Cabbe-Roquebrune
FRANCE (A.M.)
Dec. 22, 1910

DEAR DR. HOSMER:

Only a line to thank you for your letter of thanks. I will give you another fur coat gladly if I could get another such nice letter from you. However, I am in a dreadful hurry and with the usual headache.

The 25,000 words you mentioned still haunt me. I must confess, after considerable hesitation, that I never dreamt of your even attempting anything like a sketch of a life, or anything in fact except what you could draw from your own knowledge and observation and experience during the last twenty years, — a story of misery and decrepitude, to be sure, but still, a story of unceasing work and worry. You are the only man living who can speak from actual knowledge about my

## Foreword

connection with the editorial page. That feeble, invalidish activity was my only thought. As Mary Stuart said about her heart being left in France as she sailed for Scotland, my heart was and still is in the editorial page and will be in spirit. However, you know all this and if you do anything more, please concentrate on the last twenty years of your own personal knowledge and memory and don't bother about the previous parts. It could easily become a little history of the political record and thought of that period as mirrored by the *World*.

In great haste,
JOSEPH PULITZER

The desired summary was duly forwarded and produced what furnishes a better preface than any I can supply:

### S. Y. *Liberty*

SYRACUSE, Jan. 7, 1911

MY DEAR DOCTOR:

I have just read your 2500 word sketch and it has certainly filled me with amazement, first: that I should have forgotten my own life so completely, as many if not most of the incidents you name came at first as news, and second: that you should have such wonderful memory. There are astonishingly few mistakes in your general outline.

In my last note, dated Dec. 22nd, and dictated as usual in a hurry, there is a line which you might mistake as suggesting a summary of the history of the political or editorial thought of the last twenty years. I refer to the sentence: "It would easily become a little history of the political record and thought of the period as mirrored by the *World!*"

## Foreword

That would be too much work — hard work. I don't want you to have any more labor or trouble, *indeed you must not write a single line unless it gives you pleasurable occupation,* which writing often does give those who have the gift of expression and something to express in the way of thought and knowledge. What I meant was rather this thought and knowledge of yours of my relations to the editorial page, during our acquaintance, that is the last twenty years, which twenty years cover the period of my invalidism. Now I confess I never dreamt that you would write anything about the preceding period and if you don't mind the trouble I would rather you limited yourself to these twenty years of horrible invalidism and absenteeism of which you were a witness, if not a part, and which for some probably sympathetic motive you passed over too lightly. Now if you go over the last twenty years, I think you ought to tell *the precise truth* as you remember it. You need not send it to me. I would rather not have it, but as you are the only man who witnessed this part, you are the only one who can cover it. I think the story of my invalidism, if fully brought out, may explain many errors which I could not possibly prevent, although held responsible, and faults otherwise not understandable. Possibly, may also be a lesson in adversity and the fight against disadvantage, which seems to accompany my whole life to the end.

I hate the idea of passing away known only as the proprietor of the paper. Not property but politics was my passion, and not politics even in general, selfish sense, but politics in the sense of liberty and freedom and ideals of justice. However, I don't want to blow my horn to you, have a headache, dictate this too quickly and must

*Foreword*

stop with my cordial wishes for a very Happy New Year to you and yours.
               Affectionately,
                    J. P.

P.S. It may interest you to know that I dictate this about three hours from Messina on the way to Syracuse.

Unfortunately, Mr. Pulitzer's days were near their end when this was written and the good Doctor himself was smitten so that he never progressed beyond the 2500 word summary, a sketchy outline of events with some itineraries of voyages and notes on his patient's health. He died at Summit, June 2, 1914. So it has befallen that the work of making this volume came into my hands, I myself being the one person remaining with *The World* who had the longest association — eighteen years — with its owner.

No human enterprise lives so much in the open as a newspaper. Its sins of all sorts are visible each day in each of its pages. Mr. Pulitzer made *The World* in impulse and endeavor. He did not and could not make it in detail. No man can today master the complexities or control the pressure in the production of a modern journal with its wide survey and the crushing call for space. The amazing thing is not that mistakes abound, but that they are so few!

I have ventured to name him on the sub-title page as the Liberator of Journalism. I do not mean by this that he freed the press from any thrall not of its own making. In the great measure, American newspapers were organs of party or owners. They did not act freely, open to any cause. Mr. Pulitzer's belief that the paper was a public servant, bound by no other

[ xv ]

## Foreword

considerations than its duty to the community, and above any deference, even to its readers, came as a new and welcome doctrine, first to the public and at last to the press itself. He would not pander, he would not compromise and he made himself heard!

For all but four of his twenty-eight years' proprietorship of *The World*, Mr. Pulitzer was an invalid and for most of the time, blind. The elimination of sight was not total, but the vision allowed him was so dim that it served as a greater strain and irritation than if he had been wholly in gloom. In bright light he saw nothing. When the sky was gray, or at early twilight he could perceive surroundings, but never the printed page, except for a time, headlines. He had long ceased to try reading these. One eye, the right, was totally eclipsed by the detachment of its retina, the other suffered from a suffusion that completed the disaster.

I hope the following pages have been written in the spirit he wished. The limitations he set naturally could not be obeyed in a biography. His was too vast a personality. To me he seemed to have lived always, so wide was his knowledge, so deep his understanding, so swift his comprehension. Indeed, there was something uncanny in the certainty with which this man, sitting in darkness, could grasp events and discern motives.

Somehow, I think in the Beginning he must have been a Pathan from the Pamirs, who rode with Attila across the world, and as a later incarnation, one of Pappenheim's Pandours in the Thirty Years' War, riding in the van of battle, just as in his life he was always at the front for Liberty, Progress and the Welfare of Mankind.

D. C. S.

# JOSEPH PULITZER
*Liberator of Journalism*

# JOSEPH PULITZER

## HIS LIFE AND LETTERS

### 1847–1911

#### Chapter I

#### CHARACTERISTICS

Appearance and Temperament — Tastes and Fancies — Sidelights of Life and Action — A Lover of Music and Literature.

JOSEPH PULITZER was tall, six feet two and a half inches in height, but of a presence so commanding as to make his stature seem even greater. His hair was black and his beard a reddish brown. A forehead that bespoke the intellect behind it shaded a nose of the sort Napoleon admired; his chin though firm was small. To conceal this he always went bearded after he was thirty. His complexion was delicate and beautiful as that of a tender child and usually adorned with a tint of pink fit to be envied by the loveliest ladies. When angry or excited this tint took on a touch of fire that well betokened the passion raging within, and the fine forehead radiated wrath. His hands were those of genius, with long, slender fingers, full of warmth and magnetism. The eyes before they became clouded were of a grayish blue. Always weak, they never lent much expression to the face, yet his visage was animated and attractive.

Temperamentally, he was the type of the poet and musician; though loving music, he professed to care little for verse and rarely read it. Yet he appreciated the singers in his native tongue, and, I have often thought, really repressed his poetic instinct for fear it might be considered a weakness.

Unconscious proof of this may be found in the fact that in explaining why he employed as advertising manager C. M. Hammond, a young New Englander who proved anything but a success, Mr. Pulitzer said: "He looked to me like a poet, with his flowing blond hair and fine eyes. That made me try him."

Writing some instructions once to Irving Bacheller, then associate editor of the Sunday *World*, he thus expressed himself on verse: "I don't believe in poetry unless it is very strong and by a perfectly well known author. Never when obscure in thought or name."

The nose vexed him. If there had been any way of modifying its prominence, he would have greatly rejoiced. Once at Bar Harbor, walking from his secretary's office to the library, he bumped his proboscis on the hard edge of an open door, and fell into imprecations — not against the door or the wight who had left it open, but against the helpless nose. I forbear his description of this useful but unhappy member. Suffice it to say he consigned it to the pit below and wished it would stay there — it had always been a bane and a nuisance!

The organ was the delight of cartoonists, chief of whom to make use of it was his friend, Joseph Keppler. When idling together in the cafés of St. Louis, Keppler after racking his brains in vain for an idea and failing to scare one up, would remark: "Well, Joey, there's only one thing left to do. I'll go back to the office

## Characteristics

and draw your nose" — which he invariably did to the great disgust of the subject. When *Puck* moved from St. Louis to New York in 1875 and later became a powerful publication in English, he kept up the habit. It must be said that Mr. Pulitzer lent himself admirably to caricature despite his splendid figure and majestic ways. It was easy with a touch to exaggerate his facial characteristics, and in the hot politics which he courted he came in for many a savage thrust with the crayon.

Mr. Pulitzer's habits of thought and his later invalidism kept him aloof from affairs. Where a Horace Greeley became personally one of the shapers of a cause, Mr. Pulitzer, after the early days of his *World* ownership, was in but slight touch with individuals in politics and public life. While, for further example, John Thaddeus Delane, so long and so eminently editor of the London *Times*, was in close contact with the governing classes in England, Mr. Pulitzer held himself remote. He did not wish to be in touch with or in the confidence of political leaders. I recall once mentioning the visit of an eminent Democrat to the *World* editorial rooms. His instant comment was: "I don't like that. I don't want those fellows calling at the office."

He did not care to have an inside share in moulding matters, wishing all his efforts to appear openly on the editorial pages of his newspapers.

He believed in Liberty, Equality and Opportunity. Fraternity was not in his code. He lived most of his days apart from other men, having a feeling that this was the fate of the true journalist, that he must immolate himself upon the altar of his profession, devote his interest to his paper and have none other!

His initiative, strange as it may appear, was not extraordinary. Indeed, he frequently showed a hesitancy that verged upon timidity in adopting policies that were often very successful, urged upon him by the juniors. His strength lay in stimulation. Here he had few superiors. The *World* establishment under him was always like a great steamship, going over a regular route, streaming with lights, quivering with motion, and giving an impression of intense activity, even in commonplace moments, which were of course in the great majority.

He was a man of enormous impulses curbed by great reactions, who safeguarded himself from the effects of either by carefully warning his aids not to be swept off their feet by any order he might issue: all directions from headquarters were to be tempered by judgment or fuller information which he might not possess. If a very radical ukase came, the office custom was to reply, fixing a delayed day and hour for the execution. Usually a restraining telegram came about five minutes before the appointed moment.

Under his policy the virtues of the *World* were easily his own, while the mistakes and conflicts became readily the property of others. He suffered from overzeal, competition between minds, and errors of judgment. Yet without these much of the impetus would have been stayed and many of the great accomplishments impossible.

Some sayings of the wise and great he regarded as fundamental and gave them frequent repetition. One German philosopher who said no man had any sense until past forty enjoyed his high esteem. But the lines he liked most were these from Goethe (Sprüche. 72):

## Characteristics

Gut verloren — etwas verloren!
Musst rasch dich besinnen
Und neues gewinnen.
Ehre verloren — viel verloren!
Musst Ruhm gewinnen,
Da werden die Leute sich anders besinnen.
Mut verloren — allas verloren!
Da war' es besser: nicht geboren.

Wealth lost — something lost!
Must bestir thyself to get more.
Honor lost — much lost!
Must win fame, that the world may forget.
Courage lost — all lost!
Better thou had'st never been born.

Just as old King Frederick William of Prussia, father of Frederick the Great, was always hunting Europe over for tall men to recruit his Potsdam grenadiers, Mr. Pulitzer, who much resembled his Majesty in many ways, was forever seeking men for readers and secretaries. Ballard Smith, while London correspondent, and after him Frederick A. Duneka, David Graham Phillips and James M. Tuohy, all English representatives in the order named, were on perpetual assignment. The secretaries in office were frequently set to finding other secretaries, and George H. Ledlie, his general and personal representative, had a constant commission to find "the right man." He proved a scarce article, although Alfred Butes, a clever young Englishman, came closest to filling all the requirements. He had been in Africa with General Francis de Winton, was an accomplished stenographer, wrote an excellent hand, and above all was most discreet and deeper in his employer's confidence than any of the other young gentlemen ever penetrated. Indeed, he was destined to become a trustee of the vast estate and to receive

## Joseph Pulitzer

a handsome legacy, both of which he forfeited in 1907 to join Lord Northcliffe in a secretarial capacity. His departure was a real blow and left a gap never quite filled again — certainly not in the matter of close relationship. The duties of the secretaries were very exacting. Personal desires, like hope in Dante's hell, had to be left behind. This made the employment irksome except to men of lymphatic temperament and lovers of good living, who were most apt to be English, plus a German reader and pianist — a place long and acceptably filled by Friedrich Mann. Occasional Americans served between, with individual success, but the life palled on the lighter temperaments of the latter and they required frequent furloughs, which the more apathetic Britons did not crave. James Barnes, Samuel M. Williams and the late Henry D. Macdona were successful Yankees who always held his regard, while Harold S. Pollard, the last of the race in continuous companionship, gained his deep affection.

The young Englishmen were all men of parts — had to be to retain their hold. The late Arthur H. Billing was the son of a bishop; Norman G. Thwaites, later Lieutenant-Colonel in his Majesty's service, was the son of a canon, and Randall Davies, F.S.A., the son of a curate. These were all with him during the last years and constituted an unusual galaxy of talent. To their number, in 1908, was added William Romaine Paterson, a brilliant scholar and writer, of Scottish descent, and Alleyne Ireland, the eminent authority on British colonization and political economy. This group gave the entourage an intellectual atmosphere hard to duplicate.

It might be added that the defection of Butes to

## Characteristics

Northcliffe spoiled the friendly relations between Mr. Pulitzer and that energetic gentleman. Mr. Pulitzer had not dreamed that his faithful secretary would ever desert him, and blamed the supposed tempter, just as the Argonauts cursed the Sirens who lured another Butes from the Argo and his companions, in the classic tale of long ago! Apropos of the man hunting, the Pennells, in their *Whistler Journal*, note the efforts of Sir Theodore Andrea Cook to find the Impeccable One, Sir Theodore having been at the time a member of the entourage as tutor to the eldest son, Ralph, and a man who earned his title and much repute in the London literary world. D. S. MacColl, the art critic, was one of his suggestions. He allured MacColl with the opportunity to drink plenty of champagne and smoke the best of Havanas, but MacColl scented too much slavery in the job and refused to consider it. Charles Whibley, Whistler's brother-in-law, was induced to proceed as far as Paris and risk an interview, but on calling at the Pulitzer apartment, unfortunately kicked over and broke a costly Persian jardinière standing in the hall. This was regarded as indicating a clumsiness that would be unbearable, and the prospect ended. The Pennells quote Whistler as saying of the incident: "So like the British Boulevardier!" They also repeat his saying on another occasion that one of Whibley's duties would have been "the picking up of Pulitzer's eye that had a way of falling out and getting lost on the floor" — which of course was a mere Whistlerian bit of bad taste in reflecting on the greatest of bodily misfortunes.

The secretary who served Mr. Pulitzer longest was Dr. George W. Hosmer, who was both friend and physician, besides aiding in correspondence and selecting his literature, editing and reading the latter to his high satisfaction. He was nearly twenty years the senior of his patient and had an influence over his temperament such as no other possessed, partly from his firmness, tact and knowledge, and partly from the authority of a doctor. Though a medical man of high rank, he had practiced little, taking early to journalism under the elder Bennett on the New York *Herald*. As a war correspondent it was his privilege to report the battle of Gettysburg for the paper and to perform a great service for his country on the field. It was he who, crossing Cemetery Ridge in the gloom of the second evening, saw a dark mass moving across the fields below and gave the warning which enabled Gen. George S. Greene to hold his thin lines until the aid came that stopped Longstreet. For a time Hosmer was in charge of the London office of the *Herald* and it was his further fortune to be shut up in Paris during the days of horror contrived by the Commune. For the elder Bennett he had much respect; for the younger, none. He was wont to say of him that he was half Scotch and half Irish, and when sober, displayed the worst qualities of the one, and when drunk the worst of the other!

His taste in literature was of the finest and his knowledge exact and wonderful. To Mr. Pulitzer, no small reservoir of information himself, he was a perpetual marvel, outrivalling in memory even Prof. Thomas Davidson, Mr. Pulitzer's long-time friend and instructor in St. Louis.

"I never knew a man who knew so much, or knew it so well," he once observed, speaking of the doctor.

Knowing Mr. Pulitzer's passion for having only

## Characteristics

effectives about him, Dr. Hosmer carefully concealed his age. Clever traps were set to establish his birthday, all of which he successfully evaded for a long time, until one day in the heat of an argument over some saying by Daniel Webster, he clinched his point by remarking that he had heard the orator use the expression in a speech made at a New England Society dinner in the Astor House when he was a boy of eighteen. The occasion was at once located and the doctor's years were known.

To compress cables and telegrams a considerable code was developed through the years which included the names of men in the office, rivals in the profession, and others who had to do with business or politics, together with words to express figures. For himself he selected the cipher word "Andes," modestly taking the name of the second highest altitude on the earth's surface. He commonly went by the code name in office conversation. Mr. William H. Merrill, his chief editorial writer, was "Cantabo"; his treasurer, J. Angus Shaw, was "Solid" — a neat compliment; S. S. Carvalho was designated by a single syllable "Los"; John Norris became "Anfracto"; C. M. Van Hamn "Gyrate," illustrating perhaps the vicissitudes of a managing editor; Florence D. White was "Volema" on the wire. I was honored with three stage names, "Gulch," "Mastodon" and "Quixotic"; Dumont Clarke, his vice-president, was "Coin," a commodity with which he had much to do; Col. George B. M. Harvey was "Sawpit"; James Gordon Bennett came over the cable as "Gaiter," and William R. Hearst as "Gush." For William J. Bryan two code designations were used, "Guilder" and "Maxilla," the latter possibly a delicate reference to jaw. Pomeroy Burton

## Joseph Pulitzer

became "Gumbo," perhaps, as he himself said because he was "so often in the soup." The papers were respectively "Senior" (Morning); "Seniority" (Sunday) and "Junior" (Evening).

The code amused Mr. Pulitzer and he was forever tinkering it. During the Panama rumpus a cipher was constructed especially for it.

His telegrams and cables usually came unsigned save for a final word "Sedentary," which meant that a prompt reply was required. This commonly went back in a single word, "Semaphore," meaning "message received and understood." When in good humor and pleased he would sign personal messages "J. P." but when his wrath was high they came signed "Joseph Pulitzer." That meant trouble. In my eighteen years of association I received three bearing the ominous full signature!

His days after his withdrawal from active work were much the same: morning hours spent with papers and mail, a drive before luncheon, then an hour of reading and repose, after which he rode in a carriage or on horseback, saw visitors from five o'clock to six, dressed for a seven-thirty dinner, after a brief rest in bed, and then, leaving the table about nine, listened to a little music, and was read to sleep by one secretary or another.

Extravagant as he was in verbal expression, Mr. Pulitzer valued judgment and conservatism that waited on facts. In one of the changes of a generation in the office when the old heads vanished almost altogether, he caused each of the younger moulders of opinion to be given a beautiful set of gilded scales from Tiffany's, the implied meaning of the gift being quite plain.

*Characteristics*

When John S. Sargent was approached to paint Mr. Pulitzer's portrait in 1909, a sly secretary intimated that Sargent's specialty lay in divining the innermost weaknesses and powers of his sitters and putting them on canvas, the thought being that this subject might not like to be thus portrayed. Mr. Pulitzer grimly warned the painter not to spare him. "That is what I want," he said. "I want to be remembered just as I really am, with all my strain and suffering there." The painting presents the blind man, seated, holding a riding crop in the one hand and resting the other lightly against his cheek — a favorite attitude. The pain and invalidism of years show on his face, blended with high intellect, energy of character and fierceness of temper. It is Joseph Pulitzer as Time and Trouble moulded him.

Like most successful men, he had his superstitions, and one of these was a reverence for the figure 10. He was born on the 10th of April, reached St. Louis on the 10th of October, consolidated the *Post* with the *Dispatch* on the 10th of December, 1878, bought the *World* on the 10th of May, 1883 — and won. He made the superstition something of a fad and used the numerals always when he could. In buying his first New York house, he selected No. 10 East 55th Street — the two fives adding another 10.

Lastly he cut the price of his morning newspaper from two cents to one on February 10, 1896, and began the expensive duel with the millions of the Hearst estate. The result of the latter experiment was not to his liking and he lost interest in the superstition in his later years. But the dates remain milestones to be remembered in considering his extraordinary career.

## Joseph Pulitzer

Perhaps his birth, on the eve of the great revolutionary period of 1848, bred in him something atavistic, for all his life he was a passionate devotee of the cause of Liberty — liberty of action, of opinion, of Government. He opposed all sumptuary legislation, all tax law inequities, all political bossism, whether of the party or its leaders, and, above all, war!

Meal-times were play hours. At the table liberty of speech was the rule and the guests and secretaries had full freedom to express themselves without regard to the feelings of the host. Sometimes the fire became pretty hot and he would retreat to have his dessert and coffee alone. Violent disputes about music, literature, politics, history and art were the rule, with not infrequent assaults upon his own opinion and the ways of the *World* tempered by anecdotes and good stories. He loved table talk of this sort. "Tell me a good story" was his most frequent greeting to a guest. His mind was so active and projective that it was hard to set him to reminiscing; when he did venture back over the travelled road, the tale was worth hearing.

He loved art and music, a taste reflected in the great benefactions made to the Philharmonic Society and the Metropolitan Museum of Art in his will. When sight grew dim, as with most blind people, melody became a solace. The piano especially appealed to him and he heard great players whenever possible. Now and then Paderewski would pay him a visit and there would be a carnival of piano playing. The strings came next. His winters on the Riviera were made happy by the splendid orchestra maintained at Monte Carlo by the Prince of Monaco. The group of secretaries always included one excellent pianist

## Characteristics

whose duties were by no means light and whose slightest error in technique met with instant and fierce rebuke. Like Napoleon, his omnivorousness and great curiosity gave him a tremendous appetite. He was most insistent about his meals; ate often and heavily, frequently awakening in the night to satisfy his hunger with an extra meal.

He was fond of luxury; always craved and secured the best. This was from no vainglory of extravagance, following the acquisition of wealth, but was an inborn instinct, which he nearly always managed to gratify even when poor. He wished to be warm, to sleep well, to be comfortably housed and to have at his command good books and valued publications. In his later years he spent at least twelve hours of the day in bed. His afternoon nap was the trial of his valet and the terror of fellow travellers. Rooms had to be kept vacant above, below and on either side of him at hotels; and the White Star Line, upon whose steamers he usually made his European voyages, kept his good will for many years by maintaining a huge drugget made of manila rope which was spread upon the deck so that the footsteps of the idlers on the promenade deck could not jar his slumbers in the stateroom below.

This desire for silence became almost a mania. The great house, Chatwold, at Bar Harbor, had added to it in 1895 a huge granite pile, called the "Tower of Silence" by some of the humorous inmates, with specially constructed walls and partitions designed to shut out all noise — which they did not do. The new city mansion, Nos. 7 and 15 East 73rd Street, New York, built in 1902, failed to provide soundproof quarters in spite of much planning by the architects, McKim, Mead & White. Indeed, his rooms seemed to be haunted by noise, among the varieties of which was a strange knocking that nearly drove him frantic. In building the house, a living spring that could not be suppressed was found in the cellar. It was fed into a sump-pit; this in turn was emptied by an automatic pump operated by electricity, which started when the water reached a certain level and stopped when lowered. By rare fatality the pump had been placed so that the drum of the re-direct heating system acted as a sounding board and spread the incidental vibrations through the house, centring most loudly in Mr. Pulitzer's bedroom. The pump was shifted under the sidewalk, but he abandoned the room and built a single story annex in the yard, with double walls packed with mineral wool. The windows were guarded by triple glass; ventilation was by the fireplace chimney. He was sure that the jar of early morning whistles found its way to his ears by this opening. Silk threads were stretched across it to break the sound. Three doors were hung in the short passage from the main mansion, the floor of which was on ball bearings to prevent vibration. Here at last he found zero. The room was so still as to be uncanny.

Behind the Tower of Silence at Chatwold was a little balcony overhanging a rock-lined canyon through which a noisy brook went babbling to the awaiting sea. This was his favorite resting-place. Here he would sit in the cool of the morning, or in the grateful shade of the afternoon, listening to the threnody of the surf breaking almost under his feet, and gaining a tranquillity denied him elsewhere in the clatter of life.

The entourage came at times to be skeptical about Mr. Pulitzer's sensitiveness to noises, but rarely dared to experiment. Once when the *Liberty* was in dock

## Characteristics

at Marseilles a local carriage was hired by Norman G. Thwaites, then secretary, for a morning's ride. Mr. Pulitzer joined him, with Harold S. Pollard, his reader and companion. Hardly had the equipage reached the park when a wheel began squeaking outrageously. Mr. Thwaites nerved himself for an explosion. None came. Instead Mr. P. remarked sweetly: "There must be a great many birds in this park, Thwaites." Thwaites had not seen any but he assented that it was quite possible as there were plenty of trees.

"Tweet-tweet, tweet-tweet" went the wretched axle. "Really, now," said Andes, "can't you hear them singing. It is very delightful."

Just as his auricular nerves were abnormally sensitive to noises, so those of his olfactory cells shared this quality as to odors. Perfumes he especially disliked. On one occasion, while at Cap Martin, a luckless British medico who came highly recommended all the way from London to be surgeon of the *Liberty*, for the first time in his life loaded his pocket-handkerchief with patchouli. By some mischance a whiff of this reached J. P. before the candidate was presented, and roused him to fury. The doctor was taken below by a valet and deodorized before he could be examined. The incident unsettled him so that he declined the berth. A jeweller from Nice, well scented after the French fashion, boarded the yacht one day with a selection of his wares to be purchased as holiday gifts. He smelled like all the flowers of nearby Grasse, whence come the essences of the world. A thoughtful secretary placed the merchant where a strong wind blew his savor out to sea and so saved the situation and the sale.

## Joseph Pulitzer

Mr. Pulitzer cared little for the Evening or Sunday editions of the *World*, beyond expecting them to prosper, which both did amazingly, reserving his interest and affection for the six-day morning issue, which he regarded as his paper. The others were mere commercial enterprises, but the Morning *World* contained his soul — and that of the establishment. He lavished money on it, leaving the evening edition to get along with a slender force, though one of much talent. In time the Evening grew into a sort of full independence of him and his ideas and became what it is today.

The *World* was managed by its managers and edited by its editors. He suggested freely, but ordered little. Final judgment was always with the office. He once advised the business manager that he could do anything on behalf of the paper except hunt for the North Pole, or back the invention of a flying machine, both ideas seeming chimerical to him. Within less than a decade after this adjuration the Pole was located and the machine that flew became an accomplished fact. He lived to see both. Indeed, it was the *World's* award of $10,000 to Glenn Curtiss for flying from Albany to New York that enabled that aviator and inventor to establish the great business which grew about his name.

He was always interesting, seldom companionable, taking all he could from the minds of others, but rarely giving much back, his method being to dispute and to reap the benefits of an aroused defense.

Thus he became a great hunter for facts. Often at luncheon and dinner when a free-for-all conversation took place, some remark would arouse a dispute over accuracy of statement. If the question could not be

[ 16 ]

## Characteristics

settled by some one at the board, then he commanded a charge on all the reference books at hand and there was no rest until the doubt was cleared up. The waiters were prohibited from serving more food until this happened. The facts found, he would listen intently to their reading and they remained in his mind forever. The best of dinners would be much improved for him if there had been added a satisfying fact-hunt. He would puff his cigar, pat the pile of reference books lovingly with his graceful hands, and smile in deep content.

He was devoted to the memory of his mother and carried wherever he went a miniature of her comely face, which reposed always upon his dressing table.

He told with tender amusement how he grew so tall before leaving home he had to stoop in order that she could box his ears conveniently.

Usually each Fall, after election, the *World's* circulation dropped. Mr. Pulitzer would credit the slump to the errors of the editors during the campaign, and a shake-up almost always followed. One year there was no election, with the same result. Much puzzled, he called for a solution of the mystery. It proved to be due to the shortening of the daylight hours, comparative figures showing that the paper always grew in the lengthening days. Appeased, he left the staff in peace on this one count at any rate.

He disliked greed in any form. When his younger brother Albert, fresh from Europe, came to St. Louis in 1867, ice cream was a discovery for the youth, and he developed an inordinate fondness for the delicacy to the great wrath of the elder, whose reproof led to the beginning of an unfriendliness that ended in total estrangement for the last twenty years of Albert's life. Joseph had in him much of the lofty and spiritual, Albert was of the earth earthy. No two natures could have been more widely apart.

While he was interested in heredity, like Junot, he knew he was his own ancestor. "Men are made by environment, not by birth," was his final conclusion.

Discussing some passing matter, a secretary used the phrase "your friends." "My friends," interrupted Mr. Pulitzer ironically. "I have no friends. The fellows in the office will not let me have any."

This was in a great measure true. But the "fellows in the office" did not have any either, and he knew it and delighted in the singleness of their devotion to the *World*. There was no list of "sacred cows" in the place, nor any Index Expurgatorius. The facts had to warrant the story. That was the only rule.

The wide-open columns of the *World* were truly at the service of its readers. Lieut. William Nephew King, who occasionally did naval stories, was covering the sea scandal growing out of the disciplinary methods of Capt. Bowman H. McCalla. Colonel Cockerill asked him to write an editorial comment. King sought instructions as to Mr. Pulitzer's policy. "Write what you believe to be right," replied the colonel. "Mr. Pulitzer has no friends and no enemies. He has no policy that interferes with facts."

This was strictly true. In the multitude of telegrams and letters received by the *World* editors only two or three prescribe tenderness to individuals. He liked Chief Justice Ingraham, head of the Appellate Division of the Supreme Court in New York, and when that gentleman was under fire in 1907 he telephoned: "Please tell Speer Judge Ingraham is my friend, an

## Characteristics

able judge, and an honorable man. Please treat him leniently nevertheless."

With no apparent religious predilections, Mr. Pulitzer was catholic in his respect for those of others. Mrs. Pulitzer and the family were Episcopalians and he himself greatly admired Dr. W. S. Rainsford, when pastor of St. George's in New York, which was first attended. Later, when his residence was removed to 55th Street, St. Thomas' Church became the affiliation, and he transferred his regards to Dr. E. M. Stires. He rarely, if ever, went to church at all. There was a small Episcopal chapel at Jekyl Island and one Sunday morning, a visitor was surprised to see Dr. G. W. Hosmer enter its portals just as the service began and retire after a brief sojourn. Knowing the Doctor's very pronounced anti-clerical views, he asked Alfred Butes if the old boy had repented. "No," he replied. "Each Sunday morning Dr. Hosmer goes to chapel and remains until the offertory is taken up, when he places a new $5 bill on the plate and decorously retires. Mr. Pulitzer has then attended church."

His table was graced with the best vintages, the finest Moselles, burgundies and champagnes and Johannisberger from Metternich's famous Schloss. Yet he drank little, rarely more than a single glass. Indeed, he abhorred excess and doubted the ability of men to carry large cargoes of liquids. He was belittling the stories of drinking bouts one evening at dinner at Chatwold, when Arthur H. Billing remarked that in England it was quite common for a gentleman to consume a quart of champagne without visible inconvenience. "Impossible!" said Mr. Pulitzer.

Mr. Billing modestly suggested that he could

## Joseph Pulitzer

accomplish the feat himself if supplied with the bottle. "Good," said Mr. Pulitzer, "we will test it now. Mark [the butler], bring a quart of Mumm and place it before Mr. Billing. Seitz, you shall umpire and see that he drinks it to the last drop. Make sure that there is no shirking!"

The chilly quart came in. Mr. Billing drank it in the course of fifteen minutes. He was quite undisturbed by the feat and Mr. Pulitzer much discomfited. He avoided champagne himself, because the gases went quickly to his head and so he thought it would serve Billing.

His love of chess was cherished so long as his sight made playing possible. He had a special set of chessmen made, of large size, to render them plainer to his fading vision. In time it became impossible to employ even these. During the early days of his exile, when at Beaulieu, Arthur Brisbane sought to allay the tedium by reviving Mr. Pulitzer's interest in the seductive game of draw poker. All went well until Arthur's winnings at a sitting ran up to $500. Mr. Pulitzer paid up but discontinued the diversion. Long afterwards, Joseph, Jr., chanced to remark that he had taken up the game, for amusement — carefully adding that the "limit" was 25 cents, and that he found it entertaining. "I don't know about that, Joseph," remarked his father doubtfully. "I am afraid you will find it a rather dangerous accomplishment." When he played, before his eyes were quite closed, he used cards with enlarged markings.

As he must needs carry much in his memory his struggle to acquire exact information was always a severe test to the one questioned. When in Berlin, being in doubt as to the routing of a train, and having

ONE OF MR. PULITZER'S LAST WRITTEN MESSAGES

## Characteristics

no confidence in the reports brought by his staff, he sent for an official. He came in the person of a very dapper young Prussian, who went in with all the assurance of a bureaucrat and came out in collapse, saying that he had never in his life passed through such an ordeal. Mr. Pulitzer was quite bland. "That young man seemed far from a fool," he observed. "I am glad I was kind to him."

His handwriting was large, Gothic and aggressive. Its characters became exaggerated with failing sight until but a few words adorned the page. He wrote his signature as he wrote his life, big and bold.

"Forever unsatisfied" described his temperament in more ways than his use of the words in expressing his idea of the paper's public duties. He was forever unsatisfied, not so much with the results as with the thought that if a further effort had been made, a sterner command, or greater encouragement given, as the case might be, more could have been accomplished. His intense desire for the superlative often left him with not even a good comparative to pay for all the tumult raised. Curiously he was most pestiferous in his urgings and drivings when all was going at its best. In times of trouble he rested his lash. Men were left unhampered in their responsibilities; seldom chided when they failed, if there was evidence that they had tried to succeed, and richly rewarded if they triumphed.

Some one once discussing a problem remarked that it was one of extreme difficulty. "Yes," replied Mr. Pulitzer, "but what is a difficulty? Something to be overcome!"

Another high quality he had; to use poker parlance, was that he never would "call" any one. From the same characteristic no one could "call" him. People who tried it were usually sorry.

Men came and went from the *World*, and even where their going was not creditable, he rarely interfered with their return. The rigid rule once kept by the *Herald* that to leave was to mean good-bye did not prevail. He hated to have men go, was pleased when they did well elsewhere, and bore them all good-will, even some who little deserved it. Men who slipped up through the use of liquor always received consideration, and others to whom alimony was a burden in New York, were allowed to evade it in St. Louis.

Unlike his great rival, Mr. Bennett, Mr. Pulitzer was a believer in men. If any problem arose in the conduct of the *World* his first question was always: "Where is the man? Get the man and there will be no problem."

All newspapers have periods of "flattening out" when the entire editorial force needs a reinvigorating. During one of these spells on the *World*, Mr. Pulitzer was sojourning at Lakewood, New Jersey. He sent for the business manager, who, having had much experience as an editor and with editors, was usually called in on such occasions. Mr. Pulitzer wished to know the cause of the dullness. The business manager thought the boys were track-sore and suggested a "shake-up" — meaning a shifting of jobs, familiar to all press-workers in the metropolis, invented, it is believed, by the younger James Gordon Bennett, who sometimes made weird transpositions in his endeavors to stimulate the staff.

Mr. Pulitzer liked this style of experiment, but this time it did not appeal to him.

"I don't think that's the reason," he said. "I

## Characteristics

think it's because nobody on the staff gets drunk. Brad (Bradford Merrill, then editorial manager), never gets drunk; Burton (city editor) lives in Flatbush — he never gets drunk; Van Hamm (managing editor) sleeps out in New Jersey, he never gets drunk; Lyman (night managing editor) he's always sober. You live in Brooklyn and never get drunk. When I was there some one always got drunk, and we made a great paper. Take the next train back to the city, find a man who gets drunk, and hire him at once."

Returning on this strange errand, when crossing Park Row, the business manager ran into a very brilliant writer whom he had long known as a friend of the flowing bowl. He looked down-at-the-heel and depressed.

"What are you doing?" he was asked.

"Nothing," was the glum response.

"I thought you were on the *American?* What's the trouble?"

"Same old thing," was the dolorous response. "I can't let the hard stuff alone."

So he was still eligible. "Good!" cried the business manager, "I have a life job for you."

With that he dragged him into the office and nailed him to the payroll. Supplementing this the Flatbush city editor was given two weeks' board at the Waldorf-Astoria to get some acquaintance with New York.

Curiously enough, the paper responded to the prescription and became lively again.

The talented gentleman had one narrow escape of separation from his salary due to an effort to hit a blue dog which he once thought he saw in the ground-glass door of the managing editor's room, when, striking the animal in self-defense, he cut a vein in his wrist. The surgeon tied it up in the nick of time. He never lost his position, surviving even the interference of prohibition.

As Mr. Pulitzer was troubled with touches of asthma, the *Liberty* was often set in motion for no other object than to create a breeze which would pour fresh air into his gasping nostrils. "Find a breeze" was the most frequent sailing order. He was a reckless navigator, defying harbor rules and often taking great risks from storm and tide. Odd as it may seem, he knew nothing of the latter phenomenon and had to be argued with when told it was a factor to be reckoned with when the *Liberty* strayed outside of the Herculean Straits.

Five round trips he drove the noble vessel across the Atlantic, to the despair of his entourage. The idle cruising in the Mediterranean in touch with shore and many joyous ports was great fun, but the long days on the dull Atlantic were appalling to all but J. P.

"Always der cold gray sky, always der cold gray sea," moaned Dr. Friedrich Mann, his German reader and pianist. It was well described in the phrase.

Once he astounded the family by anchoring off Chatwold one bright morning, having come home, without warning, straight across the sea.

In the early days of semi-blindness, when Arthur Brisbane kept Mr. Pulitzer company with the purpose of being "developed" under the master's eye, they were making a stay at Newport. The horses were called for an early morning ride, and as the road was barred by toll-gates, Brisbane was told to get some money. He procured a $2 bill from the private secretary's funds, and stood outside awaiting J. P. The morning was misty and he came out to the street grumbling about the darkness. Brisbane had twisted the bill

## Characteristics

into an imitation of a lamp-lighter and was idly waving it in the air.

"Fog, fog, nothing but fog," growled the great man. "How can I see to ride I'd like to know, in such a mist as this? — Brisbane, give me that money!" Incidentally he never carried any cash about him, and made much of having a process server hand him a $2 fee on the street in front of his house one morning, as the first he had really received with his own hands for many years.

He liked to feel that he had his money's worth, was willing that the value should be worthy of receipt, but he hated malingering and imposition. An old associate from St. Louis was given employment in the office. He was a genial gentleman, beloved by everybody, but, if he did not think so, acted at least as if the *World* owed him a living. Summoned to Europe, as a treat, and for companionship, he returned on the same steamer with his employer and Dr. St. Clair McKelway, then editor of the Brooklyn *Eagle*. Discussing human failings on the deck one day, Mr. Pulitzer deplored the ingratitude of men who did not appreciate the consideration of employers and how much they owed to it. The gentleman from the office spoke up briskly and said: "I don't know about that. I'd a great deal rather do nothing on the *World* than work on any other newspaper."

The words sank in, and when the ship got to New York, the speaker's last "string" was measured up. He had been living up to his ideal. His $100 a week salary was stopped and he was put on space — but at $20 a column. The rate would enable him to earn his old pay, if he exerted himself, which he did not try very hard to do and so seldom lifted his earnings above

## Joseph Pulitzer

$80. Satisfied with the form of reproof, Mr. Pulitzer in time restored the salary.

Although Col. John A. Cockerill fell out of the organization and set up disastrously for himself, Mr. Pulitzer's thoughts of him were always kind. He had stood by the colonel in the Slayback tragedy of St. Louis, and had battled with many differences of opinion, but had no hard feelings over the desertion. One of his oft-repeated pleasures was to recite how he had converted Cockerill into a sincere civil service reformer. He liked to have men own up promptly when wrong. Cockerill did this. "You know," Mr. Pulitzer once said, "Cockerill was an army man. He went into the war with his father, when he was fifteen years old. He had an army vocabulary. It made him rough of speech and picturesquely profane. I have a weakness I have never been able to overcome. When Cockerill would say, 'I've been a d——d fool; wrong, d——d wrong,' I always melted."

Quoting Mrs. Elizabeth Bisland Wetmore's biography of Lafcadio Hearn, where Hearn described his adventures on joining the staff of the Cincinnati *Enquirer*, I mentioned his description of Cockerill, then city editor of that journal, as "a sort of furious young person," leaving the impression that he was brutal.

Mr. Pulitzer flared up. "Cockerill was not brutal," he exclaimed. "He was as tender-hearted as a child."

I explained that Hearn found him so later; this was a first impression. The explanation did not mollify him. He scolded poor Hearn by proxy for some moments.

When some new delight came his way, he liked to pass it on to those he wished to reward or encourage. Coming from the mild and humid central Mississippi

## Characteristics

Valley, he found the New York winter chilly and took to a fur-lined overcoat for protection. This was before the days of heated street cars or comfortable subways, and the heavy garment gave him great content. Soon the men of mark on the *World* were garbed in fur with the compliments of the owner. When his eyes grew troublesome, he secured needed shade from the flexible brim of a Panama hat. Presto! all the favorites were likewise bedecked. He had great regard for the tall silk hat and always wore one on occasions that seemed important. He usually closed all arguments with a bet when the talk grew too strenuous, and the wager took the form of a hat, frequently five hats.

In time of business stress Mr. Pulitzer would never press debtors for money. More than one large advertiser had occasion to thank him for his willingness to carry him until his load lightened.

He affected to like the play and the opera, but seldom sat through either. Unable to see, and hearing acutely, he missed the action on the stage and received full portions of the buzz in the adjacent boxes. If the piece dragged a bit he would depart after the second act. So eager was he for movement that he wanted the whole play crowded into the first act. Of actors he had varying opinions. John McCullough was a personal friend, much admired. So was Charles Wyndham, the admirable English comedian. The death of Henry Irving caused him to suggest an article on the stage in these terms: "Who is the greatest living actor left in any country? Irving himself, greatest mechanic, upholsterer, manager. Bad actor, but still deserving great fame because of high ideals. Wretched enunciation! Burial in Westminster Abbey wonderful compliment. Is there a single great actor or actress in the United States? Why not? Compare with thirty years ago. Why this decline in the United States and in England, and not in Germany and France? In Germany they give a thousand times as many classical plays as in England or the United States — even Shakespeare and other English classics."

The response to this came in the form of an article on "Irving and the English stage." Mr. Pulitzer erupted:

"The head is commonplace. Primarily heads must have more attention if they are to strike the eye, to hold the attention. Tree [Beerbohm] is a wretched actor. I'll swear to that. Why puff him? He's worse than Irving. Pay more attention to instructions. Article very, very bad throughout; hardly contains a thought. I want the topic treated again every Sunday until the real thought, the knowledge of this popular, not academic subject is made clear. 'The decay of the English stage' — Why the decay of the English stage? If I have to do this myself some one must come to me with a stenographer."

While severely critical of the *World* and its makers, Mr. Pulitzer could not brook the least disapproval of either from others. One day at Bar Harbor, after a period of very acrimonious faultfinding, he wound up with this blanket condemnation of the shop: "It has no head, no sense, no brains."

This passed in silence, but later in the day he broached a suggestion to which I replied that the idea had been tried by the *Herald* without success.

"Why do you mention the *Herald?*" he interrupted sharply. "They have no head, no sense, no brains!"

"Neither have we," I replied.

## Characteristics

He reached his long arm forward, and grasping my throat choked it vigorously and remarked reprovingly: "Stop that! You are altogether too critical and unjust to the office!"

His speeches during the Greeley campaign were all made in German, his familiar tongue. When he came to stump for Tilden, he employed English. This was not an easy task, for he thought in German and had to translate it as he talked. To facilitate clearness of expression he laboriously wrote out his addresses in English and committed them to memory as formed on paper. When he spoke in later years, after coming to New York, he had acquired the habit of thinking in English, and when asked to make an address in German during the Nicoll campaign, found it very difficult to comply. In his after years of retirement he took up German again and used it faultlessly, cultivating the language, through skilled readers, from the best books in German literature.

He liked William C. Whitney, and would occasionally visit him on Sundays, talking politics and economics, in which both were deeply versed. He always asked about Miss Dorothy Whitney, who was one of his last memories before his eyes grew dim. She married the late Willard D. Straight.

"You know," he once said, "before I lost my eyes I used to walk around and talk politics with Whitney. He was so very interesting. This young lady, then a little girl, would climb upon my knees and pull my whiskers. So she stays in my memory as among the last of those whom I could see. I shall always be interested in her."

Mr. Pulitzer read omnivorously. He was always buying books. One of his great griefs over the fire that destroyed his 55th Street mansion was the total loss of his library. He was not a "collector" in any sense, but loved his volumes for what they contained. Naturally, for one who read so much by proxy he was impatient of the prolix. For another thing, books are made from books, and much that came to his ears he had heard before. The most successful readers, like Dr. G. W. Hosmer and Harold S. Pollard, learned to edit new books in the light of what had already been read, and succeeded by tactful omission in overcoming impatience with the authors and themselves.

Of Colonel Harvey he once said, "I knew he wouldn't do as a managing editor, when I learned he refused to allow the elevator to stop to let anyone on or off while he was in it."

Beyond this penchant for monopoly in levitation, Mr. Pulitzer admired the colonel and was his firm friend all through the years. He was a frequent visitor, his touch with public characters and interest in affairs giving his host a contact of the sort he desired with men and things from which he was personally barred by indisposition. In July, 1907, the colonel was being battered more or less by the *World's* editors, the page being in charge of Frank I. Cobb and Horatio W. Seymour. Mr. Pulitzer wired from Bar Harbor:

> Tell Cobb, Seymour, etc. to treat Harvey more gently, even when he is wrong. Able, brainy fellow and one of my boys. A little joke now and then all right, but don't handle him too severely. I like him.

He had the oriental idea of democracy, that talent was the sole password to position. Inherited wealth and a place in society he ignored. He liked men who

MR. PULITZER, ARTHUR H. BILLING AND EUGENE STEWART, ON THE BRIDLE PATH, CENTRAL PARK.

## Characteristics

would make their own way and brushed aside the cultivated drones who barred their path.

He loved horses and rode with the grace and freedom of one to the saddle born. Always in good weather, at home or abroad, an afternoon ride was the rule. As he became more blind, the speed dropped to a trot, but his seat was secure and his mastery of his steed perfect. Good horses were plentiful before the automobile drove them out of use. At one time the Chatwold stables contained twenty-six animals. He was slow in taking to the auto, but once converted "took" to it amazingly. Indeed, he liked speed. To be in motion was his incessant delight. For this reason he made long and seemingly purposeless journeys. Life soon became dreary when he settled down for a time. The thought of moving cheered him up and in motion he was serenely amiable.

Like most of us who were fed educationally on Homer in our youth, Mr. Pulitzer reserved the Odyssey as a treasure to be enjoyed in riper years. He long looked forward to a reading repast when he came to the celebrated episode of the wooden horse which beguiled the curious Trojans into a trap, that cost them their city. Coming to the event, he found it described in seven rather dull lines. "I was so d——d mad," he remarked "that I could have kicked Homer!"

His passionate desire to know what was going on, and his capacity for exhausting interest, made the lot of a reader very exacting. Samuel M. Williams, a member of the reportorial staff of the *World*, was often requisitioned for this service when the others gave out, as they so frequently did. Mr. Williams was a handsome, athletic young man and besides reading the papers, rode with Mr. Pulitzer when the afternoon cavalcade went out on horseback from Chatwold, or on the Riviera. Mr. Pulitzer was also fond of swimming, and Mr. Williams sometimes kept him company in the pool at Chatwold. On one occasion Mr. Pulitzer took a deep and satisfactory dive. Just how long he had been separated from the day's doings is not recorded, but on "coming up," as soon as dripping beard and puffing lungs would permit, he called out: "Well, Williams, what's the news?"

He carried a fine repeater watch and when bored beyond expression in words would touch the spring and set it to ringing. If this failed, a long-drawn-out sigh usually suppressed the narrator.

Mr. Pulitzer delighted in refashioning the habits of thought of the men closely associated with him in the management of the *World*. By this it is not meant that he sought to warp their personal opinions, but to drill them into a catholic view of journalism and statecraft and patience with fools.

When in 1908 he decided to support William Jennings Bryan for the presidency, after twelve years of opposition to his doctrines, he put the question first up to a council of editors and department heads. The consensus was that as opposition ought to be rallied and as it refused to rally to any one else, Bryan should be supported. When the election was over and Mr. Bryan had been roundly defeated by William H. Taft, Mr. Pulitzer idly inquired how the men in the council had voted and was quite vexed to find that all of them had cast their ballots for Bryan.

"I didn't mean that they should do that," he said. "I hope no one had such a thought. I did not want to influence them at all."

*Characteristics*

He was assured that not one voted because of his determination, but that getting interested, they felt like backing their efforts, and as usual after great conflicts "went with the paper." This did not satisfy him.

To one of the young men of his shop who afterwards rose to high rank on the *World*, Mr. Pulitzer remarked: "I wish I could take your brain apart and look into it."

"I don't," the youngster said. "I am afraid you would mix up the parts and never get them in place again."

His blindness caused him to test men severely. He could learn the shape of an article by touch, but the qualities of a man could only be ascertained by intellectual pressure, and this he applied so searchingly as to seem merciless. Yet it can be truthfully recorded that no survivor ever failed at his task. It is a rather unique distinction that *World* graduates did not "fall down" when they went elsewhere.

The new men on the paper were always under scrutiny and the old ones never free from the test. One day at the lunch table at Bar Harbor, in October, 1899, the company was discussing the achievements of an able reporter, C. W. Tyler, who had just done a very good piece of work. Mr. Pulitzer was complimenting Tyler highly. Professor Thomas Davidson, who was present, spoke up and said: "I cannot understand why it is, Mr. Pulitzer, that you always speak so kindly of reporters and so severely of all editors." "Well," he replied, "I suppose it is because every reporter is a hope, and every editor is a disappointment." Apropos this attitude, a story, possibly apocryphal, that travelled after Mr. Pulitzer's death, emphasizes the point:

## Joseph Pulitzer

"Mr. Pulitzer," said the narrator, "treated his reporters like sons, and I may say without hyperbole that they respected and loved their blind and ailing and indomitable chief in a truly filial manner.

"There's a story it will do no harm to tell — a story illustrating the reporter's feelings toward Mr. Pulitzer.

"A reporter was sent to cover a revival meeting, and in the midst of the proceedings an exhorter bent over the young man and said: 'Will you not come forward?'

"'Excuse me,' was the reply, 'but I am a reporter, and I am here only on business.'

"'But,' said the revivalist, 'there is no business so momentous as the Lord's.'

"'Maybe not,' answered the reporter, 'but you don't know Mr. Pulitzer.'"

Oriental as he was, Mr. Pulitzer never divined the lines of Hafiz:

> Ten dervishes upon one mat sleep well;
> Two kings cannot within one kingdom dwell.

It was his habit to always require two men on the same job and to then let them fight it out, often to his own discomfiture and despair. The office theory was that he liked competition and sought to gain advantage by the strivings of one man to outdo the other. If this was correct, it never worked; either hopeless deadlocks followed or the men divided their domain and lived peacefully. There was probably something in the theory, but much more was it due to the habit of precaution which came upon him early in life. He always wanted to have a second resource in hand if one chanced to fail him, plus being free from hold-ups on the part of any gentleman who might think himself super-valuable.

## Characteristics

Mr. Pulitzer went to great pains to sort out men for trustees in his will. One of those put to the test was Morgan J. O'Brien, then presiding justice of the Appellate Division in New York. The editor took the jurist to ride and confided unto him his purpose. It looked good to the judge, who assumed a receptive air.

"What do you think of the *World?*" asked Mr. Pulitzer after the thing seemed settled.

"It is a great paper," replied the judge, "but it has one great defect."

"What is that?"

"It never stands by its friends."

"A newspaper should have no friends," rejoined Mr. Pulitzer tartly.

"I think it should," responded the judge sturdily.

"Well," retorted Mr. Pulitzer, "if that's your opinion, I wouldn't make you one of my trustees if you gave me a million dollars."

The considerable fortune left by Mr. Pulitzer was enhanced by the profitable outcome of wise investments in American securities listed on the New York Stock Exchange. They were not made primarily with this intent but to protect the *World*. When the paper began piling up money, with his customary caution, he looked ahead for lean years. He wished to be securely beyond the need of borrowing from banks, feeling that this might lead to his getting into the hands of the moneyed interests. So he picked out what appeared to be the soundest securities in the list for which there was always a certain market. The paper rarely needed his aid and the investments grew with the years and the increasing prosperity of the country. When his property was listed, but one

## Joseph Pulitzer

worthless item was found, a twenty-share certificate in some long-forgotten effort to build a railroad in Missouri. Every other item had held, or increased its value. Some had repaid him more than three hundred per cent!

He bought stocks in large lots — 2,000, 3,000, and 5,000 shares, always in even numbers so that the holdings might easily be carried in his memory. Some of these vast blocks were made up of Delaware, Lackawanna & Western, Lake Shore, Central Railroad of New Jersey, and like gilt-edges. They were bought at the instance of the late Dumont Clarke, president of the American Exchange National Bank, and long vice-president of the Press Publishing Company, though having no relation to the production of the *World*. To Mr. Clarke's sound judgment Mr. Pulitzer added his own with the highly satisfactory results noted. Mr. Pulitzer had himself a fear of the influence of his growing wealth upon his views and their consequent reflection in the paper. In 1907 he sent for Frank I. Cobb, his chief editorial writer. It was during tremors that preceded the "Roosevelt" panic. The editor was addressed in this wise: "Boy, I am, as you probably know, a large owner of stocks. Some of them are bound to be affected by public action. I am not sure of myself when I see my interests in danger. I might give way some day to such a feeling and send you an order that would mean a change in the paper's policy. I want you to make me a promise. If I ever do such a thing swear you will ignore my wishes."

The promise was made, but no such order ever came. It would have passed unheeded had it come, so thorough was the singleness of purpose with which the paper was suffused. Once in a while the traffic manager of

## Characteristics

the Western Union would claim a larger share of words because the owner of the *World* was one of its chief stockholders. Such visits usually increased the trade of its Postal rival. Mr. Pulitzer never mentioned his holding in the concern to any one in the shop.

He never embarked in any enterprise for making money, confining himself entirely to the investment in sound securities of earnings from his newspapers. Yet of his talents in a financial way, Lord Rothschild once said:

"If Pulitzer would devote himself entirely to finance, he could be the richest man on the globe."

His personal expenditures were enormous. The *Liberty* was always in commission and her operating cost, with repairs, ran close to $200,000 a year. In addition to this he maintained costly residences at Bar Harbor, Jekyl Island, Georgia, and in New York, to which was added the finest villa to be had at Cap Martin. Probably the bill totalled $350,000 a year, but it barely dented the great income from newspapers and investments. There was always a large annual surplus.

He cared very little about the great outlay on the *Liberty* though port charges and like annoyances vexed him. He was fohd of quoting J. Pierpont Morgan the elder, whose *Corsair* ranked with the *Liberty*, who, when asked by a friend who contemplated buying a yacht if he found it expensive, replied: "If it is of any consequence to you, keep out of it."

He loved New York. Driving once past the magnificent Columbia College Library building, the gift of Seth Low, he exclaimed: "What a wonderful city New York is, and what a more wonderful city it is destined to be. I wish I could come back and see it a hundred years from now."

## Joseph Pulitzer

He was singularly delicate about being fully clad, and could not bear to have any part of his person exposed to the gaze of another. From his earliest days he slept alone, save when he shared a bed with Professor Davidson, remarking in after years that this unwonted intimacy showed how much he thought of his learned friend. His sensitiveness in this particular developed in an amusing way at Cap Martin in the Spring of 1910, when after much negotiation the great Rodin was commissioned to execute a bust. A room for studio purposes was cleared on the top floor of the Villa Cynthia and quarters assigned to the sculptor and his wife. As Mr. Pulitzer always objected to the arrangement of details directly between principals, there was much backward and forward discussion via secretaries. Rodin insisted that Mr. Pulitzer in posing should lay bare his shoulders in order that he might correctly visualize the poise of the head. To this Mr. Pulitzer objected strenuously. Rodin was obdurate but it was not until he threatened to throw up the commission and return to Paris that his subject surrendered, and then under conditions that none but his immediate attendants should be admitted to the studio. This was agreed to and the work went on, the model proving very petulant and unruly and refusing to talk to Rodin, who naturally wished to relax his sitter and get some glimpse of his mentality. The contract was for a bronze and a marble bust. The bronze is a mere head with no attempt to indicate the shoulders. The marble goes further — and here Rodin had his revenge, for he laid a bit of ruching across the chest, playfully suggestive of the upper works of a chemise!

Personally he was singularly shy. He did not like to be pointed out publicly, or to be made a center of

RODIN, THE SCULPTOR, MODELING BUST OF
MR. PULITZER.

## Characteristics

interest. Once at Bar Harbor, I had told Mrs. Pulitzer a merry tale about him, the joke of which was on the other fellow. She repeated it to J. P. "What's this story you have been telling Mrs. Pulitzer?" he queried at luncheon. I replied that it was a good one. He was silent for a moment, then said gently, "Don't tell stories about me. Keep them until I am dead."

Chapter II

BIRTH AND BEGINNINGS — 1847-1867

Family and Early Schooling — Efforts to Enter on a Military Career — Emigration to America — Enlistment in the Lincoln Cavalry — Army Life — St. Louis.

MR. PULITZER was born in Mako, Hungary, April 10, 1847. His father, Philip Pulitzer, was of Magyar-Jewish descent; his mother, Louise Berger, Austro-German.

The family included four children, of whom Joseph was the second, the elder being Louis. Albert, born in 1851, was the third, and a sister, Irma, the youngest. Both Louis and Irma died young, the latter at fifteen.

Mako was and still is a thriving town. It is located on the right bank of the Maros River about 135 miles southeast from Budapest, and is the seat of Csnad County. Before the World War, it contained a population of some 35,000 souls. It was by no means so large in the forties, but had importance then as now as a political and business center. The population is about evenly divided between Catholic and Protestant faith, the latter slightly predominating.

As the center of a great grain and cattle growing region, it is prosperous. Flour mills grind heavy grists and there is considerable manufacturing of agricultural implements. Maros is a turbulent stream, rising in the Carpathian Mountains and subject to heavy floods that often bring disaster to the plains. Mako protects itself from the violence of the flow behind a powerful

LOUISE BERGER,
(Mother of Joseph Pulitzer.)

## Birth and Beginnings — 1847–1867

dike which, however, does not always resist the torrent when the snow melts upon the mountains in Spring. The river falls into the Theiss a little west of Mako, and below this juncture is a vast extent of marshy plain. The Theiss runs southward to meet the Danube a little to the northwest of Belgrade, with which Mako is almost in line from the North.

The city is substantially built and inhabited by an intelligent population. A Calvinist college and good schools make it an educational center.

Commonly described as a "poor emigrant lad," who had fled from poverty to better his condition in the New World, Mr. Pulitzer was nothing of the sort, save as his bold venturing brought on its own hardships.

His family was one of standing in the community, both father and mother being superior people, having means and education. The mother had great personal beauty and the father much character. Philip Pulitzer, in partnership with Mathias Reiner, established a prosperous grain business in Mako about 1840. This existed until 1853, when the firm was dissolved, the elder Pulitzer removing to Budapest with his family, having sufficient wealth to retire. The boy was sent with his oldest brother Louis to a private school and further had the advantage of a special tutor. His mother was of the Roman Catholic faith, and the early education of his younger brother, Albert, designed him for the priesthood. The family lived comfortably at Budapest until the death of the father. He had been for some years an invalid, with heart disease. The family fortune, though not exhausted, was impaired to an extent that did not permit permanent idleness on the part of the sons. After a few years the widow married, taking for her husband a merchant,

## Joseph Pulitzer

Max Blau. A stepfather did not tend to tighten the home ties of a boy full grown and adventurous at seventeen.

Early in 1864, during the excitement over the Schleswig-Holstein question, Joseph Pulitzer applied for a commission in the Austrian Army, where two of his uncles, brothers of his mother, were officers. Weak eyes and an unpromising physique, showing the ill-effects of too rapid growth, deprived him of a cadetship. Determined upon a military career, he found his way to Paris and endeavored to join the celebrated Foreign Legion for service in Mexico where his uncle Willy had gone with the Austrian Archduke Maximilian, who was being propped upon a shaky throne by French bayonets supplied by Louis Napoleon. The same weakness that excluded him from the Austrian Army operated here. From Paris, after this disappointment, he made his way to London, hoping to find a place in the British forces for service in India. He was again unsuccessful and, despairing, made a start for home via Hamburg. Here he sought employment as a sailor, but his frail appearance was against him and he found no berth. At this time Europe swarmed with agents seeking recruits, in the guise of emigrants, for the Union Army. The boy fell into the hands of one of these and was shipped to Boston. Arriving in port, in company with another who had been "recruited" in this fashion, he decided to collect his own bounty, and slipped over the ship's side at night; being an expert swimmer, he safely reached the American shore some time in August or in September, 1864. The irregularity of his arrival obscures the date. Not caring to linger in Boston, which he had invaded so unceremoniously, he made for New York, then the

## Birth and Beginnings — 1847–1867

center of military activity as well as the metropolis of the country. The City Hall Park was full of recruiting booths. Agents for country towns seeking to fill their quotas were plenty on the ground, offering attractive bounties, and he was assigned to Kingston, N. Y., enlisting for one year on September 30, 1864. His name appears on the roster as "Joseph Politzer," a form of spelling preserved today by the family in Austria. In the Adjutant-General's report on New York State it is given as "Pouletzes." The recruit reached Hart's Island in the Sound near New Rochelle on October 4th, and was detailed to Company L, First New York Lincoln Cavalry. He joined the regiment at Remount Camp, Pleasant Valley, Maryland, November 12, 1864. His age was set down as eighteen, a fiction required by law.

In after years he explained his choice thus:

"I wanted to ride a horse, to be a horse-soldier. I did not like to walk. In Europe," he added, "we knew the regiments by the names of celebrities. They were named for Kings or Princes. We had in Austria a regiment, Maria Theresa, named after the great Empress. So I inquired for the names of some of the regiments of horsemen, and was told of one called Lincoln. I knew who he was and so went to that regiment. I did not have an idea what it was like."

He found at once that there was nothing likable about it. The company was short of officers and men and belonged to a battalion that was mainly German. Indeed, the whole regiment was of a German cast at the beginning, for it was organized by Carl Schurz, with whom Mr. Pulitzer was to be so long and closely associated in later years. This did not make the scrawny, sensitive lad any more welcome. The Captain of "L" loudly remarked: "Take that —— little —— away from here! I don't want him in my company!"

This unwelcome greeting was followed with steady hazing and abuse. The rough troopers were without mercy, and the boy, ignorant of English, high-spirited, haughty and quick of temper, above all resentful of imposition and injustice, had a hard time. He was unmercifully pestered, and in the frenzy brought on by ill-treatment struck one of his tormentors, a non-commissioned officer. This was a serious offense. One of the seniors, Captain Ramsey, who had found the strange lad a good chess player, became his friend and staved off punishment, but the episode did not make him more popular.

The regiment itself had seen long service before the newcomer joined. Organized in response to the first call issued by President Lincoln for volunteers, April 15, 1861, it served all through the war. Mr. Schurz had intended to be its commander, but his appointment as Minister to Spain took him from the country. Gen. Philip Kearny advised that the command be offered to Capt. A. T. McReynolds, of Grand Rapids, Mich. He accepted. He was then fifty-five years old and a veteran of the Mexican War. When McReynolds reached New York, June 15th, he found his regiment more of a problem than a command. There was but one well-organized troop. That was "C," which came from Philadelphia. William H. Boyd was its Captain. This company was the first to move, reaching Washington July 22d, in time to greet the flood of fugitives from the first battle of Bull Run.

## Birth and Beginnings — 1847–1867

Three squadrons were composed of Germans and Austrians who had rallied to Schurz, who was an exile of '48, as many of these men were. The regiment established a camp in what was then called Elm Park, in New York, near where the present American Museum of Natural History stands. Here it loafed and drilled, awaiting orders and equipment from Washington. Neither came.

Simon Cameron was Secretary of War and never caught up with his job. The men were growing demoralized when Capt. F. C. Adams, an outsider, with no other interest in the regiment than a patriotic desire to make it useful, went to Washington, and after much trouble succeeded in securing from President Lincoln the required order which set the slow machinery of the War Department in motion. His hardest task was to procure funds to take the command out of pawn, it being some $20,000 in debt. This he finally did, thanks to Mr. Lincoln, and in gratitude the regiment took the President's name. On the 25th of August, after several months of idling, it marched down Broadway en route for Washington, arriving at the capital on the 27th.

In season the regiment became part of the cavalry forces of the Army of the Potomac, and saw long and hard service under Custer and Sheridan. McReynolds remained Colonel until June 14, 1864, three years almost to a day. He then became a Brigadier-General. He was succeeded by Alonzo W. Adams, who was not popular in the regiment, being especially objectionable to the Austro-German element. It had fought valiantly at Winchester on October 19, 1864, a few weeks before the boy's arrival in its ranks. For the moment after his coming there was not much fighting, though there was plenty of rough riding. He shared in skirmishes at Antioch, Liberty Mills, Waynesborough and Beaverdam Flat. The grand strategy of the war was to develop in 1865 when Sheridan began his circling movements about Lee. In these, however, the recruit bore no part. The regiment was divided, the company to which he belonged being detailed to the Valley of Virginia, while the main body kept with Sheridan. Here he got along no better than before, being at odds with his comrades and entirely out of sorts with army food and rough customs of his older associates. Finally, Major Richard J. Hinton, who had been one of John Brown's men, and was on special duty in the Shenandoah Valley, succeeded in having the boy detailed as his orderly. This took him away from the company — Hinton not being an officer of the regiment — and his remaining army days were fairly peaceful.

The battalions with the Army of the Potomac kept in motion until the grand wind-up at Appomattox. They had the honor of taking Robert S. Ewell, the hammer of Lee's army, and five other Confederate Major-Generals at Sailor's Creek, April 6, 1865, almost the last conflict of the war.

With all its service the regiment lost in killed but three officers and twenty-two men, though in scores of conflicts. Besides its part in battles and skirmishes it matched Mosby's Guerrillas, furnished a corps of admirable scouts and vigorously policed the valley. Following Lee's surrender on April 9, 1865, the scattered companies were pulled together and rendezvoused finally near Alexandria, Va. It marched in the great review of the Grand Army on May 23d, and returned to camp to prepare for mustering out.

## Birth and Beginnings — 1847–1867

In May, 1896, when Mr. Pulitzer occupied the John A. Logan house for a short stay, we were driving together in Washington. He asked where we were. I said between the west wing of the Capitol and the Baltimore and Ohio depot.

"I was here once before," he said.

"When?" I asked.

"I rode with the Army in the grand review after the war was over. The reviewing stand was just at the corner of the Capitol. We rode by and then went to quarters to be mustered out."

I had in mind the vision of that historic grand stand — of the great Commanders bidding their men goodby — of Sherman turning his back on Stanton — and reached for his recollection.

"What did you see?" I asked.

"The man and the horse on either side of me. Not another thing. But how sore my knees became riding in close formation and pressed against the others in line."

The muster occurred on June 5th, but the rolls were not completed until the 24th. On the 26th the regiment broke camp and rode together for the last time to the B. & O. depot, where horses and equipment were surrendered and train taken for New York. It was necessary to change cars at Baltimore and to do this march through the city. The command reached New York on the morning of the 28th and went to the Armory of the Eighth Regiment, where it was given a warm reception and a feast. From the Armory the men marched to the Battery and took steamer for Hart's Island. Here in barracks and tents they were held until July 7th when they were paid off and departed, each on his own way.

## Joseph Pulitzer

While he rarely alluded to his military experiences, no member of the old regiment who was in need ever asked for aid in vain, and one venerable veteran was kept on the *World's* pension roll as long as he lived, even though Mr. Pulitzer had no memory of him as a companion-in-arms.

For many years, he once said, he believed that he had seen Lincoln. His service with the Lincoln Cavalry, the ever presence of the great name, the common portrait, all combined to create the delusion in his mind. Finally, so to speak, he took himself aside and firmly figured out that by no chance could he have ever set eyes upon the martyred President.

The lot of the soldier returning from a prolonged war is hard indeed. This was peculiarly the case after the American Civil conflict. It was fought by boys, most of them under twenty, who left home half-educated, without trades and unplaced industrially. They came out of the army men, unequipped for industrial effort and, what was worse, with their minds so charged with their great adventure as to be unable in many instances to adjust their mentality to the changed conditions. Moreover, society did not welcome them. They were out of step. The country was saved, why bother about its saviors? They were left to take care of themselves. The attitude of all communities was repellant if not hostile. It was not until a generation grew up to which the war appealed as a glorious tradition that any real attention was paid to the soldier; then he was old and it came as a charity.

If, therefore, the social position of the native born was difficult, even more so was that of the young foreigner,

## Birth and Beginnings — 1847-1867

still badly equipped in the matter of his vocabulary, and having no trade with which he could employ his hands. In this state he idled about New York, living on the slender sum left him from his $13 a month of army pay, vainly seeking work. The city swarmed with ex-soldiers, all in the same predicament. Not only were they not wanted as workmen, but they were frowned upon in places of public resort. In French's Hotel, which stood where the great Pulitzer Building now looms, at the corner of Park Row and Frankfort Street, was a boot-blacking stand made up of a long row of cane-bottomed chairs. The boy, in his worn uniform, was particular about his appearance and, poor as he was, would drop in from his loafing place on a City Hall Park bench occasionally to have his shoes polished. Finally the porter requested him not to come any more as the hotel's patrons resented the presence of soldiers! This gave rise to the legend that he had once been put out of the hotel which he lived to buy.

A crimp sought to sell him for a long sea voyage, but alarmed at the vile looks of the Water Street dive, where he was taken to "sign up" he fled on a full gallop for City Hall Park.

Despairing of finding work in New York, in company with another stranded youngster, he went to New Bedford under the impression acquired before he entered the army that it was easy to ship as a whaleman. He found that the whaling industry had not recovered from its destruction by the Confederate cruisers. There was but one whaleship fitting and the captain, not liking his looks, rejected him. Disgusted and discouraged he returned to New York.

## Joseph Pulitzer

One of the difficulties about finding work in that city, beside the superabundance of soldiers, was his lack of English speech. There were too many like him to be absorbed. Realizing that he must learn the tongue to get on, he determined to strike out into the interior where he would not hear German but would be compelled to use English. Some one, evidently a joker, now told the boy to try St. Louis, as there were no Germans there. He was properly astonished, as may well be conceived, to find it overwhelmingly German, but this fact was to turn his fortunes, as the event proved.

With several others in the same plight he decided about the first of October to start West. His army overcoat had been stolen and the sole article of value in his possession, a fine silk handkerchief, to which he had clung through all his adversities, he now sold for seventy-five cents to supply food for the journey. He never told how he made the trip, but a stream of out-of-lucks worked their way on the bumpers of freight cars and by chance lifts on the expresses. At any rate he reached East St. Louis on the evening of October 10, 1865. It was cold, with a sleety rain falling. He did not know that a river had to be crossed to reach the city of his desire and was appalled to find a wide stream barring the way. From the railroad yard he stumbled to the Wiggins ferry. Here is his version of what followed:

> There was no bridge across the Mississippi. Passengers had to cross on a ferry boat for which an extra charge was made. I don't remember how much the charge was, but it made no difference for I had not a cent. I was hungry, and I was shivering with cold. I had no dinner, no overcoat. The lights of St. Louis looked like a promised land to me. But how to get

## Birth and Beginnings — 1847–1867

across the river was a problem. A ferry boat came into the slip. I edged my way down to the gates, hoping something might turn up to help me. Two deck hands of the ferry boat came to the end of the boat near the gates. I heard them speak in the German language. I ventured to call out to them in German. What I said I don't recall, but one of them came up to the gate and I got to talking with him, finally asking if there was any way I could get aboard and across the river. He said that one of the firemen had quit and they might need a man in his place. He went to the engineer, who came and asked whether I could fire a boiler. I said I could. In my condition I was willing to say anything and do anything. He said he would take me and opened the gate, letting me on the boat. The boiler was on the open deck. He put a shovel in my hand and told me to throw some coal on the fire. I opened the fire box door and a blast of fiery hot air struck me in the face. At the same time a blast of cold driven rain struck me in the back. I was roasting in front and freezing in the back. But I stuck to the job and shoveled coal as hard as I could. I don't remember how many trips back and forth across the river I made that night, but the next day I went ashore and walked the streets of St. Louis. I still have a painful recollection of firing that ferry boat with its blasts of hot air in my face, and the rain and snow beating down on my back.

Landed in St. Louis and scanning the "want" advertisements in the *Westliche Post*, he found there a chance for a job at the old Benton Barracks, as hostler for the mules there quartered in the Government service, ex-cavalrymen preferred. He walked four miles to the post, only to find that he had left his discharge papers behind with his bundle in St. Louis. The weather had turned deadly hot, but he ran all the way back and got them. He was then given a place as caretaker for sixteen mules of the Missouri temperament. "I still remember those mules," he remarked long afterwards. "Never in my life did I have a more trying task. The man who has not cared for sixteen mules does not know what work and troubles are."

As a matter of fact, however, he nursed the mules but two days. He could stand their idiosyncrasies, but not the barrack food, "horrible" he recalled it, so he threw up the place and tramped back to the city. Remembering the shortness of hands on the ferry, he applied to the kindly engineer and was set to work operating the gates. This bridged him over his first crisis. The job was temporary, however, and he next found a place on a river steamer, faring to Memphis. The cholera was raging in the Tennessee city and he aided, between trips, in caring for the dead. Coming back to St. Louis and again in need, he joined the roustabouts on the levees unloading steamers. The rough stevedore who employed him did not like the spectacle of a white boy, slender and delicate in looks, rolling bales and barrels with the negroes and set him to checking the deliveries. Getting the knack of it he took to stevedoring himself and operated a small gang with living profit. The work was desultory and to eke out a livelihood he hired a livery hack and drove it for a time to the ferry landing; he even tried his hand as waiter in a restaurant, the experiment lasting but one day, however, the nervous landing of a beefsteak upon a customer's head terminating the engagement. In this fashion he struggled along for weeks, doing any odd jobs that came to hand. Among others he worked on a building construction, where, the fore-

UDO BRACHVOGEL AND JOSEPH PULITZER

## Birth and Beginnings — 1847–1867

man falling ill, his pay was not forthcoming on the day it fell due, which happened also to be the date when he should have paid his board. Ashamed to face his hostess without funds, he did not return to his lodgings, but "slept out" all night. He had but 10 cents in his pocket which he invested in apples. The next day the money was paid and he returned to his room. When he explained his absence, the landlady roundly scolded him for his sensitiveness.

St. Louis enjoyed then as now an admirable institution, the Mercantile Library, and here the eager youth soon found his way. Between jobs he haunted its rooms, reading omnivorously. One of the librarians, Udo Brachvogel, who became a lifelong friend, remembered how the boy would be waiting on the steps in the morning for the doors to open and had to be driven out at evening. He would not leave his book for lunch, but always brought two apples in his coat pocket to serve for refreshment at noon. This liking for apples continued all his days. He had the fruit follow him from South Africa and Van Dieman's Land when out of season in America.

Always prudent, he made it a practice when paid off, to invest all but a little change in advance board and lodging. "Thus," he said, "I was secure. I did not have to worry and could look about for something better." The longest period of the security thus attained was six weeks, during which he "looked about" to good purpose, connecting with a number of lawyers having offices in the building at the corner of Fifth (now Broadway) and Market Streets, among whom William Patrick and Charles Philip Johnson, then Circuit Attorney of St. Louis, and later Lieutenant-Governor, gave him much aid and were always

## Joseph Pulitzer

his steadfast backers. Here he picked up a meagre living serving papers and doing like errands for the legal gentlemen. The ground floor was occupied by the drug store of Jones & Sibley, a favorite meeting-place for the tenants above, who included a number of physicians, among whom was Dr. Joseph Nash McDowell, the eminent surgeon. In this company the boy became known as "Shakespeare" from his classic profile, which, with a little tuft on the chin, did suggest the Bard of Avon, somewhat remotely. During the terrible cholera of 1866, which devastated the city, at the instance of Dr. McDowell, the jack-of-all-trades assumed the wardenship of Arsenal Island, where many of the dead were buried. He took his belongings and a few books to the island and remained on duty as an officer of the Department of Health until the plague subsided, when he returned to the city and resumed his uncertain career.

The Deutsche-Gesellschaft, a society formed by Carl Schurz and Dr. Emil Preetorius to assist newly-arrived Germans, next placed him as an assistant bookkeeper in Strauss's Lumber Yard. He soon became popular with his employer, as a person of superior taste and education, speaking as he did excellent French and unquestionable German. He was accurate with his work and gave general satisfaction. The head bookkeeper leaving, the tyro thought himself entitled to the succession, but his heavy, vertical handwriting did not look well on the ledgers and he was not promoted. Miffed at this he resigned and renewed his search for better opportunities, one of which he soon found among his friends the attorneys.

The work of securing land rights under a plan to build the Atlantic and Pacific Railroad was under

JOSEPH PULITZER AT TWENTY-ONE.

## Birth and Beginnings — 1847–1867

way. This made it necessary to record its charter in every county through which it was proposed to run the line, twelve in all, and he was engaged for the purpose.

The dangers of the employment were considerable. The region he must traverse was a wild and thinly inhabited country which had been the home of guerrillas during the war and was half a century in acquiring settled habits. In company with a negro companion, both riding horseback, he cruised the country, learning the articles of incorporation by heart, so that he wrote them into the county records from memory. The hardships were great in the ill-favored land. Fording the Gasconade River at a flood, the negro and both horses were swept away and drowned. Having breasted the Danube in his boyhood, the youth made the shore, clinging to the saddlebags that held his documents. In this manner he completed his task to the high satisfaction of his employers, and upon the foundation of the Charter thus laid, the St. Louis and San Francisco railroad exists today.

This exploit gave him renewed standing with the lawyers. He took desk room in the building where his friends were located, and making liberal use of Mr. Patrick's library, fitted himself for the bar. Having "found himself," as the saying goes, he determined to become an American citizen and was duly naturalized in the "Saint Louis Court of Criminal Correction," as the certificate reads, on the sixth day of March 1867. He is described as subject of the Emperor of Austria with whom he permanently parted company. Then to his diversified employments he added the office of Notary Public and further enlarged his horizon by securing admission to the bar. There is no record of the date in St. Louis, nor did he appear to practice the profession much beyond the collection of bad debts, being too young and too foreign still to secure clients who would risk their cases in court with him.

It was his good fortune at this period to make the acquaintance of Professor Thomas Davidson, then an instructor in the St. Louis High School, a Scotchman of marvellous learning; indeed, one of the foremost minds of the day. The greed of the youth for education pleased Davidson, who was a little the elder and a born pedagogue. He responded liberally to the yearning with an outpouring from a mind crammed with knowledge. Nights and Sundays "Joe" would lie on the bed in his room, or that of the Professor, while Davidson transferred intelligence in colossal quantities. He literally knew everything!

The friendship with Davidson remained Mr. Pulitzer's closest relationship until the wise and kindly Professor left this life at Cambridge, Mass., September 14, 1900. He had been born in Aberdeenshire, Scotland, October 28, 1840, and so had not quite ended his sixtieth year.

Connected with the admirable Mercantile Library was a chess room, largely frequented by the educated Germans who played that intellectual game. As a frequenter of the Library the youngster, who was an accomplished player, found his way into the circle which included Dr. Emil Preetorius and Carl Schurz, the conductors of the *Westliche Post*, the leading German daily of the town. Some correction the boy made to a play which he was watching caused him to be told to try it himself if he could do better, which he straightway sat down and did. This gave him an entrance into German society, slight but destined

## Birth and Beginnings — 1847-1867

to become the road to fortune. The secretaryship of the Deutsche-Gesellschaft became vacant, and through Schurz and Preetorius he secured the place to become active in looking out for the welfare of the newcomers. The position did not occupy all of his time or afford an income of much substance. It was, however, a foothold, and coupled with his notarial business and minor law jobs gave him a living.

German society in St. Louis was very active in musical, social and charitable affairs and the young man now found a considerable place in it. Mrs. Preetorius was a special friend to the youth, who all his life held her memory in deep affection.

His love of literature led him to frequent the German bookstore kept by Fritz Roeslein, at No. 22 Fourth Street. Here many congenial spirits forgathered, including a bright young Austrian artist named Joseph Keppler, who established a German comic weekly called *Puck*, which was to be heard from thereafter in a wider field, Carl Schurz, Dr. Emil Preetorius, Udo Brachvogel, Prof. Louis Soldan, late Superintendent of Schools, Carl Daenzer, founder of the *Anzeiger*, Dr. George Engelman, botanist and meteorologist, Dr. Frederich Kolbenheyer, Lt.-Gov. H. C. Brockmeyer, Judge J. G. Woerner and others of note in their day. Indeed, he never sought any company but the best.

The activities noted carried him well into the year 1868, when the door to his future life opened wide.

## Chapter III

### ST. LOUIS — 1868–1877

Entry Into Journalism — The "*Westliche Post*" — Election to the Missouri Legislature — The Independent Republican Movement — Reforming the Missouri Constitution.

THE *Westliche Post* needed a reporter. Carl Schurz, Dr. Preetorius and Louis Willich, the city editor, took counsel together about filling the vacancy. Mr. Pulitzer's various activities in German circles and his more or less unattached station in life caused his name to be brought up in the conference without his knowledge, together with that of one Ahrenberg, a man of experience. Both Schurz and Preetorius were inclined to give the place to the man with a training; but Willich, fearing a rival in Ahrenberg, pleaded for Pulitzer, and as a result he was accepted. When Willich sent for him and revealed his good fortune the recipient was amazed.

"I could not believe it," he once said. "I, the unknown, the luckless, almost a boy of the streets, selected for such a responsibility. It all seemed like a dream."

There was not much dreaming after he set to work.

Willich was both wrong and right in his point of view. He was in no danger from the newcomer, so far as his position went, for the young reporter did not pause much between the bottom and the top. Besides

## St. Louis — 1868-1877

Schurz, Preetorius and Willich the staff consisted of two reporters. Schurz was absorbed in politics and Preetorius ill with a nervous affection which limited his energies. It was the new man's chance. Indefatigable, pervasive, he stopped at nothing in his eagerness to excel. No task was too hard, no hours too long. His working day was from 10 A.M. to 2 A.M. He literally contributed columns to each issue and soon leaped over the head of Willich to editorial association with Schurz and Preetorius. He dominated the shop with his electrical energy and overwhelming capacity for production. News, politics, public opinion — he grasped them all, both as reporter and interpreter. He awed the establishment by his prodigious efforts and made at once a large place for himself in the life of the town, becoming conspicuous and establishing himself as a force in Missouri politics.

His eagerness in the search of news, his still imperfect English, and his gaunt figure topped by a bulbous head with its small pointed chin, tufted with a few strands of red, made him a figure to be laughed at by his rivals on the local press other than German. He was guyed and misled unceasingly, but his good humor and persistence soon turned this attitude into one of respect, hastened somewhat when his "stories" took the form of frequent "beats" on important local and political matters. It was not long before the editors of the English sheets were advising their young gentlemen to cease guying "Joey" and endeavor to imitate him if they expected to hold their jobs, as it was becoming a little monotonous to be compelled to secure the best stuff by translating from the columns of the *Westliche Post*.

One of the English writing reporters, Henry Morton

## Joseph Pulitzer

Stanley, was destined to join the immortals as the explorer who was to turn light upon the dark continent. Another, William Fayel, has left this impression of the youth in action:

> In those days the alley back of the old Post Office, at Second and Olive Streets, was a very important and lively thoroughfare. One sultry day nearly all of the reporters of St. Louis were drawn there by some incident, the exact nature of which has escaped memory. Suddenly there appeared among us the new reporter, of whom we had all heard but whom we had not yet seen.
>
> I remember his appearance distinctly, because he apparently had dashed out of the office, upon receiving the first intimation of whatever was happening, without stopping to put on his coat or collar. In one hand he held a pad of paper, and in the other a pencil. He did not wait for inquiries, but announced that he was the reporter from the *Westliche Post*, and then he began to ask questions of everybody in sight. I remember to have remarked to my companions that for a beginner he was exasperatingly inquisitive. The manner in which he went to work to dig out the facts, however, showed that he was a born reporter.
>
> He was so industrious, indeed, that he became a positive annoyance to others who felt less inclined to work, and inasmuch as it was considered quite fitting and proper in those days to guy the reporters of the German papers, the English reporters did not hesitate to undertake to curb his eagerness for news. On more than one occasion the new reporter was sent out from the Coroner's office on a wild-goose chase. But it was soon observed that, while taking this banter in good part, he never relaxed his efforts. The consequence was that the city editors of the English papers soon discovered that the *Westliche Post* often contained news which the other reporters had failed to obtain. Major

MR. PULITZER AT A SUABIAN CHURCH FESTIVAL
(Cartoon by Joseph Keppler in the St. Louis *Puck*.)

## St. Louis — 1868-1877

Gilson was then city editor of the *Democrat*, and every reporter on that newspaper had occasion to remember an order which he posted on the bulletin-board. It was brief, but to the point. I do not recall the exact words, but in substance it directed the reporters to give less time to attempts to delude the German reporters and more time to work in competing with them. That ended the efforts to curb the new reporter's activity, and we all soon learned to appreciate and make the most of his extraordinary capacity for news gathering.

He was quick, intelligent and enthusiastic, but of all his qualities the most notable was his determination to accomplish whatever he set out to do. I recall an incident which illustrates this characteristic. He was at Jefferson City as the correspondent of the *Westliche Post*. I represented the *Republican*, a Democratic organ. One night there was a secret Democratic caucus, to which only representatives of the Democratic papers of the State were invited. Early in the session there was a noise in the corridor. Suddenly the doors were broken open, the doorkeepers went sprawling on the floor, and through the open casement calmly walked the correspondent of the *Westliche Post*. He stepped to the reporters' table without a word, placed a pad of paper before him, took his seat without question or objection from the members, and the next day his was the only Republican paper in the State which contained a report of the caucus.

Mr. Pulitzer's chief ambition at that time seemed to be to root out public abuses and expose evildoers. In work of this kind he was particularly indefatigable and absolutely fearless.

While representing the *Westliche Post* at Jefferson City, through the influence of Carl Schurz, Louis Benecke, of Brunswick, Missouri, then chairman of the State Senate Committee on Banks and Banking, made Mr. Pulitzer his clerk so that he had some near-at-hand views of affairs at the State Capitol, as well as a closer touch with the Republican politics of the day. This gave him the opportunity to observe legislative and lobby methods at first hand, the knowledge of which he was soon to turn to good account.

In December, 1869, chance took Mr. Pulitzer into active political life. There was a legislative vacancy in the Fifth District, caused by the resignation of John H. Terry, a Democrat, which had to be filled by a special election. The young writer was a delegate to the Republican convention and there was so little hope for winning that no one would accept the nomination. The convention met in Turner Hall, on Tenth Street, below Market Street. While the delegates were hunting a candidate Mr. Pulitzer left the room for a moment and advantage was taken of his absence to give him the doubtful honor, rather in the light of a joke. On returning he tried to decline, but the body stuck to its decision and he decided to take the joke seriously. Both convention and candidate overlooked the fact that he was under the age required to qualify. He threw himself into the canvass with all the fury of his soul. Day and night he exhorted his constituency, made a personal canvass of the voters and roused unusual interest in the campaign. On the morning of the day set for the balloting, December 21st, the Missouri *Democrat* (Republican in politics) said of him:

> Mr. Pulitzer is neither an old resident, a great man nor a rich man. He is young and has lived here only since his return from service in the army. But he is a young man of thorough honesty, whose business it has

been as local editor to understand the workings of our City Government, and he has a fine education and natural ability.

The outcome was his triumphant election, defeating Samuel A. Grantham, his Democratic opponent, by a vote of 209 to 147.

The adjourned session opened at Jefferson City on January 5, 1870. He was duly seated despite the lack of age qualification and attended both as a representative and as correspondent of the *Westliche Post*. The two positions did not go well together. A Southwestern Legislature, during the reconstruction period, was anything but idyllic. The halls were filled with adventurers and the lobby with agents of corruption. These he assailed in print and on the floor with all the zeal of his fiery soul. He was soon in a very unhappy position. The old hands in the lobby tormented him incessantly, while his high sense of duty and lofty ideas put him much out of place among his careless and often corrupt colleagues. He fought for honesty, against the sale of law, and engendered much hostility. To be in a position to follow up his crusades on the floor with the power of a newspaper of such strength as the *Westliche Post* then enjoyed was held unfair in the eyes of his fellow members, with the result that he soon became a storm center.

St. Louis was under a dual government. The Mayor and the City Council were elected by the people of the whole community, the officials of the County Court by a part. By familiar devices the Judges of the County Court exercised large powers that affected the general welfare of the city. Up to the time the Missouri Pacific, Iron Mountain and North Missouri Railroads were sold under foreclosure, the County Court had the power to name the directors of these corporations. The Court appointed all the County officials, ruled the Poorhouse and Insane Asylum. It named the assessors with whom tax-dodgers fared well. There was no check on the Charity Superintendent. The County Treasurer, a Court appointee, placed the funds where he pleased, the County getting no interest, such return as there was being graft to the official. The Court was made up of five members; the majority ruled as it willed, with vast peculation. One member furnished material in great quantities for a new county poorhouse, and as chairman of the committee in charge of the work, approved of bills made out in his own name. Single-handed, as a reporter Mr. Pulitzer fought the system in the *Westliche Post*, much to the astonishment of the ring. Here was some one quite different from the German reporters whom they had contemptuously known as "Schnorrers" — spongers. The work he had done as a reporter he now followed up as legislator and correspondent. His first move was to introduce a bill to abolish the County Court, which at once aroused the powerful opposition of that body.

It chanced at the moment that a new insane asylum was being hurried along at Allenton, to continue the grafting enjoyed in building the poorhouse. To make sure of the game the old buildings were sold before the new were well under way. Several hundred thousand dollars had already been spent and a million was the easy limit. The contract had been given to Captain Edward Augustine, Supervisor of Registration for St. Louis County, and a court favorite. When Mr. Pulitzer's measure came up for consideration he backed

## St. Louis — 1868-1877

it up in the *Post*, attacking Augustine, who was much in evidence at Jefferson City in company with several notorious lobbyists, all out to kill the bill. This Mr. Pulitzer made clear in his dispatches. Augustine, incensed at the reference, made known to Theodore Welge, an estimable citizen, who was also a friend of the legislator, his purpose to insult Mr. Pulitzer publicly, and force him to stop advocating a bill that would take away his profitable contract. Augustine was a huge man with the neck of a bull and the arms of a prize fighter; Mr. Pulitzer, very slender and boyish.

What followed is best told in the language of his friend and fellow correspondent, Wallace Gruelle, writing for his paper, the St. Louis *Dispatch:*

### PULITZER AS A SHOOTIST.

*Jefferson City, Jan. 27, 1870* — To-night, about half past 7 o'clock, Mr. Pulitzer shot at and wounded Mr. Augustine in the office of the Schmidt Hotel. It appears that Mr. Pulitzer — and, by the way, I am on Pulitzer's side, not because he is a newspaper man, but he is a clever, affable gentleman, whose portrait I intend to paint some day, and he voted right on the Richland County bill — had sent an article to the *Westliche Post*, at which Mr. Augustine took offense, and mildly told Mr. Pulitzer that he was a liar. Mr. Pulitzer cautioned Mr. Augustine against using such strong language. Mr. Pulitzer left the hotel and got a pistol and returned and went for Mr. Augustine. Had not his pistol been knocked down, Missouri would have been in mourning this day for a slaughtered loyal son. As it was, only two shots were fired, one of which took effect in Augustine's leg. Augustine struck Pulitzer on the head with a Derringer, or some other kind of pistol, cutting his scalp and ending the battle. Mr. Pulitzer was arrested and gave bond for his appearance before the City Magistrate of Jefferson City.

The Missouri *Democrat's* account printed on January 29th, a day late because of some delay on the wire, gave this version of the affair:

*Jefferson City, January 27, 1870* — Mr. Joseph Pulitzer, a member of the Legislature from St. Louis, shot Capt. Edward Augustine, of St. Louis, this evening, about 7 o'clock. A dispute had arisen between them relative to a statement in the *Westliche Post*, of this date, to the effect that Augustine was here in the interest of the County Court. Augustine pronounced this statement a lie, and the man that made it a liar. The parties were in the office of Schmidt's Hotel, where there were many other persons.

Pulitzer left the room in haste and was gone ten or fifteen minutes, it is said, to go to his room which is on High Street, it is supposed, to get his pistol. On returning he again approached Augustine and commenced anew his conversation in an insulting manner. Augustine called him a puppy, when Pulitzer called him a liar. Augustine started toward him, when Pulitzer drew his pistol, aiming at his breast, but Augustine seized his arm and that directed the shot downward, which took effect in the right leg below the knee. A second shot struck the floor, when Augustine pressed him into a corner and knocked him down, cutting his head severely. Parties then separated them. There is great excitement and the act is generally declared one of shameless and murderous intent. The ball was extracted by Drs. Hurtt and Thompson. The St. Louis delegation held a meeting, but took no action, although there was general mortification and no one justified Pulitzer. It will doubtless be brought up in the House to-morrow,

## St. Louis — 1868–1877

as all agree it is a disgrace to St. Louis. The pistol was taken away from Pulitzer by C. C. Cady. It was a Sharp's four-barrelled weapon and two balls were discharged.

This statement caused Wallace Gruelle to reply in his paper, the *Dispatch*, with a "card" published also on January 29th, reading:

A CARD.

*Editors of Dispatch:*

In the Jefferson City correspondence of the *Democrat* this morning Gerald is more severe than just on Mr. Pulitzer. I want it understood in the beginning that I am not Mr. Pulitzer's special companion. I know the correspondent of the *Democrat* to be a perfect gentleman. I don't believe he would do any man a wrong intentionally; yet, misled doubtless by rumor, he has done Mr. Pulitzer injustice in making the following statement: "As he moved to the sidewalk he met two or three gentlemen of the press and said: 'If you wait a little while, you'll have an item.'" The idea conveyed is that Mr. Pulitzer told the gentlemen of the press, who happened to be T. D. Rapp and myself, before he left the hotel or as he was leaving it, to "Wait awhile"; which is correct.

The whole thing is this: Understanding that a meeting of the St. Louis delegation was to be held in the parlor of Schmidt's Hotel, Rapp and I went down there. We found several German members and Mr. Augustine talking over an article which had appeared in the *Westliche Post* and of which Mr. Pulitzer was the author. He had ascribed Mr. Augustine's visit to Jefferson City to improper motives and that gentleman was correspondingly indignant.

Mr. Pulitzer entered from the street door, went up to

## Joseph Pulitzer

them and asked what was the subject of discussion. Some one answered "you." Mr. Augustine then spoke to him and told him that in writing what he did about him to the *Westliche Post* he was a liar, or words to that effect. Mr. Pulitzer told him to be more cautious in his language. Mr. Augustine, very excited, told him he was a "d——d liar." Mr. Pulitzer then left the crowd and came over to where Waters, of Ray; Moon, of Livingston and T. D. Rapp and myself were standing. I said to him, "Pulitzer, why didn't you knock that man down when he called you a d——d liar? You must keep up the *esprit du corps*, man." Pulitzer replied: "Oh, it's all about the County Court." In a minute or two he left the house.

About five minutes afterwards I had a message to send off and asked Mr. Rapp if he felt like walking to the telegraph office with me. He said he had no objections. We started, and about twenty feet from the door we met Mr. Pulitzer returning to the hotel. It was then he told us to come back, that we would get a good item. Thinking he alluded to the meeting of the delegation, I told him we would be back in a few minutes. At High Street we separated, going down that street to the telegraph office. When about half way across the square I met three of the committee clerks of the House, all of them out of breath and running. One of them told me to go to Schmidt's Hotel and I would get an item. I told him I had just left Schmidt's. He said a shooting scrap had occurred. I turned back and found that Pulitzer had shot Augustine.

I am no upholder of assassination, but because a man unfortunately gets himself into a scrape, I do not see the necessity of hounding him down. Politically Mr. Pulitzer and I are enemies. Personally we are friends. I have stood by him and I will stand by him. I may not justify the step he took, but then I want justice done the man. His case may be bad enough

## St. Louis — 1868–1877

in its best aspect, but I cannot see the necessity of making it worse than it really is.
Respectfully,
WALLACE GRUELLE.

Mr. Gruelle kindly supplemented his card with this dispatch:

*Jefferson City, Jan. 28th, 1870* — The exciting topic this morning is the shooting affair at Schmidt's Hotel. I think this is overdone. At least, Pulitzer is blamed more than he ought to be. As I told him last night, after he reached his room, I had a great notion to shoot him for aiming at Augustine's breast and hitting him only in the leg. Bad marksmanship is to be deprecated on all occasions, and when a member of the press — and a legislator, to boot — essays to burn gunpowder I want him to go the whole hog.

As I am the political guardian of Pulitzer, I have got him all right on important questions — his cue is to vote "no" whenever Mr. McGinnis, who sits directly in front of him, votes "aye." I will have to practice him at pistol shooting — have to make him understand that when he wants to shoot a gentleman he must take distance at such a pace that the party to be shot cannot knock the pistol down with his hand. Shooting is a science and ought to be scientifically done. I am going to turn the alley-way of Miss Lusk, just back of my room, into a shooting gallery and put Pulitzer under a severe course of training for about two weeks, day and night, and I will bet, at the end of that time, he can snuff a candle at ten steps. If he can't, I now and here pledge you my word of honor that I will shoot him myself.
WALLACE GRUELLE.

Naturally great commotion followed. Mr. Pulitzer roomed with Anthony Ittner, a fellow member from

## Joseph Pulitzer

St. Louis, in the house on High Street, who chanced to be in the room when the young hothead came in to get his pistol. Ittner saw him ransacking his valise but did not notice that he had taken out a weapon. He was excited, said that Augustine had insulted him and he was going to return the compliment with interest. They parted on the street, Ittner going to a bowling alley where he had left his coat, and his roommate to the Schmidt Hotel, where the affray took place in the interim. Returning, Ittner was told of the shooting and went at once to the hotel. Inside he found "J. P." washing blood from a slight cut acquired during the melee, but quite cheerful. He greeted Mr. Ittner with "Hello, Tony" accompanied by what in after years the latter described as a broad grin. Ittner then looked up Augustine and found him sitting in an armchair in his room, smoking a big cigar, the slight flesh wound causing him no great discomfort. An excited group of friends surrounded the captain, one of whom, Joseph P. Colcord, was urging that they take the case into their own hands, as the officers of the law in Jefferson City were not in his opinion very eager to protect citizens from assault.

Mr. Pulitzer was not molested but went to his room. Ittner followed and soon an officer came who escorted him to headquarters. Ittner went along and gave bail.

The outlook was ominous. He was plainly guilty of felonious assault, and the hostiles intended to use the mishap to get rid of him and so smooth the path of much questionable legislation. He had few friends and his foes were numerous and powerful, while the act itself was hardly defensible. The incident came up in the House the next day under a resolution to appoint a committee of three to investigate. In the debate

## St. Louis — 1868-1877

Assemblyman Leeper voiced the majority sentiment. He hoped the resolution would not pass. It would lead to the investigation of the conduct of other members. If a member went to a wine party and did something not pleasing to some other person, the House might investigate that. If he happened to kiss a pretty woman there, must the House investigate that? Let the law take its course. Suppose the House should undertake to find out whether this member was guilty, it might have some effect on a court or jury.

Mr. Jones, of Nodaway, said the matter did not concern the House. If the resolution were passed, the House would be called on to inquire into many things that happened on the outside. He moved to lay the resolution on the table, and it was so ordered by a vote of 58 to 42.

In the police court the morning after the shooting Mr. Pulitzer was fined $5 for violating a city ordinance. This did not suffice, quite naturally, in so stormy a moment. He was accordingly rearraigned on a charge of assault with intent to kill, under an indictment by the State.

There was an instant rally to his support among citizens of St. Louis who believed in his sincerity and approved of his course. Charles P. Johnson, Circuit Attorney of the city, and Britton A. Hill volunteered to defend him and despite the pressure for an immediate prosecution succeeded in delaying trial until the heat died down. The case was often called and as often postponed.

Mr. Pulitzer's small resources were unequal to the costs, which with a $100 fine finally imposed on November 20, 1871, ran up to $400. Ex-Mayor Daniel G. Taylor, Lieutenant-Governor E. O. Stanard, and

*Joseph Pulitzer*

Henri C. Yaeger, a prominent miller, among others, made up the sum. In later and better years Mr. Pulitzer wrote to Mr. Johnson for the list of contributors and repaid all in full.

The fading out of the prosecution was aided by Theodore Welge's knowledge of Augustine's purpose and somewhat unexpectedly by the coming forward of a professional lobbyist, old at the game, who coldly told the opposition that unless they ceased their prosecution of the youngster he would reveal all of their rascalities and wreck a number of reputations. "If that boy goes to prison, he will not go alone," was his ultimatum. This "argument" prevailed.

"It was the first hit I ever made," observed Mr. Pulitzer thirty years afterwards.

He had made much more of a hit than the one referred to. His bill passed and became a law. The corrupt court was done away with and the people were given a chance to elect upright, honest men like Judge John H. Fisse and Charles Speck. The Augustine contract was annulled, despite many threats of personal violence against the new judges who felt it well for the time to go armed.

Upon the taking of office by Lieut.-Gen. Ulysses S. Grant, as President, March 4, 1869, there followed a shocking orgy in American politics. Privilege was rampant. The whiskey ring, the railway land-grabbers, the various grades of spoilsmen who scavenged upon patriotism were all present in full force. To this was added the corruption and oppression of the Reconstruction era in the South. The ideals of Charles Sumner, William H. Seward and Horace Greeley were brushed aside by the rough leadership of Thaddeus

## St. Louis — 1868–1877

Stevens, Benjamin F. Wade and Zachariah Chandler. Sumner was driven from his position as Chairman of the Senate Committee of Foreign Affairs; two high-minded members of the cabinet, Attorney-General Ebenezer Rockwood Hoar and General Jacob D. Cox, Secretary of the Interior, were forced out in 1870, and John Lothrop Motley was removed from the post of Minister to England. These acts were indicative of an intolerable condition, resentment over which soon made itself manifest throughout the country and first took form of an independent movement in Missouri, under the leadership of Carl Schurz, vigorously aided by his young lieutenant who became secretary of the organization. Col. B. Gratz Brown was nominated for Governor and elected.

Brown's election greatly stimulated what became a nation-wide revolt, which shaped up in New York on November 22, 1870, at a conference attended by Carl Schurz, Charles Francis Adams, William Cullen Bryant, Samuel Bowles, Gen. Jacob D. Cox, and others. Here was laid the foundation for the great fight against Grant that was to follow two years later and to become a vain thing, through the mistake of selecting Horace Greeley for leader. In the interim the war on Grant was furiously carried on in the columns of such newspapers as the Chicago *Tribune*, Cincinnati *Commercial*, Springfield *Republican*, New York *Tribune*, and, of course, the *Westliche Post*.

When Governor Brown took office he appointed Mr. Pulitzer one of the board of three Police Commissioners governing St. Louis. The term was two years and the salary $1000 a year. His period of public service was stormy, as might have been expected. He was not yet twenty-four and full of fire. He warred with the local gambling ring, was often assaulted and much accused, but all the while held himself fair.

The independent movement continued to grow not only in Missouri but in the land at large. With others Mr. Pulitzer drafted and signed a call for a convention to be held at Jefferson City, January 24, 1872. It was issued in the name of the Liberal Republican party and named delegates to attend a convention at Cincinnati on the first Wednesday of the following May. Mr. Pulitzer was one of those elected. At Cincinnati he was selected as one of the secretaries of the convention which nominated Horace Greeley for President and Governor B. Gratz Brown for Vice-President.

As a paladin of political purity, Mr. Pulitzer plunged deeply into the movement. He took to the stump and made sixty admirable speeches, in German, mainly in Missouri and Indiana.

The Republican party, however, was not destined to be reformed. Grant was triumphantly re-elected; the defeat, coupled with the loss of the *Tribune*, manoeuvred out of his hands by a Republican combination, killed Greeley. Mr. Pulitzer ceased to be a Republican and ever after upheld the principles of Thomas Jefferson.

One of the results of the defeat of Greeley was the opportunity it gave Mr. Pulitzer to acquire his first newspaper interest. How it came about is best described in this excerpt of a letter written by him to St. Clair McKelway, editor of the Brooklyn *Eagle*, early in 1911:

> About forty years ago, when I was only twenty-five, some of the proprietors of the *Westliche Post*, in

MR. PULITZER AS A LEADER OF LIBERAL
REPUBLICANISM.
(Cartoon by Joseph Keppler in the St. Louis *Puck*, March 30, 1872.)

## St. Louis — 1868–1877

St. Louis, became nervous, wanted to retire, thought the paper was ruined by the Greeley campaign, and sold me a proprietary interest in that paper on very liberal terms. They thought I was necessary to the paper. They probably would have done the same thing to any other man who worked sixteen hours a day, as I did through that campaign.

As he progressed on the *Westliche Post* Mr. Pulitzer became more and more a figure in St. Louis. He lived at the Lindell Hotel, where a number of young unmarried men made their homes, and became one of the gayest of the group, an old associate recalling him as "a good story teller, full of fun and much inclined to practical joking." He acquired a good saddle horse and took long morning rides as a relaxation from his indefatigable work on the paper, in whose affairs he now played a large part, writing editorials as well as keeping up his political reporting.

Murat Halstead once described his first view of Mr. Pulitzer, which came at this period. "I was visiting Carl Schurz in the office of the *Westliche Post* in St. Louis," he said. "We were talking shop and considering men. 'I have a fellow here who is going to be heard from,' said Mr. Schurz. He added with a laugh: 'They say he looks like me.' Just then the door opened and through the crack came the very tall, thin figure of Joseph Pulitzer, red-bearded and scrawny. We were introduced and were always friends. I was interested in independent Republicanism and so was he. This drew us together."

Life was a little dull after all the excitement of the great campaign. The *Westliche Post* had suffered from the defeat and Mr. Pulitzer was too high-geared for

## Joseph Pulitzer

his elder associates. Therefore in a few months he sold his interest in the paper to Schurz and Preetorius for $30,000 and took a holiday. He visited his old home and relatives in Hungary and enjoyed an extended tour of the Continent.

In 1872, George W. Fishback forced a receivership of the St. Louis *Democrat* to exclude other interests that had declined to sell. The result was a court order to dispose of the property, and at the resulting sale, March 22, 1872, Fishback secured control. He incorporated a new company with $500,000 capital, the majority of which he held, allotting portions to associates in the management, including J. B. McCullagh, a news editor of extraordinary ability. D. M. Houser, who had held a sixth interest, and William McKee then determined to enter the field. On July 18, 1872, they issued the *Morning Globe*, with Charles B. Davis as its editor. Mr. Davis died July 20, 1873, and in the fall Mr. McCullagh transferred his talents to the *Globe*. The paper lacked an Associated Press franchise, a costly handicap.

St. Louis had a number of struggling German dailies, one of which, the *Staats-Zeitung*, possessing an Associated Press franchise, was on the rocks. Returning from Europe in the midst of the newspaper changes noted, Mr. Pulitzer, seeking an opening, bid in the bankrupt German sheet for a song, on January 6, 1874. He ran it but one day, selling the franchise to the *Globe* for $20,000, and disposed of the machinery to a German group who used it to establish a short-lived *Courier*.

With the franchise in hand, McCullagh showed such energy and skill in newspaper making as to put the *Democrat* at a disadvantage, though both suffered

## St. Louis — 1868–1877

from the competition. Accordingly, on May 18, 1876, the two were consolidated as the powerful *Globe-Democrat*, which holds the morning field in St. Louis to this day. Mr. McKee died December 20, 1879, after a notable newspaper career that began under Major M. M. Noah in the office of the New York *Enquirer*.

The proceeds of the *Westliche Post* stock and the profits of this sale placed Mr. Pulitzer for the moment in easy circumstances. He invested some of his funds in Capt. James B. Eads's schemes for improving the Mississippi, and awaited events as a gentleman of leisure. He took rooms at 1547 Papin Street, and bought another saddle horse, one of the handsomest in the city, and rode much. Each morning as he set out he would usually have for companions Col. J. C. Normile and Col. J. L. Torrey. The three were exceptional horsemen, splendidly mounted, and the cavalcade usually brought the ladies of the neighborhood to the windows to admire their grace and splendor.

Carl Schurz was a neighbor, making his home with Felix Costé, while a very agreeable family, the Balmers, resided at 1548 Papin Street. The daughters were quite musical and when the German Opera stars came to St. Louis their home became a center of delight to music lovers, of whom Mr. Pulitzer was one. He always called the young ladies of the family "The Nightingales." Sunday nights were gala affairs at the Balmer mansion and none contributed more to their gayety than "J. P."

Social life in St. Louis in the early and mid-seventies was very congenial. The people associated with each other and public affairs were large and agreeable. The balls and parties were numerous and enjoyable.

## Joseph Pulitzer

Charles Jump, a local dealer in liquid refreshments, who had a talent for making composite pictures, constructed a reproduction of one of these affairs, in which Mr. Pulitzer was a central figure. It is given herewith and shows him in the center of the dancing throng, towering above his neighbors with an ineffable expression that was in time to vanish from his features.

Idleness, however much embellished, was never to his taste and he soon turned his attention to public affairs.

The Republicans had nominated William Gentry for Governor, representing what Mr. Pulitzer thought to be thorough incapacity for the place. In an effort to reclaim the Independents, they disguised themselves as a "People's Party," which soon became known as the "Tadpoles." The Democrats named Charles M. Hardin, and Mr. Pulitzer at once took the full plunge and came out in his support. The "Tadpoles" dubbed their opponents "Bourbons" and a hot campaign followed. William S. Grosvenor, Editor of the *Democrat*, had been associated so intimately with Mr. Pulitzer in the Independent movement that they became noted locally as the political firm of "Bill and Joe." The dissolution of the partnership followed the convention and Mr. Pulitzer's position was made public in an alleged interview published in the St. Louis *Globe* on September 7, 1874, which read:

> The only importance that could be attached to an interview with Hon. Joseph Pulitzer just now arises from the fact that he is the positive circulating radiator of the Schurz element and was Bill's right-hand bower from the birth of the puny and deformed Tadpole baby until that miserable infant breathed its last at Jefferson

MR. PULITZER AT A ST. LOUIS BALL

## St. Louis — 1868–1877

City. Joseph mourns the loss of the baby, but would feel much better had Bill and the other nurses poisoned it long before, rather than let it die such a horrible death.

"Mr. Pulitzer," asked a reporter yesterday, "do you approve of the manner in which the People's Convention threw Weigel overboard?"

"Certainly. They did excellently well in making their choice. Oh, yes! I wanted the 'Tadpoles' to commit suicide, but they have decided to die a lingering death. This will give them a chance to repent. Yes, they did excellently well."

"Then you really mean that they have done excellently wrong?"

"Why," said he, "the fools could not have done worse if they had tried. The ticket is so very mean and miserable that I like it. It is an excellent joke."

"What do you think of the head of the ticket?"

"Mr. Gentry is, I believe, a gentleman, but I am not aware of any fundamental law or provision to be found in the Constitution of the State of Missouri which forbids a man to have ideas beyond the culture of hogs. Mr. Gentry is an excellent farmer, but because he is an excellent farmer is no reason why he should make an excellent Governor. I've known farmers in my time who were as excellent as he is, but they would be fools in the Governor's chair. I'm a good fellow and I believe you think so; you are a good fellow, I know that; but what an absurdity it would be for either of us to aspire to the office of Governor of the great State of Missouri. The man Gentry is an ass, and he was nominated by asses."

When questioned in regard to his opinion of the whole ticket, he expressed himself as being disgusted with it from first to last.

The firm of Bill and Joe did not last long, but it was a grand firm while it lasted.

## Joseph Pulitzer

Mr. Pulitzer corrected the language, but not the facts in a statement written for the *Republican*, in which he said:

Is it necessary for me to say that the pretended interview in the *Globe* is a fiction, and not a fact? While I have used no such language as that imputed to me, I do not deny having exercised the great privilege so stoutly advocated by the *Republican*, and the one upon which the so-called People's movement is based — the inalienable right of bolting. The political firm of Joe and Bill is dissolved. Neither the unquestionable personal honesty of Farmer Gentry, nor the ingenuousness of the platform, nor the power of old associations, the natural reluctance to sever them, the sympathy and admiration for honored friends, nor the participation in the incipiency of the movement before it had any form, unity or aim, can reconcile me to so palpable a result of politics without principle. For one, the appeal to personal and political independence shall not have been in vain.

I bolt both the platform and the ticket. Not that I fail to recognize in the movement some excellent men and good intentions. But without referring to that particularly warm place said to be paved with good intentions, the result of the convention reminds me very much of that leg of mutton on which old Dr. Johnson dined on the way to Oxford, and which he declared to be as bad as could be: "ill-fed, ill-kept, ill-killed, and ill-dressed." Platform and ticket are ill-born, ill-reared, ill-principled and ill-led. To men of thought and principle both platform and ticket are deaf and dumb. Selecting candidates upon the whole very much inferior to those of the Democracy, the convention remained still further behind by failing to protest against the real causes of the prostrate condition of the country — the corruption, the lawlessness, the usurpation and the profligacy of the national administration.

Is it justifiable either by principle or policy for the people of one state to declare for self-government and reforms, and calmly see their brethren of the next state robbed and ruined and turn a deaf ear to their appeals for help and sympathy? Is it either patriotic or honest for the people of one state to declare for self-government and reforms, and appeal for votes to the very political party which has reduced the principles of self-government to a farce, and fastened a government of force and fraud, of robbers and robbed, upon sister states, members of the same union, parts of the same grand republic and people of the same race and nation? Is Missouri an island in the South Sea that she should know nothing of the political issues of the country? Or if she does, is she like the ostrich that, by hiding his head under the sand, thinks his whole body is hidden?

Not agreeing with that part of the Democratic platform which fails to distinctly repudiate any idea of inflation or repudiation, I find still less excuse for a new movement without courage to express any idea upon national affairs, without new or old principles, without protest against the alarming centralization and corruption of power at Washington, and with clearly no other aim than to have one set of state officers rather than the other, and that, too, the more unknown and unreliable set.

Had the convention, instead of cowardly truckling to the Grant party of this state, imitated the bold and manly course of the Illinois Democracy and declared against inflation and centralization, corruption and mis-government and robbery in the South, it would have commanded the sympathy of all independent voters, no matter what the chances of success had been. But when, to allure as many votes as possible, it sacri-

## Joseph Pulitzer

ficed principles and ideas in order to unite Grantites and anti-Grantites, Democrats and Republicans, hard-money men and inflationists, home-rulers and centralizations, Rebels and Union soldiers, postmasters and people, white and black men, it sacrificed not only success, but what was more valuable, the honor and independence of its professions and the respect of its thinking and independent sympathizers. However, I lack both time and inclination to go into the merits of the case more at length and subscribe myself with respect,

          Yours Independently,

                    JOSEPH PULITZER.

True to his belief and under a hot fire from his old associates, Mr. Pulitzer stumped the State, making many vigorous speeches assailing Grant's administration and the Carpet Baggers. In one address at Sedalia, on October 9, 1874, he paid warm respects to John B. Henderson, with whom in after life, when the Henderson family resided in Washington, he became a very intimate friend. In addition to the Congressional and State tickets in the field, a contest was on for delegates to a Constitutional Convention called to meet at Jefferson City, May 5, 1875, to revise a constitution passed in 1865, based not upon human rights, but on evil conditions growing out of the Civil War. The Democrats triumphed. Mr. Pulitzer was elected a delegate to the Constitutional Convention on December 20th, and served with distinction during its deliberations.

The convention opened with the usual turmoil of popular convocations, and came to a deadlock at once over the question of employing a chaplain and paying him for his prayers. It was not possible to extract

## St. Louis — 1868–1877

compensation for the service and the perplexity was solved by Rev. William Priest, a Primitive Methodist from Marion County, who volunteered to open the sessions with a Divine appeal without fee.

Mr. Pulitzer was not spontaneous as a rule and usually prepared his speeches carefully. It is recalled that he was much interested in a certain clause and wrote out an elaborate argument for use on the floor. Unfortunately, the question at issue came up while he was absent and was debated and disposed of. He came in breathless and began his address, only to be blandly ruled out of order by the chair. After that he managed to be present on all occasions.

The great problem was to restore State rights, tempered to meet the nationalism resulting from the outcome of the conflict. In this Mr. Pulitzer stood against the extremists of both sides. When one delegate declared that "it would do no harm to insert a clause declaring the allegiance of Missouri to the United States," Mr. Pulitzer replied in part:

> The gentleman seemed to be absolutely afraid that unless we recognized that we live in the United States of America, in the Western Hemisphere of the inhabited globe, on the west bank of the Mississippi River, that some morning we will wake up and find ourselves slipped out of the American Union! I have no such apprehension. We are the weaker of the two. Our relations are those of the infinitely weak child compared with the strong parent. Why, then, call upon the child to define the power of the parent, the Federal Government? Are we not all aware of the power of the Federal Government? Do we not all know of the revolutionary changes irrevocably wrought in the last fifteen years? Is it necessary to show bad

conscience by reiterating needlessly that we love and cherish the Union?

Mr. Pulitzer then at length defined his objections to running either to the extreme of State's rights as before the war, or the extreme of centralization as then indicated at Washington with an alarming accumulation of power in a few hands, concluding:

> As a child will naturally seek refuge in the arms of a kind and tender mother from the rude, strong and oppressive hand of the father, which may be laid upon it, so, sir, I think it is time that the States should remember their original form of government, that form of government which guaranteed to them self-government, which gave them birth before this Union and which today administers to their most important necessities, before they should needlessly fall upon their knees and exclaim that "They do love and cherish the United States Government," lest somebody might think that they did not. Mr. Chairman, I cherish the United States Government. Perhaps I have more reason to do so than some gentlemen upon this floor. Surely I stand here not as a Missourian in a local, sectional or national sense of the word, but in the consciousness of the pride of being an American citizen, and I say that it is needless and superfluous to repeat declarations that are self-evident and hence no declarations.

Among the many characteristic utterances of Mr. Pulitzer in this convention, indicating that he then held opinions which he never changed, were these:

> I am not here, sir, as a trader or a trafficker; we are not selling and bargaining. Principles, convictions and motives are neither sold nor bargained for!
> Let one idea and one spirit actuate us — that the

constitution which this convention will prepare shall not only represent the very highest standard of intelligence and statesmanship but that it shall also be acceptable to the people of this State.

I believe that the State of Missouri desires for her citizens at least the capacity to write their own names and be able to read before they vote in a government that should be based upon intelligence and not ignorance.

Mr. Pulitzer sturdily opposed all efforts to take from the people of Missouri the right to amend their constitution by constitutional convention every ten years. He did not believe in delegating to the State Legislatures such authority, pointing out how dangerous this power might be in the hands of unscrupulous politicians. As usual, he pleaded for preservation of the rights of all the people. In like manner he fought against giving the Legislature the right to change at any time the charter of St. Louis, citing in support of his argument the gigantic corruption under Tweed in New York, declaring: "Tweed derived all his power and based his entire system of public plunder on such an amendment as is proposed. The power of Tweed and his coadjutors lay in making charters in Albany and in carrying out charters in New York. It was thus they could make the system of public plunder possible. Without it such public plunder could never have reached the magnitude it did."

One of Mr. Pulitzer's most vigorous fights in the convention was in behalf of the public schools and the broadest possible education of the poor at the expense of the State. He believed then, as always, that there rests upon the State a greater moral responsibility to prevent crime by education than to punish crime committed through ignorance of moral and State laws.

He dealt with the subject of trusts and corporations in these still living words:

> I heartily despise demagogical appeals against the rich, or any particular class, but this question is so grave that it must be treated without gloves. The growth of the money power in this country has been fabulous, and its connections with and interest in the Government is alarming. We all want prosperity, but not at the expense of liberty. Poverty is not as great a danger to liberty as is wealth, with its corrupting, demoralizing influences. Let us have prosperity, but never at the expense of liberty, never at the expense of real self-government, and let us never have a Government at Washington owing its retention to the power of the millionaires rather than to the will of the millions.

His most important service, however, lay in completing the work begun with his pistol shot. He secured the adoption of an amendment giving St. Louis the right to a new charter that would end the dual government and county rule — a reform from which the city has benefited to this day.

## Chapter IV

### THE POST–DISPATCH — 1878-1883

A Washington Correspondent — Marriage — Rescuing a Wreck — Consolidation and Establishment of His First Newspaper — Success From the Start — On the High Road — Eyes Turned to New York.

WHEN the convention adjourned, Mr. Pulitzer was without active occupation. He went to New York and attempted in mid-1875 to buy the *Belletristische Journal*, a German weekly conducted by Rudolph Lexow. The negotiation failed and he went again to Europe for a long stay, including an extended ramble on the Mediterranean shores, filling his eyes with the joyous vision of the azure coast, which he was to frequent much, but never more to see.

He returned to America in 1876 and took active part in the celebrated Presidential campaign when Samuel J. Tilden of New York, as Democratic candidate, opposed Rutherford B. Hayes of Ohio.

From the independent Republicanism that fought the Republican Party to Democracy, and particularly to the Democracy that assailed public robbery, the large-minded patriotic Democracy of the Tilden campaign was but a very short step, and Mr. Pulitzer cut loose from his old political associates in all ways. He went into the Democratic campaign heart and soul, making speeches that were illuminating and convincing and had great success with the masses.

## Joseph Pulitzer

He had an early passion for public speaking, had admired with enthusiasm the great orators and always regarded oratory as the most direct method of appeal to the people. He was also personally well equipped for it. His tall figure, his fine appearance on the platform, his good voice, his capacity for rapid reasoning, his command of language, all contributed to make him a great force in campaigning activities. The speeches he made in Indiana and Missouri ranked far above the level of campaign eloquence, in that or in most other political campaigns.

Democracy stood for his strong love of individual liberty, his belief in equality before the law and his opposition to centralization of governmental powers. Carl Schurz had returned to the Republican ranks, and the national campaign of 1876 found these two former associates pitted against each other on the platform. Mr. Pulitzer challenged Schurz in St. Louis, "stumped" the old battleground of Indiana, and made his initial public appearance in New York, where he was first heard on October 31st of that year, when to a great audience in Cooper Union he proclaimed these principles:

> I stand here to say that the war is over, and it is time that it should be. When the South was wrong I did not hesitate to enlist against it; but today, when the South is not wrong, but wronged, I do not hesitate to enlist for it. The rebel of today is he who robs the Government; the traitor to the Union is he who tries to make peace and unity impossible. The enemy of the Government is he who disgraces a position of public trust.
>
> The Southern people belong to us, and we belong to them. Their interests are our interests; their

## The Post-Dispatch — 1878-1883

rights should be our rights; their wrongs should be our wrongs. Their prosperity is our prosperity; their poverty is our poverty. We are one people, one country and one government; and whoever endeavors to array one section against another and endeavors to make the union of all people impossible is a traitor to his country.

Mr. Pulitzer threw himself into the campaign with his customary impetuosity, with all the enthusiasm of a passionate advocate, and he had to pay a perilous penalty. He outran his physical strength, and developed a weakness of the lungs that was manifested by spitting blood. The election over, in delicate health, without employment, he came to New York and, calling on Charles A. Dana, suggested the idea of a German edition of the *Sun*, which he desired to conduct. Mr. Dana was interested, but Isaac W. England, his publisher, vetoed the project. The contact was to Mr. Pulitzer's advantage, for it resulted in his being added to the Washington staff of the *Sun*, with a chance to do some excellent reporting of the contest which resulted in depriving Mr. Tilden of the Presidency. Not only were his dispatches signed, but he was invited to contribute to the editorial page, where his name also appeared, a most unusual distinction to receive from its exacting editor. When the disappointing result was reached and Mr. Tilden patriotically accepted the decision of the Electoral Commission, Mr. Pulitzer dropped his pen and made another journey to Europe. With the Fall he returned to Washington and completing the requirements for admission to the Bar in the District of Columbia, was duly qualified to practice law. His was an unsettled mind. He had not returned to Washington for the sole purpose of ornamenting the District Bar. During his stay in the city he had met, through his friend Gen. John E. Clarke, a Missouri Congressman, afterwards clerk of the House, Miss Kate Davis, a charming and accomplished young woman, and a growing regard, fostered by absence, drew him back, with no certainty as to what his next move would be to establish himself in life. The courtship, like all things in his career, was rather stormy. The lady was very beautiful, highly connected and in no hurry to be captured by an unknown. Her father, William Worthington Davis, of Georgetown, was a distant cousin of Jefferson Davis, late President of the Southern Confederacy; her mother, Catherine Louise Worthington, a member of the Maryland family of that name. The parents were cousins. His impetuosity won, but more than once there was considerable doubt as to whether the engagement would endure. He had no occupation and no great amount of money. The opportunities at the law in Washington were more in the lobbies than the courts, and therefore distasteful. Besides, he had newspaper in his blood and could not content himself with the commonplace. Therefore, he had no serious purpose in establishing himself in Washington, but kept on the lookout for a journalistic opening — not as an employe, but as a proprietor.

Openings were not numerous, though newspapers were plenty. He seems to have had some inkling of a chance in St. Louis. What it was does not appear in his correspondence or in any memory left behind. His courtship, running parallel with an unsettled mental state, became unpromising and, after a tiff, he went to St. Louis to be there followed by a letter, which while not extant, judged by his response, was

MRS. KATE DAVIS PULITZER AT THE TIME OF HER MARRIAGE.

plainly in the nature of a challenge. The reply bears no date, merely "St. Louis, Sunday noon, 1878," but is, he says in the context, his first love letter. It reads:

> MY DEAREST KATE: What better answer can I make than this, that I shall return tomorrow evening? Have *you* not conquered, No? Yes. I shall make every effort to get through with my matters here and leave tomorrow evening. If nothing happens to prevent my departure, I shall be in Washington 24 hours after you read this. Need I say that there will not be many hours after my arrival before I hope to have the pleasure of seeing you? Need I say that I long for that moment? If you knew how much I thought of you these last days and how the thought of you creeps in and connects with every contemplation and plan about the present and future, you would believe it. I have really felt miserable here in spite of the most cordial signs of friendship, the most gratifying flatteries to vanity, the most absorbing pressure of business. Why? I don't know. But I suspect there is a woman in it. I have an idea that you had a good deal to do with it. I have an ideal of home and love and work — the yearning growing greater in proportion to the glimpse of its approaching realization. I am almost tired of this life — aimless, homeless, loveless, I would have said, but for you. I am impatient to turn over a new leaf and start a new life — one of which home must be the foundation, affection, ambition and occupation the corner stones, and you my dear, my inseparable companion. Would I were not so stupid always to be serious and speculative! Would I had your absolute faith and confidence instead of my philosophy! I could not help thinking, I could not help feeling, how utterly selfish men are in love compared with women, when I read your letter and feel its warmth. I cannot help saying that I am not worthy of such love, I am too cold and

selfish, I know. Still I am not without honor, and that alone would compel me to strive to become worthy of you, worthy of your faith and love, worthy of a better and finer future.

There, now you have my first love letter. I hope it will be read in a less serious spirit than the one in which it is written. Don't of course, show my letters to anybody. I can't bear that thought. Confidential correspondence, much more even than conversation, depends upon strict privacy. Men would certainly not make certain declarations in the hearing of others. But I must stop. Have kept a friend waiting all this time, and now another arrived.

Good-bye till Wednesday,

J. P.

There was no business outcome to the visit, but he returned to Washington properly subjugated, and resumed his search for something to tie to. His old friend Joseph Keppler had brought his German *Puck* from St. Louis to New York in 1875, and in 1877 established an English edition, in company with Adolph Schwarzmann. The colored cartoons were new to the metropolis and Keppler's dashing crayon already pointed the paper toward success. Mr. Pulitzer now began a negotiation to join the partnership, but terms could not be agreed upon.

Two letters of the moment reveal nothing but his state of mind and a reflex of that of the lady, as they are without date. The first reads:

WASHINGTON, Wednesday,
11/12 A.M.

MY DEAREST KATE: Yesterday, at this hour, my friend McCullough (the actor) sat at the table and in this chair and we agreed to arrange it so as to cross the

## The Post-Dispatch — 1878-1883

ocean together — he to put off his departure until after the 15th inst. — I to put off mine on the 6th of July — to go earlier. Two hours afterwards I sent a telegram to New York insisting upon an answer. This morning I received a brief reply that a letter had been mailed without the remotest allusion as to its contents. Also, a letter from St. Louis with a definite and rather advantageous looking proposition about my purchasing an interest in a newspaper there. Also, your note, my dear, which impressed me Europeanward.

I give you this brief outline of my day's doing, and you can now see yourself what an utterly inconsistent, uncertain and inconstant chap I am. Here I am within, perhaps, less than a fortnight, of our possible or probable departure for Europe, and for the life of me I cannot venture a positive opinion, whether, after all, we will go at all, nor whither we will go, where we will settle down. Funny situation, isn't it? As if to give you a foretaste of the future, you are met by difficulties even before you start on that lifelong journey which philosophers call so perilous; whatever may be thought of your discretion, my child, your pluck is really splendid.

I do not expect that letter from N. Y. until tomorrow morning, and doubt whether it will contain anything definite. If it should I'll telegraph. But, once more, don't wait for it or any other further information from me. Get ready. With my very much growing inclinations to go to Europe, I feel as if, after all, the chances are in that direction. Still, my dear child, while you may regard that as the probability, think also of the possibility of our not going abroad and like a sensible girl be ready for that contingency too. And do all you can to be ready by the 17th or 18th. I have an idea that, after all, you would care more about the presence of some of my friends than I.

I will probably come over to-morrow (Thursday)

and telegraph you before I do. I said probably, so don't rely upon it and by no means let it interfere with your great mission. That takes precedence over everything now. I never dreamt how much interest I myself could take in — dresses. But I do, I assure you.

Write me every day, my child, and not so briefly.

J. P.

The second epistle is from:

NEW YORK,
Wednesday, 5 P.M.

MY DEAREST KATE: I write this downtown in the greatest haste, hoping that you are well, that you received my letter written before I left Washington, and that perhaps I shall find a letter from you at the hotel when I return this evening. Have been downtown since a very early hour, busy as a bee in the negotiations about the matter known to you. Prospects look quite favorable for a consummation of a bargain, though there is by no means any certainty of it whatever. I know and feel that you regret my absence, dear Kate, but I also know that your good head will not let your impatient heart run away with it. It is an important opportunity, perhaps a fortune, and you ought not expect me to neglect it. I must have business to occupy my mind and heart. You do the latter. Occupation will do the former, and unless all indications are grossly deceptive, the paper which I expect to purchase will turn out to be a great fortune both pecuniarily and politically. But then I am a sceptic, and leave you to be sanguine.

The worst of it is that I see no hope of getting away from here before Saturday or Sunday. I beg you, my dear child, to believe me that I am all the same with you in spirit. Make all arrangements, complete every preparation upon the assumption that

## The Post-Dispatch — 1878–1883

I will certainly be with you on Monday for that important ceremony, thereafter to stay with you forever. What you think best, do. I'll accept cheerfully any arrangement you may make, hoping only that there will be so little ceremony, so much quiet, that there will be but little need of arrangement and few preparations necessary. Of course, I shall endeavor to return sooner. If I can, I certainly shall. You may depend upon that. But as I said it looks as if I absolutely had to stay here all of this week.

Don't fail to write me every day, dear.

In haste,
Yours ever truly,
J. P.

Address: "Gilsey House."

Whatever the great prospects were they faded out. Brushing the future aside for the moment he kept his engagement and the young couple were married by the Rev. J. H. Chew, at the Episcopal Church of the Epiphany, Washington, June 19, 1878, where the bride's parents had been wedded thirty years before. He took his wife to Europe and during his stay contributed a number of letters to the *Sun*, short studies of European conditions, revealing a deep and prophetic vision, as lighted by events. The first article, printed September 22, 1878, compared conditions in Germany with those in the United States. He found the weak Germany he had known as a lad made strong by the war with France, just as a weak America had been made strong by its own conflict. "On this side of the ocean," he said after finishing his comparisons, "we have passed through the worst and light is dawning. On the other, the worst is to come, and darkness with it. . . . I cannot remember a single person of either nationality who did not clearly intimate or express a belief in the utter inevitability of another war between France and Germany. This dreadful thought was firmly impressed upon the minds of both nations. Women speak of it as a matter of course. Children are brought up in it. . . . This may not occur for years. But it is liable to occur any day, so Bismarck thinks it necessary to be prepared for it every day. The only way to prevent war is to be amply prepared for it, seems to be the German theory. And so that great nation enjoys a peace that is practically no peace, but only preparation for another struggle. Like gladiators or prize-fighters both Germany and France are in training for the next match. It is as ridiculous to call the present state of Germany a real peace as it would be to call the severe and trying work of training a member of the ring, pleasure. It is but a pause, not peace."

Writing on October 13th, he gave a plain picture of German political conditions, as they prevailed up to and through the war:

> . . . so that the people of Germany while they have to pay heavily for all these princes and rulers do not profit by them. They pay for the fiddlers but have execrable music. The more princes, the less principles. The more rulers, the worse ruled. This is what I called in my previous letter over-government. It was bad enough if it only affected the pockets of the people. But it becomes worse by affecting their manhood and freedom. . . . the limited freedom of the people is to be still more curtailed. The powers of the government over the people are to be still more arbitrary and absolute. . . . Instead of more liberty the people will have more military and more police.

## The Post-Dispatch — 1878-1883

Further letters considered conditions in England and France. He found the French had learned moderation and how to govern themselves, and he described England as an unhappy country, because burdened with aristocracy and inherited wealth. "A happy people never leave their native land" was his apothegm, and the emigration figures were used to prove the point. He believed, though, that middle-class England was wedded to the aristocracy and would not abolish it if it could. "Great wealth and great pauperism were the dominating features of the land."

Returning from Europe in the late Fall, he made his way to St. Louis, with the idea of establishing himself in the practice of law.

As usual he took much counsel, one of his advisers being Roswell Martin Field, father of the celebrated Eugene, accounted the wisest, if not the most successful, lawyer in the city. Another was his friend Charles P. Johnson, who, continuing his unceasing interest in the young man, more discerning of the true vocation of his confidant, told him plainly to keep out of law and get into journalism; that he was unfitted for the bar, but pre-eminently equipped for newspaper work.

While Mr. Pulitzer was hesitating over his future course an opportunity on the lines advised by Johnson was ripening. St. Louis had always been a well-newspapered town, from the foundation of the *Republican* in 1808, though there had been no great prosperity in the profession. Among the living in 1878 was a flickering evening sheet called the *Dispatch*, which had descended through a series of luckless ownerships from the St. Louis *Union*, established in 1862 by

Frank P. Blair and sundry associates to fight the *Democrat*, in which at the time Blair held a stock interest. William McKee and George W. Fishback, its chief owners, fell out with Blair over Major-General John C. Fremont's political and military course when that strange figure began acting very independently of his Washington superiors in St. Louis. Blair opposed Fremont and was instrumental in securing his removal. To this the *Democrat* took violent dissent and the *Union* was the consequence. O. D. Filley, John Howe and Barton Able were among those associated with Blair in the ownership. Peter L. Foy was editor-in-chief, A. W. Alexander, leader writer, and Col. William Cuddy, managing editor. The *Union* stood by Lincoln and the *Democrat* held firm for Fremont, even to the extent of following him to the Cleveland convention where he was foolishly nominated for the Presidency, but faded out. The *Democrat* then switched to Lincoln and pushed the *Union* out of any influence it might have justly earned.

In 1864, the *Union* was taken over by a new company including Richard T. Coburn, Charles P. Johnson, Josiah Fogg, James Peckham, E. B. Thomas and John S. Cavender. It had failed as a morning competitor of the *Democrat* and was placed in the evening field. Mr. Coburn acted as editor, with Mr. Johnson as his assistant, Mr. Peckham having charge of its business affairs. After six months of ill-fortune the paper was returned to its former owners. In April, 1868, Peter L. Foy and William and E. B. McHenry took over the property and changed the policy to the support of the Democratic party. Foy sold his interest to George W. Fishback and in December, 1871, the firm of William H. McHenry & Co. became publishers.

## The Post-Dispatch — 1878–1883

Mr. Fishback, on securing control of the *Democrat*, disposed of his interest to D. R. Barclay, who then bought out the McHenrys and became sole proprietor. After a period of loss Mr. Barclay sold the paper to Stillson Hutchins, an adventurous journalist, for $120,000. John N. Edwards, afterwards editor of the Kansas City *Times*, ran the news. Mr. Hutchins, in 1875, took over the St. Louis *Times*, and managed both papers. This experiment was not a success. Before the end of the year he sold the *Dispatch* to William R. Allison, of Steubenville, Ohio, for what he could get. Allison soon lost his stake and unloaded the paper on Messrs. Wolcott & Hume, publishers of the *Journal*, who steered both papers into bankruptcy.

The *Journal* was merged with the *Times* and the *Dispatch* was offered for sale by the Sheriff on the Court House steps, December 9, 1878. Advised of a possible bargain, Mr. Pulitzer counted his change and decided he could bid up to $2,500 for it and have $2,700 left. He consulted Daniel M. Houser, of the *Globe-Democrat*, as to how long he could keep going on that sum. Houser estimated that he could last seventeen weeks, and he decided to attempt the purchase. The creditors of the *Dispatch* thought it worth $40,000, but William Hyde, an experienced newspaper man, expressed the view that it was not "worth a damn." Its plant was a wreck, its type worn out, its credit in the community gone, and its whole outlook completely forlorn. Great sums had been sunk in it, and no one dreamed that any of the lost money could be retrieved. The assets of the *Journal* were sold as junk for $600. Samuel Arnold, acting for Mr. Pulitzer, offered $2,500 for the *Dispatch*, and its belongings, subject to a $30,000 lien. His was

## Joseph Pulitzer

the only bid and the paper was knocked down at that price. A few minutes later several substantial citizens came running up out of breath and asked a chance to bid. They were too late. Putting $300 cash in a safe place, as an insurance against family need, Mr. Pulitzer ventured upon his new undertaking. He did not arrive at the office of his purchase until about ten o'clock the morning of December 10th. The staff of writers and mechanics, who had held on to their jobs with uncertain pay and more uncertain future, had gone ahead in the absence of guidance and put some copy into type. So forlorn was the equipment that there were no ropes to lower the elevator from the composing room to the press room, and the forms were slid perilously down the stairs. The press could turn over and that was about all. Shortly after noon an edition on the old lines of 1,000 copies was turned out and the new owner had a chance to look around.

It is by no means certain that he had the idea in mind of attempting to revive the paper. Indeed, it is more the probability that another speculation in franchises was in his main thought, anticipating a possible "killing" such as had followed his bid for the news rights of the *Staats-Zeitung*. This was the local opinion as manifested in a cartoon published in *Die Lanterne*, the current week. It showed the *Dispatch's* new owner carting off his possession in a wheelbarrow under a sign crediting him with being a dealer in broken-down newspapers and indorsing his own action with this sentiment:

> Well, not so very cheap after all. But I think if I put on a good coat of *Reform* varnish and an *Independent* crank in it and get the whole up on a sound *Post* it will make a pretty good *Organ*.

CARTOON FROM DIE LANTERNE ON BUYING THE ST. LOUIS DISPATCH.

## The Post-Dispatch — 1878-1883

A rival evening paper, the *Post*, had been established January 10, 1875, by John A. Dillon, a member of the *Globe-Democrat* staff. It was a creditable but not prosperous sheet. The news that J. P. was in the field roused Mr. Dillon to deep interest. He sent his reporters about town interviewing the newcomer, and the dissatisfied creditors, printing a column on the 10th, headed with the query: "What will he do with it?" which really concealed Mr. Dillon's anxiety as to "what will he do with me?" The *Dispatch* had a press franchise, the *Post* had none. As it turned out, the joker who framed the cartoon hit a bull's-eye, for before nightfall Mr. Dillon had called on Mr. Pulitzer and proposed a consolidation on equal terms. It was agreed to, and on the afternoon of the 12th, the two papers were issued as the *Post and Dispatch*. In two weeks the heading was shortened to the *Post-Dispatch*. Before the $2,700 was exhausted the paper began to pay and never again lost a dollar.

The creed of the consolidated journals was short and crisp: "The *Post and Dispatch* will serve no party but the people; will be no organ of Republicanism, but the organ of truth; will follow no causes but its conclusions; will not support the 'Administration,' but criticise it; will oppose all frauds and shams wherever and whatever they are; will advocate principles and ideas rather than prejudices and partisanship. These ideas and principles are precisely the same as those upon which our Government was originally founded, and to which we owe our country's marvellous growth and development. They are the same that made a Republic possible, and without which a real Republic is impossible. They are the ideas of a true, genuine, real Democracy. They are the principles of true local self-government. They are the doctrines of hard money, home-rule and revenue reform." Though some of his best friends thought the "hard money" declaration was imprudent, he declined to change it.

Filled with his theory of public service Mr. Pulitzer began to clean up abuses in the City Government of St. Louis, the chief of which was systematic tax dodging on the part of the well-to-do. Declarations of property and investments were required by law. Investigation of the returns filed in the Assessor's Office showed that people of wealth habitually made false inventories and so evaded the payment of their just dues. The more modest citizens obeyed the law. The *Post-Dispatch* began printing in parallel columns the returns from rich and poor, to the shame of the former, with the result that the abuse was reformed.

The city, though old, was yet a border town and as such gave harbor for border vices. Gambling on a large scale was the rule, sheltered by the authorities. Not only were faro banks and like devices plentiful, but the marketing of lottery tickets had risen to the dignity of an industry. The Police Commissioners were named by the Governor and certain nominees were quietly investigated by a local committee which designed to keep its work secret. The *Post-Dispatch*, on February 18, 1879, gave full publicity to the committee's findings and two of the appointees were withdrawn. It followed this up on March 24th, giving details concerning the existence of the gambling ring, headed by Alanson B. Wakefield, a local power of the first magnitude. This exposure led to an investigation, one of the fruits of which was the indictment of

## The Post-Dispatch — 1878-1883

Wakefield for perjury on April 24th. Four days later some fifty employees of the gambling establishments were arrested and heavily fined.

The warfare thus begun continued unflinchingly. On August 23d the St. Louis Lottery Company retired from business, and on October 29th following Wakefield, hitherto invincible, was sent to the Jefferson City Penitentiary for two years. The issue lived to influence the election of the next Legislature. The business died hard, and it was two years before Missouri made gambling a felony under the law.

Civic matters continued to interest Mr. Pulitzer. He brought about the erection of a permanent exposition building, forced the cleaning and repairing of the streets and the beginning of the park system that has done so much to make the city attractive. These things were not done without friction and much rattling of dry bones, but they were real accomplishments and as such stood to the paper's credit. Naturally, serving the public instead of an interest was so novel as to be much condemned, but the public soon learned where its welfare lay and support was never lacking.

Some of the liens against the rickety plant held, and, mindful of his former franchise transactions, sundry creditors assailed Mr. Pulitzer's right to it. Here his acquaintance with Murat Halstead stood him in good reserve. Halstead was then President of the Western Associated Press and at once brushed aside the theory that the tail went with the hide, and that a franchise could not continue beyond the life of its original owner. Mr. Pulitzer waved his telegram in triumph from the steps of the *Post-Dispatch* building in the face of a crowd of disputants, and held the fort. The creditors persisted and the case was carried up to the United States Supreme Court by Charles Gibson, then his attorney, and he was confirmed in his possession.

The *Post* had been issued from the presses of the *Globe-Democrat*, having no equipment of its own beyond type and talent. Operations were therefore consolidated at the *Dispatch* office, 111 North Fifth Street, where the rattle-trap equipment was made to do until a better could be procured. For a year the partnership continued, when, as in the case of the other owners of the *Westliche Post*, Mr. Pulitzer's speed proved too fast for Mr. Dillon, with the result that a buy-or-sell proposition was made. Mr. Pulitzer bought and became sole owner. Put in corporate form, he became President and made his physician, Dr. Frederich Kolbenheyer, friend of the bookstore days, Vice-President.

The paper now being fully his own, Mr. Pulitzer's instinct for gathering talent about him began to assert itself. He brought in as his chief editorial aid Col. John A. Cockerill, who had already achieved considerable eminence in his profession and who was selected as the person most likely to equal the redoubtable J. B. McCullagh of the very powerful *Globe-Democrat*. Colonel Cockerill, born in Adams County, Ohio, December 5, 1845, was slightly Mr. Pulitzer's elder, while his active newspaper experience had been much wider. He was son of Col. Joseph R. Cockerill of the Seventieth Ohio, whose regiment felt the first advance of the Confederates at Shiloh. Of himself a "Colonel" he once said:

## The Post-Dispatch — 1878-1883

When it comes to military titles, I'm out of it. My father was a Colonel, and so I presume my friends think the title is hereditary. My war record is soon told. I enlisted in the army as a drummer boy in 1861, and served until 1863, when we were mustered out by general order of the War Department. I again enlisted as a bugler in the artillery and served for a short time. I was in Southern Ohio at the time of Morgan's raid, when we did all running and no fighting. I saw all that I cared to of war and prefer reading about it to being in it. From '73 to '75, I was aide-de-camp to Governor William Allen of Ohio.

Before entering the army the boy had been playing "devil" in a local printing office and when through with the army, he went back to the case in the office of the *Scion of Temperance*, printed at Columbus, where he also became one of the clerks in the State Senate. He worked later in Hamilton and next became associated with Clement L. Vallandigham, in the publication of the Dayton *Empire*, later known as the *Ledger*. This not being a successful enterprise, he transferred his talents to the Cincinnati *Enquirer*, under the leadership of J. B. McCullagh, then Chief of its staff. By 1872, he had become managing editor. In 1877, he left his desk to become the *Enquirer's* correspondent in the Russo-Turkish War. He retired from the paper on his return, and, after a brief experiment on the Washington *Post*, became managing editor of the Baltimore *Gazette* in 1878. It was after a year in Baltimore that he joined Mr. Pulitzer, who found in him a man after his own heart, and one who had wit, quick decision and a willingness to face the music on all occasions, no matter how loudly it played. To this Cockerill added indefatigable industry, a keen

## Joseph Pulitzer

news sense and the ability to write pungent paragraphs. He could be highly agreeable or effectively repulsive as the occasion required and had the faculty of acquiring the affection of his men. The *Enquirer* had been the boldest of news-gatherers under his hand, and, although an evening paper had no such range as one in the morning field, he soon made his presence felt in St. Louis.

Intensely interested in politics, Mr. Pulitzer was elected a delegate to the National Democratic Convention, held at Cincinnati, in June, 1880, which nominated Major-General Winfield Scott Hancock for President, and William H. English of Indiana, for Vice-President. He served on the Platform Committee which evolved a tariff-for-revenue plank that became the issue of the campaign. Gen. Hancock's remark that the tariff was a "local question" brought upon him the scorn of the Republican orators and editors, though its truth was destined to become clear even to that party in after years. It was seized upon, made much of both in argument and as a means of "frying fat" out of tariff beneficiaries, with the result that the ticket was beaten, James A. Garfield of Ohio and Chester Alan Arthur of New York being elected.

Continuing his interest in politics, Mr. Pulitzer became a candidate for Congress at the Democratic primary held September 25, 1880, contesting for the nomination with Thomas Allen, President of the Iron Mountain Railroad. Mr. Allen had the support of the Missouri *Republican*, and two German dailies, the *Anzeiger* and the *Amerika*. Evidently the aid given Mr. Pulitzer by his own paper, the *Post-Dispatch*, was not very potent. Mr. Allen carried the

MR. PULITZER WELCOMING BEN BUTLER
TO DEMOCRACY.
(Cartoon in Die Lanterne, September, 1880.)

## The Post-Dispatch — 1878–1883

primary by a vote of 4,254 to 709 for the editor, was nominated by acclamation at the convention and elected in November; Mr. Pulitzer was thereby enabled to give his entire time to the *Post-Dispatch.* This he did with unremitting energy, coming to the office after dinner to work late on editorials and suggestions for the next day's issue.

Giving heavy blows he received many in return, some of them physical. He was twice bodily attacked, once by Col. W. B. Hyde, editor of the *Republican*, and once by a man who, the *Post-Dispatch* declared, was the avenger of its gambling crusade, though the assailant insisted he acted because of a local story which reflected on a relative. Mr. Pulitzer did not resort to arms, but treated the incidents as part of his stormy task.

He worked ceaselessly. At noontime his luncheon was usually a sandwich taken with a glass of beer at the place of refreshment operated by Anthony & Kuhn at 112 North Broadway, at a table with a friend or two, Joseph Weill, a wholesale dry goods merchant, and James Reed, agent for A. Booth & Sons, the great firm of Baltimore oyster shippers, being his most frequent companions. He drove to the office in a brougham drawn by a big iron-gray horse, driven by Eugene Stewart, an astute colored man who remained with him as long as he lived, driving his equipages in Europe as well as America. Usually, Mrs. Pulitzer kept him company to the office and would come after him when the paper was out. It was his practice to return after dinner and remain "working," as an acquaintance, Charles A. Hoffman, of St. Louis, has written, "every night at his desk in the editorial rooms of the *Post-Dispatch*, then at 111 Broadway, by the light of a single gas jet. I would pass by on my way home between eleven and twelve o'clock, and he was always there."

His desk in the office of the *Post-Dispatch* was in an alcove masked by a curtain, from behind which he would leap out from time to time with some new thought or criticism for his associates. One of his firm rules, based perhaps upon his own lingering accent, was that there should be no dialect used in the paper's columns, that might seem to reflect on comers from other lands. This he continued on the *World*. Nor would he permit men to be distinguished by nationality.

July 9, 1880, he was able to write to William C. Steigers, his advertising manager, then on a New York hunt for business, that the circulation of the paper "was more than twice that of the *Dispatch*, more than twice as large as that of the *Post*, and double that of the two papers consolidated." The *Post-Dispatch* continued to progress mightily. For eight months in 1881, John Pope Hodnett, John B. McGuffin and A. B. Cunningham kept a little *Star* a-twinkling. When it flickered out, Mr. Pulitzer took over its list and McGuffin, who rendered him important business services both in St. Louis and the invasion of New York.

December 31, 1881, the paper moved to Nos. 515–517 Market Street, where there was plenty of room and where two Hoe presses had been installed to meet its steadily rising needs. It was easily first in the evening field and challenged the robust *Globe-Democrat*. The profits ran from $40,000 to $85,000 per year.

Mr. Pulitzer was able to gratify his desires for travel and his position in life was assured. For a man

## The Post-Dispatch — 1878–1883

of thirty-five he had gained what would have been the summit of ordinary ambition. Apparently he had prepared the way for a comfortable, prosperous existence with the certainty of reasonable wealth and a strong place in the community. His health, however, was not good and he began to seek relief from the office work and the climate, leaving the general conduct of the paper more and more to Colonel Cockerill.

On settling down in St. Louis, Mr. Pulitzer first took up his residence at No. 2920 Washington Avenue, where his oldest son, Ralph, was born on June 11, 1879. The last year or so of his life in this city was spent at No. 2648 Locust Street.

The even tenor of his life was abruptly changed on October 5, 1882, when the shining hours of the *Post-Dispatch* were darkened by a tragedy. Mr. Pulitzer had been absent much during the summer and at the time was in New York. Colonel Cockerill, who was in editorial charge, had been opposing the candidacy of Col. James O. Broadhead, of the law firm of Broadhead, Slayback and Haeussler, for Congress,' the reason being that Colonel Broadhead, after accepting a retainer of $10,000 from the city in a suit against the Laclede Gas Company, had later abandoned his client to defend the case for the corporation. Cockerill's articles were severe and reflected not only on the character of the candidate but of the entire firm. This he supplemented by taking the stump and reiterating his paragraphs with more force at the hustings.

Col. Alonzo W. Slayback, one of Broadhead's partners, was a strong, determined man, who resented the reflections on his firm and determined to stop them. In the course of his excitement he consulted Gen.

William T. Sherman, then a resident of St. Louis, and a member of the Elks Club, to which both Slayback and Cockerill belonged, as to what sort of a personage the latter might be. The General told him Cockerill's father had served with him in the army; he was a fighter and his son was like him — he would fight too. The two colonels met at the club one afternoon, when they declared a truce over a bottle of wine and parted friends. A week later the storm broke out anew. In a speech at a ward meeting Slayback denounced the paper and called it a blackmailing sheet. The next afternoon the *Post-Dispatch* reprinted a personal card, which had been written by John M. Glover, an attorney afterward elected to Congress, and published a year before, in the Fall of 1881, in a first edition of the paper, the card being taken out by Mr. Pulitzer before the next edition was issued. In reprinting the Glover card, which impugned the valor of Slayback, the *Post-Dispatch* directed special attention to it in an editorial paragraph. On its appearance Slayback decided to go to the *Post-Dispatch* office and "have it out" with the editor. He took with him William H. Clopton, later appointed United States District Attorney by President Cleveland, with the purpose, as he declared, of slapping Cockerill in the face and forcing him to retract.

Cockerill was at his desk a little after 5 P.M. conversing with John B. McGuffin and Victor T. Cole, one the business manager of the paper, and the other foreman of the composing room, when the door opened and Slayback walked in, closely followed by Mr. Clopton. None of those present could, afterward, give a clear idea as to what occurred. Slayback uttered some excited words and rushed at

## The Post-Dispatch — 1878-1883

Cockerill who, taking a revolver from his desk drawer, fired. Slayback fell with a bullet through his chest, expiring in a few minutes.

Two widely different stories were told at the inquest next day. Mr. Clopton testified that Slayback was unarmed and that he was shot while he was in the act of taking off his coat for a fight with his fists alone.

Cockerill claimed, in a prepared statement read by him at the inquest, that Slayback was pointing a revolver at him when he, Cockerill, fired, and that for him it was either to shoot or be shot.

The shooting caused intense excitement in St. Louis. A great throng gathered about the office and there were threats of vengeance against Cockerill and the paper. Some of the hotheads in the crowd wished to burn the building. The other newspapers gave great space to the story. Cockerill went of his own volition to police headquarters to await the outcome. As it was an affair between gentlemen, the Coroner's Jury did not presume to pass upon the culpability of the survivor, leaving it for a court inquiry, which was never held. Cockerill was bailed and the incident faded into history. Broadhead's candidacy, which was for both a short and a long term in Congress, resulted in his election for the short term, and that of his opponent, Dr. J. H. McLean, for the long one. Some years later Broadhead was appointed Minister to Switzerland by President Cleveland.

The effect upon the paper was at once visible. It lost circulation and was bitterly denounced, the "personal" character of its policy coming in for deep criticism. All communities are well supplied with citizens who dislike being disturbed, and who believe that whatever is, is right. Of these St. Louis had its full share. On the other hand, a strong following felt that the paper was a true public servant, however roughly it might have made its way. Mr. Pulitzer stood by Cockerill through the storm, but it was soon apparent that neither owner nor editor could hold his former standing in the city and that the paper required another pilot. In this emergency Mr. Pulitzer turned to John A. Dillon, his former partner, and induced him to take over the general management. Mr. Dillon stood high in St. Louis. He was a nephew of Col. James B. Eads, the eminent engineer, who devised the Mississippi jetties, bridged the river and performed other notable feats. His wife was a granddaughter of Pierre Choteau, the great fur trader and rival of John Jacob Astor. He was a gentleman of talent and charm, who floated serenely with the best element in the community. Mr. Dillon assumed full charge, in the face of the popular resentment. If his coming did not at once restore the paper to its former place in the community, it stopped its descent.

The circumstances, however, bred in Mr. Pulitzer a feeling which he never lost: that he was unwelcome in the town. Ill health increased and, following the excitement and anxiety of the tragedy, so affected him that his wise physician ordered a long and complete rest. With this in view he departed for New York early in May, 1883, with the design of taking a trip abroad.

He had from time to time looked over the New York newspaper field, starting negotiations for Benjamin Wood's evening *News*, and John Kelly's *Star*, one prosperous and the other a weakling, kept alive by

THE ST. LOUIS POST-DISPATCH BUILDING

## The Post-Dispatch — 1878–1883

the funds of Tammany Hall. Nothing had come of these and he had dismissed the idea from his mind. Following the Cockerill-Slayback affair, November 16, 1882, his brother Albert, who had been a valued member of the New York *Herald* staff, on a capital of $25,000 to which Joseph made a small contribution, with apparently no great faith in the enterprise, had established the *Morning Journal* as a one-cent paper. It succeeded from the start and this was not without its effect on the elder brother's mind.

The Democratic field in New York was poorly covered. The *News* and *Star* had no standing. The *Times* and *Tribune* were Republican, the *Herald* and *Sun* mischievously independent and the *World* in the power of Jay Gould. Mr. Pulitzer's belief in true democracy was still his uppermost thought; he desired to become a national figure, to do something greater for the cause he loved. A Presidential campaign — 1884 — was approaching. The defeat of Hancock in 1880 and the split in the Republican party caused by the Garfield-Conkling row, bred a belief that a Democratic victory could be brought about. Conkling had been Grant's master and could not brook the independence of his successor. The assassination of the President, though it gave the haughty Senator from New York a President of his own selection in Chester A. Arthur, promoted from the Vice-Presidency, did not soothe his feelings. He had thrown up his office in an appeal to the New York Legislature for re-election as a vindication and had been beaten. He had also forced the nomination of Judge Charles J. Folger for Governor in 1882, and the latter had been buried under a hostile majority of over 183,000 for the little-known Grover Cleveland.

## Joseph Pulitzer

The time seemed ripe for Democracy and the place for the best effort on its behalf was New York.

With all these reflections, nothing was farther from Mr. Pulitzer's immediate thoughts than undertaking a new enterprise. He had adjusted his affairs for at least six months' absence to be spent in tranquil travel or pleasant repose. During the few days at his command in New York, he looked about among the papers and politicians, as was his wont, and made the discovery that Jay Gould was winding up his affairs as an active operator in Wall Street and, having found the *World* a liability rather than an asset, either financially or as a utility, was willing to consider a sale. As a result he opened a negotiation, the outcome of which was to have compelling influence on his fortunes.

## Chapter V

## THE OLD "WORLD" — 1860-1883

Founding by Alexander Cummings — Consolidation With the "Courier and Enquirer" — Manton Marble's Regime — Suppression of the Paper — The Gould-Hurlbert Period.

IT WAS a newspaper of no inconsiderable journalistic, if not material repute, toward which Mr. Pulitzer turned his expanding ambitions. The *World* had been important and influential for more than twenty years. In 1860, New York, though well provided with publications, both morning and evening, had another added to the supply through the belief of Alexander Cummings, a Philadelphian, that the community would support a one-cent daily, edited on religious lines. He had launched, some years before, the *Evening Bulletin* in Philadelphia, which had attained a measure of success, enough at least to give him prestige in selling stock for the new venture. He made a wide appeal to the pious and succeeded in getting together enough money to make the start. This was done on Thursday, June 14th. The salutatory was half-prophetic in that it proclaimed this central thought: "We seek public estimation: We do not seek popular favor."

Mr. Cummings was none too affluent and the *World* soon taxed his purse beyond its strength. Charles Godfrey Leland (Hans Breitmann) had been the editor of the *Bulletin* and, being poorly paid, mostly in promises, came to New York some years

*Joseph Pulitzer*

before Cummings, and in his autobiography gives this gl‿ⁿpse of his status, in the later fifties:

> Mr. Cummings [1] had once, during a financial crisis, appealed to my feelings very touchingly to let my salary be reduced. I let myself be touched — in the pocket. Better times came, but my salary did not rise. Mr. Cummings, knowing that my father was wealthy, wanted me to put a large sum into the paper, assuring me it would pay me fifteen per cent. I asked how that could be possible when he only could afford to pay me so little for so much hard work. He chuckled and said: "That is the way we make our money."

According to Leland, his employer had a very ingenuous way of "paying his debts." His friend, Simon Cameron, later and briefly Secretary of War, had a bank — the Middleton — "which if not wildcat, was far from tame, as its notes were always from five to ten per cent. below par — to our loss — for we were always paid in Middleton. I have often known a clerk to take a handful of notes at par and send out to buy Middleton wherewith to pay me." Losses were continuous and considerable from the start. To stay the deficit the price was raised to two cents on November 24, 1860. This did little good. The sum

---

[1] Mr. Cummings had an active and interesting history. Born in Williamsport, Pa., in 1810, he acquired the printer's trade in the office of the *Lycoming Gazette*, of which his brother was proprietor. He later edited the *Williamsport Chronicle*, and in 1846 established the *Philadelphia Bulletin*, the first afternoon newspaper in the Quaker City, selling at two cents. After his retirement from the *World* he engaged in sundry Philadelphia publishing ventures, with poor success, until 1866 when President Johnson appointed him Territorial Governor of Colorado. This post he filled for several years, when, returning East, Senator Simon Cameron secured his appointment as American Consul at Ottawa, Canada. He held the office until his death in 1881. The *Bulletin*, in the hands of William L. McLean, lived to become one of the great newspaper successes of America.

## The Old "World" — 1860-1883

extracted from stockholders aggregated $200,000 and in a year it was gone. Mr. Cummings, looking about for salvation, contrived a union with the *Morning Courier and New York Enquirer*,[1] once the chief of the Whig organs under the powerful editorship of General James Watson Webb. The dissolution of the Whig party, the onrush of the new Republican organization, in which Horace Greeley of the *Tribune* and Henry J. Raymond of the *Times* had most benefited, together with its old-fashioned blanket-sheet form and archaic methods, had reduced the paper to a small place in the city field. It held some circulation because of its long history and close relation to commercial interests.

The consolidation took place on July 1, 1861. The best value brought to the newer enterprise was a membership in the highly important Associated Press.

Despite 30,000 circulation promised in the *Courier and Enquirer's* valedictory, the paper did not thrive. It was well supported by the commercial and financial part of the community but there was little local advertising in the New York of that day; the war made newspaper production costly and soon Mr. Cummings abandoned the paper. It was a stock company, and its securities had been used among bankers to replenish the treasury. August Belmont

---

[1] The *Courier and Enquirer* was itself the result of a number of amalgamations, to wit:

1826 — *New York Enquirer*, founded by Mordecai M. Noah.
1827 — *Morning Courier*, started by James Watson Webb.
1829 — *Courier and Enquirer* united.
1832 — Webb purchased Noah's interest and becoming sole editor made the *Courier and Enquirer* the first politically independent newspaper with this motto: "Principles not men."
1845 — *New York American*, that had been established by Charles King in 1819, absorbed by the *Courier and Enquirer*.

was credited with being a leading factor in keeping the paper alive. John Anderson, the tobacconist, who became rich by the discovery that "fine cut" packed in tin-foil, kept moist as well as in cumbersome "crocks," Fernando Wood, Mayor of New York, Augustus Schell and General S. L. M. Barlow, were all involved in its affairs, together with Dean Richmond and some wealthy up-state Democrats. Manton Marble, a journalist of capacity, became part owner and editor. The *New York American* of that day, a struggling sheet, and the *Weekly Argus* were absorbed in course.

During the war time the paper was well served at the front. Edmund Clarence Stedman was one of its correspondents and Robert H. Newell (Orpheus C. Kerr) a member of the staff. Indeed, the paper never lacked talent. Mr. Marble was in the difficult position of being loyal during the period of the rebellion — and he was loyal — and conducting a newspaper in defense of the Democratic party, the battered remains of which represented much of pro-slavery and copperheadism, exasperated a good deal by the zeal with which Republicanism of the Ben Wade, Zach Chandler and Thad. Stevens type was emphasizing its own merits and casting odium on any form of opposition that might interfere with its permanence in power. To read back over the columns of the *World* during Mr. Marble's editorship is to find that it was sane and sound in its reproof of the extremists and in the light of events. The hysteria of Greeley, the ferocity of the abolitionists and the horrors of reconstruction are well visualized against the cooler, conservative and, at this distance, sensible attitude of the *World*.

The sensation of the paper's career was its suppression

## The Old "World" — 1860–1883

for three days, May 19, 20 and 21, 1864, by General John A. Dix, Provost Marshal for New York, because it printed in its late city edition, on the morning of the 18th, a bogus proclamation in which President Lincoln purported to order a day of fasting and prayer and a draft of 400,000 men. The hoax was sprung in the midst of General Grant's bloody and inconclusive Wilderness campaign, and for a few hours caused intense excitement in the city, though it appeared only in one other paper, and that of limited circulation, the New York *Journal of Commerce*. Secretary William H. Seward sent out an instant denial on the part of the Government at Washington, and the excitement died down, but at half-past eight o'clock on the evening of the same day Lieutenant Tuthill, commanding a squad of the Tenth Veteran corps, took possession of the *World* office and another file of the same forces under Captain William H. Cundy seized the establishment of the *Journal of Commerce*. Orders for the arrest of the editors and owners of both journals accompanied instructions to take over the plants and stop the publication of the papers. The order of arrest was rescinded. Both papers were, however, suppressed, to the wrath and dismay of all concerned. Mr. Marble and Messrs. Prime, Stone, Hale and Hallock, proprietors of the *Journal of Commerce*, united in a public protest which appeared in the other New York papers on the morning of the 19th, this copy being taken from the *Herald:*

*To the Editor of the Herald:*

Will you oblige us by publishing in your columns the following statement of the proceedings of the government this evening towards the *World* and the

## Joseph Pulitzer

*Journal of Commerce,* regarding the publication in our morning's issues of the forged proclamation, purporting to be signed by President Lincoln, appointing a day of fasting and prayer, and calling into the military service 400,000 men.

The document in question was written on the manifold paper, such as used for all the despatches sent to the several newspapers of our association, and had every external appearance and mark to identify it as a genuine despatch arriving in the regular course of business.

It was delivered at our office late at night at the time of the receipt of our latest news, too late, of course, for editorial supervision, but, as it happened, not before our printing offices were closed.

It was delivered at all, or nearly all of the newspaper offices, and published in a part of the morning editions of the *Journal of Commerce* and *World,* and, as we are informed, in a part of the editions of one or more of our contemporaries.

Early this morning the fact that the despatch had not been sent by the Agent of the Associated Press became known to us, and its fraudulent character was at once announced upon our bulletin boards, and a reward of five hundred dollars offered by us for the discovery of the forger. The Executive Committee of the Associated Press also offered a similar reward of one thousand dollars, as the fraud had been attempted to be perpetrated upon all the journals composing our association.

We took pains in the afternoon to apprise General Dix of the facts in the case, and gave him such information in regard to the circumstances of the forgery as might assist him in the discovery of its author. The government was at once put in possession of the facts in the case. Nevertheless, this evening General Dix, acting under peremptory orders from the Government

## The Old "World" — 1860-1883

placed our offices under a strong military guard and issued warrants for the arrest of the editors and proprietors of the *World* and *Journal of Commerce* and their imprisonment in Fort Lafayette. A vessel was lying, under steam, at one of the wharves to convey us thither.

Chancing to meet one of the officers of General Dix's staff, charged with the execution of this order, we proceeded in his company to the headquarters of the Department of the East and were informed by General Dix that the order for our arrest had been suspended, but that the order for the suppression of the publication of the *World* and *Journal of Commerce* had not been rescinded, and that we could not be permitted to enter our offices, which continue under the charge of the military guards.

We protest against this proceeding. We protest against the assumption of our complicity with this shameless forgery, implied in the order of our arrest. We protest against the suppression of our journal for the misfortune of being deceived by a forgery not less ingenious, nor plausible than the forged report of the Confederate Secretary of War, which Secretary Seward made the basis of diplomatic action.

PRIME, STONE, HALE & HALLOCK,<br>
*Journal of Commerce.*<br>
MANTON MARBLE, *World.*

New York, May 18, 1864.

Meanwhile the secret service machinery of the Government was promptly set in motion to discover the perpetrator of the fraud. There were two theories of the motive behind it, one that it was designed to provoke a flurry in the stock market, the other that it was planned by some traitor, so as to get the papers into the early morning European mails that went

[ 121 ]

out on the day of issue with the idea of influencing foreign powers further against the North. This last suggestion was put out by the *Herald*. The first theory proved correct. A clue was found in the Wall Street brokerage office of Kent & Knapp, which pointed to Joseph Howard, Jr., City Editor of the *Brooklyn Daily Eagle*, who was put under arrest Friday afternoon at his home in Willow Street. He owned up to General Dix, and admitted the stock jobbing purpose behind his performance. On the day the forgery appeared, William Henry Sutton, long foreman of the *Eagle*, not dreaming that Howard had a hand in the concoction of the document, spoke doubtfully of its authenticity to him when he came to his desk in the *Eagle* office on the 20th, to which he replied:

"It is not Lincoln's style; it may not be genuine," and then added reflectively:

"I guess it's all right, but it seems to be premature."

It is a fact that but two months later a call for 400,000 men was issued by the President, so "premature" was at least true.

On Saturday the authorities arrested as a fellow conspirator Frank W. Mallison, a member of the *Eagle's* staff who "covered" Williamsburg not only for the *Eagle*, but for the morning *Times* and *Tribune* in New York. Both were promptly taken to Fort Lafayette by United States Marshal Murray. Mallison told the whole story, though acclaiming his own innocence of anything worse than making the manifold copies from Howard's original, which were distributed to all the members of the Associated Press, except the *Tribune*. It appears that this was done between three and four A.M. The *Times* scented "fake" and did not use the "proclamation." The *Sun's* edition was

## The Old "World" — 1860-1883

already printed. The *Herald* put the proclamation into type and into the form for the city run but stopped the presses after several thousand had been printed and succeeded in keeping them out of the public's hands.

On the evening of the 20th, the soldiers were withdrawn from the two newspaper offices, but the order came so late that Mr. Marble did not attempt to call his force together for an edition on Saturday, the 21st. The *World* published no Sunday edition and so did not appear again regularly until Monday, the 23d of May. In this issue a full account of all the happenings was given. It showed nothing worse on the *World's* part than extreme carelessness. Howard was an experienced newspaper man, had been City Editor of both the *Tribune* and *Times*, and knew the ways of the various night desks. He had contrived the delivery of the "flimsy" so that it came into the office on the heels of the last batch of the same sort of copy from the Associated Press. The night clerk in the *World* office had just received the final envelope from the A. P. and putting it in the copy box whistled up the tube as a signal to have it pulled to the editorial rooms. The boy whose duty it was to do this did not respond and when the envelope with the forgery was thrown on the counter by a very hurried messenger, the clerk, pausing to reprove the lad for letting the door slam, threw it into the waiting box and again whistled "upstairs." This time the box was elevated with the considerable consequences noted.

Howard's father, John Tasker Howard, was a deacon of Plymouth Church and had been instrumental in bringing Henry Ward Beecher from Indianapolis to become pastor of the parish. Mr. Beecher

## Joseph Pulitzer

was a powerful personage at the time both as a preacher and a Republican. His good offices secured the release of Howard from Fort Lafayette after a few months' duress. The luckless Mallison was allowed to remain a year, and hated Howard and Beecher with great cordiality as long as he lived. Neither of the blithesome gentlemen was ever brought to trial. Howard survived the incident 44 years, dying March 31, 1908, at the age of 75.

Following the war years the paper continued its policy, supporting the ideals of Democracy, but by no means supinely. It bolted the party nominees, Seymour and Blair, on the eve of the Presidential election in 1868, advising a stronger selection against Grant and Colfax. It was in a fair way to be first in news-leadership by heading an uprising in the Associated Press in 1866, which its management, according to Frederick Hudson, in his "History of Journalism," failed to grasp, that would have given it a great advantage — a mistake never repeated in the several after-time news-buying jumbles.

December 29, 1869, Mr. Marble secured full control of the paper by stock purchase and continued his policy of conservative democracy, plus a good paper. All was going well. It almost ranked in income the mighty *Herald* despite the latter's lead in circulation. The tax returns for the first three quarters of 1869 show respectively receipts of $200,958, $214,694, $127,281, against the *Herald's* $188,395, $199,757 and $204,919. The party break-up, in 1872, affected the paper adversely, coupled with the revival of the *Sun* under the masterful hand of Charles A. Dana, and his publisher, Isaac W. England.

St. Clair McKelway, so long the accomplished editor

## The Old "World" — 1860–1883

of the *Brooklyn Daily Eagle*, who became the *World's* Washington correspondent from 1866 to 1870, and an editorial writer later, said of it once, that it "was the best written and least read paper" in New York.

This was true as to the first part. Though weak in circulation compared with the *Times, Tribune, Sun* and *Herald*, it was influential. Its readers were largely persons of means, the aristocratic old Democrats of New York. A much greater number read Ben Wood's *Daily News*, partly because it sold for a cent and partly because it regularly printed the policy and lottery drawings.

After the election of 1876, when Samuel J. Tilden, though victor on the face of the returns, gave way to the Electoral Commission's selection of Rutherford B. Hayes as President rather than risk the rising of civil strife, Mr. Marble felt that little hope remained for the survival of the Democratic Party or for the successful maintenance of a newspaper published in its interest. In this mood he unloaded the paper nominally on his editorial associate, William Henry Hurlbert, though the "angel" in the case was Col. Thomas A. Scott, the Napoleonic head of the Pennsylvania Railroad, who felt that a newspaper would be a good adjunct to the pursuit of public privileges. Hurlbert was a man of great talent, who had long been an editorial writer on the paper, with much previous newspaper experience. He had been foreign editor of the *Times* in the late fifties, for one thing, and was succeeded by Charles Godfrey Leland, who gives this note of him, at that early day, in his autobiography:

> Hurlbert was, even as a boy, very handsome, with a pale face, and black eyes, and extremely clever, being

## Joseph Pulitzer

*facile princeps* the head of every class, and extensively read. But there was a screw loose somewhere in him. He was subject, but not frequently, to such fits of passion or rage that he literally became blind while they lasted. I saw him one day, in one of these, throw his arms about and stamp on the ground as if unable to behold any one. I once heard a young lady in New York profess unbounded admiration for him, because "he looked so charmingly like the devil." For many years the *New York Herald* always described him as the Reverend Mephistopheles Hurlbert.

There was not much change in the tone of the paper after Hurlbert assumed editorial control. Indeed, if anything it was higher. He had a style of great polish, and careful editing was his law. Scott wearied of his possession after three years of "putting up" had severely taxed his purse, and passed the *World* on to Jay Gould, whose sinister course in Wall Street as the promoter of panics and wrecker of railroads had made him hated even there. Mr. Gould did not take the paper because he really wanted it but as part of a railroad trade with Scott. This is his own story of its acquisition:

I never intended to have the paper and got it more by accident than by design — almost against my desire. The way of it was this: In the summer of 1878 or 1879 I met Mr. Tom Scott, of the Pennsylvania Railroad, in Switzerland, in Berne. Mr. Scott was very much depressed and broken up — financially, physically and mentally. I felt a profound sympathy for him. He asked me as a favor to take his Texas Pacific Railroad off his hands and I concluded to do so. In arranging the details Mr. Scott appealed to me to include the *World* in the transaction. He owned it absolutely. I cared nothing about it but finally yielded. And that

## The Old "World" — 1860–1883

was the origin of the purchase. It was really a mere accident. I never cared anything about the *World* while I had it. It was simply an accidental trade of mine.

He was, however, sustaining about the same time, 1882–3, a little one-cent *Evening Star* in Boston, having some design on the welfare of New England in his mind.

Mr. Gould did not like to lose money and once blandly offered his broker, Washington E. Conner, a third interest in the *World*. Conner found the paper was costing Gould $40,000 a year and, guessing that the gift meant toting a third of the load, declined the proffer with thanks. If Gould expected any results in the way of financial benefit from the ownership of the *World* they were never achieved. The public at once sensed an interest not their own and the paper went into a slow but steady decline.

The *World* had long shared with the *Times* the triangular block between Park Row, Beekman and Nassau Streets, in later days occupied by the Potter and Jones buildings, but abandoned these quarters in 1881 and removed to a new structure built by Gould at Nos. 31–32 Park Row. Hoe presses were installed and the plant considerably modernized.

On the 31st of January, 1882, the old *World* building was destroyed by fire. Six lives were lost and the memory of the disaster survives as one of the horrors of the city. The disused Bullock presses in the basement were destroyed and the files of contemporary newspapers that had not been removed were lost.

Mr. Marble, born in Worcester, Mass., November 16, 1834, survived until July 24, 1917, on which date he died in London. Most of his life after the sale of the *World* was spent in England, much of it at Bourne-

*Joseph Pulitzer*

mouth. His brilliant successor, Mr. Hurlbert, born in Charleston, S. C., July 13, 1827, died at St. Augustine, Florida, February 18, 1905, after a strange career abroad. The intellectual disturbances of his younger days, noted by Leland, culminated in a clouded mind.

CHAPTER VI

THE NEW "WORLD" — 1883-1885

Purchase of the Property From Jay Gould for $346,000 — Principles Laid Down — The Policy of Public Service and the Support of True Democracy.

MR. PULITZER was never slow in testing out his impulses. An appointment was made with Mr. Gould at his office in the Western Union building at 195 Broadway, and the two men were not long in reaching an agreement. By May 8th, terms were settled and the next day was fixed as the time for signing papers and making the initial payment. Departing from Gould's presence late in the afternoon a sudden panic seized the would-be purchaser. He saw many difficulties ahead. New York looked vast and appalling. The efforts needful to secure success seemed for the moment beyond his strength. In this state of mind he determined to abandon the project, tell Gould to keep his paper and start forthwith upon his European holiday. There was some reason to hesitate about plunging into the sea of New York journalism, especially as rejuvenator of a semi-moribund and discredited sheet. The city was strongly held journalistically. The *Herald*, though outstripped by the two-cent *Sun* in circulation, had the lead in advertising and profits. It usually issued ten or twelve pages daily, in sections labelled according to the size of the sheet, based upon the four-page unit; triple sheet was twelve, and so on. The *Sun*, restricted always to

## Joseph Pulitzer

four pages, was a model of condensation and interest, with a vitriolic and learned editorial page. The *Times* and *Tribune* kept their price at four cents and gave eight pages week days for the money. The Sunday *Sun* sold for three cents — usually an eight- or ten-page sheet. The *World* was two cents daily and three on Sunday, the others five cents. There was also still in existence the feeble, flickering *Star*, owned by John Kelly, Boss of Tammany Hall, which sold daily for two cents and on Sunday at three, aping the make-up of the *Sun*. Two one-cent morning papers were in existence — *Truth*, owned by Josh Hart, a theatrical manager, and Albert Pulitzer's *Morning Journal*. Charles A. Dana controlled the *Sun;* James Gordon Bennett, the younger, then in his highest estate, the *Herald;* George Jones, the *Times*, and Whitelaw Reid, the *Tribune*.

Another factor in Mr. Pulitzer's indecision was the attitude of his brother, who promptly opposed the proposed invasion. When Joseph called to announce his purpose a violent discussion arose between them as to whether New York could stand two Pulitzers. Albert was naturally of the opinion that it would not. In the wordy dispute that followed Joseph expressed the stout belief that it would. The difference, however, disheartened him. Returning to the Fifth Avenue Hotel, where he was lodging, he told Mrs. Pulitzer to pack up and arrange to sail the next day. She laughed at his fears, and by her optimism and courage drove them away. After a sleepless night he met Gould to conclude the bargain. Just as he was about to affix his curious zigzag signature to the document the cunning financier withheld his pen and observed gently:

## The New "World" — 1883-1885

"By the way, Mr. Pulitzer, I had quite forgotten that some time ago I gave a small block of this newspaper stock to my son George. I would like to have him retain his interest. I assume you will have no objections to the boy's keeping this little holding."

"Not if you do not object to seeing it stated each morning in the year that the Gould family has no control or influence in the property," was the emphatic reply.

"Oh, well!" replied Mr. Gould, seemingly a trifle hurt, "if you view it in that light never mind. I only thought you might like to have the young man in with you."

The price paid for the property was very high, all things considering, $346,000, delivered in installments. Mr. Pulitzer never gave notes and the payments were arranged for on honor. The profits of the *Post-Dispatch* provided amply from a reserve in bank to meet the first installment. For the rest of the time the *World* paid for itself, making money almost from the hour the new proprietor took hold. The sum was the amount Mr. Gould claimed the paper cost him, plus its losses, for the four years of his ownership. Mr. Pulitzer once said that any man could capitalize a property upon earnings of ten per cent., but that Mr. Gould was the only one in the world who could capitalize upon a loss of twenty per cent.!

A further quotation from the letter written by Mr. Pulitzer to Dr. St. Clair McKelway, previously quoted, gives his version of the purchase:

> Nearly three years ago you were kind enough to write a flattering account about me on the occasion of the *World's* twenty-fifth anniversary. I meant to thank you many times. I do so now, sincerely. You were cer-

tainly always more generous than I deserved, but there was one error in your statement which I have reason to regret. The publication in the *World* itself has led some other writers to accept the statement as authoritative. This statement, as you may remember, was that Mr. George W. Childs of Philadelphia furnished the capital I needed to buy the *World*. Now forgive me if I trouble you with the exact truth in correcting the entirely unfounded statement.

I did not know Mr. Childs at the time I bought the *World*, had never laid eyes upon him, did not know anybody who did know him and never had any pecuniary or business transaction with him in my life; of course never received in any shape, form or manner one dollar or one cent from him. It is true I met him and we became friends a year or two after I bought the *World*, when its sudden and complete success was already the talk of the profession.

It is also true that if I had received any assistance or capital from him I could not be ashamed of it, as he was a high-minded, honorable and public-spirited man. But it so happens that I did not.

You doubtless ask why I am so earnest and emphatic on this point. This is my answer, my only motive. If there is anything in my melancholy life's work which I hope and wish may do good, it is that it should give encouragement to thousands of hardworking journalists who honestly believe that they have no chance of ever becoming owners or part owners of newspapers because they have no capital. If there is anything that a hardworking newspaper man really needs, it is encouragement, hope, belief that he may rise from the smallest to the highest position.

I should particularly like to feel that after I have passed away there will be more men than there are now in the profession and work which I have loved so much, possessing hope and confidence of rising to the highest

## The New "World" — 1883–1885

position, and it is solely for this reason that I will tell you the secret in a few simple words where the capital came from.

In December, 1878, I bought the *Post-Dispatch*, in St. Louis, at public auction, for $2,500. When I bought the *World*, a little more than four years after, the *Post-Dispatch* had become a highly prosperous paper for those days, and its prosperity enabled me to pay the necessary purchase money for the *World*. This is the simple story of the capital that went into the *World*.

Napoleon said that every private carried the marshal's baton in his knapsack. I hope that every reporter, copy reader, city editor or editorial writer will believe that he can carry his capital in his head if he will only work hard enough and stick to his convictions and sound principles. There are more dead papers to resurrect to-day than there were in 1878 and many reporters of to-day may be great revivalists a generation hence. I like reporters. I want to encourage them.

The news of the change was made known to New York in the issue of the *World* of May 10th, in the form of an announcement from William Henry Hurlbert, reading:

> The undersigned has this day transferred to Mr. Joseph Pulitzer, well known as the founder and editor of the St. Louis *Post-Dispatch*, the entire control of the *World* newspaper, which will be issued under Mr. Pulitzer's editorial management on and after tomorrow morning, May 11, 1883.
>
> Mr. Pulitzer's experience as a journalist and his loyalty to sound Democratic principles warrant the confidence and good will with which the undersigned cordially commends the *World* under his direction to the public of New York.
>
> Wm. Henry Hurlbert.

New York, May 9, 1883.

*Joseph Pulitzer*

The routine employees, at Mr. Pulitzer's instance, received a letter from John Gilmer Speed, the General Manager, who retired almost at once from the paper's service, of which this is a specimen:

May 9, 1883.

DEAR SIR:

Mr. Hurlbert asks me to inform you that he will transfer the control and management of the *World* to-morrow morning to Mr. Joseph Pulitzer. He wishes me in his name to thank you for the fidelity and ability with which you have discharged the duties confided to you and to say to you, at the request of Mr. Pulitzer, that you will oblige him by retaining your present position on the paper at your present salary and upon your merits as heretofore.

Mr. Hurlbert begs me further to express to you personally his sincere good wishes for your welfare and happiness.

And I am,
Very truly yours,
JNO. GILMER SPEED,
*General Manager.*

Mr. Hurlbert's staff at the moment included Jerome B. Stillson and Montgomery Schuyler as editorial writers; J. H. Coplestone, Night Editor; A. C. Wheeler (Nym Crinkle), Dramatic Critic; H. G. Crickmore, Sporting Editor. Mr. Wheeler and Mr. Crickmore remained long with the paper "on their merits." The others had a short survival.

Mr. Pulitzer made his initial appearance in the *World* office on the evening of the 10th of May. His coming, of course, disturbed the sleek routine of the place. Under Hurlbert the office was most decorously conducted. There was never any excitement within

## The New "World" — 1883-1885

its walls, no furious endeavors to go to press with everything in the forms at the last minute; no racing for trains, no rivalries with contemporaries. Instead, the pages closed peacefully after Mr. Hurlbert had carefully polished his leader and the copy of his writers. He usually topped off the night with the contents of a cold bottle kept in the composing room refrigerator.

In a twinkling all this was changed. The tall young adventurer from the West, his language still laden with the accent of his foreign tongue, radiating excitement and diffusing energy, came in like a tornado. Soon all was confusion. The old-fashioned staff viewed his coming with tremulous dismay.

One man moved in with him, E. C. Hancock, who had formerly been New Orleans correspondent of the *Herald*, and reaching New York, had become the Managing Editor of Albert Pulitzer's *Morning Journal*. This was the earliest of J. P.'s many raids on other offices and the result was not satisfactory. He found the new man so flustered that he mentally resolved to ship him at the first opportunity. But the luckless recruit performed one great service. During the evening he pestered the excited owner beyond endurance, among other things to make some sort of an announcement proclaiming the change. This Mr. Pulitzer was loath to do. He could think of nothing to say; had not thought of a salutatory at all. Hancock insisted so persistently that Mr. Pulitzer sat down and wrote at an outburst this creed for the new journal he intended to make, and by following which he won his great success:

The entire *World* newspaper property has been purchased by the undersigned, and will from this

## Joseph Pulitzer

day be under different management — different in men, measures and methods — different in purpose, policy and principle — different in objects and interests — different in sympathies and convictions — different in head and heart.

Performance is better than promise. Exuberant assurances are cheap. I make none. I simply refer the public to the new *World* itself, which henceforth shall be the daily evidence of its own growing improvement, with forty-eight daily witnesses in its forty-eight columns.

There is room in this great and growing city for a journal that is not only cheap but bright, not only bright but large, not only large but truly democratic — dedicated to the cause of the people rather than that of purse potentates — devoted more to the news of the new than the old world, that will expose all fraud and sham, fight all public evils and abuses — that will serve and battle for the people with earnest sincerity.

In that cause and for that end solely the new *World* is hereby enlisted and committed to the attention of the intelligent public.

JOSEPH PULITZER.

This was taken to the composing room and fell into the hands of Joseph N. Quail, an eighteen-year-old compositor, who put it into type. Mr. Quail graduated downstairs and some time after the *Evening World* was established, became its City Editor. He held the place as long as he wished, and when wearied of an outside position, which had tempted him away, returned to the office, where he was always welcome. Mr. Pulitzer gave the managers a standing order that "Joe" should always have a place if he wished it. He was on and off the staff a number of times.

## The New "World" — 1883-1885

Following the above announcement was an editorial entitled "True Democracy," which set forth that an intelligent newspaper must be independent, but not indifferent or neutral on any question involving public interest. Its rock of faith must be true Democracy, not the Democracy of a political machine.

The *World* promised under its new management to maintain such a Democratic character; to oppose organized monopolists, who, coveting and possessing exclusive rights under the aegis of public charters, were undermining a political freedom won more than a hundred years before. It was for true Democracy to preserve political freedom now, as it established political freedom in former days.

The heading of the newspaper had been slightly altered four times in its history and radically changed a fifth. Originally the text letters used at the top of the first page had between "The" and "World" a vignette of two globes, surmounted by a hand printing press from which irradiated rays of light. Bannerets across the base carried a motto "Its field, The World." When the consolidation with the *Courier and Enquirer* took place, the words "Morning Courier and New York Enquirer" were added in Roman capitals beneath the vignette. On November 17, 1862, the Roman capitals were replaced with full-faced type, a little smaller. This remained until December 16, 1876, when the subheading vanished, together with the vignette and the paper became simply "*The World.*" On August 20, 1881, the text heading was replaced by a full-face heading, reading "*The New York World.*" This remained the title until the morning of the 11th of May, when Mr. Pulitzer issued the first number under his own auspices. He restored the first heading, with the globes in vignette, surmounted by the printing press as before, but without the motto. This remained until after the erection of the Statue of Liberty, when that figure was added to the vignette.

The paper was eight pages in size, with six columns of the standard $13\frac{1}{2}$ ems pica in width. The headlines were set in capitals of Roman condensed with two hanging indentations each. There were four "display" headings on the first page, each extremely modest. One covered an account of a local storm — which led the page; another that of a murderer's last hours in the White Plains jail; the third, James R. Keene's sale of his pictures and giving a mortgage on his real estate, because of financial pinching, and the fourth, over a cable from St. Thomas, doubting the use of dynamite in a Haytian revolt. It was a dull looking paper, judged by any standard.

Mr. Pulitzer's first move was to call for local harmony between the Tammany and County Democracy factions, and he published an editorial on the 12th quoting various eminent Democrats like William C. Whitney and Abram S. Hewitt as indorsing the idea, which finally came to pass through the extinguishment of the County Democracy. On Sunday, May 13th, there was an editorial on "Our Aristocracy," which reprehended the upper phases of society. It averred:

> There is the aristocracy of Central Park. The low Victoria, adapted to exhibit boots, stockings and skirts as freely as hats and shoulder wraps. The sleigh with more nodding plumes than would deck out a company of lancers.
>
> There is the sordid aristocracy of the ambitious matchmakers, who are ready to sell their daughters for

## The New "World" — 1883-1885

barren titles to worthless foreign paupers, and to sacrifice a young girl's self-respect and happiness to the gratification of owning a lordly son-in-law.

The new *World* believes that such an aristocracy ought to have no place in the republic — that the word ought to be expunged from an American vocabulary.

It was proclaimed, in sequence, that the new *World* was nevertheless the organ of a true aristocracy — the aristocracy of labor — the man who by honest, earnest toil supports his family in respectability, who works with a stout heart and a strong arm, and who fights his way through life courageously, maintaining his good name through privations and temptations, and winning from his children respect as well as love.

This and much more of the kind followed. It was a large contract, but it appealed to the popular mind and the man who made it was sincere, coming as he did wide-eyed from the Middle West and believing more than he saw!

It must not be assumed, however, that the affairs of the "aristocracy" were ignored. On the contrary, they received the utmost attention, but not in the style of the celebrated Jenkins. The glitter was stripped off and the mystery of exalted doings dispelled. This process spread to the press generally and destroyed social exclusiveness in the old sense — and with it interest in the antics of any "set."

One of the first things the *World* did on the same Sunday, May 13th, was to interview Jay Gould, the former proprietor of its columns, an evident bit of disinfecting.

On Monday, the 14th, John Roach, the shipbuilder, was interviewed on the Gould interview. The headlines proclaimed that the "boss monopolist" indorsed the "stock waterer's" views. Mr. Gould had announced himself in the interview as being out of Wall Street and never expecting to go back again. The retirement of William H. Vanderbilt had been noted a few days before. The *World* speculated on the effect of the departure of two such strong men and rather likened them to the backers in a faro bank, expressing some hope that the withdrawal of the whales from the speculative waters would give the smaller fish a better chance. In this way a new atmosphere was steadily created both on the news and editorial side. Incidentally there was considerable response to the "aristocracy" editorial, one "Mary" breaking into song in this fashion:

> No more shall dawdling Duke or dreary dude,
>   With languid lisp or aspect strained and solemn,
>   Deepen the sadness of the solitude
>   That lately brooded o'er thy *beau monde* column.

Eager to succeed, Mr. Pulitzer took counsel everywhere with success. George W. Childs, publisher of the Philadelphia *Public Ledger*, was an oft-sought adviser, while another, the most valued of all, was Gen. Charles H. Taylor, of the Boston *Globe*, who after a long struggle with adversity had placed that paper upon a pinnacle of prosperity from which it has never been removed. Neither of these mentors had the same attitude toward the province of the press that Mr. Pulitzer adopted, but both were farseeing, wise and kindly gentlemen, much interested in the fiery adventurer.

The first move for public service came on Wednesday, May 16th, when a demand that the Brooklyn Bridge, not yet open, be made toll free was voiced and this in due season came to pass.

On May 17th, the paper announced these new *World* doctrines:

## The New "World" — 1883-1885

1. Tax Luxuries.
2. Tax Inheritances.
3. Tax Large Incomes.
4. Tax Monopolies.
5. Tax the Privileged Corporation.
6. A Tariff for Revenue.
7. Reform the Civil Service.
8. Punish Corrupt Officers.
9. Punish Vote Buying.
10. Punish Employers who Coerce their Employees in Elections.

This is a popular platform of ten lines. We recommend it to the politicians in place of long-winded resolutions.

It may be noted that nine out of ten of these propositions came to pass. Mr. Pulitzer himself weakened on a Tariff for Revenue in after years and it ceased to become a part of his doctrine. The rest stood, and are embodied in the laws of the country.

By May 18th the circulation had begun to move and a number of complaints were reaching the office from people who could not secure the *World* from newsdealers. Emphasis was laid on the fact that it would do its best to catch up, but years were to pass before it did. The number of copies circulated on May 11th was 22,761. On August 11th, the paper took stock of its progress in a three-column canvass of the newsdealers. The output had risen in the three months to 39,000 per day and was going strong. Commenting on this growth, Mr. Pulitzer wrote:

> We feel as if our work was hardly begun. We have spoken in the cause of true Democracy, and we take the growth that has rewarded our efforts as proof that the people have watched our cause, have given it their

approval and that they are daily offering us new encouragement to continue as we have begun.

He could not stand the luckless Hancock, and sent at once to St. Louis for Col. Cockerill and John B. McGuffin. Both arrived within the first week of the new ownership and set to work carrying out the changes due. Col. Cockerill took charge of the news end of the paper and Mr. McGuffin that of the business department. The establishment was not large. But 33 frames occupied the composing room and 55 printers comprised the force. The office was non-union, though under pressure to join the closed shops. A number of union men were working, "planted" by the union, which welcomed the chance to play on a stranger's nerves. There was dire need for economy and Mr. McGuffin, unused to luxury in St. Louis, cut off the ice and soap that the office supplied the composing room. This led to a revolt which the union advocates had hitherto been unable to foment. The suspension bridge between New York and Brooklyn, a model of engineering and architectural grace, was due for its formal opening on May 24th, Queen Victoria's birthday. The *World's* new editors looked forward to it as an occasion for their first spread. They had been writing it up for several days and on the 22d had printed a wood-cut of the structure, the first in a long line of illustrated endeavor. The evening of the dual event, when Mr. Pulitzer and Col. Cockerill came to the office to exploit the story, they found no printers on hand. They had gone on strike for soap and ice. John R. O'Donnell, Night Editor of the *Herald*, was President of Typographical Union No. 6, and at once took advantage of the situation. In company with

## The New "World" — 1883-1885

Col. Cockerill Mr. Pulitzer adjourned with him to Keenan's Cafe, next door to the office, and there surrendered not only on the ice and soap question, but as to the wider one of letting card-bearers openly work in the office, which was what the Union had been playing for as the first step toward a closed shop. The nonunion scale of 40 cents per 1,000 ems was accepted on the part of the organization. This gave rise to a queer complication and later to a story that the Union had aided the struggling proprietor. The wage scales of the other papers ran out during the life of the arrangement and they were raised to 46 cents. The *World* stood on its agreement but accepted an offer from the Union to pay 5 cents per 1,000 to the men out of its treasury until the contract terminated in November. The total amount thus paid was not great — $1,797.80, according to the Union records, but it held the men in place at a time when a strike was about to break in the book offices, and until full recognition and the entire scale were granted. The prudent Mr. McGuffin saved ice one night in the week — Sunday — by not ordering a supply for two days on Saturday. This was endured until Mr. Pulitzer himself, seeking to slake his thirst on a warm Sunday evening at the composing room spigot, found the Croton lukewarm and restored the refrigeration for the seventh day.

His little office was on the same floor as the composing room and he came into constant contact with the compositors and make-up men, with whom he was soon on the best of terms and for whom he always showed the utmost regard.

There were no restaurant accommodations in the building and the busy force was supplied by a basket vender of delicatessen, whose first name was also

Joseph, though shortened to the more colloquial "Joe." All hands, including Mr. Pulitzer, bought their midnight refreshments from "Joe" standing at case or imposing stone and taking bites between pauses in the make-up. Later the editorial rooms and Mr. Pulitzer's office were transferred to the third floor on the front, facing Park Row and the old Post Office. Here he and Col. Cockerill occupied rooms adjoining. The editorial writers shared a large office together.

Settling himself down to the hardest kind of work the newcomer soon had enough to do.

The bridge ceremonies were well reported in the issue of the 25th, despite the strike, but the opportunity for a "spread" that had in it a great lift in circulation came on the 30th, Decoration Day, when a throng of holiday sightseers crossing the structure became panicstricken and a dozen lives were crushed out, while a score were injured. To this tragic event the *World* gave one of its eight pages. The headlines were but one column in width and only two inches or so in depth; such was the journalistic restraint of the day.

Grover Cleveland was in the last days of the first six months of his term of office as Governor of New York, and had given frequent and unmistakable evidence of the kind of metal in him. The next year a President of the United States was to be chosen. On June 6th the *World* took a step in the direction of its greatest political opportunity, as the event proved, by asking for "Another Cleveland" to lead the National Democratic hosts. It did not urge his nomination, but "one like him" — perhaps "an unknown"—must certainly be produced. Under this warrant, as there were no duplicates, the Cleveland

## The New "World" — 1883-1885

boom, in proper time, got under way, and the rest is history.

On the 3d of July a neat typographical innovation was introduced. The vacant spaces on either side of the title were filled with what became known as "ears." These were circles in which the *World* was advertised as the only eight-page paper selling for two cents in the United States. In time the "ears" were used for all sorts of announcements affecting the interests of the paper, with the weather report added to lure the eye of the reader.

Mr. Pulitzer, always modest about his own achievements, used to say that Mr. Bennett and Mr. Dana made him a present of the town, one by an economic move and the other by a shift in policy, which was in a measure true. By September 18th, the newcomer's progress was so marked that the *Times* cut its price from four to two cents. Mr. Bennett, on September 25th, dropped from three cents to two, which was greeted by Mr. Pulitzer as "Another victory for the *World*." "The *Herald*," he wrote, "has reduced its price to two cents and the *World* is still booming. Brother Bennett, like Brother Jones, now believes in Western journalism. Owing to the pressure of advertisements the *World* will enlarge its size to at least eight columns more than the *Herald*."

Agreeable to this promise the paper was expanded to ten pages on the daily and to twelve on Sunday by the addition of a four-page "Sunday supplement." Mr. Bennett rose to the occasion by inserting a number of page advertisements in the *World*, the new proprietor gladly taking his money for, much as he boasted of his increased advertising, the amount published was puny gauged by later days. There were no dry goods pages and the only firm to begin using the *World* at this stage was that of Edward Ridley & Sons, on Grand Street, which sometimes risked a double column and had the paper to themselves. So Mr. Bennett's spreads were really events. They advertised the *Herald* at two cents as "the cheapest paper in America."

Unfortunately for his fortunes in cutting his price, Mr. Bennett also trimmed the profit of the newsdealers from $\frac{1}{2}$ to $\frac{1}{3}$ of a cent per copy. When in 1876 the *Herald* lowered its price from four to three cents, it allowed the dealer but $\frac{1}{2}$ cent margin, against $\frac{3}{4}$ when on the four-cent basis, causing much dissatisfaction; but so strong was its position with the public that the protests came to nothing. This time, however, the dealers organized under the leadership of a shrewd and able member of their trade, Stephen J. Richardson, in after years celebrated as a circulation manager on the *Recorder*, *Journal* and *World*, who led a strong and exhausting fight against the *Herald*, compelling it to establish a special delivery and agencies, at great cost and loss of circulation, much of the increment from which went to the *World*, attracted by its new methods and energetic management. The papers of the city generally sided with the dealers, although supplying the *Herald* agencies with their own publications for retail sale. Major George F. Williams, a Civil War veteran, ran the enterprise with much effort, backed powerfully by Mr. Bennett, but without avail. The drain was too much for the Scotch part of Mr. Bennett's psychology and after a year of contention, which kept the town in disorder with parades and mass meetings, he surrendered. Incidental to this mistake he raised his advertising rates, already high and arbitrary, and thus further amplified the "present" to Mr. Pulitzer.

## The New "World" — 1883-1885

Following the others, the *Tribune* went from four to three cents. None of these moves checked for an instant the momentum of the *World*. Indeed, it gathered strength from the several surrenders. People were moved to renewed interest in a publication which had so soon brought all rivals to their knees, and the result was increased circulation, increased advertising and increased prestige.

As the circulation conflict died down the election of 1884 loomed up and here Mr. Dana came in with his share of the giving. Grover Cleveland, as Governor of New York State, had offended the brilliant editor of the *Sun* by the curt rejection of a request for the appointment of a junior in the Bartlett family, stockholders in the paper, for appointment in the Adirondack Survey, then under the supervision of Verplanck Colvin. The editor, blind to the signs of the times, heedless of the great independent wave then rising, or rather contemptuous of it, assailed Mr. Cleveland with unmeasured bitterness and lampooned his independent followers, picking a word, "Mugwump," out of the Mohegan tongue, with which to characterize men who desired better things in politics than the high tariff and bloody-shirt doctrine of the Republican leaders. That party had nominated James G. Blaine, for whose support there would have been some excuse, but Mr. Dana, to emphasize his scorn for Mr. Cleveland, came out instead for Benjamin F. Butler, who ran on the Greenback Labor ticket for the chief office.

Eugene Field, then rising into the light in his "Sharps and Flats" column in the Chicago *Daily News* had blithely prognosticated Mr. Dana's performance in the following lines, published July 5, 1884:

## Joseph Pulitzer

> I gather them in, and I never care
> How the victims rage or the people swear;
> Thurman, McDonald and Flower, too,
> Have gently flocked to my hullaballoo,
> And now I am patiently waiting here
> For the Grover Cleveland boom to appear;
> And blind to the chances it has to win,
> I'll gather it in — I'll gather it in.

The effect on the fortunes of the *Sun* was immediate and deplorable. Its circulation, which alone of all city morning papers was proudly printed each day, shrank from 137,000 to 85,000 and finally became so attenuated as to disappear altogether from its place at the top of the first column over the editorial page, vanishing June 7, 1886.

Mr. Pulitzer, in the meantime, seized upon the situation with avidity, and made Mr. Cleveland's candidacy the special property of the *World*. With a political prescience for which he was notable, he picked Mr. Cleveland as the best possible nominee, feeling that much of the great majority gained by him when a candidate for Governor of New York in 1882, from Republican halfbreeds who resented the nomination of Charles J. Folger by the Conkling-Platt machine, could be counted on again. The *World* urged him strongly upon the National Democratic Convention held at Chicago, predicting that he could carry New York, New Jersey and Connecticut, and he was duly named. The prophecy proved correct.

The election of Mr. Cleveland was in doubt for several days. There was great excitement in the city. Jay Gould, as master of the Western Union Telegraph Company, was accused of holding back the returns and an angry mob with ropes in hand made a demonstration in front of the company's headquarters at

## The New "World" — 1883-1885

Broadway and Dey Street that presaged an outbreak. Fortunately, the result in Indiana, the key of the doubtful states, soon became clear. The determination of the Democrats not to have another Tilden-Hayes affair was not put to the test.

The potency of the *World's* support cannot be better described than in these words of Mr. Cleveland, written nearly a quarter of a century after, when the *World* celebrated its Twenty-fifth Anniversary under Mr. Pulitzer's guidance:

I never can lose the vividness of my recollection of the conditions and incidents attending the Presidential campaign of 1884 — how thoroughly Republicanism was intrenched — how brilliantly it was led — how arrogant it was — and how confidently it encouraged and aided a contingent of deserters from the Democratic ranks.

And I recall not less vividly how brilliantly and sturdily the *World* then fought for Democracy; and in this, the first of its great party fights under present proprietorship, it was here, there and everywhere in the field, showering deadly blows upon the enemy. It was steadfast in zeal and untiring in effort until the battle was won; and it was won against such odds and by so slight a margin as to reasonably lead to the belief that no contributing aid could have been safely spared. At any rate, the contest was so close it may be said without reservation that if it had lacked the forceful and potent advocacy of Democratic principles at that time by the New York *World* the result might have been reversed.

In the presidential canvass of 1892, I was again a witness of the *World's* democratic zeal and its efficient party work. In that struggle it left nothing undone that any newspaper could do to aid the cause, and it certainly accomplished much.

## Joseph Pulitzer

I have spoken specifically of the two campaigns with which I was personally most familiar, and in which I had the opportunity to share campaign activities, though I do not intend to speak of them as exceptional instances of the *World's* achievements.

Mr. Cleveland touched the real point of the case in this statement of influence, for the significance of Mr. Pulitzer's great and immediate success with the *World* was that he enforced a radical change, he renewed the vigor and vitality of the press in that special phase of its force, the editorial page. For him that page was the paper. Mountains of figures have been given to show how the *World* grew in his hands, for indeed prosperity came almost before he knew it; but that prosperity was not his foremost thought in this adventure. Naturally he wished to make the paper pay and pay well, but he contemplated his relation to it in a far higher sense than that of money making. For him the newspaper was not a mere chronicle; it was rather an opportunity in another sense than that of a sordid money maker. His passion was to be felt in the strife of public forces then in play, and to be heard in the consideration of national concerns.

In this conception the editorial page was the arena of public life — the place where all the forces involved in the conflict for or against the welfare of the nation were to be met and fought every day in every year. Here are some words of William H. Taft that come very near to his thought:

> The Press is essential to our civilization, and plays an unofficial but vital role in the affairs of government. The discipline of a fear of publicity, the restraining and correcting influence of the prospect of fearless criticism are of much value in securing a proper ad-

## The New "World" — 1883–1885

ministration of public affairs. The exercise of power without danger of criticism produces an irresponsibility in a public officer which, even if his motives are pure, tends to negligence in some cases and arbitrary action in others.

There were few radical publications of respectable parentage in the country; indeed the most progressive ideas were to be found in the more conservative sheets, such as the New York *Evening Post*, the Boston *Herald* and the Springfield *Republican*. However sensational Mr. Pulitzer's ideas of news presentation might have seemed in the staid days of his first appearance in New York, his editorial views were then and always of the soundest and highest character in the interest of a free government and the public welfare.

Soon after acquiring the *World* Mr. Pulitzer brought his family from St. Louis to New York, leasing the furnished residence of James W. Gerard at No. 17 Gramercy Park, where he had Samuel J. Tilden and Clarkson N. Potter for next-door neighbors. Mr. Gerard was father of the future Ambassador to Germany, who was to serve in the trying times of the World War.

The high hopes of Democratic success aroused by the nomination of Mr. Cleveland led to a renewed activity in the two clans of Democracy in New York, the County Democracy and Tammany Hall. Some young men like John M. Bowers, William C. Whitney, W. Bourke Cockran and Hugh J. Grant were making themselves felt in party councils. Mr. Pulitzer's force of character and the power in the *World* were recognized as factors in the hoped-for result, and the group persuaded him to take a nomination for Congress in the solid Ninth District on the assurance that his

## Joseph Pulitzer

election was a foregone conclusion and that it would not be necessary for him to make a campaign. He accepted, defeating Herman Thum, Republican, by a majority of 7,021 votes.

Mr. Pulitzer took his seat in the 49th Congress, which did not begin to function until the first Monday in December, 1885. He felt the need of a secretary and consulting his always wise contemporary, Gen. Charles H. Taylor, of the Boston *Globe*, selected Edwin A. Grozier, an exceptionally well-adapted young man, born in San Francisco, but at the time private secretary for Gov. George D. Robinson of Massachusetts, a place filled after three years' service as reporter on the *Herald* and *Globe* in Boston. Mr. Grozier accompanied him to Washington and looked out for his political affairs.

The editor had taken the nomination with great reluctance and only to help the ticket. He soon found he had made a mistake. The demand upon his time in the office was so great that he could give his Washington chair but little attention. The frequent journeys backward and forward were tiresome and he was seldom in his seat, though much on the road. He took more interest in the work of the *World's* Washington bureau than that of Congress. T. C. Crawford was the paper's very able correspondent. A vivid Congressional inquiry was under way and Mr. Crawford in discussing it with his editor used the phrase "Album of letters." Mr. Pulitzer pounced upon "Album." "That's the word," he exclaimed. "Album! Make it conspicuous in your dispatches." He did and the next day the country was talking about the "Album."

He stopped at John Chamberlain's hostelry when in

## The New "World" — 1883-1885

the city, keeping in seclusion and dealing with a huge correspondence that constantly piled up. His absenteeism was seized upon by the unneighborly *Sun* and severely criticised. Moreover, holding a place in the House of Representatives was incompatible with the severe duty of running a vigorous, critical newspaper devoted to public service. This with the fact that the Tiger declined to change its stripes caused him to resign, taking effect April 10, 1886. He was greatly relieved by this step, which freed him from an unpleasant entanglement and once more made it possible for the *World* to act as a defender of popular rights, regardless of party interests or relationships.

A revolution in press building had been under way for several years. Luther C. Crowell, a Cape Cod fisherman with rare mechanical talents, had invented a folding device for attachment to the rotary press perfected by R. M. Hoe in 1871, which like its predecessor, the Bullock, delivered uncollated sheets. By this it was possible to make a neat half-page fold, up to eight pages. Mr. Pulitzer was the first publisher to install one of these machines in the office of the *Post-Dispatch*. Its vagaries nearly drove him mad and bred in him a strong prejudice against new devices. Quoting this experience, he would ever after add: "Let the other fellow pay for the experimenting." The folder in time became a success, and was followed by an even greater improvement made possible through its adaptability. The first arrival was a double insert press by which it was feasible to increase size from eight to ten or twelve pages. The first of these was offered to Mr. Pulitzer, who, timid from his recent experience, declined it. The more venturesome James Gordon

*Joseph Pulitzer*

Bennett bought it for the New York *Herald*—"Press No. 140" on the Hoe factory books. Being operated nearer home, it worked better and Mr. Pulitzer promptly purchased the second one manufactured. The *World* press room was equipped, when he found it, with single eight-page machines of the early type. The pressure on its columns soon became so great as to force an increase in their number from six to seven.

Soon it was certain that eight pages could not long contain the growing news and business and more presses were called for. Mr. Crowell had now expanded his invention so as to produce the familiar quadruple machine, the base of all the monsters of to-day, capable of producing any size inserted up to sixteen pages, and collected, at half capacity, up to thirty-two. Mr. Pulitzer was compelled to forego his desire to let the other fellow pay for the experiment and installed the first to come from the factory. One press could not take care of all his troubles and two of the eight-page machines were rigged tandem to do what they could in producing a bigger and better *World*. Soon there was always a press on the stocks in the Hoe factory designed for the *World* establishment.

None of his competitors was better equipped. The *Sun's* cellar was full of Bullocks and with a four-page size, it was not embarrassed. The *Times* was printed on a battery of Walter presses, invented by the owner of its London namesake, each driven by a separate engine. They did duty for many years after. Until Sunday papers became mammoths the quadruple press was adequate, though the *World* was never, in all its history, able to keep its press requirements up to the demands.

## Chapter VII

### THE DAY'S WORK — 1885–1891

Statue of Liberty Saved — Boodle Aldermen and the Broadway Franchise — Strenuous Hours on Park Row — Breakdown — Blindness — Retirement.

THE OPPORTUNITY to perform a great public service and at the same time aid in erecting a monument to the dearest longing of his soul — Liberty — arrived for Mr. Pulitzer in 1885. Commissioned by the people of France, who raised more than 1,000,000 francs for the purpose, Auguste Bartholdi, the sculptor, had executed a gigantic figure of the goddess, wonderful in art and magnificent in conception, designed to stand on Bedloe's Island in New York Harbor, holding a torch of freedom to welcome the oppressed of all the world. A committee had been formed, of which William M. Evarts was Chairman and Richard Butler Secretary, to secure funds for the construction of a proper pedestal. The work lagged until the statue, boxed and ready in France for shipment to America, bade fair to remain there. Enough money had been gathered to lay a concrete base, but not a cent was in sight to pay for the construction of the great pedestal designed to lift the statue a hundred feet above the level of the sea. The committee had vainly sought aid from Congress to avert the shame. This failing, it announced its inability to proceed further and in effect threw up its hands. It was then Mr. Pulitzer

*Joseph Pulitzer*

made his first great appeal to the American public. On March 16th, he published in the *World* this effective editorial:

> Money must be raised to complete the pedestal for the Bartholdi statue. It would be an irrevocable disgrace to New York City and the American Republic to have France send us this splendid gift without our having provided even so much as a landing place for it.
>
> Nearly ten years ago the French people set about making the Bartholdi statue. It was to be a gift emblematical of our attainment of the first century of independence. It was also the seal of a more serviceable gift they made to us in 1776, when, but for their timely aid, the ragged sufferers of Valley Forge would have been disbanded and the colonies would have continued a part of the British dominion. Can we fail to respond to the spirit that actuated this generous testimonial?
>
> The statue is now completed and ready to be brought to our shores in a vessel especially commissioned for the purpose by the French Government. Congress, by a refusal to appropriate the necessary money to complete preparations for its proper reception and erection, has thrown the responsibility back to the American people.
>
> There is but one thing that can be done. We must raise the money.
>
> The *World* is the people's paper, and it now appeals to the people to come forward and raise this money. The $250,000 that the making of the statue cost was paid in by the masses of the French people — by the workingmen, the tradesmen, the shop girls, the artisans — by all, irrespective of class or condition. Let us respond in like manner. Let us not wait for the millionaires to give this money. It is not a gift from the millionaires of France to the millionaires of America

## The Day's Work — 1885-1891

but a gift of the whole people of France to the whole people of America.

Take this appeal to yourself personally. It is meant for every reader of the *World*. Give something, however little. Send it to us. We will receive it and see that it is properly applied. We will also publish the name of every giver, however small the sum given.

Let us hear from the people. Send in your suggestions. We will consider them all. If we all go to work together with a firm resolve and a patriotic will we can raise the needed money before the French vessel bearing the Bartholdi statue shall have passed the unsightly mass on Bedloe's Island that is now but a humiliating evidence of our indifference and ingratitude.

The response was instant and popular, as these excerpts from the daily files of the paper show:

Please receive from two little boys one dollar for the pedestal. It is our savings. We give it freely.

Inclosed please find five cents as a poor office boy's mite toward the pedestal fund. As being loyal to the Stars and Stripes, I thought even five cents would be acceptable.

The inclosed dollar comes from a party of poor artists who dined in University Place this evening.

A lonely and very aged woman with very limited means wishes to add her mite to the Bartholdi fund. Hoping that the inclosed dollar may induce multitudes all over the country to respond and that the enterprise may be very speedily accomplished is the earnest wish of the writer.

A few poor fellows whose pockets are not as deep as a well but whose love of liberty is wider than a church door, hand you the inclosed $7.25 as their mite toward

## Joseph Pulitzer

the Bartholdi fund. May Heaven help your good work; it seems that New York's rich men do not.

I am a young man of foreign birth and have seen enough of monarchical governments to appreciate the blessing of this Republic. Inclosed please find $2 for the Bartholdi fund.

I am a cash boy with a salary of $5 per month, and I contribute 50 cents to the Bartholdi fund.

I am a wee bit of a girl, yet I am ever so glad I was born in time to contribute my mite to the pedestal fund. When I am old enough I will ask my papa and mamma to take me to see the statue, and I will always be proud that I began my career by sending you $1 to aid in so good a cause.

On August 11th, following, the *World* was able to announce in triumph the success of its undertaking. The $100,000 was in hand. Work had not been delayed. The money was turned over, first in a $25,000 check and later as needed, while the work went on.

General Charles P. Stone, late of the American and later of the Egyptian Khedive's army, was the engineer. When the French transport *Isere* brought the statue to New York the pedestal was ready and, as Mr. Pulitzer wrote, the nation had been "saved from disgrace."

The statue was dedicated October 28, 1886, with a great naval and civic demonstration. The sculptor was present to witness the crowning of the work. "It is as I wished," he said. "The dream of my life is accomplished. In this work I see the symbol of unity and friendship between two nations — two great republics."

How that symbol endures the world learned in 1917 and 1918, when America stepped across the sea and paid her debt to France, principal and interest, compounded a thousand fold!

JOSEPH PULITZER AT FORTY.

## The Day's Work — 1885–1891

President Cleveland, in accepting the statue, used these notable words:

> We are not here to-day to bow before the representation of a fierce and warlike god, filled with wrath and vengeance, but we joyously contemplate instead our own deity, keeping watch and ward before the open gates of America, and greater than all that have been celebrated in ancient song.
>
> We will not forget that Liberty has here made her home; nor shall her chosen altar be neglected.

As the paper prospered so famously Mr. Pulitzer wished all who had to do with it to prosper accordingly. He was always giving rewards to bright reporters and enterprising editors. Each new press as it came in was the warrant for some sort of celebration. Christmas and Thanksgiving brought turkeys for all. When the *World* passed 100,000 in circulation 100 guns were fired in City Hall Park and every employee received a tall silk hat.

He was anxious that the men should enjoy themselves and actually bought a section of the old Elysian Fields in Hoboken as a playground. It was too far off and there was little time to play, so the experiment was no great success. He then sought to use the ground as a site for a *World* village, offering to aid the men in building houses. They preferred to select their own abiding places, so the project came to nothing. He was disappointed but took some small consolation in taking shares in the World Building and Loan Association, keeping up his payments until everybody else had "bought out" their shares. Then he caused it to be wound up with no record of having provided a home for anybody. He evolved a number of mutual benefit plans, none of which was welcomed by the unions, who in time controlled all departments, and so gave up his efforts to uplift beyond providing a good workshop, plenty of employment and decent pay.

The paper was now too much for the unaided efforts of even two such workers as Mr. Pulitzer and Colonel Cockerill. Accordingly, Ballard Smith was taken from the New York *Herald* and made managing editor, Colonel Cockerill becoming editor in charge. Mr. Smith was born at Carmelton, Indiana, September 20, 1849, of New Hampshire ancestry, his forbears coming from Durham, in the Granite State. He graduated at Dartmouth in the class of 1871 and took to journalism as a reporter on the Louisville *Commercial* under Col. R. M. Kelly. Here he became city editor and was then taken over by Col. Henry Watterson to fill the same position on the *Courier-Journal*, eventually becoming managing editor. Having metropolitan aims, Mr. Smith came to New York where Manton Marble made him city editor of the *World* in 1876. After a very short service here, Mr. Dana invited him to become managing editor of the *Sun*, a place he retained for two years, going thence to the *Herald*, and making room for Chester S. Lord, who was to hold the office for twenty-nine years with distinguished ability.

Mr. Smith was a typical Kentuckian, of fine appearance, dash, and a keen nose for news. He was also something of a social figure, then a novelty among working newspaper men in New York. The ill-natured *Sun* was sponsor for the story that the successful proprietor of the *World* had acquired Mr. Smith more for his social graces than his editorial abilities, desiring to use his "drag" as a door opening for a parvenu. Nothing could have been more absurd.

## The Day's Work — 1885-1891

Mr. Pulitzer needed no door openers and had no use at all for what was then called society and which the *World* under his leadership was doing so much to destroy.

Mr. Smith's coming added to the vigor of the news hunt and considerably to Mr. Pulitzer's troubles. Cockerill and Smith were alike in being abrupt in conclusions and highly sensitive about authority. There were constant clashes between the gentlemen which called for intervention on the part of their employer, who often found himself in a trying position. He esteemed them both and did his best to harmonize their differences, though coming to the safe conclusion that "temperament" was something that could not be dealt with.

To Mr. Smith was due the "page" story and the emphasizing of headlines, together with sending reporters upon big assignments in carload lots. There was small limit to his daring. Notable interviews were his specialty, some of the best of which he did himself, including one with Grover Cleveland in 1887, while President, that made a general stir.

To the editorial page at this period was also added Mr. William H. Merrill, from the Boston *Herald*, who became chief writer and long held the post with skill and discretion; Edward S. Van Zile, who produced a bright "Personal and Pertinent" column; and A. B. Kingsbury, a Harvard graduate, whose clever touch graced the *World's* columns for a third of a century.

The great news "stunt" of the Cockerill-Smith days was the unveiling of the boodle Aldermen, who had been bribed by Jake Sharp to give a street car franchise on the sacred limits of Broadway, which for

## Joseph Pulitzer

nearly a century had been filled with lumbering "busses" because the property owners would not permit track-laying on their noble thoroughfare. It is not necessary here to recite the detection, arrest and trial of the boodlers. The *World*, under Mr. Pulitzer's hard driving, made the scandal a great occasion for cleaning up New York politically, paving the way incidentally for William C. Whitney and Thomas F. Ryan to make themselves multi-millionaires by taking over the corrupt franchise and building up the colossal pyramid of high finance that went to smash with the Metropolitan Street Railroad.

The reports of the trial were unique. The late Ira Shafer was chief counsel for the boodlers. The gay reporters of the *World* made much of him to his intense and angry disgust. Walt McDougall, the *World's* cartoonist, "did" him in thumbnail sketches and Henry Guy Carleton impaled him on witty shafts of description. Never was there a more delicious line than Carleton's describing Mr. Shafer's beginning of the cross-examination of Katy Metz, the maid-servant in the next house, who had noted the coming of the conspirators to call on Alderman Jaehne, the single statesman who was to go to prison.

"Even as Antinous tiptoed up to the stranded Aphrodite on the Paphian shore," wrote Carleton of Ira's approach to Katy. It put Shafer into a frenzy to no avail.

To gather notable contributors and make good use of their names, was one of Mr. Pulitzer's strongest moves. Valerian Gribayedoff, the artist who first made intelligent newspaper illustrations, Walt McDougall, cleverest of the early every-day cartoonists, were samples developed in the office. Mrs. Jefferson

## The Day's Work — 1885–1891

Davis enjoyed a comfortable salary for the last ten years of her life as a special contributor, though latterly seldom called upon. When Ward McAllister made New York's Four Hundred famous, Mr. Pulitzer kept after him until he "edited" society news for the paper with decorous comment on the upper world — now a universe without interest, society as such having happily disappeared. It was much of a mystery to the public up to the eighties.

Bill Nye, the humorist, was one of the first annexed. Charles B. Lewis, "M. Quad" of the Detroit *Free Press*, was another early acquisition. John B. McGuffin died, and, on the recommendation of Gen. Charles H. Taylor, George Walter Turner came from Boston to succeed him as business manager.

How well the paper was doing during this period of hard work is evidenced from this letter to William C. Steigers, Advertising Manager of the *Post-Dispatch:*

*The World.*

EDITOR'S ROOM,
NEW YORK, May 13, 1887.

Personal.

DEAR MR. STEIGERS:

Please do not for the future make any bets with regard to the *World's* earnings, especially with Captain Slattery, who is a good fellow. At the same time, as you have blundered into this thing, I am bound to say that the earnings of the *World* for 1886 were over five hundred thousand dollars.

Yours truly,
JOSEPH PULITZER.

An exhilarating episode of this busy time was a physical encounter with Joseph Howard, Jr., whose

## Joseph Pulitzer

bogus draft proclamation had caused the *World's* suppression twenty odd years before.

Howard was bold and insolent in manner and brushed aside an assignment given him with the announcement that he intended, instead, to cover the Winter Carnival at Montreal, then a novelty. When Mr. Pulitzer objected Howard replied hotly and followed it up with a blow, in delivering which his glasses fell to the floor. He demanded a cessation of hostilities until he could find his eyes and while in a stooping position in search of the spectacles, his tall employer lifted him by his collar and the seat of his unmentionables and deftly tossed him out of the room. He never came back but made a good living for years with his "Howard" letters, the leading customer for which was the Boston *Globe*.

The evening newspaper field in New York had been negligible. The *Daily News* held the largest circulation, chiefly among the tenements. The *Evening Post* had for rivals the *Mail and Express* and the *Commercial Advertiser*, of the same class. The *Evening Telegram* was a small annex to the *Herald*. All had slim outputs; none was generally circulated. Into this neglected field, on March 17, 1887, came the *Evening Sun*, edited by Amos J. Cummings, an editor par excellence. It was an instant success at one cent and revived the fading fortunes of the *Sun* establishment. The *World* took no cognizance of the new arrival until October 10, 1887, the twentieth anniversary of Mr. Pulitzer's arrival in St. Louis, when the progress of the *Evening Sun* had pushed its circulation well up over 100,000 per day. On that date the first issue of the *Evening World* appeared — four pages — one cent. The determination to start it had been rather hastily arrived at. E. Tracy Greaves was managing editor and

## The Day's Work — 1885–1891

S. S. Carvalho, an indefatigible and talented member of the morning *Sun* staff, came over to be city editor. He took ten days to organize a force and get under way. The *Evening World* soon met and passed its rival. The loss for the first year was about $100,000. This it overcame after 1889 and always continued as a powerful earning factor in the establishment, though, of course, competing with its parent, dividing the business and forcing the *World* to do two dollars' worth of work for one.

There had been no revision of the New York State Constitution since 1867 and Mr. Pulitzer, mindful of the struggle to correct that of the State of Missouri, supported a demand for a Constitutional Convention voiced by the Anti-monopoly League. The politicians in both parties were cool toward the suggestion and failed to provide ballots for the required popular vote. The *World* furnished 5,000,000 and the proposition carried at the election in November, 1887. The Legislature of 1888 passed the necessary act, but it was vetoed by Gov. David B. Hill. Revision had to wait until 1892.

To cap his strenuous labors Mr. Pulitzer, in the fall of 1887, threw his personality into the local campaign for District Attorney. Tammany held the place and had for its candidate Col. John R. Fellows, an ex-Confederate soldier, brilliant and easy-going, who ran the office on the comfortable lines of pull and complaisance. The opposition nominated De Lancey Nicoll, then a young and shining figure, a New Yorker of long lineage and great fitness for the office. The campaign was one of the fiercest in local history and ended in defeat, Fellows receiving 99,798 votes; Nicoll 77,556. Mr. Pulitzer had spoken powerfully

## Joseph Pulitzer

from the stump and doubly so in the paper. He was deeply disappointed at the result, and coming out of his office on Election night, November 8th, after the paper had gone to press, chronicling his first New York failure, had paused for a moment in the telegraph room on his way to the elevator. The staff and heads crowded around him in silent sympathy.

"Gentlemen," he said, "we have been getting out a fine political paper. From now on I want a fine newspaper every day!"

But there was more than political discomfiture to depress him. He was undeniably ill, though on his feet. His nerves were shattered and, what was worse, eyesight, never strong, became troublesome. He had, indeed, much abused his powers of vision. Long hours of reading in poor light and in bed while a boy in St. Louis had laid the foundation of weakness; longer hours writing and poring over proofs in the dim hot gaslight of the day had complicated the preparations for disaster. Added to the nervous crisis there were symptoms of a weakness of the lungs, which had before threatened him. In this state of health it was deemed unwise for him to remain during the winter of 1888 in New York and by the advice of Drs. Herman Knapp and James W. McLane, he departed for Monterey, in California, taking with him for a companion Charles B. Fearing, of New York, and later adding Charles J. Merrill, son of William H. Merrill of his editorial staff, as secretary.

He took up headquarters at the Hotel Del Monte, where a glimpse of his state can be had from a letter of regret sent to the New York Press Club declining its invitation to a dinner given its President, Col. John A. Cockerill, February 16, 1888:

## The Day's Work — 1885-1891

I sincerely regret my inability to be present at to-night's banquet. I would have answered your kind invitation sooner, but owing to serious trouble with my eyes, am unable to read or write. Particularly do I regret this to-day, as it deprives me of the long cherished desire of paying public tribute to Colonel Cockerill's high talents and charming amiabilities of character which to-night you meet to honor. I know of no one more faithfully devoted to the highest purposes and noblest missions of the press than he. I know no one more entitled to a complimentary banquet than your President, John A. Cockerill.

JOSEPH PULITZER.

The fair skies and sunshine of the Coast failed to bring any relief. Indeed, he grew more nervous and out of sorts. He was uncomfortable and made every one else so. A few months demonstrated that no quick recovery was possible, as his physicians had hoped. California supplied too close contacts with the very affairs that had worn him out. He therefore returned to New York, disconcerted and no better, visiting St. Louis for the last time on his way.

The paper was enormously successful, the establishment well organized, and there was really little for him to concern himself about, so he bestirred himself for some new action. The quarters at 31–32 Park Row, in addition to being owned by Jay Gould, were cramped and inconvenient. In a few years they were entirely outgrown and Mr. Pulitzer, who had now begun to believe that his venture would last, looked about for a building site. Always desiring to complete his triumph over the *Herald*, which had so far been confined to circulation, Mr. Pulitzer early planned to overtop Mr. Bennett's mansard roof at Park Row and Ann Street.

*Joseph Pulitzer*

With this purpose in mind he had purchased the lot at No. 11 Park Row, with some frontage on Ann Street. The space would have been too small at the best and as needs grew Mr. Pulitzer abandoned the idea of facing his rival, and instead erected an annex at 250 Adams Street, in Brooklyn, where several of the older presses were installed for reserve in case of fire and to help out on the Sunday runs, now becoming heavy because of size and circulation. This annex was opened February 5, 1887, the Rev. Henry Ward Beecher making the address and saying some kind words on behalf of newspaper enterprise. The relief was slight, however, and too distant for daily use.

The *Evening World* was now a lusty infant crying for room and the issue of the Sunday *World* always a problem in the press room. French's Hotel, at Park Row and Frankfort Street, came into the market and on April 10, 1888, his forty-first birthday, Mr. Pulitzer completed the purchase of the property for $630,000 in cash, and plans for the construction of a permanent home for the property became uppermost in his mind. The site stood on historic ground where the first fight for liberty, unavailing though it was, occurred in the British Colonies of North America. It was originally granted in 1642 to Covert Lockerman and one Van de Grist, under Dutch rule. Elsie Lockerman, who inherited the property, married Pieter Cornelius Vanderveer, who built the first brick house on Manhattan Island and also constructed the first three-masted vessel to hail from New York. On the death of her husband, Elsie married Captain Jacob Leisler, who, on the advent of William and Mary, deposed the officials who had been appointed by King James, and acting on behalf of his fellow citizens set up as Lieu-

SITE OF THE PULITZER BUILDING, 1854

## The Day's Work — 1885-1891

tenant-Governor over the liberated community. He duly notified King William of his acts on behalf of the new dynasty, but his letter brought no response. Instead, King William sent Col. Henry Slaughter with a company of regulars to take over the governorship. Leisler and his son-in-law, Jacob Milborne, were seized, convicted of treason and hanged in front of the Leisler residence at the junction of Park Row and Frankfort Street on May 16, 1691. To Mr. Pulitzer also, the site bore an interesting personal reminiscence, for it was from French's Hotel that he had been asked by the head porter to depart in 1865, as the guests objected to the presence of lounging ex-soldiers!

With the uncertainties of his beginnings and the unsettling due to his health, Mr. Pulitzer had not established a home in New York. After two years in the Gerard mansion, he shifted to another rented house at No. 9 East 36th Street. He then purchased No. 10 East 55th Street from Charles T. Barney and in 1888 was installed there. Later a narrow house, No. 12, was bought and the two thrown together.

Here a large library accumulated, many choice paintings were gathered, together with a great collection of gobelin tapestries.

Mr. Pulitzer's eyes and nerves continued to be disturbing, and he kept away from the office, spending some of the summer at Lenox.

The year 1888 carried a Presidential campaign. Mr. Cleveland had given great satisfaction to his supporters and his renomination came as a matter of course, with tariff reform as the issue. Benjamin Harrison of Indiana was named by the Republicans. In New York, David B. Hill ran again for Governor. While the paper supported the Democratic ticket, the force exerted was not the same as that of four years before. Mr. Pulitzer's illness stayed his hand and Colonel Cockerill had turned Republican, not liking the tariff policy of the President. In New York State Governor Hill, controlling the convention, had failed to indorse Mr. Cleveland's views on the tariff. He combined with the liquor element, then being assailed by the Republicans, and his henchmen traded shamelessly with the opposition for votes on the Presidency, the shrewd and unscrupulous Matthew Stanley Quay being in charge of the national Republican campaign. As a result Hill carried New York State by 650,444 to 631,293 for Warner Miller while Mr. Cleveland lost it by a vote of 635,737 to 648,759 for Harrison, and with it, the election, although his popular vote was 98,000 over that of his opponent in the country at large. There was every confidence that Mr. Cleveland would win and this had proven fatal when coupled with the tactics of Hill.

No improvement being visible in his health, Mr. Pulitzer determined to submit his case to the best European specialists and arranged for an extended absence from affairs. The problems of the new building were considerable and as there was much friction between George W. Turner, the business manager, and Colonel Cockerill, he established what he was pleased to call a regency, adding to these two gentlemen, his brother-in-law, Col. William L. Davis, a mining engineer of agreeable personal qualities and fine presence, but without newspaper experience, who was to have a trying time umpiring for the pair of experts, each of whom was endeavoring to outplay the other in the crisis. This step taken, he sailed, on what was to be the beginning of intermittent exile and

## The Day's Work — 1885-1891

complete absence from the *World* establishment for the rest of his life. Accompanied by his physician, Dr. James W. McLane, he went first to London, where Sir Andrew Clarke confirmed the early diagnosis, and wrote out a régime for his daily life, the essential point of which prescribed the absolute separation from all interests and scenes which would stimulate the passion for work that had wrecked his physique.

Proceeding to Paris, this verdict was confirmed by the famous Dr. Charcot, Dr. Brown-Séquard, Dr. Dupuy, Dr. Bouchard and Drs. de Wecker, Lamboldt and Meyer. It was advised that the best results might be reached by a slow journey home around the world. The suggestion was accepted and preparations made for the journey via Constantinople, Suez and India. In London Mr. Pulitzer had acquired the first of his long line of English secretaries in the person of Claude Ponsonby, son of Sir Henry Ponsonby, and he was included in the entourage as an agreeable companion, along with Dr. McLane and a due retinue. The eye weakness caused Mr. Pulitzer to make a stay in Wiesbaden, where he received the attention of Dr. Hermann Pagenstecher, the first oculist of his time, whose brother Albrecht had been a friend in America.

In the midst of his distractions the great Pulitzer Building had gotten under way. The cellar walls had risen to the level of Park Row, and on October 10, 1889, the twenty-fourth anniversary of his arrival in St. Louis, the cornerstone of the structure was laid by his son Joseph, Jr., then aged four years. From his sickbed in Wiesbaden the invalid sent this message:

God grant that this structure be the enduring home of a newspaper forever unsatisfied with merely printing news — forever fighting every form of Wrong

## Joseph Pulitzer

—forever Independent—forever advancing in Enlightenment and Progress—forever wedded to truly Democratic ideas—forever aspiring to be a Moral Force—forever rising to a higher plane of perfection as a Public Institution.

God grant that the *World* may forever strive toward the highest ideals—be both a daily schoolhouse and a daily forum—both a daily teacher and a daily tribune—an instrument of Justice, a terror to crime, an aid to education, an exponent of true Americanism.

Let it ever be remembered that this edifice owes its existence to the public; that its architect is popular favor; that its moral cornerstone is love of Liberty and Justice; that its every stone comes from the people and represents public approval for public services rendered.

God forbid that the vast army following the standard of the *World* should in this or in future generations ever find it faithless to those ideas and moral principles to which alone it owes its life and without which I would rather have it perish.

JOSEPH PULITZER.

The laying of the stone was made an occasion of consequence. Attending the ceremonies were David B. Hill, Governor of New York, Chauncey M. Depew, William C. Whitney, Daniel Dougherty, the silver-tongued orator, as he was widely known, George W. Childs of the Philadelphia *Ledger*, Gen. Charles H. Taylor of the Boston *Globe*, and others of note. Mr. Depew made the oration and Governor Hill an address.

Overmatched as they were by the *World* and in the presence of a daily decline in their prestige and profits, the owners of other old-established New York newspapers cherished the delusion that its growth was

## The Day's Work — 1885-1891

mushroom and would in season wilt and vanish. The *Herald* was contemptuous of the *World* as "a gift enterprise" concern, because of some coupon and voting schemes used to advance circulation. The setting *Sun* could only vituperate and hug the hope of a collapse. When, however, the columns of the new Pulitzer Building, late in 1889, began to show their shadows against the *Sun*, some misgiving that the new *World* had come to stay sunk into Mr. Dana's ample mind. Standing in his window on the second story of the *Sun* office watching the riveters place the girders, in company with Julian Ralph and William M. Laffan, his publisher, Mr. Dana remarked:

"Laffan, that begins to look serious."

"A mere episode, a mere episode," replied Laffan.

For the *Sun* it turned out like Mr. Artemus Ward's twins, to be "2 episodes."

From Wiesbaden Mr. Pulitzer went to Paris, preparatory to continuing his journey around the world. Though he had been ordered to keep his hands off affairs, this was not possible, then or thereafter. The instruction to his brother-in-law, Col. William L. Davis, left as his personal representative in New York, showed that he at least did not intend to travel in blissful ignorance. Under date of November 23, 1889, these items occur:

> Get a list of Belmont's correspondents in India, China, Japan, generally, and keep it for the use of the office, with the understanding that my mail is to be sent in their care, unless otherwise ordered; for instance, to illustrate, if I send the cableword to send mail to Bombay, you look at the list and send my mail care of Sallagrun, Khumah & Co., and so forth.

Remember that the mail to India goes by way of England, allowing about four weeks from New York; and remember also that the Indian mail leaves London every week on Fridays. Don't therefore mail anything by the Saturday steamers, as that mail would simply stay over in England from Monday till Friday; but instruct everybody in the office to mail by the Wednesday steamers, either North German Lloyd, Inman or the Teutonic. Those steamers generally go into Southampton or Queenstown on Thursday, and should connect with the Indian mail which leaves Friday evening. In this way the mail should reach Bombay in 24 days.

After I leave India the mail will reach me by way of San Francisco, both to China and Japan, as you can see by the regular post office notice published in the *World* every week.

As to the amount of letters and correspondence to be sent, you may judge from this simple rule. As many pleasant and agreeable reports as possible. No unnecessary questions for my decision. Nothing disagreeable or annoying unless of REAL IMPORTANCE. Any question that can be settled at the office should be settled there, and for that very purpose you, Cockerill and Turner should have a regular daily sitting and consultation. I do not mean to revive the regency, which seems to have died without formal abdication; but I really do wish to emphasize this point. You three gentlemen have ample power and discretion to settle any of the ordinary questions that may arise during my absence, and I do not want to have my trip spoilt by ordinary bothers, nor to pay a dollar or two per word for such things. But if an extraordinary thing of real importance, you need not hesitate, and I want you to cable me fully, no matter whether I am in Singapore or in Yokohama, even if it costs four dollars a word or forty. Of course anything concerning the paper

**THE PULITZER BUILDING.   53 TO 63 PARK ROW**
(From an Etching by Walter Hale.)

## The Day's Work — 1885-1891

and our people will interest me just as much in the Himalayas as in St. Moritz, perhaps even more, and regular, full and, I trust, favorable reports will be specially agreeable.

In the same communication he showed concern over the building plans, which, though the cornerstone was in place, were by no means closed, saying among other things:

> The finish of the building is something I know very little about. I want to be sure that no *false* economy or niggardliness will mar the building inside. I want the finish to be creditable at least, if no more, and first-class in every respect, as the contract with Post requires. What are the exact facts, or rather what is promised as to the character of the interior finish? How is the *Times* building finished? Have you ever been through it? Can anything be suggested by which our finish can be improved? You remember Post's contract requires it to be at least as good as that of the *Times*.
>
> I think it already time to look out for a particularly bright man who is to have charge of the renting of the building. He ought to be the brightest and most experienced fellow attainable. We and he ought already to begin thinking, he studying the exact rents paid on the respective floors of the surrounding buildings, like the *Times*, Potter and *Tribune*, the character of tenants we can obtain, and in what way and from what localities. By using our paper in advertising we might perhaps secure leases in advance for whole floors by specially adapting them for certain purposes.

Post was George B. Post, the architect whose general plans had been accepted. Mr. Pulitzer added to them the two most striking features of the building, the great

## Joseph Pulitzer

archway of an entrance and the gilded dome. With further interest in the building he wrote under the same date:

Please send me the sketch of the figure of Atlas as drawn by MacMonnies. If I like it I will order it, but send with the sketch full information about the process of the casting, its color, the material, beauty and durability, how long it will last and how much like bronze exactly will it look. Consult the other bright minds in the office as to the sketch. I want a figure of some kind in the corner, and the only question is whether this is the best and most appropriate artistic design. Could not something more original be drawn? The globe or world I want; and the only question is whether it could not be carried by some other figure than Atlas, or in some other way. However, if Post and his people and our people conclude that the Atlas design as submitted is the best that can be had, you can order it.

I am anxious that Post should keep to the original agreement, and put in a temporary roof over the press room, with a view to its earliest possible completion and the actual removal of the press room long before the building is finished. I am afraid there is a great deal more trouble in this one point than in all the others put together.

The big point to be made with Hoe, and the one that is truly of the greatest importance to him, is that, in getting the new order for new-sized presses, he not only receives the most extraordinary order ever received by his firm but that it will lead to a quasi revolution in press machinery, forcing the other leading papers to imitate this change, as they have imitated every change introduced by the *World*. It will mean a great many presses to Hoe, besides those ordered by the *World*. This point ought to be very strongly used

## The Day's Work — 1885-1891

by you and Mr. Turner, and with variety of illustrations and emphasis for which I have no time.

The prophecy as to Hoe turned out to be correct. The orders from the *World* led to the vast development of his establishment just as Mr. Pulitzer predicted.

From Paris, Mr. Pulitzer now began what was to be the leisurely trip around the world. He designed to go through the Aegean, thence to Constantinople, with India, via Suez, the next objective. He had been warned that one of the dangers of his condition was a hardening of the arteries of the brain, one of which might rupture at any time. This was to caution him against undue excitement, something he was never able to control. At one of the Grecian ports a cablegram from Colonel Davis revealed some office dissensions that threw him into a quick passion, which kept him overwrought until the party reached Constantinople. Here as the ship was about to leave port, while standing at the rail, Mr. Pulitzer turned to Ponsonby and remarked:

"How suddenly it has gotten dark."

"It's not dark," replied the secretary.

"Well, it's dark to me," was the reply.

And dark it had become! The detachment of the retina had broken the machinery of his eyes. Instantly all was consternation. The best doctors at hand could only advise his return to Europe for treatment by a specialist. He therefore took ship for Europe, not totally blind, but with dim vision held by only a slender thread. The first port made was Naples. Here he was at once put into a darkened room, where he lay many long days. To add to his misery the heavy guns of the fortifications near the city were roaring all day in artillery practice, and the tremendous detonations and vibrations of their discharge threatened a total destruction of the invalid's nerves. This was reported to the authorities in Rome, and the gunnery was considerately discontinued for the time. All his life thereafter was spent in evading noises, though with unerring ill-luck he invariably managed to be at the center of whatever clatter abounded. Extreme debility and depression were natural concomitants of his condition. When strong enough to bear removal he was taken to St. Moritz in the Engadine where, it was believed, the mountain air, so helpful to most invalids, would bring relief. Instead, the atmosphere, freighted with the chill of the glaciers, gave him bronchitis and added another item to his discomfort. Lucerne was selected as the best place to fight the new affliction. There was some improvement, upon which he went to Paris and thence to Trouville, where he found himself greatly benefited. Several weeks here so increased his bodily strength that he determined to return, partly to prepare for the opening of the new building, but mainly to consult with Dr. S. Weir Mitchell, who was considered, both abroad and at home, high authority on nervous diseases, as well as a capital writer of fiction.

He reached New York in October, 1890, and found the usual clutter over the building and its occupation.

Consultation with Dr. Mitchell produced the same old story. If he was to regain his health he must abstain from the stress of affairs. This, of course, was a sentence of exile. He took steps accordingly and decided to put the control of the *World* in other hands. His purpose was made known on October 16, 1890, in these words:

# The Day's Work — 1858-1891

### Announcement

Yielding to the advice of his physicians Mr. Joseph Pulitzer has withdrawn entirely from the editorship of the *World*.

For the past two years Mr. Pulitzer has been unable, by reason of a misfortune to his sight, to give a personal supervision to the conduct of his journal. In the opinion of his physician the irksomeness of this imperfect and unsatisfactory connection with its management has prevented a completer restoration of his sight.

To secure relief from what is felt to be a hindrance to recovery, the entire control of the *World* has been vested in an Executive Board of its principal editors, who have been long in its service, and have conducted it in the absence of its chief. The change is thus more nominal than otherwise. It involves no change of men, of methods, of principle or of policy. The *World* will continue to be guided by the ideas of the man who made it what it is. It will follow the lines marked out by him in dedicating this journal to the public service — to the cause of justice, of good morals and good government.

Those to whom the management of the *World* is intrusted will miss the inspiring direction, his sure intuitions of what is right and best, and his constant enforcement of a high and still higher ideal of excellence. But they will endeavor to prove their loyalty to him and to fulfill their obligation to the public by keeping the *World's* course true to the chart which he has so plainly marked out in his splendidly successful direction of its progress in the past.

They, and all connected with this journal, in common, we are sure, with its vast multitude of readers, will hope for the speedier and surer recovery of his full capacity for work which is confidently promised by the

*Joseph Pulitzer*

medical advisers as the result of a period of complete rest.

The *World* had long ceased to have any New York rival except the *Herald*. On October 17th, following the announcement of Mr. Pulitzer's retirement, Mr. Bennett took this editorial note of the event:

> Mr. Joseph Pulitzer the other day resigned his direct control of the New York *World*. It is needless to say that if this is really the case a great vacuum is made in the present actuality of American journalism.
>
> What the Greeleys and the Raymonds and the Bennetts did for journalism thirty years ago, Pulitzer has done to-day. It is true his methods have been queer and peculiar, but after all they have suited the present American public.
>
> As for us of the *Herald*, we droop our colors to him. He has made success upon success against our prejudices; has succeeded all along the line; has roused a spirit of enterprise and personality which, up to this time, has not been known. This man, however, who has given us a new line of thought and action now becomes a part of the past.
>
> We have not always agreed with the spirit which has made his ideas a journalistic success, and we cannot refrain from regretting that he did not encourage us in the new departure which he made, instead of merely astonishing us, frightening us, and, we may add — now that it is past — perhaps a little bit disgusting us.
>
> But, *le Roi est mort, vive le Roi!* The *New York World* is dead, long live the *World!* Pacet!

The drooping of the colors pleased Mr. Pulitzer immensely, and never after were there any acrimonious encounters between the two. Indeed, in matters of mutual interest to his last day Mr. Bennett usually

## The Day's Work — 1885-1891

instructed his business associates to follow the *World*.

Sometimes the gentlemen in the office would overexult in rejoicing over outfooting their rival, but they were usually checked. Mr. Bennett once in a moment of wrath announced his purpose to kill the *Evening Telegram*. He was stayed by his business manager, Albert Fox, and the pink publication continued to sap the life-blood of the *Herald*. The latter did something the *World* office did not like and it took to frequently reproducing the patricidal editorial in its evening edition. Mr. Pulitzer stopped the practice, saying that he could never forget Mr. Bennett's kindness on the occasion of his breakdown.

Mr. Pulitzer always ascribed his collapse to his exertions in the Nicoll campaign. This might have been the last straw, but the real cause lay in twenty years' misuse of a frail physique. He was a driver of men, but of none more than himself. Working far into the night, racking his sleepless brain for new and better ideas, crowding long journeys between days that knew no rest, the calamity came almost as a mercy to bid him pause.

When the Pulitzer Building opened its doors on December 10, 1890, it was something more than the tallest building in New York and a landmark to be known for long years to come; it was truly a monument of achievement. In six and one-half years its creator, the *World*, had returned its price to Jay Gould and built and equipped its home at a cost of about $2,500,000, every cent of which it had earned and all of which it had paid without recourse to loans of any sort. Mr. Pulitzer abhorred debt and he was very particular to make it known that the new building carried no obligations of any sort, by securing from County Register Frank T. Fitzgerald, a certificate to that effect.

This desire for untrammelled possession was his strongest characteristic. Later when Mr. Bennett leased the square at Broadway and Thirty-fourth Street, upon which he built the beautiful *Herald* Building, as low in contrast with the surroundings as the *World's* home was lofty with its neighbors, Mr. Pulitzer, meeting the Commodore in Paris, asked him how he could do such a thing. "I could not sleep nights," he observed, "if I thought another owned the ground upon which my building stood."

"I shall not be here to worry about it," was Mr. Bennett's reply. He was not, but the *Herald* was no more the *Herald* of a dynasty either when he left it behind, while the building became a patent-medicine signboard.

The day chosen for the public opening was the twelfth anniversary of the taking over of the wreck of the St. Louis *Dispatch*. Unable to face the strain Mr. Pulitzer had the day before sailed for Europe, leaving the event in other hands. Mr. William H. Merrill, chief editorial writer, made the welcome address in his name, and it was responded to by Gov. David B. Hill of New York, Gen. Charles H. Taylor of the Boston *Globe*, Gov. James A. Beaver of Pennsylvania, Congressman Roger Q. Mills, Governor-elect Robert E. Pattison of Pennsylvania, Gov. Morgan G. Bulkley of Connecticut, Murat Halstead, the veteran editor of the Cincinnati *Commercial*, Daniel Dougherty, Gov. Leon Abbett of New Jersey, St. Clair McKelway of the Brooklyn *Eagle*, former Senator Warner Miller, and other notables.

## The Day's Work — 1885-1891

In a little booklet issued to commemorate the occasion, Mr. Pulitzer paid a special tribute to George W. Turner, the *World's* business manager, as one to whom the shaping of the structure was due, crediting to his ingenuity and devotion the solving of the many problems involved in its construction. But as the old saying goes, "Death comes with the new house," the new building, instead of bringing joy, soon became full of discontent. In creating an organization to control the property in his absence Mr. Pulitzer, who was himself President of the Press Publishing Company, the corporate name of the *World's* ownership, made his brother-in-law, Col. William L. Davis, Vice-President. Between Turner and Cockerill there was a feud of the first magnitude as to who was really IT in the establishment, with a perpetual conflict over size fixing and office details. Neither was longer paying close attention to affairs. Turner had a small yacht and other pleasures, while Colonel Cockerill had established himself in Room 1, at the Astor House, where he spent the major part of his time. He was also at odds with Ballard Smith and to placate him, Smith, who had also become indifferent, was sent to Brooklyn to take charge of the extra page devoted daily to that city.

Mr. Pulitzer's health had not improved with his visit to America, and the reports that reached the office of his physical and mental state were not reassuring. The rivals in the office made life a burden for Colonel Davis, but the paper under the impetus of the new building and the enormous advertising that it produced had made a record year in 1890. Ninety-one promised equally well, despite the neglect of the official powers. It fell out that both Turner and Cockerill felt that they

## Joseph Pulitzer

had earned an interest in the property. The former, late in the spring of the New Year, so far overestimated his value to the paper as to make a flat demand for a controlling share. This was met by his instant dismissal. Feeling that he might as well have a round-up Mr. Pulitzer ordered Colonel Cockerill to St. Louis, and brought on John A. Dillon, who had been in general charge of the *Post-Dispatch* ever since Mr. Pulitzer's removal to New York, to take Turner's place. He came at once, bringing Mr. George H. Ledlie with him as assistant.

Colonel Cockerill declined the St. Louis assignment and resigned. Some time before, C. P. Huntington and Mark Hopkins, feeling the need of press work, had purchased the New York *Star*, a morning daily of limited circulation, from John Kelly, the Tammany boss. This had been given over on a six months option to Frank A. Munsey, who, following his first success with a juvenile weekly called the *Argosy*, was ambitious to invade daily journalism. He had turned it into a tabloid sheet called the *Continent*. Its office was at the corner of Broadway and Park Place and it had made some progress when the starting of the New York *Recorder* gave it a competitor too great for Mr. Munsey to meet. The result was that he turned it back to its owners. Hooking up with the Huntington interests Colonel Cockerill engaged them to buy the *Commercial Advertiser* from the estate of Hugh Hastings, and to convert the *Continent* into a one-cent morning edition, under his editorship, which was done, as the *Morning Advertiser*.

Colonel Cockerill's stay with the two *Advertisers* lasted until September 28, 1894. On that date he

## The Day's Work — 1885–1891

retired, having notified Messrs. Butler, Stillman and Hubbard, the law firm which attended to the affairs of Huntington and the Hopkins estate, that the place was no longer compatible. He joined the staff of the *Herald* and in January, 1895, was assigned to the Far East, where he did some notable work as a correspondent in China and Japan. Returning by way of Egypt, he died at Shepheard's Hotel, in Cairo, where he was stricken with apoplexy, on April 11, 1896. Of his departure from this life the *World* said editorially:

> The sudden death of John A. Cockerill at Cairo, Egypt, on Friday night, removes one of the best-known and most widely popular newspaper workers of this country. Col. Cockerill was for some years the managing editor of The World. He brought to the discharge of his responsible duties trained ability as a journalist, unsurpassed fidelity and industry, great personal loyalty, and qualities of mind and heart that endeared him to all his associates. No "newspaper man," as he preferred to call himself, ever had more friends or better deserved them. At the time of his death he was in the service of the New York Herald as special correspondent, and his letters from Japan to that journal have been exceptionally interesting and valuable.

The *World* also reprinted the *Herald's* editorial regrets, with the head line "A Merited Tribute." To further dispose of the accepted theory that there was rancor between the two old associates, the concluding paragraph of Colonel Cockerill's will read: "I name as my executor Joseph Pulitzer, who has been a faithful and sincere friend to me, and to whom I am indebted for much that I enjoy."

Colonel Cockerill's body was brought to America and

after a service in Calvary Baptist Church, New York, taken to St. Louis and there interred in the Elks lot, Bellefontaine Cemetery, where in 1891 he had erected a monument for the local lodge of the Order.

The only cognizance taken by the *World* of Colonel Cockerill's departure at the time was a curt paragraph written by Mr. William H. Merrill to the effect that "the indispensable man was not numerous."

In spite of Mr. Merrill's assumption, Colonel Cockerill was never replaced on the *World*, though many were called and some chosen. That is to say, no one ever came into the editorship who fitted in so well with Mr. Pulitzer and at the same time was able to rally men to himself and inspire them with his zeal and energy. The two were "John" and "Joe" to each other and the frankness of speech between them was electrifying. If Mr. Pulitzer was a Napoleon, Colonel Cockerill was his Murat.

The New York *Recorder*, established in January, 1891, had begun floundering after a first flush of success under the management of Howard Carroll, son-in-law of John H. Starin and a New York *Times* graduate. It had been founded at the instance of one J. D. Douglass, who had become acquainted with James B Duke when he came up from Durham, N. C., to push the brand of tobacco packed by his family. The two lived in a side street hotel opposite the St. Denis, and Douglass, when wealth came Mr. Duke's way, led him to start the paper. Could Mr. Duke have given it needed attention it would have succeeded. As it was it made a dent in the local situation and jarred the *World* more than any rival that ever came into the field. To this rocking ship Mr. Turner appeared as a savior in 1891, and was promptly taken on board.

## The Day's Work — 1885–1891

The paper advocated Free Silver, but perished a fortnight before the defeat of Bryan in 1896. Mr. Turner lived on the receivership until 1901 when he left the country for Japan, taught English in the schools at Nagasaki for five years and, returning to America, died at Berkeley, California, November 11, 1914, after having lived the life of a recluse for eight years — a strange ending for one who had risen so far.

Thus it will appear that May, 1891 was a moving month in the *World* office. In addition to the departures noted, Mr. E. A. Grozier resigned to take over the Boston *Post*. This, however, was a friendly migration, Mr. Pulitzer advancing him $40,000 to aid in the purchase, from which he built up for the *Post* the largest strictly morning circulation in America.

These commotions naturally filled Mr. Pulitzer with anxiety and stirred him out of his invalidism. Against the advice of family and physicians he determined to return and did so, arriving in New York about June 10, 1891, in a period of terrific heat, to which he was always supersensitive. He had also long desired a steam yacht of his own, and before the disturbance Mr. Turner came across a craft, once the *Sans Peur*, which had been the property of the Duke of Sutherland, sold to E. D. Morgan, and renamed the *Katerina*, which after being wrecked off the east end of Long Island, had been rebuilt by a speculator, Daniel W. Sullivan. Mr. Turner himself had a taste for yachting, and after sundry trips on the *Katerina* recommended her acquisition.

Mr. Pulitzer accepted the recommendation, and the yacht had been purchased in April for $100,000. The new owner rechristened her *Romola* after George Eliot's novel of that name — a favorite book. The

Navy then had a surplus of officers and on the suggestion of ex-Secretary William C. Whitney he borrowed Lieut. A. P. Nazro to command the craft, that excellent officer securing a year's leave for the purpose. She was put into commission and lay in the North River. He had half planned to return to Europe in her if found to his liking. Taking a test dinner on board, the heat of the cabin nearly killed him. He therefore abandoned her for the return trip and went back by steamer, ordering the yacht to meet him at Leghorn. He sailed for Europe on June 17th, after a week's stay. During this time he filled the gaps in the *World's* machine by making Ballard Smith acting editor in charge and Col. George B. McClellan Harvey, managing editor.

The *Romola* went on her way to Leghorn where she duly arrived. In due season her new owner came on board. There he spent one night. The heat and poor dining quarters were too much for him. In wrath and disgust he ordered the luckless craft back to New York. Here after several years of languishing in the Erie Basin she was sold to Venezuela as a gunboat for $25,000, Mr. Pulitzer charging $75,000 up to experience.

## Chapter VIII

### THE VENEZUELA AFFAIR — 1892-1895

Col. Charles H. Jones — Silver Repeal — President Cleveland's Challenge to Great Britain — Services for Peace — The Great Bond Fight.

THE OUTSTANDING event of the summer of 1892 was the riot at Homestead, Pa., where many strikers were killed by hired Pinkertons and the Coal and Iron Police, a private body employed by the steel and mining interests. This was a labor conflict of the first dimensions and the *World* wholeheartedly took the side of the men. The rights of labor were more obscure then than now. Most of the rioters were Slavs who had been imported to work at starvation wages while their employers fattened under a tariff passed to "protect American workmen." Naturally, as the men became a little enlightened they had discerned the unfairness of their position and, having no backing but their own hands, resorted to violence.

The *World's* support of the strike brought it much criticism and Mr. Pulitzer was roundly blamed for the animus shown by the news editors in charge. The reproofs of his contemporaries led Mr. Pulitzer to believe that the paper had suffered from overzeal and he put a damper on. The reform in methods of dealing with labor, the abolition of hired mercenaries and the establishment of the State police in Pennsylvania, as we now look back, would indicate that the "overzeal" of the day was an impulse for justice.

The diligence and intelligence of Mr. Carvalho had all the while been making a strong appeal, and although he was nominally managing editor of the *Evening World* he was in constant use for other things. In July, 1892, he was summoned to Paris and interviewed as to his staying powers and the chances of unshaken devotion. These were strongly enough evidenced to send him back with instructions to remove Ballard Smith from the post of acting editor in chief, though supplying no other situation. The gossip of Park Row ascribed this to the course Mr. Smith had allowed the *World* to take during the Homestead troubles, Colonel Cockerill's *Morning Advertiser* and the vicious *Sun* lending currency to the tale. The truth was, he had lost the power of action, and besides he had not been able to bring about any accord between himself and the much-absent proprietor. He had vibrated between the Brooklyn office and the position of editor in charge without producing much in either place — due, it can now be said, to the beginning of a mental breakdown that was to follow and cloud the last seven years of his brilliant life.

On August 24th, Mr. Pulitzer, though absent in Europe, gave a dinner to Mr. Smith at Delmonico's, the guests at which were fellow members of his staff, to which the absent host cabled this message:

> Grateful memories for loyal services, sorrow for parting and confident hopes for happy career. The *World* will always be a tender Alma Mater, proud of your talents, watchful of your fame and helpful of your high aspirations.

## The Venezuela Affair — 1892-1895

Mr. Smith did not, however, leave his kindly Alma Mater for good. After a short rest he became London correspondent of the *World*, but in a year his fine mind gave way. He died in a sanitarium at Waverley, Mass., July 31, 1900.

Mr. William H. Merrill quietly assumed the duties of chief editorial writer and for the moment the *World* had no editor-in-chief. On September 30, 1892, Mr. Carvalho was made assistant vice-president with "absolute power" over all expenses and stern instructions to reduce them. The paper was always growing out of its clothes, and just as parents are apt to be distressed at the perpetual wants of children, Mr. Pulitzer at a distance could not understand the ever-expanding pay rolls, even though they brought with them no special retrogression of profits.

Mr. Dillon had not been successful in the business office and was transferred to the editorial page, while Frederick Driscoll, the younger, took his place. He did not wear, and John Norris, who was a factor in the success of William M. Singerly's Philadelphia *Record*, applied for the place. Mr. Pulitzer had made it a policy not to take men from positions, in view of possible failure, and so rejected the application. Mr. Norris boldly resigned and came back to take a chance. He camped in the pressroom and made radical recommendations. His persistence pleased Mr. Pulitzer and he was engaged as business manager.

The *World* was now approaching the tenth anniversary of its history under Mr. Pulitzer's ownership. This it celebrated on Sunday, May 7, 1893, by the issue of a one-hundred page edition of the *World*. Many Sunday newspapers, including the *World*, now contain this amount of white paper regularly, but at the time this was a prodigious exploit, forty-eight pages being the greatest space normally occupied with the wonders of Sunday journalism. The edition had a sale of 400,000 copies and was heralded as a new milestone in journalistic endeavor, which indeed it was. Many tributes were received. Sir Edwin Arnold contributed a poem, "The Tenth Muse," and the decade of progress was properly reviewed. An interesting item in this summary was the statement that during the period $17,680,442.02 had been expended in the *World's* production,

On the morning of Wednesday, May 10, 1893, Mr. Pulitzer arrived from Europe for the purpose of celebrating the tenth anniversary of his ownership of the *World*. He gave a dinner that evening to twenty selected members of the staff. The night was one to be remembered. William H. Merrill, chief editorial writer, sat at Mr. Pulitzer's right and S. S. Carvalho, then publisher of the *World*, at his left.

Col. George B. McClellan Harvey, the managing editor, John A. Dillon and George Cary Eggleston, of the editorial staff, vied with each other in proposing toasts and drinking healths until they seriously affected their own. It was well past midnight when Harvey rose solemnly for the twenty-fifth time, glass in hand, and drawled out what proved to be a final toast:

"Let us — ah — drink," he said, "and when we — ah — drink let us — ah — drink to the — ah — King!"

"O, damn it, Harvey," replied Mr. Pulitzer, sharply, "No Kings! No Kings!"

On Saturday he was away again across the Atlantic. Soon after reaching Europe, having become weary of Colonel Harvey's habit of editing the paper by telephone

## The Venezuela Affair — 1892-1895

from uptown clubs, his frequent absences and general preference of society to work, he applied such strictures as to force a parting of company, Colonel Harvey becoming "advertising manager" for the Metropolitan Street Railway Corporation, then fast growing under the ingenious financing of William C. Whitney and Thomas F. Ryan. E. O. Chamberlin, a capable graduate from the *Sun*, took his place.

Mr. Pulitzer's European stay was brief. He returned in June to take up his residence for the summer at Bar Harbor, in the beautiful villa called Chatwold, belonging to Mrs. Louise Livingston, on the ocean shore, beside Bear Brook, a mile and a half from the village. *World* problems continued to vex him. The relations between Mr. Carvalho and Mr. Norris in the business office had become reduced to correspondence and Mr. Norris came in for disciplinary measures that cut his salary in half and subordinated his powers until they were negligible. At this juncture he applied for a leave of absence and took a trip to Alaska to cool off. Full charge downstairs and upstairs was therefore given for the moment to Mr. Carvalho, as publisher, and I was brought over from Brooklyn to assist, sitting in the seat of Norris, remaining there until he returned in the late summer. Just as we were becoming comfortable, in July Mr. Pulitzer astonished the managers in the *World* office by putting Col. Charles H. Jones in complete editorial charge. Mr. William H. Merrill, chief editorial writer, never assumed any authority other than that delegated to him in almost daily instructions, and these rarely extended beyond his page. Colonel Jones was to be a real editor, with control over all phases upstairs. Mr. Pulitzer examined him for a week at Bar Harbor and

## Joseph Pulitzer

sent him to the office unannounced, with a blue envelope in hand giving him his plenipotentiary powers.

The astonishment of the shop was not at the colonel, but at the wide scope seemingly given a man with no knowledge of the field, and Mr. Pulitzer's disregard of those who had done much to hold the paper together successfully. Mr. Carvalho was quite flattened out, so to speak, while the editors looked upon the new man with deep distrust. He was an experienced journalist, a Georgian by birth, who had gone into the Confederate Army at fifteen, and was forty-five at the date of his arrival in the *World* office. At an earlier period he had edited *Appleton's Journal* and the *Eclectic Magazine*, but his start had been made in Jacksonville, Florida, where he had put together the *Times* and *Union*, and made a success, "riding in" on the early development of the State as a winter resort by the Flagler interests. Selling out to advantage, he had gone to St. Louis and revived the dying *Republican*, renaming it the *Republic*. Mr. Pulitzer always respected vigorous opponents and the colonel had been a lively one. He had just sold his interest in the *Republic* to David R. Francis and was eligible for further exploits.

It was soon manifest that the new man would not do. Personally he could not impress the hardened old hands. He wore whiskers in a smooth shaven vicinage and his ladylike manners were objectionable. He was soon flustered, between the proprietor and the staff; the Sunday *World*, for example, printed a drawing by Walt McDougall of a flirtation on the Asbury Park board walk, which included a very accurate portrait of a lady, who turned out to be Mrs. Jones!

Aside from all this Colonel Jones's ideas reflected

## The Venezuela Affair — 1892-1895

much of the Populism that was soon to capture the Democracy, remote from those ideals which had solidified in the *World*, and they involved the dawning Free Silver heresy. His beginnings were full of mistakes. He was fortunately under guard of the established forces and could not, luckily for the paper, enforce obedience. The summer passed, however, without great friction, Mr. Pulitzer was within reach and no amazing breaks occurred, such as were to follow.

When Mr. Cleveland placed before Congress the duty of repealing the Sherman Act and staying the Silver stream, Colonel Jones left his desk and went to Washington, where to the astonishment of Mr. John H. Tennant, in charge of the news at the *World's* Washington Bureau, he assumed the duty of writing the dispatches covering the situation, all against the repeal, which Mr. Tennant had been forecasting in his own articles. He was brushed aside while the colonel filed 4,000 words on the opposite tack. When the *World* reached Washington, not a line of the Silver stuff appeared. The colonel's wrath fell upon Mr. Tennant, who, taking him to the telegraph office, proved that all the Jones message had gone to New York, while he himself had sent nothing.

What had happened was quite simple. When the flood of Silver advocacy came into the office, a council of war was held, Mr. Carvalho presiding and the copy was "canned." Its author returned to his post with diminished powers and the repeal stoutly supported by the *World* went through and became a law November 1, 1893. Colonel Jones's hands were pretty well tied for the moment, and matters drifted along.

On June 25, 1894, the American Railway Union declared a strike against the Pullman Car Corporation, with resulting violence at Kensington, near Chicago, in the great railway yards of the city. Much damage followed and on July 2d, the United States Court issued an injunction forbidding interference with train operations by the Union. Colonel Jones then wrote a celebrated editorial, "Government by Injunction," stoutly reprehending the action and endorsing Eugene V. Debs, leader of the strike, who disregarded the mandate of the law. This was the last straw. He was suspended from the conduct of the editorial page and his activities were limited to the supervision of the news. Undaunted by the adverse attitude of Mr. Pulitzer, the colonel insisted that his views represented those that would control the next Democratic Convention, and that he would write "Government by Injunction" into the National Democratic platform.

He did not exert himself much in his suspended state and Mr. Pulitzer, knowing that his contract was valid and not wishing to waste him, put before the editor at Bar Harbor, in July, a proposition to return to St. Louis and take over the control of the *Post-Dispatch*. The colonel had $80,000 cash in bank, and it was suggested that he purchase a half-interest for $300,000, paying the $80,000 down, and allow the balance due to accrue from the earnings. The proposition at the moment did not seem attractive and was not accepted. The colonel returned to New York, doing nothing in particular during the summer and early fall. The *Post-Dispatch* was not progressing. The Scripps-McRae League was conducting a vigorous competition and the *Star-Sayings*, its other evening rival, had acquired a new angel. Both were parasiting on the *Post-Dispatch* through a deal with the newsboys, whereby all three papers were vended on the street

## The Venezuela Affair — 1892-1895

for five cents, no single paper being sold. This was a strangling process and its effects were painfully visible on circulation. The colonel being coy, Mr. Norris was sent to St. Louis to shake things up.

War had been declared between China and Japan on July 27th, and a new epoch, not well divined at the moment, began in world affairs. The *World* disengaged James Creelman, the ablest reporter of his time, from the *Herald* and sent him to the scene of the conflict. Mr. Creelman's dispatches were notable instances of newspaper enterprise. One of these, charging a massacre of Chinese by the Japanese troops at the taking of Port Arthur, November 21, 1894, was the cause of a controversy of international proportions. The Japanese Government denied the charges. Mr. Creelman always stoutly maintained their truth. The tale lingered disagreeably in Japanese minds. Mr. Bennett celebrated Mr. Creelman's departure with almost life-size pictures of Mr. Pulitzer "The Great Editor" and Mr. Creelman "The Great Reporter," displayed side by side in the *Herald*.

The city election of 1894 took up a considerable share of Mr. Pulitzer's attention. A fusion was effected by which Col. William L. Strong, a Republican merchant, was nominated to oppose Hugh J. Grant, the Tammany mayor. Against strong personal appeals from eminent members of the organization the *World* supported Colonel Strong with its customary energy, and he was elected.

The season had been spent pleasantly at Bar Harbor, with a few weeks in the early fall at Newport. Elections past, Mr. Pulitzer turned his thoughts again to the Jones-*Post-Dispatch* problem. Mr. Norris's efforts at shaking things up had not been successful beyond the shaking, and Colonel Jones was being wasted in the *World* office. He was again asked to consider moving. He again declined. Mr. Norris was all the while getting into deeper trouble. He had aroused antagonism within and without the office. The one cent newspaper was coming into vogue and he endeavored to make it effective in a five-cent town. The newsboys revolted. He was assaulted and in many ways his life made a burden. He was a man of courage and stuck to his post and his policies, but the results were to the disadvantage of the property. In this emergency Colonel Jones was appealed to once more in December, when Mr. Pulitzer, who was preparing to leave for a winter's stay at Jekyl Island, persuaded him to visit St. Louis and give him the benefit of a ten-day survey. This he did, with the result that on the 24th he was asked to go to St. Louis and personally carry out his suggestions. The invitation, written from 10 East 55th Street, was characteristic:

> I have accepted your advice about St. Louis, and must seriously ask you to go out there, at least for a time, to help in the new departure and to carry out your suggested changes in the character of the paper.
> There are obvious reasons in our difficulties and your present environment in the *World* office which to my mind should make this an agreeable change and opportunity, especially if you return here with fresh laurels of Western success.
> I am leaving town for the winter and should like to have your answer at the earliest moment.
> ... If you are going out tomorrow, I will be glad to see you at half past eleven. I leave next day.
> With kind regards and best wishes for a pleasant Christmas, faithfully yours.

## The Venezuela Affair — 1892–1895

As an upshot Colonel Jones tendered his resignation as editor of the *World* to take effect January 1, 1895, and agreed to go to St. Louis on the condition that he could have "absolute control." He required also that he be permitted to acquire a majority stock interest on the terms originally proposed. To this end he had drawn up a contract providing for the purchase of 5,003 of the 10,000 shares. Mr. Pulitzer had in the meantime departed for Jekyl Island. The contract was forwarded to him and sent back after a week with many emendations. It was redrawn and returned. In a few days a message came to Mr. Carvalho, declining to execute the document, Mr. Pulitzer having discovered under its terms that he was paying for the colonel's stock himself and parting with the control of the property. He offered to sell the latter all the stock he could then pay for, and to make him president, editor and manager, with as much "control" as if he held a majority of the stock. On this basis Colonel Jones bought a one-sixth interest, 1,667 shares, for $80,000. The agreement was concluded at Jekyl Island on February 3d. Colonel Jones proceeded at once to St. Louis to take charge.

Following his departure Mr. Pulitzer was seized with misgivings as to what the new head would do to his old hands in the *Post-Dispatch* office, and became greatly concerned. He had asked the colonel to show them every consideration and had been told they would be judged on their merits. He was especially disturbed as to what might happen to his managing editor, Florence D. White, William C. Steigers, his veteran advertising manager, and other trusted employees. While the colonel had as yet taken no special action, in mid-February Mr. Carvalho and Mr. H. D. Macdona, of Mr. Pulitzer's secretarial staff, appeared on the scene with a plan to so amend the by-laws as to restrict the "control" conferred upon the colonel by his contract. To this he took prompt exception and immediately acted according to his own purposes. The executives named were turned into the street, his brother, George W. Jones, was made business manager, and the *Post-Dispatch* became a privateer sailing as her captain listed.

Mr. Pulitzer brought the dismissed gentlemen to New York and placed them variously on the *World*, in the meantime beginning legal proceedings to get back his property.

He now purchased Chatwold and adopted Bar Harbor as his permanent summer residence. Extensive additions and alterations were set under way and he departed for a spring in London, taking up his residence in Moray Lodge, Kensington. Nothing very eventful occurred. Chatwold was set in order and he returned in July to enjoy its new aspect under his own roof.

Following the repeal of the Sherman silver act, President Cleveland undertook the reform of the tariff, and encountered the "Ohio idea," fathered by Frank Hurd, of a tariff for revenue with incidental protection. A bill introduced by Congressman William L. Wilson of West Virginia was finally passed. It was not satisfactory to Mr. Cleveland, who allowed it to become a law on August 27, 1895, without his signature.

Thus far the *World*, and this meant Mr. Pulitzer, had proceeded in fair harmony with the doughty Democrat in the White House. The *World* had never failed to criticise or alertly watch all the moves of the Administration, but there had been no overt difference

## The Venezuela Affair — 1892–1895

on lines of public policy. One of the first magnitude now arose above the political horizon.

In 1844–45 Richard H. Schomburgk, a Prussian naturalist and surveyor employed by the English Government, had drawn a line on the map between Venezuela and British Guiana. Allowed, it gave to England a vast territory, but Venezuela never accepted the line and it had been more or less in dispute for half a century. In 1895, for some reason not clear at the time, the matter became acute, soon took an important place in the press and found its way into politics. England had always refused to consider any question raised by Venezuela, declining to admit that one existed between the two countries, implying, indeed, that she knew of no such nation. Appealing to the United States from under the aegis of the Monroe Doctrine, Venezuela worked up much feeling in this country, especially as President Cleveland did not outwardly appear to regard the dispute as of much consequence. Because of this, for weeks preceding the December meeting of Congress the jingo press, principally Republican, had been hurling criticism at the President. Individual jingoes in and out of Congress added their vituperations to that of the editors. He was dubbed a coward and a "fat stuff," with ill-considered malice. On December 18th, he confounded his critics with a special message that took their breath away. In cold terms he made public the demand of his Secretary of State, Richard Olney, upon Great Britain, that it should arbitrate its dispute with the South American Republic and, in case of refusal, proposed in his message that the United States should intervene, investigate the boundary and determine who had a rightful claim to the wilderness, and that if England then

## Joseph Pulitzer

proceeded to occupy by force any territory we thought belonged to Venezuela we should stand ready to fight her on that dispute. He concluded with these words:

> In making these recommendations, I am fully alive to the full responsibility incurred and keenly realize all the consequences that may follow. I am nevertheless firm in my conviction that while it is a grievous thing to contemplate the two great English speaking peoples of the world as being otherwise than friendly competitors in the onward march of civilization, and strenuous and worthy rivals in all the arts of peace, there is no calamity which a great nation can invite which equals that which follows supine submission to wrong and injustice and a consequent loss of national self-respect and honor, beneath which is shielded and defended the people's safety and greatness.

As usual on such occasions loud applause greeted the defiance in Congress and the press joined in reckless approval. The old anti-English spirit rose to full limits. The *World's* was the first voice to be heard in the madness.

Mr. Pulitzer saw the fearful consequences of a world conflict, such as war between England and America was likely to bring, with the German Emperor's hand over his sword, and began an anti-jingo campaign of surpassing vigor. The morning after Mr. Cleveland's message and the dispatches between the State Department and the British Foreign Office had been read the *World* said in Mr. Pulitzer's own words:

> President Cleveland's message to Congress on the Venezuelan matter is a grave blunder. It is a blunder because it is based on a wrong conception, because it is not sustained by international law or usage and because it places the United States in a false position.

## The Venezuela Affair — 1892–1895

The President in his message, like Secretary Olney in his despatches, assumes that the policy of Great Britain in Venezuela involves a menace to this country. To interfere in South America and bring on a war between two great, free and highly civilized nations on any account less serious than a menace such as the President described would be the monumental crime of the century.

Are our peace and safety as a nation, the integrity of our free institutions and the tranquil maintenance of our distinctive form of government threatened by an extension, however unwarranted and arbitrary, of the British possessions in Venezuela? The assumption is absurd. And with it falls the structure of ponderously patriotic rhetoric reared upon it by the President.

It is a grave blunder to put this Government in its attitude of threatening war unless we mean it and are prepared for it and can appeal hopefully to the sympathizers of the civilized world in making it.

The *World* showed in successive editorials that the Monroe Doctrine was in no way affected by the dispute between Venezuela and Great Britain. Its arguments were made upon a dispassionate array of facts and existing conditions; its conclusions were based upon the principles of international law.

"War is not impossible," said the *World* on the third day. "War, on the contrary, is being made every day more possible by the reckless and inconsiderate clamor of men who should know better, who fill the air with bombast about the pregnability of Great Britain's vast commerce and the impossibility of war." It said further:

When grave and reverend bishops, ministers of peace in the world, announce that they place implicit

## Joseph Pulitzer

confidence in Mr. Cleveland and indorse everything he does, even to the extent of war, what can be expected of the great body of people?

Danger of war lies not in the point at issue but in the irritation of the public mind which all this talk creates. If Great Britain should yield every point in Venezuela and the craze which possesses this country were still to drive the Administration into war, it would be nothing stranger than when Germany yielded to France all that she had asked, and yet the French spirit, thirsty for blood and glory, forced the Government to war. Let the war idea once dominate the minds of the American people and war will come whether there is cause for it or not.

It is absurd to say that war is impossible so long as blatant jingoes echo the President's tocsin in Congress, while leading divines and other messengers of peace, in blind idolatry of a personality, egg on the clamor, and great leaders of thought and sentiment stand as spectators.

On December 21st, at the instance of Congressman R. R. Hitt of Illinois, the House passed a resolution authorizing the appointment of a commission to investigate the boundary and appropriating $100,000 for its expenses. This was signed on the same day. The unthinking country had made its challenge over a matter with which it had no concern and about which it knew nothing. The reaction came quickly. First it fell upon the Stock Exchange where a panic of the first dimensions got under way. Values crumbled, firms went down and consequences became visible. The Stock Exchange had so far treated matters as a joke. London bankers, recalling recent yacht racing controversies, cabled to the members of the New York Stock Exchange: "When our warships enter

## The Venezuela Affair — 1892–1895

New York Harbor we hope your excursion boats will not interfere with them." The Wall Street wags cabled back: "For your sake it is to be hoped that your warships are better than your yachts."

As stocks tumbled, loud grew the protests for peace, not from principles of morality, not from the promptings of conscience, but because values were being squeezed. Moral sense came next to the surface. Bishop Henry C. Potter, of the Episcopal Diocese of New York, wrote to the *World:* "Though the nation seems to have gone mad, it is most comforting that one journal remains sane. The leader in the *World* this morning is as conclusive as it is dignified and courageous. It disposes of the message with a force and finality that leaves nothing to be desired."

But it was necessary to present to the country at large some stronger appeal than the arguments of international law. The *World* turned to the great men of England. They responded with messages of conciliation, of fraternity, of good-will and of sentiments of peace on earth that were published on Christmas morning.

From the British throne came this message sent by the Prince of Wales with the knowledge and consent of Queen Victoria: "Sir Francis Knollys is desired by the Prince of Wales and the Duke of York to thank Mr. Pulitzer for his cablegram. They earnestly trust and cannot but believe the present crisis will be arranged in a manner satisfactory to both countries, and will be succeeded by the same warm feeling of friendship which has existed between them for so many years."

The venerable William E. Gladstone cabled: "Only common sense is necessary" — a phrase that stood out like a beam of light. Lord Rosebery wrote: "I absolutely disbelieve in the possibility of war between the United States and Great Britain on such an issue as this, for it would be the greatest crime on record. History would have to relate that the two mightiest nations of the Anglo-Saxon race, at a time when they appeared to be about to overshadow the world in the best interests of Christianity and civilization, preferred to cut each other's throats about a frontier squabble in a small South American republic. The proposition required only to be stated to demonstrate its absurdity. I congratulate you on the good work that your paper appears to be doing in this direction."

There were many more messages from men of note. All save one of the bishops of England contributed sentiments of peace through the *World*. The Freemasons of England used the same channel to reach their American brethren. Cardinal Gibbons and Bishop Potter rallied the American clergy. The New York Chamber of Commerce led the business men back into paths of reason. Christmas sermons from a thousand pulpits echoed the expression of peace and good-will that the *World* had voiced and telegraphed everywhere throughout the country. A few days later, reviewing the events of the week, it said:

> The effect was instantaneous and gratifying. The war clamor ceased. Within two days the reaction was complete. The truth told and the facts presented proved to the country that it had been made a victim of false alarm. Publicity had done its work. Truly "peace hath her victories no less renowned than war." Benjamin Constant was right: "The press is mistress of intelligence, and intelligence is mistress of the world."

## The Venezuela Affair — 1892-1895

The Venezuelan boundary dispute was relegated to the realms of diplomacy, and nearly four years later an international commission rendered a decision that was peacefully accepted by all concerned. A further and most important outcome was the signing of an arbitration agreement between the United States and England.

Joseph Chamberlain, member of British Cabinets and keen observer of many countries, remarked in later years: "The *World* led public thought when it secured expressions and opinions from leading men of America and Great Britain and performed an inestimable service to the English-speaking people of the whole world. War between the two countries would be a terrible calamity, and the *World* performed a patriotic service to its country. It did not wait for a leader, but led the people."

Looked at from this distance and in the light of clearly exposed efforts to foment discord between other nations and the United States, as in the cases of Mexico and Japan, it is now easy to believe that the Venezuelan crisis was the outcrop of German machinations, the influence of Berlin having always been the strongest at Caracas. The Emperor William II, but new on the throne, had dismissed Bismarck and taken autocratic charge of his Government, with much rattling of the sword. That the world did not then take him seriously, postponed, if it did not prepare, the war that came twenty years after. A pity indeed, that the People of the Nations could not have had such a note of warning in 1914 as the *World* sounded in 1895!

Recurring to Mr. Pulitzer's own affairs, his suit to oust Colonel Jones from the control of the *Post-Dispatch*

*Joseph Pulitzer*

came up for hearing before Judge Woods in St. Louis, on September 30, 1895. The colonel had been having a very good time indeed. He was booming Free Silver, took the side of the governor, William Joel Stone, and made local politics lively.

Frederick N. Judson defended the Jones régime and F. W. Lehman headed the Pulitzer forces. In the end Colonel Jones was upheld and cavorted gloriously.

Although the Sherman Silver Act had been out of operation for two years its consequences were still in motion. The gold reserve which the Treasury thought needful to protect national credit was constantly slipping. It had been necessary in February to float a bond issue of $64,000,000 for the purpose of buying bullion. These were sold to J. P. Morgan & Co. for $104\frac{1}{2}$ and were soon worth 120 on the market. In August the *World* had warning from its alert Washington correspondent, Mr. Tennant, that another bond issue was in contemplation and on the 15th the paper editorially advised the Treasury not to vend any more bonds to brokers at $104\frac{1}{2}$, which the people were eager to take at 120 or more. Following close on the heels of the Venezuela affair the Washington office learned that the bond issue was settled, and on December 26th, the *World* repeated its warning. Mr. Pulitzer, at Lakewood, instantly set the machinery of publicity in action. He caused all the national banks in the country to be queried and overwhelming evidence was soon accumulated to show that the people would take any amount by popular subscription at prices far above the contemplated syndicate operation. Mr. Pulitzer himself offered to buy $1,000,000 at the top price, whatever it might prove to be. As a result of the agitation, though deeply indignant at the inter-

## The Venezuela Affair — 1892-1895

ference, Secretary of the Treasury John G. Carlisle, on January 5, 1896, placed the loan before the public. The issue of $100,000,000 was oversubscribed six times.

There was an amusing anti-climax to Mr. Pulitzer's share in the operation. He left the bidding for his $1,000,000 to Mr. Dumont Clarke, his banker, who offered 114. In a few days it was apparent that this price would yield an immediate profit of $50,000. Mr. Pulitzer was deeply concerned as to how he could rid himself of the unearned increment. A council was called of all the wise heads in the office to advise him. About a dozen of the sages were present. All sorts of queer suggestions were put forth, including one from Arthur Brisbane, that the unfortunate incubus should be given to West Point Military Academy, which of course could not receive gifts. Finally, after two hours of wearisome debate, the business manager remarked, speaking for the first time:

"Why not keep it?"

This advice was duly presented to the agitated gentleman at Lakewood — and accepted!

## Chapter IX

### BRYANISM — 1896-1897

The Coming of William R. Hearst — Bolting the Democratic Ticket — Defeat of Bryan — *Post-Dispatch* Changes.

EARLY IN 1895, John R. McLean, owner of the Cincinnati *Enquirer*, had paid Albert Pulitzer $1,000,000 for the New York Morning *Journal* and proceeded to reorganize it on the lines of his own paper — a very powerful sheet in its way. To do this he found it necessary to raise the price to two cents. This increase, together with the change in character from a light and irresponsible sheet to one of a different, if not higher, grade brought disaster. The circulation dropped from around 100,000 a day to about 20,000 and the *Journal* began industriously losing money. In this posture it attracted the attention of William Randolph Hearst, owner of the *Examiner*, in San Francisco, whose father, George Hearst, late senator from California and a noted mining operator, had accumulated great wealth, half of which was at the service of his son. Mr. Hearst had pushed the *Examiner* into the first place in Pacific coast journalism. He had followed the *World* very closely; his New York offices were on the eleventh floor of the Pulitzer Building, where he had picked a large corner room, panelled its walls with redwood brought from California and fitted it with fine furniture of the same

## Bryanism — 1896–1897

material, while his newspaper enjoyed the *World's* special news service. Negotiations with Mr. McLean were undertaken by Charles M. Palmer, Mr. Hearst's business representative, and on September 25, 1895, the *Morning Journal* became his property though no announcement of the new ownership was made until November 6th, the morning after election. The plant, a small one, located in the Tribune Building, began to be overworked and soon all traces of McLean vanished. The *World's* size of page and length and width of column were adopted and the price of the paper restored to one cent. The town was well supplied with one cent newspapers, the chief of which, the *Press*, had been started in 1884 by a group of New England manufacturers, at the behest of Robert P. Porter, who became editor, to oppose Mr. Cleveland's election on a low-tariff platform. The others were Colonel Cockerill's *Morning Advertiser*, and a last attempt of the venerable *Sunday Mercury* to survive with a penny offspring. The new venture at once began to grow, not at the expense of the high-priced but of the low-cost papers. The *World* was not affected at all. Though no great signs of extravagance or energy were at first manifested, the paper grew, and it was evident that Mr. Hearst had a powerful purpose behind him, to say nothing of money. That he had picked the *World* as his antagonist soon became apparent. His assaults were made within and without the office. The *Sunday World* had become strong under the editorship of Morrill Goddard and his special staff. Mr. Hearst began a quiet negotiation to acquire the *World's* entire Sunday outfit, using the *Examiner* office, in the Pulitzer Building, as the place of conference. Mr.

Goddard yielded to the offer in late January, 1896, and to the consternation of the establishment moved out, taking all hands with him. Mr. Pulitzer, taken completely by surprise and well appreciating the value of the young editor, took measures for his recall. Mr. Carvalho foregathered with him, held out inducements, and the outfit returned. They remained in their nest in the dome for twenty-four hours, when Mr. Hearst, resuming his check-book argument, prevailed and the young men vanished, as it were, in thin air. Not only were the editors gone, but all of the paraphernalia. The most extraordinary dollar-matching contest in the history of American journalism had begun.

Mr. Pulitzer was mightily stirred by this episode and feeling doubly grieved that the "assignation," as he called it, was made in his own building, demanded that the *Examiner* give up its office in his property. This was accordingly done, the Boston *Globe* taking over the lease and remaining therein ever after.

By this time the *Morning Journal* had touched the 150,000 mark. This was within 35,000 or so of the Morning *World's* average, and Mr. Pulitzer, ever impatient of rivals, began considering measures to match the newcomer and head him off. While the *World* was not losing it had ceased to grow, more from the competition of its one-cent evening edition than that of the *Morning Journal*. Mr. Norris, who had grown up with the success of William M. Singerly's one-cent Philadelphia *Record*, urged a break in the *World's* stagnation by cutting the morning price in two. Mr. Carvalho sided with Mr. Norris and argued strongly to make me see the case his way. I could not, and put my views into a brief. On February 7th, Mr. Pulitzer turned about after an overnight stay in town and

## Bryanism — 1896-1897

departed for Jekyl. He took Mr. Norris and Mr. Carvalho along. They went only as far as Philadelphia and returned that night with the announcement that the die was cast, and that the price would go down on Monday, February 10, 1896, following.

The immediate effect was electric, but not as its owner had anticipated. The *World's* circulation increased 88,000 per day. Mr. Norris had figured that it would logically go to 1,000,000. Mr. Pulitzer believed the move would wreck the *Herald* and stop the *Journal*. It did nothing of the sort. The blow fell heavily on the *Advertiser*, crushed the little *Mercury*, nipped the *Press*, sent the *Recorder* reeling into the evening field for a short survival, and lifted Hearst, full grown, into the public eye.

In announcing his purpose editorially, Mr. Pulitzer proclaimed that he "preferred power to profits." He soon found his power doubtful and his profits reduced about two-thirds. Mr. Norris had argued that the "ideal newspaper" would have no advertising solicitors and predicted that business would follow the change with a rush. The result was quite the contrary. A number of old *World* readers went elsewhere — readers who had buying capacity — and the newcomers were not responsive to its advertisers. To cap this an increase in rates was made leading to a warfare with advertisers, which ended in a compromise that recognized a group of merchants as a business body and perpetuated for years a combination of interests that forced down rates, and was extremely difficult to deal with. The classified advertisement columns were also asked to yield more. On top of this, size was rigorously curtailed to meet the appalling drop in earnings, Wall Street cut to a mere column or less, and book reviews were entirely excised in the insistence on saving space for news alone, thus killing two sources of important, if limited, circulation and much advertising.

Mr. Hearst felt that he had his antagonist staggering and began a furious assault. He spent money as it had never been spent before on newspapers in any field. Enormous posters pasted in huge gilt frames proclaimed his enterprise, and the response in circulation came quickly. The advertisers, however, were chary and have always remained so in regard to his morning edition, then the *Journal*. As Mr. Pulitzer was accustomed to observe out of the wealth of his newspaper knowledge: "Circulation is the first thing a newspaper gets; advertising the last; circulation is the first thing it loses; advertising the last."

The *World* grew too under the competition and with the renewed effort excited by it, so that from the standpoint of circulation honors were even. There was one important difference in the conditions affecting the rivals. The *World* at all times earned the money used in the fight, while the *Journal* cut huge holes in the resources of the Hearst estate, for the time being and for many years to follow.

Long after, in one of his musing moments, Mr. Pulitzer remarked: "When I came to New York Mr. Bennett reduced the price of his paper and raised his advertising rates — all to my advantage. When Mr. Hearst came to New York I did the same. I wonder why, in view of my experience?"

As to his opponent, Mr. William R. Hearst testified on the settlement of his mother's estate (San Francisco, 1921) in explaining the disappearance of the half that she had given him after the death of his father, Senator George Hearst, that the conflict brought on by the *World's* cut in price had been "very expensive." It had been, indeed, to eat up something like $8,000,000!

Strong as he was in imitating the *World* Mr. Hearst was weak in originating. His vast expenditures were all devoted to outdoing. His newsgathering was mainly a "pick up" from others. Indeed, it used to be asserted that when the first edition of the *World* reached the *Journal* news room, a grateful copy desk would set up this refrain:

Sound the cymbals, beat the drum!
The *World* is here, the news has come!

While Mr. Pulitzer did not feel that Mr. Hearst had any sound principles — personal or political — he regarded him as he once said, as "a master of the great art of attracting attention," but never accepted him as in any sense a rival, the *Herald* continuing until the last day to be his standard of measure in achievement.

The price cut as first made was confined to the city area. This status existed for some months, when, Mr. Norris's logical million being still far distant, the country cost was reduced to one cent, with only proportionate results and further loss in revenue. Economy became the order of the day and the summer was rendered uncomfortable by demands for reduction in expenditure, little of which was possible in the face of Mr. Hearst's unremitting outgo.

With the departure of Mr. Goddard, Arthur Brisbane, who had spent most of his time with Mr. Pulitzer and on special assignments, became Sunday editor. There was no further effort to put an overlord on the editorial page, Mr. William H. Merrill continuing

## Joseph Pulitzer

serenely in charge, subject only to Mr. Pulitzer's supervision. During the latter end of the Jones régime Mr. Richard A. Farrelly had been taken from the city desk of the morning edition and made managing editor of the evening, Charles Edward Russell coming from the *Herald* to take his place on the city desk. Mr. Pulitzer now determined upon a further shift. He sent E. O. Chamberlin to the evening and transferred Mr. Farrelly to the morning headship — that is, he so ordered. The occasion was to be celebrated with a birthday dinner to Farrelly, at which a number of guests corresponding with his seventeen years on the paper were invited. The dinner was set for a Monday night. On a Sunday the invited guests were astounded to receive telegrams from Mr. William H. Merrill, who was to act as chairman of the feast, announcing that Farrelly had "gone over to the enemy." He had, indeed, and there was another considerable gap in the ranks of the *World's* effectives.

Recruiting becoming necessary, Mr. Pulitzer brought over Mr. William Bradford Merrill from the New York *Press*, where he had gone after service on the Philadelphia *Press*, and he took up the duties of managing editor.

A more surprising secession than that of Mr. Farrelly was soon to follow. Mr. Pulitzer's dissatisfaction with the outcome of the one-cent move was more than considerable and he bore heavily upon those who had the financial burden in hand and the heaviest weight fell upon Mr. Carvalho. The strike of the dry goods combination was on and the exchequer suffered heavily from the curtailed circulation revenue and the huge increase in the mechanical cost of handling the larger edition. Conferences were under way for a settlement with the advertisers in March when Mr. Carvalho was sent to St. Louis to observe the actions of the rebellious Jones. Some word reaching the office that he was dealing with the "combine," as it was known at long distance, on a basis that did not seem sound to the others concerned caused Mr. Norris to wire Mr. Pulitzer at Jekyl Island to ask Mr. Carvalho to withhold any action until the former could pass on certain facts then on their way to him by mail. Mr. Carvalho was at once served with a blanket notice to do nothing. On his return he evinced deep resentment at the situation in which he felt himself placed and on the last day of March, 1896, telegraphed Mr. Pulitzer that unless his powers could be restored on all matters before five P.M. he would consider himself no longer in the *World's* employ. At 5.30 he called me into his office, apprised me of the facts stated, and, having received no reply, asked me to announce to the other newspapers and the men in the office that he was through, which I did with very great regret. Mr. Pulitzer's only comment that ever reached me was that he had "allowed Carvalho to relieve himself." In a few days the retiring publisher was enrolled under the broadening banners of Hearst. His powers were transferred to Mr. Norris and mine were enlarged.

Mr. Pulitzer finished the cold weather of 1896 at Jekyl Island, spent part of April in Washington and made a start for England in May, returning again to his comfortable residence at Moray Lodge, Kensington. His health was comparatively good and he went about much, for one thing attending a dinner given in honor of Gen. Patrick A. Collins of Boston, American Consul General at London, on May 30th, at which Col. Henry

*Joseph Pulitzer*

Watterson was a fellow guest and gave the British lion's tail a terrible twist.

June 6, 1896, a deputation from the leading peace and arbitration societies of England called upon Mr. Pulitzer, then at Moray Lodge, Kensington, and presented him with an address, which read:

> We desire, on behalf of all who wish to see knit even more firmly the ties of history and kinship between the two great branches of the English-speaking race, to proffer our hearty thanks for the prompt efforts made by you through the great journal you direct towards that noble object, and to congratulate you on the immense and gratifying success resulting from that beneficent exemplification of the marvellous facilities of modern journalism in the dark days of last December. Your prompt intervention evoked from the best, wisest and most influential persons of the day so united and emphatic a protest that the counsels of moderation and sanity were enabled to exert their rightful sway over true public sentiment.

Cardinal Vaughan made the address on behalf of the delegates, and Mr. Pulitzer responded with the last speech he ever prepared, read by his son Ralph. It follows in full:

> I am deeply sensible of the great compliment of your presence. Yet I feel that you come to do honor to a principle and not to a person. It is a natural desire with men of earnest conviction to find expression for that conviction.
>
> I know of no purely moral sentiment that has been advanced in England since the abolition of slavery that appeals so strongly to the mind and heart as this idea of substituting civilized methods of peace and reason for barbarism and needless war.

[ 218 ]

## Bryanism — 1896-1897

It is encouraging to feel that there are men in the world like those constituting your various peace and arbitration organizations; men who, putting aside their own interest and pleasure, and neglecting their own comfort and their own affairs, labor for the public good and a high ideal. We beyond the Atlantic have watched with admiration your devoted enthusiasm, often under discouragement and not seldom in the face of misapprehension. I congratulate you upon the fruit of your labors in the progress of this sentiment which I have observed during my present visit.

In America there is not — or, at least, recently there was not — a single organized society such as yours. But this is not because the American people are opposed to the principle you represent. Just the reverse. It is because all of the people in the United States, regardless of parties and sections, are in favor of arbitration and, as it were, form one national arbitration society, which has grown from a membership of 7,000,000 that it had when arbitration was provided for in the treaty of Ghent to 70,000,000 to-day. It is growing at the rate of over a million a year, and will number over a hundred millions in twenty years.

True Americanism means arbitration. If the great Republic across the sea stands for anything it stands for the reign of reason as opposed to the reign of force; for argument, peaceful discussion and lawful adjustment as opposed to passion and war.

America is proud of the fact that arbitration is an American idea.

Even our jingoes all were and are for arbitration, and the dark cloud that recently passed over America was only made possible by an unfortunate refusal of arbitration.

It was a noble idea that stirred the American people, even though that idea was based upon a mistaken conception of fact. The spirit of protest was called out by a natural sympathy with the under dog, as we say — with the weak against the strong — and not by any personal feeling for Venezuela, with which country Americans have hardly anything in common. It was produced by the regard of our people for the very appearance of justice though the substance itself were not there and by their determination to protect American ideas against foreign intrusion even outside our boundary line.

In the mind of every American the cherished Monroe doctrine stands alone side by side with the Constitution and the Declaration of Independence, and if, from their great devotion to that doctrine — which in an impulsive enthusiasm they thought was involved — Americans espoused the Venezuelan cause, is that not more creditable to them than if they had acted from mere personal sympathy?

If the New York *World* has been to any degree helpful in this Venezuelan affair, your warm words of appreciation are welcome, and are an encouragement to all members of my profession on both sides of the Atlantic who have fearlessly discharged their duty under great difficulties. For it is not pleasant both to criticise the Government and offend the people in free countries, where popular opinion is always the force behind the Government. Where that opinion is subject to impulses, often from an excess of enthusiasm, the responsibility of the press becomes most grave.

It is a duty to interpret the right, to expose the wrong, to teach the moral, to advocate the true and to oppose the false, constantly and conscientiously, judicially and fearlessly.

Without sacrificing conscience to the natural desire of plaudits and popularity, it must attack error,

## Bryanism — 1896-1897

whether emanating from the Cabinet or from the people themselves.

It must do its duty against that false and perverted patriotism called jingoism.

True patriotism, true Americanism, mean love of a pride in country. But we love our great Republic not because it has 70,000,000 of people, not because of its vast area and exhaustless resources, not even because of its wonderful progress. We love her because her cornerstone is enlightened intelligence, and her foundations are freedom, equality, public morality, national honor, tolerance and, above all, justice.

Jingoism is not confined to any one country, but is found in England as well as in America; in Germany as well as in France; in Russia as well as in Japan. Jingoism is an appeal to national vanity, national prejudices or national animosities.

Every day there rests upon the conscientious press the responsibility of combating these prejudices and of teaching lessons of enlightenment.

Arbitration, as I have said, is an American idea. The very first treaty of peace into which the United States entered, the treaty with England in 1783, provided that any dispute that might arise under it should be settled by arbitration. The second treaty of peace, the treaty of Ghent, made in 1814, also contained an arbitration clause, which was the means of settling several acute disputes that otherwise might have reopened the smarting wounds of war.

Three times since the war of 1812 peace was threatened more darkly than in the Venezuelan incident. The first occasion was the dispute as to the northeastern boundary, which came to a crisis in 1828. War seemed inevitable, but the arrangements for arbitration gave time for passion to cool and for reason to have a fair hearing, and the crisis ended in a compromise. Then there were the difficulties arising from the Trent affair and the Alabama claims.

In the Trent affair it was averted because both nations listened to reason. In the affair of the Alabama claims the treaty of Washington was made in 1871 providing for the Geneva Arbitration Tribunal.

The force of the idea of arbitration in America is well illustrated by the settlement of the Canadian fisheries dispute in 1878. The Arbitration Commission decided in favor of England. After the decision was announced it was discovered that the award was based on false evidence. But America honorably insisted upon abiding by the decision of the commission and paid the award of $5,000,000 to our Canadian friends, — a gigantic sum for a few fish.

In the eighty years since the treaty of Ghent America has an unbroken record for arbitration. Only a short time ago, in 1890, both houses of the American Congress joined in a resolution authorizing the President to negotiate with the powers to the end that differences and disputes which cannot be adjusted by diplomatic agency may be referred to arbitration. In all, the United States have taken part in twelve great arbitrations. Ten of these were arbitrations of disputes with Great Britain. Also, we have acted as arbiters in six international disputes.

In no case have the United States ever refused arbitration. In no case have they made war, except for independence and self-preservation. Those facts go far towards assuring peace as an outcome of the Venezuela case.

But the chief danger was passed when England recognized the American Commission now sitting at Washington. That was really the first step towards arbitration.

When England accepted our commission, when

## Bryanism — 1896-1897

she made a courteous and tactful offer of facilities, she insured a peaceful settlement of the question. She might have refused to recognize the commission. She not only did recognize it, but she also submitted her claim and case to it with all the evidence in her possession.

You may feel assured that the decision of the American Commission, composed of four Judges and scholars, will be as fair and judicial as would be the result reached by any four of your own Judges. The American Commission, gentlemen, will justify both the moderation and the confidence of the British Government.

The outcome will be peace; peace with a better understanding, with friendlier good-will, with kindlier feeling.

But I hope and believe that both nations will provide against the recurrence of such a crisis. If you will vigorously carry on your campaign of education you can make it most improbable that any government will refuse to arbitrate such trifling disputes again.

But as to the future danger, let us trust that there will be either a treaty or a tribunal making it impossible for the two nations to go to war about any issue that does not involve the national independence, the national honor or the national existence.

Civilization means that disputes and differences, whether individual or international, shall be settled by reason or by some judicial process, and not by force. Civilization is no more possible without peace than permanent peace is possible without arbitration. Yet this does not mean peace at any price.

There are certain issues that are not arbitrable.

War against a cruel despotism or slavery Americans regard as not only just, but as inevitable.

They believe in the French revolution. They

naturally sympathize with the uprising of any people against despotism, whether in Greece or Hungary, or Poland in the past, or in Cuba to-day.

I cannot help feeling that you, as Englishmen, share with the Americans at least in some of these sympathies. I have always held it one of England's greatest glories, almost equal to her matchless literature, almost equal to her genius for conquest, colonization and government in the remotest parts of the globe, unsurpassed since the days of the Romans, that for a century she has been for all Europe the strong place of refuge for political offenders.

She, with Switzerland, has been practically the only European asylum for liberty-loving revolutionists and political exiles. She has protected all alike, whether anarchist or monarchist, whether rebel or pretender to a throne. And since England has shown this devotion to political freedom, Englishmen will understand a similar spirit in America.

However we may differ on many questions, we have common sympathies for liberty and humanity, just as much as we have a common language.

We speak, we read, we think, we feel, we hope, we love, we pray — aye, we dream — in the same language. The twentieth century is dawning. Let us dream that it will realize our ideals and the higher destiny of mankind.

Let us dream not of hideous war and butchery, of barbarism and darkness, but of enlightenment, progress and peace.

So deep were his convictions that he could not believe there would be another war in the face of common sense, modern wealth and military improvements. He was soon to be disabused in the matter of our own conflict with Spain, where the *World* was quite as aggressive for free Cuba as any other force. He did not live to see the great World War, but such a thing he believed entirely improbable and any opinion to the contrary was severely reprehended.

Returning to America for the usual summer at Bar Harbor Mr. Pulitzer was at once face to face with a great political problem.

The repeal of the Sherman Act in 1893 set the forces of the silver miners into motion. Under the leadership of Marcus Daly, head of the great Anaconda group, coupled with the Nevada interests, plans were laid to capture the national conventions of both parties. William McKinley, Governor of Ohio, who as a Representative had fathered the tariff legislation that lived under his name, had been groomed by Marcus A. Hanna as the Republican nominee.. The Democrats were at sea. A strong following would have renominated Mr. Cleveland, but they were without voice in the convention, the Populism of the West having fused with the Democrats and elected a full outfit of wild asses' colts. Mr. McKinley was known to favor silver, but what the party platform would convey was another matter. To make sure, the American Bankers Association raised a fund of $85,000, which Oscar E. Leach, President Harrison's comptroller of the currency, and then cashier of the National Union Bank of New York, took to St. Louis, where the convention was held, and gave to Thomas C. Platt, Boss of New York, to use in preparing a sound money platform. Mr. Platt gathered many black and some white delegates to his bosom, and when the platform came out of committee as sound as could be desired it was adopted. Garret A. Hobart of New Jersey became Mr. McKinley's running mate.

In the interim the silver men had been attending to

## Joseph Pulitzer

the Democratic situation. Mr. Pulitzer had foreseen what was to come as early as April, when the free silver element captured the Missouri Democratic convention, for it was thereby made plain that the coalition between the Populists and Democrats, so far as it was to be effective, would result in substituting the political theories of the former for Democratic principles, and as he saw that a free silver man would be nominated at Chicago, he warned the Democratic party that to make such a nomination would be to commit suicide.

His belief was justified by the outcome at Chicago. The carefully collected body of delegates, gathered together at a cost to the mine owners of $289,000, as Mr. Daly's books showed when examined after his death, responded to William J. Bryan's carefully staged rhetoric and did not press a "crown of thorns" upon the "brow of labor" or crucify mankind upon a cross of gold. Arthur Sewall, a rich shipbuilder of Bath, Maine, a State that had fallen for the Greenback doctrine a few years before, was named for Vice-President. Just as in the opening days of the *Post-Dispatch* he had stood for sound money against much advice from his well-wishers, Mr. Pulitzer now took firm stand against the heresy. On Mr. Bryan's receiving the nomination the *World* said:

> There is no doubt as to the result of the election, except as to the size of McKinley's popular and electoral majorities. To question this is to doubt the intelligence, the underlying honesty and the public morality of the people. Opinions as to the result, upon the issue which the free silver mono-metallists have forced, are a test of faith in the people. The *World* believes, it must believe, in the abiding good sense and the active conscience of the American people. It is absolutely

confident that the proposal to debase the currency, to the standard of a few semi-civilized countries, against the standard and the experience of the most enlightened and prosperous nations cannot stand the trial of a four months' discussion.

It may be here interpolated that among the most conspicuous figures at the Chicago convention was Col. Charles H. Jones, President, Editor and Manager of Mr. Pulitzer's St. Louis *Post-Dispatch*. He was there to make good his promise that he would write his celebrated "Government by Injunction" editorial into the Democratic national platform, and as chairman of the committee that framed the document he did, on July 9th.

Mr. Pulitzer, located at Chatwold, spent one hundred and twenty days in unceasing labor, never for a waking moment out of touch with the telegraph, dictating, urging, informing. The fever of the fight revived his bodily strength and he labored as few in the fullness of their powers could do, sustained by his devotion to the right. Mr. Bryan was beaten by a heavy electoral vote, but his popular following was so great that the change of thirty-seven thousand votes properly distributed would have seen him through. The country escaped by a narrow margin, but the disease was long endemic and some of the resulting remedies were nearly as bad.

Mr. Hearst and the dying *Recorder* were the only newspapers in New York to support Mr. Bryan, the former gathering all the advantages, which were not inconsiderable. Following the election Mr. Pulitzer sailed for the Mediterranean on the Hamburg-American liner Colombia, a poor choice, as it turned out. He was unable to curb the noises of the ship or to suppress its vigorous brass band, which had a mania for playing at all times, and landed in Genoa after a voyage of much discomfort.

He had designed to spend the winter at Monte Carlo, but the confusion of sounds repelled him. The yachts in the basin were seemingly always striking eight bells and there was too much music in the air for a nervous man. Several hotels were tested, each with a like result. In the search for silence that followed, Cap Martin, a rugged pine-clad peninsula lying between Mentone and Monaco, was discovered. Here in the Hotel Cap Martin he found the ideal stopping-place. The peninsula itself was a bit of medieval Italy, though just inside the borders of France; a few small farms, a little village on the heights, some groves of century old olive trees and a scattering of shy villas amid the pines made the surroundings to which he came. The noises in the hotel had been subdued already to suit the nerves of that fine lady, the Empress of Austria, who was to be assassinated five years later by an American-made anarchist. Weary of a vapid court and an empty life, she spent much of her time here and was a guest at the time of the former subject's arrival. The place was exactly to his liking.

Though desiring quiet, Mr. Pulitzer never cared to be dull and at Cap Martin he indulged in his fondness for playing with doctors. The great Dr. Ernst Schweninger, Bismarck's physician, was summoned from Berlin and came with his régime of heroic treatment. He laid his patient upon his back on the floor and almost literally jumped on him, under the theory perhaps that a man who could stand his system could

## Bryanism — 1896-1897

survive anything. Then, with advice to avoid work and worry, the professor departed, staggering under the load of a gigantic fee, back to his beloved Bismarck. After two months at Cap Martin, Mr. Pulitzer returned again to America, where he found a fine storm awaiting him.

Mr. Brisbane had been a very successful Sunday editor. With the aid of a superior colored "comic" edited by Alexander Kenealy, son of the attorney for the Tichborne case, later editor of the London *Mirror*, and his own ideas the paper had taken on a huge impetus. His 1896 Easter number had touched 600,000 circulation in response to vigorous advertising, and big figures ruled. Moved by this, Mr. Pulitzer gave him complete charge of the Sunday paper, news and all, outside of the editorial page. The city editor was Charles Edward Russell, since noted as a Socialist writer and speaker. The pair had great talent and, coupled with the doubling of the comic sheet from four to eight pages, the paper took on a tremendous rise, reaching a Christmas high-water mark of 623,000 copies. Unhappily the extension of the "ideas" to the news offended the conservative reader who, before, could throw away the "magazine" section, but was helpless against the flood of freaks. There was a royal struggle between Morrill Goddard, the "idea" editor of the Sunday *Journal* and a *World* graduate, and the Brisbane forces. This led to such an overdoing that the contest was seized upon by the *Sun* and *Post*, followed by "conservative" newspapers elsewhere, amazed at the astounding growth of both *World* and *Journal*, until a threatening wave of hostility was engendered. Clubhouse committees excluded both papers from their libraries and Sunday School workers enlisted for their extirpation. All the hullabaloo did not check circulation, which kept on mounting, but the effect on Mr. Pulitzer was severe. As soon as he recognized the size of the disturbance he called for details and demanded to know how his paper could have been so degraded, and who did it. It was hard to locate the sinners, for despite the impression created by the fusillade that the *World* must be conducted by a combination of ghouls and perverts, at no time in its history had the paper been so respectably manned. Brisbane, whose bizarre brains had provoked the rumpus, was the son of the eminent social reformer, Albert Brisbane. He had, before coming to the paper, been the London correspondent of the *Sun*, and by far the most brilliant American newspaper writer ever sent overseas. His cables glowed with interest and met with wide appreciation. He had also held the managing editorship of the *Evening Sun*. William Bradford Merrill, the managing editor, was the son of a Congregationalist clergyman, born in Salisbury, New Hampshire, educated in Paris, and trained on the very respectable Philadelphia *Press* under Charles Emory Smith. Robert Hunt Lyman, the night editor, was a New England Lyman, graduated from Yale, who arrived in the *World* office by way of the Springfield *Republican* and New York *Herald*. Joseph J. Eakins, the sporting editor, originated with the Louisville *Courier-Journal* and had made a high name for himself in the field of sports. John Norris, the business manager, came from the staid Philadelphia *Record*, while his assistant (myself) was the son of a Universalist clergyman and a graduate from the conservative office of the Brooklyn *Daily Eagle*. The editorial writers included David Graham Phillips, who came from the *Sun* to the *World;* George Cary Eggleston, brother of Rev. Edward Eggleston, the famous author of "The Hoosier Schoolmaster," and John A. Dillon, Mr. Pulitzer's former partner on the *Post-Dispatch*, all gentlemen of the highest grade; while to cap the sheaf, the editorial page was in charge of William Henry Merrill, who before coming to the paper had been a writer on the editorial side of the Boston *Herald* and editor of W. H. H. Murray's religious weekly, the *Golden Rule!*

Looking back over the files and comparing with present-day journalism, it is hard to discover what it was all about, but Mr. Pulitzer, greatly alarmed, placed Brisbane under stern restrictions. The "ideas" disappeared, and with them much of the circulation. That it was made up later on sounder and better lines is no special vindication of the reading public of the day. The *Journal* did not reform and survived the shock without loss of sleep or sales. Brisbane, after a brief trial on the Evening, joined Hearst in September.

The outcome of the clamor was the dubbing of both papers as "yellow" journals, a name that has gone around the world as appended to the unusual in newspaperdom. The use of the color that was to make the phrase came about in this wise: With the growth of the comic section the weekly publications began to copyright their pictures, which could no longer be taken with credit for fillers. Outside the work of McDougall original material had to be gathered from contributors. Among these was a clever young illustrator, R. F. Outcault, who brought in several half-page drawings showing scenes in the tenements, which were christened "Hogan's Alley." The pressman in charge, William J. Kelly, owed most of his experience

## Joseph Pulitzer

with colors to printing block samples for George Mather's Sons, the ink makers. When his efforts were criticised he replied that no one could print the wishy-washy color schemes that came to him in plate form; give him something solid and he would show results. Charles W. Saalberg, the colorist at the time, happened to be painting up one of Outcault's drawings; with his customary quickness, he replied: "All right, I'll make this kid's dress solid yellow." He did and a one-tooth infant in the group of ragamuffins stood out like a sunrise. Kelly was good as his word. The "Yellow Kid" became enormously popular. Outcault was bought by Hearst, but the *World* continued to use "Hogan's Alley" drawn and colored, however, by George B. Luks, since famous as a painter of the first rank. The two kids ran against each other in the rival comics, lent their "yellow" to the extravagant competition, and added a new designation to newspaper vernacular.

Mr. Pulitzer, returning from abroad, spent several Spring weeks in Washington, occupying again the fine mansion belonging to Mrs. John A. Logan. General Logan had been dead ten years and his widow turned a wing of the house into a museum of relics of her deceased husband. Here were displayed a remarkable collection of swords, uniforms, portraits, documents, etc. The layout as arranged was rather doleful. Mrs. Pulitzer called it the mausoleum.

Here Mr. Bryan visited him to exhibit his hoofs and horns, so to speak. The interview was prolonged and argumentative, Mr. Pulitzer seeking to persuade his brilliant visitor to see the error of his ways and the latter firmly standing his ground. Toward the close of the interview Mr. Pulitzer, remarking that his guest had made him "a great deal of trouble," asked permission to pass his hand over Mr. Bryan's face. The latter took the delicate fingers in his own heavy fist and passed them over his adamantine jaw. "You see, Mr. Pulitzer," he observed, "I am a fighter."

Mr. Bryan's jaws were clean shaven; Mr. Pulitzer's well upholstered. He asked the former to lend him his hand. This he passed over the foundation of his whiskers. "You see I am one, too" he commented. Mr. Bryan saw. And so they parted never to meet again.

The disagreement with Colonel Jones came to an end in June, 1897. The defeat of Bryan and the pressure of going it alone in St. Louis had made him amenable to reason. It manifested itself in the form of a willingness to surrender his stock for the $80,000 it cost him plus one sixth of the profits during the period of his independence — some $45,000. The understanding arranged, Mr. Pulitzer, then at Bar Harbor, was strongly inclined to let the colonel remain in charge, under salary. For one thing he was a success, and for the other, as he telegraphed Mr. Norris, who attended to the transfer in St. Louis, Mr. Pulitzer "shivered at the thought of resuming a new trainload of thoughts, details and care." "There is nothing in reason," he added, "that I would not do if he stayed." The colonel preferred to take his profits and depart. John A. Dillon was sent on a short stay to start the machine over again and Messrs. Johns and Steigers returned to their posts. Mr. White was made general manager, but performed his duties in New York mainly thereafter, becoming a permanent part of the *World's* machine.

*Joseph Pulitzer*

Upon his retirement Colonel Jones came to New York with his brother, George, and bought the trade publications of the Lockwood *Press*, which kept him in affluence until his death, January 27, 1913, at Ospedaletti, Italy.

On the whole the adventure fell well for Mr. Pulitzer, who came out of the scrape with his usual good fortune. Colonel Jones was the foremost trumpeter for free silver on its own ground, while the *World* greatly peeved many Democrats by bolting Bryan, though safe inside the gold belt. Following this policy, the sound-money Chicago *Chronicle*, then verging on success, was wiped out in the storm of adverse opinion which greeted its stand. In St. Louis, however, the local rivals made no headway against the *Post-Dispatch*, which came back to its owner much improved and sure of its constituency. It might be noted that Mr. Frederic N. Judson, the colonel's victorious counsel, continued in that capacity for Mr. Pulitzer the rest of his life and became one of the executors of his will.

Several times after this experience Mr. Pulitzer considered selling of the *Post-Dispatch*, once seriously. The would-be purchasers were David R. Francis and Charles W. Knapp, owners of the now deceased *Republic*. They planned making it an evening annex to their morning paper. The two came to New York and the bargain seemed closed at $1,500,000, all in 5 per cent. bonds, running for a long term. I had been out of town and on reaching the office received an early call from Alfred Butes, Mr. Pulitzer's secretary. Mr. Butes gave me an outline of the proposed sale and said papers were to be signed at one o'clock. Mr. Pulitzer, although his mind was made up, would appreciate an opinion. I called it a foolish deal. The paper

## Bryanism — 1896-1897

would be wrecked just as the *Republic* was being destroyed by a rich politician's ownership, and he would get it back as damaged goods. At one o'clock Mr. Pulitzer had a headache and the deal went no further. Some days later I was asked if I had a safe deposit box. I had a small one. A bundle of sealed papers were sent me to stow until called for. They were the documents in the case and were left in my custody for many years. Why? I rather think it was for the purpose of confounding me with the evidence in case the prediction went wrong. This did not prove to be the case as the *Post-Dispatch* thrived and the *Republic* did not. In season the package went back to its owner by request and without comment.

In August, 1897, William Rockefeller, in a moment of wrath at the progressive raise from $150,000 to $2,500,000 in the assessment of Rockwood Hall, his residence near Tarrytown on the Hudson, by the tax officers of the town of Mt. Pleasant, announced that he would sell the place for $350,000 rather than submit to the extortion.

Mr. Pulitzer commissioned John A. Dillon and myself to look it over with the design of buying if satisfactory for a near New York residence. We recommended the purchase, but Mr. Rockefeller repented and would not sell. For a time Mr. Pulitzer looked up other locations in the suburban area, but finding nothing to his liking, abandoned the idea.

During the fall of 1897, the paper was greatly strengthened by acquiring the services of Charles G. Bush, long the cartoonist for the *Herald*. He was an accomplished artist and always drew to a purpose. He was Boston born and a graduate of the United States Naval Academy, being in attendance at the outbreak of the war between the States and present at the excitement when Annapolis was abandoned from fear of a rebel invasion. The students were packed on the old frigate *Constitution* and a ferry boat, which was impressed to tow them out of danger. The engineer's sympathy was with the South. Brig.-Gen. Benjamin F. Butler was in charge and when the engineer mutinied Cadet Bush was sent to get the warrior's sword, not at his side for the moment. The sight of the blade got up steam.

Mr. Bush was an agreeable addition to the staff personally, as well as a cartoonist. As usual no place had been arranged for his studio. When Mr. Bradford Merrill became editorial manager, that title had been gilded on a door in one of the fifteenth floor rooms. He preferred to manage on the twelfth floor, where all the work was done. Mr. Pulitzer suggested that this title be "quietly removed" from the door and the quarters given to Mr. Bush. This was duly done. The job vanished with the erasure.

In September, 1897, immediately following a coming-out party given in her honor at Chatwold, Mr. Pulitzer's oldest daughter Lucille Irma, was stricken with typhoid fever. The attack was followed by complications that continued the illness until the last day of the year, when she died on December 31st. Of all Mr. Pulitzer's children she was most like him, with the same eager mind, the same restless energy, and the same desire for accomplishment.

## Chapter X

### THE WAR WITH SPAIN — 1898–1903

Cuban Revolt and Consequences — Greater New York — British Boer Conflict — Home Destroyed by Fire — Roosevelt becomes Governor and Vice President.

THE consolidation of Greater New York, for which the *World* was responsible more than any other force, was due January 1, 1898. The election of 1897 was therefore to choose a Mayor. In pleasant anticipation of capturing the office, Thomas C. Platt, boss of the Republican party in New York State, had extended the Mayor's term to four years. He nominated Gen. Benjamin F. Tracy of Brooklyn, for the place, refusing a fusion with the Independents who named Seth Low, whose distinguished record as Mayor of Brooklyn for two terms in the early '80s, and as President of Columbia College, had made him highly desirable for the post. Tammany named Robert A. Van Wyck, while the old single-tax party revived and nominated Henry George. Mr. Platt, figuring on Mr. McKinley's 60,000 majority in the city in 1896, thought he could win with a straight Republican. Instead, Tracy received but 105,863 votes against 151,540 for Mr. Low. Van Wyck polled 233,979. Near the end of the campaign Henry George died and his son, Henry, Jr., received his vote. It was 21,693. The *World* vigorously supported Mr. Low.

On the night of the New Year the Pulitzer Building was the center of a gorgeous pyrotechnic display, while editorially it indulged in a striking experiment. Mr.

## Joseph Pulitzer

Pulitzer had invited Alfred C. Harmsworth, later celebrated as Lord Northcliffe, then on a visit to America, to edit the paper for a night. He elected to issue it in tabloid form and the novelty added something like 100,000 to the circulation, despite the fact that his lordship did not get out a very good sheet. The entire staff honored the occasion by performing their duties in full dress, with the exception of Pomeroy Burton, the city editor, who refused to participate in what he thought was an affectation. Not so many years afterwards he joined the Northcliffe forces, forsook his American allegiance and became "Sir Pomeroy" in 1923.

Strong as he had been for peace in the dispute with Great Britain over Venezuela, Mr. Pulitzer veered about radically in the quarrel between the United States and Spain. For one thing liberty was involved; for another his rivalry with Hearst created a longing for bigger things to happen. He once confessed that he had rather liked the idea of a war — not a big one — but one that would arouse interest and give him a chance to gauge the reflex in his circulation figures. The second Cuban revolt, following the suppression of the ten years' war in 1879, had evoked wide sympathy in the United States long desirous of Cuba Libre. The sentiment in support of the insurgents was almost unanimous. When General Valeriano Weyler assumed command of the Spanish forces and began his infamous policy of "concentrating" the people in camps so they could not aid the insurgents, where they starved and perished, American indignation rose to a fever pitch. President McKinley and his advisers were adverse to a conflict and no doubt would have freed Cuba without it, but for an untoward incident. The battleship Maine, which had been anchored for some time in the harbor

## The War with Spain — 1898-1903

of Havana, was destroyed during the night of February 15, 1898, by a mysterious explosion. In all 259 men lost their lives. The country was thrilled with the horror, for which there has never been an explanation. Popular opinion believed the ship had anchored over a harbor mine and that some Spaniard in the secret had touched this off. The Spanish authorities insisted that the calamity was due to an internal accident. This was not possible. A seaman from the Ward liner *Saratoga*, in port at the time, brought the *World* a foot square block of cement from the bottom lining of the battleship that had fallen on the deck of his vessel following the explosion, showing the force had been upward, not outward. There was another theory, that the rebels had blown up the ship to arouse public opinion in America. The affair remains as much of a mystery as ever. It did arouse opinion. Demands were made upon Spain, which, with the usual Castilian lack of diligence, dallied over the situation and though quite willing to make terms, failed to give them expression in time to prevent the declaration of war, which came April 23, 1898, and cost Spain not only the last of her possessions in the Western world but the Philippine Archipelago in the distant seas of the East, Admiral George Dewey having swooped down upon Manila with the Pacific squadron on the 1st of May and destroyed the Spanish fleet of eleven vessels. Word of this did not reach the United States until May 7th, when E. W. Harden, the *World's* correspondent with Dewey, having hurried to Hongkong, sent this dispatch:

> I have just arrived here on the United States revenue cutter *Hugh McCulloch*, with my report of the great American triumph at Manila.

*Joseph Pulitzer*

The entire Spanish fleet of eleven vessels was destroyed.

Three hundred Spaniards were killed and four hundred wounded.

Our loss was none killed and but six slightly wounded.

Not one of the American ships was injured

E. W. HARDEN,
(*World's* Staff Correspondent.)

The message reached the office only in time to receive publicity in a few copies of a late morning edition, but all the New York evening papers fattened their figures that day on the *World's* news.

The destruction of Cervera's fleet, off Santiago de Cuba on July 4th, by Admiral W. T. Sampson's forces was soon followed by the fall of Santiago. By this time the cost of conducting a fleet of tugs and voluminous cables had wiped out the *World's* profits. Dealers failed to cut their orders between battles and the paper was swamped with returns. Mr. Pulitzer lost interest in war and turned to urging an early peace. This soon came in Cuba. A protocol was signed on August 12th, by Jules Cambon, the French Ambassador acting for Spain and Secretary of State William R. Day. On August 13th, Manila surrendered to forces under Major-Gen. Francis Vinton Greene. December 10th, formal articles of peace were signed, the United States paying Spain $20,000,000 for the "Spanish property" in the Philippines.

The troops suffered severely in the tropic summer and Mr. Pulitzer, with a war experience of his own in the ranks, urged their prompt recall. "Make your demand to send the soldiers home stronger," he wrote W. H. Merrill. "The cry for investigation is secondary. The instant, urgent necessity is to break up the

## The War with Spain — 1898-1903

pest camps and disband the volunteers. There is not the slightest reason nor the slightest necessity for this immense army. The navy has force enough to take care of remote contingencies."

The outcome of the war was far from satisfying the owner of the *World*. He never wanted another. Aside from the single dispatch detailing the Dewey victory, the news results were meagre, the circulation was wasteful and the general expense great. Stephen Crane, the rather unusual genius who was hired as a war correspondent on the strength of "The Red Badge of Courage," sent only one dispatch of any merit and that, accusing the Seventy-first New York regiment of cowardice at Santiago, imperilled the paper. It was seized upon by Hearst as a slander on heroes and bade fair to do much damage, which was arrested by an official report confirming Crane's account of the command's conduct. Mr. Pulitzer sought to counteract the clamor by raising a fund for a memorial. This was rejected by the regiment and as much of the money as could be traced was returned to the donors. The rest, after some time, was quietly accepted by the officers and used in beautifying the regimental lot in Kensico Cemetery and so vanished from the books. To conclude the uncomfortable chapter, Sylvester Scovel, the most enterprising of the *World's* correspondents at the front, struck Major-Gen. W. R. Shafter in the face, resenting an insult at the raising of the flag over Santiago de Cuba. Fortunately his friendship with President McKinley saved him from the consequences of his act, however much it may have been justified.

Another misery for the owner that grew out of the war was the headlines in huge type. These were invented by Foster Coates, managing editor of the *Evening World* during the period. They made a great hit with the public, but not with Mr. Pulitzer. Coates used them in a conflict of extras with the *Evening Journal*, which Arthur Brisbane now edited and improved the big block letters by ornamenting them with stars and stripes. Between type and the absurd numbering of extras, both papers became discredited, but the chief condemnation fell on the *Evening World*. Mr. Pulitzer endured the screaming typography until the end of the fighting, then he ordered the foreman to collect all large letters and melt them up. This he did, but they refused to stay dead. The rival sheet continued their use with profit, and after a short subsidence they reappeared to stay not only in the *Evening World* but in afternoon papers generally.

Mr. Pulitzer had not cared to open Chatwold for the season of 1898, but took the W. A. Miles mansion at Narragansett Pier for the summer. This was but a few hours' ride from New York and enabled him to keep some one of the staff on the road most of the time. The house was very comfortable, on the bluffs facing the sea. His health was good, but the exasperation of the war period and the falling off in the paper's prosperity vexed him greatly. For the first time since he had owned the *World* he had to call on his resources for working capital, as between the one-cent depletion in earnings and the great cost of the news service, the paper drew heavily upon him. He got it all back later and the year showed no real loss, but he did not enjoy the experience. Following his own family affliction, another occurred at the Pier. Mrs. Jefferson Davis, widow of the President of the Confederacy, and so a cousin by marriage of Mrs.

## The War with Spain — 1898–1903

Pulitzer, came to the resort for the summer with her daughter, Varina Annie Davis, widely known as "Winnie," who had been elected "Daughter of the Confederacy." She was a beautiful girl, sombered by sustaining the shadows of the lost cause. Taken ill, she died on September 18th. Mr. Pulitzer admired her greatly, although as he once remarked, "privately" he had "a very poor opinion of the Southern Confederacy."

It had been the rule for George Cary Eggleston to take charge of the editorial page on Mr. Merrill's day off. Mr. Pulitzer rescinded this and gave the duty to David Graham Phillips. "Tell Eggleston," he said in giving the instructions, "only reason is desire to develop and encourage young men."

To Merrill he wrote further on August 17, 1898, urging that it was time to "reopen the school house" and in "twenty or thirty questions and answers articles" give the facts about Manila, Havana and San Juan — these facts "to be gathered from books, papers and magazines, and people who have lived in these places, of whom there must be quite a number in New York." This he followed with some simple questions of his own:

> What are the Philippines? What is Porto Rico, Etc.
> What are the habits of the people?
> What their fitness for America; self-government?
> How do they live?
> What is their character?
> What is a Malay — What a Negrito?
> How far are they below the American Negro — former slaves?

That suggests the class of questions to be treated, and further light and information can be given by

## Joseph Pulitzer

printing little stories, incidents, examples and illustrations. And if, in reply to your requests for information, you get good, well-written letters from men with experience, you might print some of them. The one thing to avoid is any expression of *your own opinion*.

One by one the features cut out in the early one-cent days crept back. The books were allowed a modest space and were noticed by Mr. Eggleston, brother of Edward, the eminent author, who had earned considerable distinction himself in literary lines. Mr. Pulitzer did not like the style he followed and wrote him thus:

> Will you pardon an old admirer for a word of criticism on a critic.
>
> Try to make the most interesting points of the book you review your first object of thought.
>
> The second object is, in looking for the first, to be sure that you have not forgotten to pick up the salient, interesting, striking kernel, idea, pith, or essence of the book.
>
> Then, after that, if there is any room left you may express your opinion. But don't reverse the order of this proceeding.

Following closely upon the war excitement came the election for Governor in New York State. Thomas C. Platt picked Col. Theodore Roosevelt for the Republican nominee and started him on his glittering political career. Mr. Pulitzer sought to enlist Judge William J. Gaynor as the candidate for the Democrats. His urgings took this editorial form:

> Judge Gaynor certainly possesses many qualities desirable in a candidate. There can be no doubt in any mind as to what the man who sent McKane to

prison would do to the Canal Ring if he were elected Governor. No Force bill would receive his approval. No corporations with interests inimical to the public interest could either buy or dictate legislation if Gaynor were Governor. He is as brave as Roosevelt, and is superior as a stump-speaker. No boss could control him. He has shown himself to be a reformer who reforms evils.

Judge Gaynor declined to run and Judge Augustus Van Wyck, of Brooklyn, was selected. He was a brother of Robert B. Van Wyck, the city's unpopular Mayor. Roosevelt won by a plurality of 17,786. Here is exhibited another instance of Mr. Pulitzer's political prescience. Gaynor was at the height of his popularity and would undoubtedly have beaten Roosevelt, so changing considerable history.

While there was much criticism of the colonel during his term as governor, nothing notable occurred that concerned Mr. Pulitzer. The *World's* revelations of Ice Trust scandals involving Mayor Robert A. Van Wyck, Charles F. Murphy, John F. Carroll and Charles W. Morse did not impress the governor enough to cause him to remove the mayor, though pressed to do so, the influence he was then seeking to sustain him for renomination, or something better, that of Republican State Chairman B. B. Odell, keeping him tranquil during the disturbance and unmoved in the presence of guilt.

The rivalry with the Hearst papers had been furious during the war — and exhausting, financially. Mr. Pulitzer was approached for a truce and pending it wrote Merrill:

There is a proposition before me to stop all unfriendly utterances between the *World* and *Journal*.

## Joseph Pulitzer

> I don't know whether the proposition will be carried through or not, but in the meanwhile you might suspend such utterances unless there is provocation.
>
> You might tell the others also, but very discreetly, as I doubt whether the thing will finally go through. This until further notice.

The "further notice" dragged along until the fires in both offices cooled down and professional warfare ceased.

In the fall Mr. Pulitzer sailed for England, and previous to departing strove to suppress politics on the editorial page. Just as Frank Buckland's railway guard decided that "frogs is toads, but turtles is hinsects," Mr. Pulitzer defined "politics" as "anything involving corruption." "Anti-trust," "anti-monopoly" or "anti-franchise" topics, also were "politics." Each of Mr. Merrill's assistants, George Cary Eggleston, David Graham Phillips, James W. Clarke and John A. Dillon, was forbidden to write on the subject. Clarke was to "try for a month" to show that "solemnity and statistics are not his forte". Further, he wrote Mr. Merrill:

> Indeed, you might talk to Dillon and Phillips and request them "for the 400th time" to write in a similar vein. Make them promise that for a fortnight they won't write anything serious. Let them take a serious subject and present it with satire, sarcasm and irony. Tell Eggleston the same thing, when he returns.
>
> You and you only are privileged to be solemn — as a reward for your past services, your great age and high merit!

These inhibitions did not tend to improve the page, which wobbled a good deal for the rest of the year, and during the early part of the next. July 12, 1899,

## The War with Spain — 1898–1903

Secretary of War Alger resigned and Elihu Root was appointed in his stead, on July 22d. The page failed to rise to the occasion, Merrill calling for instructions. Mr. Pulitzer, then at Bar Harbor, broke out on July 24th:

> I sharply protest against the second class, second hand opinionless character of the page. Since my return, in three days, Alger's resignation, Chicago meeting, Bryan's speech, the strikes, the shocking collapse of the canal frauds and the appointment of Root were among the events uppermost in the public mind. And nethermost on the page.
>
> Your request for my opinion about Root's appointment I particularly resent, as comment was too self-evident.
>
> Either the editors have opinions which they are afraid to express, or they have no opinions. In either case they do not do their duty. I am tired of being both a scapegoat and scarecrow; held responsible for the very things I dislike.
>
> I am tired of this 'possum policy and, to remove any excuse, formally and fully withdraw every word I said to you or to Phillips on the subject of politics or anything else, leaving you full freedom guided only by your common sense and conscience. Is this clear?
>
> Please read this to Mr. Phillips and to Mr. Eggleston. It is dictated, as you see, angrily but yet deliberately for telegraphing. As a measure of precaution, however, it is now sent by mail.
>
> What is the use of having an editor if he cannot, dare not, express his opinion about the appointment of Mr. Root?

Richard Croker was, in 1899, the full-fledged "boss" of Tammany, and being much under fire from the *World*, he conceived a plan for vexing its owner by

## Joseph Pulitzer

using the power of the Tax Department to rate Mr. Pulitzer's "personalty" at $500,000. This was from two to five times as much as had been paid upon by men like Carnegie, Rockefeller and the Astors, whose wealth was vastly beyond that of the victim. "Personal taxes" were taken lightly and rarely collected in New York. Mr. Pulitzer was quite willing to pay and did not fight the assessment, but he felt the time had come for some real reform in taxation. He took personal charge of the campaign, one of the results of which was the passing of the franchise tax law, which added $100,000,000 to the borrowing capacity of the City and considerable to its revenue. Further, the single-tax principle of assessing land and improvements separately became the ruling policy.

The "encouragement" to Mr. Phillips proved a difficult matter. He was out of line with traditions and impatient of his associates. He soon came in for chiding, as this characteristic letter shows:

Bar Harbor, Aug. 17, 1899.

My dear Phillips: Let us make a bargain, apropos of your imperious insensibility, referred to in your pleasant note. Promise me, upon oath, that when you come here you will insist upon my telling you the truth about your work, your development and your ambition during the last three years.

Promise me also to insist very emphatically, for I am so cowardly about criticising sensitive and delicate, likeable persons, that I am sure to run away from it unless you use a club. Promise me further that you will use that club, with the understanding that it is for your own good, and for the sake of your future. Mine is behind me, as you know.

I hope you will be here September 1st, but my engagements may be such then as to make a later day preferable. You had better enquire of old Merrill, about a week before then, or keep me informed of your address. Then I will let you know in time.

J. P.

Looking toward 1900, in a desire to head off the renomination of Bryan, Mr. Pulitzer started a boom for Rear-Admiral George Dewey, who had returned with amazing éclat from the conquest of Manila. The effort did not get very far. Dewey was too simple for politics and upset the possibility by several indiscretions that showed he was not sophisticated enough for life on shore.

The friction between the South African Republics and the British Empire that began with the Jameson raid, December 29, 1895, came to a head in September, 1899, keeping company with the international yacht races for the America's cup between Sir Thomas Lipton's first *Shamrock* and the American defender, *Columbia*, and Admiral Dewey's return from Manila. With his deep interest in peace, Mr. Pulitzer moved at once to avert war. On October 4th, the *World* began piling up a petition to President William McKinley, asking him to proffer his good offices to the disputants with the aim of preventing a resort to arms. The petition was signed by many eminent people and backed by a great public meeting in New York. Events, however, moved too rapidly for any form of intervention. The day managing editor of the *World*, John H. Tennant, had been eagerly cabling direct to the Boer authorities to get some word, and on October 11th, received a reply from President Kruger that electrified the chancelleries of Europe, roused England and sent a thrill through the United States. It read:

## Joseph Pulitzer

*World*, NEW YORK: Through the *World* I thank American friends most sincerely for their sympathy. Last Monday the republic gave England forty-eight hours' notice within which to give the republic assurance that the present dispute will be settled by arbitration or other peaceful means and troops will be removed from the borders (of the Transvaal). This expires at 5 (P.M.) to-day. The British agent has been recalled and war is certain.

The republics are determined that if they must belong to England a price will have to be paid which will stagger humanity. Have, however, full faith that the Sun of Liberty shall arise in South Africa as it arose in North America.

Mr. Pulitzer was at Bar Harbor at the time. His sympathies were decidedly pro-Boer, and the English members of the circle had a hard time bearing up under his bitter denunciations of the British cause. One day in a burst of excitement he fiercely expressed the hope that every English soldier in Africa would be killed: "Yes, killed . . . them!"

Alfred Butes mildly suggested that this might affect Arthur H. Billing, who was present, as his brother was a member of the South African Horse. Mr. Pulitzer had one of his quick revulsions:

"My God!" he exclaimed, "The poor fellow may be dead now!"

"Very likely, sir, very likely," replied Billing. And it was true. In a few days word came that the boy had been slain in battle and was no more at the moment of the remark.

When it became apparent that Bryan would again essay to make himself President in 1900, Mr. Pulitzer endeavored to redeck the Democratic ship with new

## The War with Spain — 1898-1903

planks that would banish the memory of Free Silver, and in view of America's possession of Porto Rico and the Philippines, he selected Imperialism as the issue for the campaign. Despite much urging, Mr. Bryan was coy and the Chicago platform of 1896 remained his shibboleth. It was hard to take much interest in such company and the *World* did not try.

The dissatisfaction that always follows war suggested the possibility that Mr. McKinley might not be renominated. In the editorial speculation, Governor Roosevelt received criticism as a Presidential possibility. Mr. Pulitzer reproved the writer tentatively, in this fashion: "Don't you think attacks on Roosevelt are premature and a little intemperate, considering that you don't know what situation will be created by the conventions?" Later he instructed Mr. Merrill thusly: "Tell Roosevelt he has no chance and he had better make a good Governor, regardless of Platt."

Whether because of this advice or not the Governor seemed quite "regardless" of Platt, who soon found a neat way of removing the strenuous one to what he thought would be a political desert island. Vice-President Garret A. Hobart had died, and when Mr. McKinley was renominated at Philadelphia Mr. Platt deftly placed Mr. Roosevelt on the tail of the ticket. He protested much in public and private over the proceeding, but accepted.

Though by no means popular at the moment, thanks to the Commoner's stand, Mr. McKinley had a plurality in the Electoral College of 137, and Mr. Bryan's vote was 150,000 smaller than in 1896.

In 1900 George Cary Eggleston retired from the editorial page to devote himself to literary work. His place was filled by John L. Heaton, taken from the

## Joseph Pulitzer

Sunday force, who had been a leader writer on the Brooklyn *Daily Times* and the defunct *Recorder*, between which experiences he had founded the Providence *News*.

Early on the morning of January 9, 1900, Mr. Pulitzer's fine house at Nos. 10–12 East Fifty-fifth Street was destroyed by fire. Fortunately he was at Lakewood. Mrs. Pulitzer, her two young daughters, Edith and Constance, and her infant son, Herbert, then three years old, were rescued, together with the servants, but Mrs. Morgan Jellett, the housekeeper, and Elizabeth Montgomery, governess, lost their lives. The large library and many family portraits, valuable paintings and choice Gobelin tapestries went up in the flames.

In February following the fire Mr. Pulitzer leased the Henry T. Sloane house at 9 East Seventy-second Street and installed his family therein, pending the search for a purchasable location.

Looking about for a home site Mr. Pulitzer selected the lots Nos. 7–15 East Seventy-third Street, New York, and made their purchase April 17, 1901. Messrs. McKim, Mead and White were commissioned to design the mansion, and the plan-making gave him amusement and irritation in about equal proportion. He required that a detail of the façade should be modeled in plaster. This was done and sent to him at Bar Harbor, in the midsummer. He studied it by touch and a very limited remnant of vision, to which any strain did harm.

The lot was 77 ft. 6 in. x 57 ft. 4 in., and on this was constructed a five-story structure of limestone and granite. It was elaborately furnished and contained, besides a great library, a ball room that was

## The War with Spain — 1898–1903

destined to be little used and a swimming pool that met with like fate. The water meter had been recently introduced and it competed so liberally with its brother of the gas corporation that the pool was allowed to go dry and remained so.

During the period of planning and constructing his 73rd Street mansion, the architects, Messrs. McKim, Mead and White, were employed by President Theodore Roosevelt to remodel the White House in Washington, and some of his idiosyncrasies, together with those of the architects, afforded opportunity for mirthful comment on the part of Samuel George Blythe, then the *World's* very able Washington correspondent, who was not slow to make the most of his chance. After a number of "joshes" had appeared, Mr. Pulitzer telegraphed Mr. Blythe:

> If you have no compassion for the architects, please have some for me. I am an old man and hope to pass my few remaining years in a house I am building here. These architects are my architects and unless you allow me to show them more respect in my own paper they never will finish the house for me.

This was the only direct word of repression or criticism that Mr. Blythe ever received from headquarters during his ten years of admirable service on the *World*, though his employer often "kicked" to the office over the space given his humorous articles, in which the great Roosevelt was pictured to a hair. Mr. Pulitzer took his politics seriously and demanded news instead of persiflage, especially when it ran into columns.

Although so magnificently quartered he spent almost none of his life in the New York house. A few weeks in the Spring or Fall at the most found him in the city. For the rest he was forever flitting between Europe, Bar Harbor and Jekyl Island.

Unfortunately for good government in New York City, Mr. Platt reduced the term of Mayor from four to two years, in bitterness over Van Wyck's victory in 1897 and the resulting riot of graft. In 1901, when a Mayor was again to be chosen, Tammany set its best foot forward and selected Edward M. Shepard, a distinguished Independent Democrat, who practiced law in New York, but lived in Brooklyn. His father had been Grand Sachem of the Hall. A fusion was formed behind Seth Low, and this, though in something of a political dilemma, Mr. Pulitzer supported. Low won by a vote of 296,650 to 265,940 for Shepard.

October 15, 1902, Mr. Pulitzer's old associate, John A. Dillon, died at Chatwold, the victim of a fall from his horse. This had broken some ribs and led to a fatal attack of pleurisy. He had retired some months before from active service on the editorial page, to which he had long been a bright contributor.

David Graham Phillips now resigned to take up the production of fiction, with signal success, after writing anonymously "The Great God Success," in which he had used his employer as a leading and not very delectable character.

Mr. Pulitzer was keenly hurt when he discovered that the author of the novel was Mr. Phillips. He was very fond of him and had striven hard to develop in him a fitness for first place on the paper. Phillips died tragically January 24, 1911, as the result of a bullet wound received the day before at the hands of

*The War with Spain — 1898–1903*

a madman, who imagined a character in one of his books bore a reflection on himself.

In the year 1903, Mr. Pulitzer was largely occupied with his plans for the School of Journalism. Beyond this the period was placid and not notable for efforts inside or outside of the *World* office.

## Chapter XI

### PARKER-ROOSEVELT CAMPAIGN — 1904

Editorial Changes — Coming of Frank I. Cobb — Efforts to Expose and Combat Political Corruption — Some Vivid Letters.

WITH the incoming of 1904, Mr. Pulitzer began to feel that the responsibility for the editorial page always his chief concern, was more than he cared to carry every day. Mr. William H. Merrill had been an admirable editor for eighteen years, but had now passed well into his sixties. He possessed to a nicety the art of grasping Mr. Pulitzer's ideas and requirements and putting them in polished form, but he would not initiate. On days when no inspiration came from above, the page was apt to be perfunctory. Urged to lead, he would always take the ground that he "knew Mr. Pulitzer's mind." As it turned out, he did not. Persistent proddings failing to produce Mr. Pulitzer took action.

Samuel M. Williams of his personal staff, was sent on a survey to the several cities of size, to read the dailies there published and seek talent. Landing in Detroit he discovered much vigor in the *Free Press*' editorial page, and found it due to the pen of Frank I. Cobb, a young native of Kansas, born in Shawnee Township, August 6, 1869, who grew up in Michigan timber towns, where he acquired a fighting instinct of the first order. He had worked in sawmills, taught school and served as reporter and political correspond-

## Parker-Roosevelt Campaign — 1904

ent on Grand Rapids and Detroit newspapers before taking to leader writing. He was soon annexed and brought to New York. Previously, Samuel E. Moffett, son of Mark Twain's sister Pamela, had been added to the force, and Mr. Ralph Pulitzer had joined the page. Introducing the new man to Mr. Merrill, after sundry conversations, Mr. Pulitzer put his desires into writing thus:

> I did not make one delicate point clear enough, I fear, when I spoke to you about increasing age and declining vigor, emphasizing the need on your part of overseeing and suggestion, of thought, study, revision, editing, reading, *directing*, and *far less*, mere writing. That you are a good writer, that at times you must write, goes without saying; but you must not write *as a rule*. You must not indulge in the pleasure of or feel satisfaction in writing; must not think that I shall be satisfied with your work in proportion to the amount written by yourself. Indeed, the reverse is true. You must try to write as little as possible, just as I did, but you must try to *think* just as I did, to *suggest* as hard as I did, to edit copy as I used to do, and to feel satisfied in proportion, as you furnish to the other writers, not only thoughts and topics that would occur to *them*, but thoughts and topics that would *not* occur to *them*. That is to say, topics of a more independent character — unexpected things they would hardly dare to treat — things that the editor alone, the real editor, has the right to decide.
> 
> This is the way I hope you will maintain your position as chief of the writers for a very long term, to your satisfaction and my own. That is, you must get more work out of the others; you must keep them spurred to the largest possible suggestiveness, impulse, courage; develop independent thought and fearless comment; get ideas beyond the common-

place for them, and yet keep judgment, decision and responsibility in your own hands.

The most important work lies in thought and decision. You have now: Moffett, Cobb, Osborne, Kingsbury and Ralph. I shall be disappointed if the page does not show force, vigor, and above all, *independent* leadership. There is a great deal of rottenness in Denmark, if you can only see it. And don't forget that *leader*. I will forgive dullness in all other articles, if you will only manage to have one leader strong, striking and respect-commanding. After a while people will be educated to look for that leader, and therefore the man who writes it should touch no other thing the same day. Indeed, I will give him forty-eight hours, making him re-write it sixteen times.

Do please take a little pains with Ralph. Talk to him on the topics and questions of the hour. Also show him all my notes, directions, cables and perhaps, this too. And don't forget the clippings.

Cobb, the newest recruit, did not have a very good time at the beginning, nor did his style at once appeal. Mr. Pulitzer had sailed for Europe when he began his labors and judged by samples, somewhat sharply, as this note written to Mr. Merrill on the Baltic while returning from abroad shows:

*S.S. Baltic,* 5 July '04.

MY DEAR OLD MAN: I hope Cobb will improve with age, but I must tell you that the two first editorials you sent as excellent specimens of irony, (one on Cortelyou's selection as chairman of the Nat. Committee; the other on Rockefeller's wife going to church) were to my mind or taste, very poor.

Flippancy, dear old fellow, triviality, frivolity, are not irony — please underscore these few words and put them into Cobb's brain.

## Parker-Roosevelt Campaign — 1904

Irony requires a delicacy of touch which triviality does not supply — indeed, destroys.

I dwell upon these two articles because they are the only ones I have read by Cobb, and because they present a very good example of what I detest — certainly dislike, if detest is too strong. I would not have printed either of them had I been in your place.

The moral is you must be more careful in reading so called *ironical* articles than in reading serious ones — as I am the final judge. Much better leave them out if you have any doubt.

In addition to this, the Cortelyou article should not have been treated in any except the most serious spirit. No more shameless offense against public morality or public intelligence was ever committed by Mr. Roosevelt. As to Mrs. Rockefeller, I think it was worth a paragraph — *not* an editorial.

Ralph has a sense of irony, because he has delicacy of touch.

The Presidential contest of 1904 was between Theodore Roosevelt and Alton B. Parker, who had acquired repute as a political manager under David B. Hill, and some distinction as chief Judge of the New York State Court of Appeals. Bryan had twice tried and failed to reach the apex of American ambition. He yielded to pressure in a Convention where William R. Hearst had 263 votes and allowed Parker to have the nomination. From the start the candidate did badly. He was slow about putting his feet on a gold plank; did so only after much pressure and not very solidly in an interview reluctantly given the *World*. Mr. Pulitzer was anxious that he should seize upon Republican campaign corruption as a great issue. This he failed to do. In addition the factionalism between David B. Hill and Judge D-Cady Herrick was not assuaged

## Joseph Pulitzer

by the nomination of the latter for Governor of New York on the Democratic ticket. Mr. Pulitzer was at Carlsbad when the national nominations were made. He thus expressed himself concerning the campaign in a letter to Samuel E. Moffett:

CARLSBAD, June 15, '04.

DEAR MR. MOFFETT: I have just read your very interesting observations on the political situation and quite agree with you. The chief trouble of the ostrich policy is that it may be justified by lack of intellect — by the consciousness of inability to formulate issues, to give expression in the right form to the right thing. If Parker lacks that ability I think he is exceedingly wise — not otherwise! By the way, here is a thought — though unfortunately late. Shut yourself up for two or three days; at home, if you prefer, and write one editorial on Roosevelt, reviewing his career apropos of his nomination and presentation for re-election. Of course, the article ought to have appeared the very day after his nomination, but it may not be too late even three or four days after. It may be hung upon the unquestionable shouting, yelling, yellow-plush eulogiums brought out by his nomination. You might refer to some expressions of that sort.

These, very crudely and hurriedly, are the main points: (1) Absolute fairness. Indeed, the headline ought to put that into some winged word or phrase, say, "Justice in Opposition" or "Justice and Opposition" or "Opposition Without Injustice." Put together all that can possibly be said about the wonderfully interesting career of the young man, who less than ten years ago held only a little local office — noted for his teeth. Do him full justice for whatever he has done, whatever ability he has shown, whatever courage, physical or moral, he has displayed. For instance, his treatment of the negroes — the Booker Washington incident —

## Parker-Roosevelt Campaign — 1904

the appointment of Crum — the Northern merger decision, &c, &c. Then, having done him full justice, unroll the indictment. I will not trouble you by giving you the specifications. My idea is that his real weakness and vulnerability lie in his jingoism, blatant militarism, unconstitutionalism, in the personal Government he has substituted for that of *law*, in, what Nelson very well termed, his lawless mind — Panama, Philippines, Wood, pensions, the Cuban letter. You must remember other instances.

Don't forget, guardedly, to indicate that in spite of all his follies, even political crimes, his re-election seems probable unless the Democrats act with considerable wisdom both in presenting the opposition candidate and putting him on the right platform. But, in that case, intimate that Roosevelt could be beaten.

I hope I am not too late to thank you for your little book, as you call it, which I have read with much pleasure — real interest. Altho I cannot agree with some of its theories, I fully agree to the fact that it shows a good deal of thinking and reading. I take it for granted that some of the theories were developed when you were young and that age and ripeness either have or will modify them. I hope I may have the pleasure some time of discussing some of the principles involved.

I wish I knew what or whom you really meant by that reference to the *managing editor*. I swear *I* don't know who the man is.

With kindest regards,
   Faithfully yours,
     JOSEPH PULITZER.

Returning to Bar Harbor in July for the Summer and Fall, Mr. Pulitzer devoted much time to the campaign. On the evening of September 19th, fol-

## Joseph Pulitzer

lowing a conference of national Democratic editors at the Waldorf-Astoria, a banquet was held, Josephus Daniels, of the Raleigh (N.C.) *News and Courier*, presiding. On request, Mr. Pulitzer sent the diners a cheering message, ending:

> It is because I so strongly desire Judge Parker's election that I speak so plainly on this subject. I admire his judicial temperament. I appreciate the great personal sacrifices he has made in accepting the nomination. But having accepted it I earnestly beg of you, when you see him to-morrow at Esopus, to urge that he accept also the full responsibilities of his position; that he will not permit the campaign in New York, the pivotal State, to be mismanaged by the small politicians who beset him; that he will in the next sixty days be even more than heretofore the People's leader and teacher, their tribune and advocate.

His liking for good apples found expression during the campaign, in this note addressed to William C. Steigers, business manager of the *Post-Dispatch:*

> I see advertisements about apples en exposition from Washington State Department. If they are really excellent, as advertisement says, send me some samples here regardless cost.

Mr. Pulitzer also forwarded a few views on the Missouri and general situation to George S. Johns, editor of the *Post-Dispatch*, saying:

> Unquestionably support Folk, giving him the benefit of the doubt.
> Unquestionably he will be re-elected; all the more certain if Butler and the machine should go against him.

## Parker-Roosevelt Campaign — 1904

Unquestionably all these little tricks and manipulations about Folk are absurd. Public sentiment will brush them away.

Unquestionably you must fight Cook and Allen, if they are corrupt and identified with corporation lobbying and machine.

Unquestionably you can make splendid fight on this latter and concentrate upon it more vigor, force and independence than anything else. They represent no political principle; not even political offices, but represent the perversion of political machinery and political party for purely private and pecuniary ends. You ought to be able to educate the people that Democratic principles and Democratic honor demand their defeat; that the election of Folk would be all the more triumph if accompanied by defeat of these two men on his own ticket. You ought to welcome the chance. Is this clear?

Telegraph the nominations. Don't hem and haw about Folk unless he does something absolutely, clearly and concretely, forfeiting public opinion, public confidence and respect. I dictate this, not having seen a copy of P. D., or received one single word from anybody, on instinct not knowledge.

After forcing Judge Parker to make a pronouncement in favor of sound money Mr. Pulitzer tried to stir him into a fight on campaign corruption. On October 1st, he served an editorial demand on Roosevelt to answer these ten questions:

1. How much has the Beef Trust contributed to Mr. Cortelyou?
2. How much has the Paper Trust contributed to Mr. Cortelyou?
3. How much has the Coal Trust contributed to Mr. Cortelyou?

4. How much has the Sugar Trust contributed to Mr. Cortelyou?
5. How much has the Oil Trust contributed to Mr. Cortelyou?
6. How much has the Tobacco Trust contributed to Mr. Cortelyou?
7. How much has the Steel Trust contributed to Mr. Cortelyou?
8. How much have the national banks contributed to Mr. Cortelyou?
9. How much has the Insurance Trust contributed to Mr. Cortelyou?
10. How much have the six great railroad trusts contributed to Mr. Cortelyou?

Naturally, Mr. Roosevelt did not answer, although he knew, his former private secretary, George B. Cortelyou, then secretary of commerce and labor — a handy position under the circumstances — being in direct charge of collecting the cash. Parker did not respond until the 29th of October and then with a few feeble words to the effect that he was sure Trust money was behind his rival. It was indeed, as the sequel will show.

The *World* supported Herrick with vigor. He was beaten by Francis W Higgins, Republican, who had a lead of 80,560. Parker fell 175,552 behind Roosevelt in the State and lost the Nation by 5,082,754 to 7,624,489 for the Colonel, who had a majority of 196 in the Electoral College. Bryanism was still triumphant.

The exhortations written and spoken to Mr. Merrill failed to produce the desired result, and Mr. Pulitzer, with much heartburning, decided to replace him at the head of the *World's* editorial page. From the

## Parker-Roosevelt Campaign — 1904

vantage of Jekyl Island he spent the winter of 1905 testing the juniors with Merrill on a sidetrack a good part of the time. That is, the younger men were given days "in charge." Mr. Cobb developed the most spirit of initiative, and was correspondingly tried.

He was criticised sharply, and not infrequently, on imperfect understandings. This with the vastness of New York and the lack of friendly associations wore on him. In the Spring, the owners of the Detroit *Free Press* made him a proposition to return that had a strong appeal, carrying as it did, an interest in the property. The great automobile boom had not begun and the paper was something of a burden on its owners. So the thing was a gamble. Sore over his frequent lashings, Cobb decided to accept. He was under contract and asked Mr. Pulitzer for release. The request reached him in New York the day before Easter Sunday. He devoted the holiday to its consideration. Summoning one of the elders in the office, he took him riding through Central Park in a snow storm and near its conclusion, advised him of Cobb's request and desired an opinion. The elder thought the young man might as well be humored; what was the use of trying to drive an unwilling horse? Mr. Pulitzer seemed to assent.

"I liked that young man," he murmured. "I liked the way he swore."

For a while he was silent. Then just as the carriage reached the Seventy-second Street exit from the Park, he stopped its motion and in a voice full of fury, shouted:

"Go back to the office and tell that . . . young fool I will *not* let him resign . . . him!"

The message was delivered as received. Cobb bowed amiably to the mandate. The next morning he was sent for. Expecting some fireworks, he was upset to have Mr. Pulitzer pull his ear playfully, after Napoleon's habit when pleased, and observe tenderly: "My dear boy, don't you know you quite spoiled my Easter?"

One outgrowth of the incident was an agreement that both would not get mad at each other at the same time.

Once in a while thereafter Cobb would throw up his hands, but Mr. Pulitzer would always receive the intelligence placidly. "I suppose you know Cobb has resigned again," was his usual presentation of the fact. It never went into effect. Indeed, Mr. Pulitzer had found in him precisely the man he wanted; one who could decide and act. He never waited for "instructions" and led, more often than he followed.

Mr. Merrill now departed for the Adirondacks in pursuit of early trout. At the end of the prescribed vacation it was extended, and re-extended into midsummer. The period was a trying one for both Mr. Pulitzer and himself. He solved it, however, after a clash had reduced his compensation to a pension basis, by resigning to become editor of the Boston *Herald*, filling that position until his death, September 6, 1907.

## Chapter XII

### INSURANCE REFORM — 1905-1907

Uncovering of Equitable Corruption and Its Extraordinary Results — Discovery of Charles E. Hughes — His Election as Governor — Yacht *Liberty* Built — Sixtieth Birthday.

THE year 1905 was notable for news. Japan fought Russia to a finish; President Roosevelt began his masterful manoeuvers, political and otherwise, from the security of his second term in the White House, and the *World* accomplished the greatest feat in all its history, unmasking insurance corruption, reforming the practices of the gigantic corporations centered in New York and, incidentally, starting Charles E. Hughes upon an exalted public career.

The insurance expose and its results followed a quarrel between James William Alexander, President of the Equitable Life Assurance Society, and James Hazen Hyde, who as heir of Henry B. Hyde, founder of the corporation, held a controlling interest in its shares. The "Society" was ostensibly "mutual" and its shares had small earning power by legal limitations, but they controlled the workings of the concern and gave to the junior Hyde vast power in the financial field, which, it is fair to say, he did not use greatly for his own account, but allowed to be employed to the advantage of others, notably Edward H. Harriman, who through access to its funds was able to acquire control of the Southern Pacific railway system and build for himself a fortune in securities of $75,000,000.

The policy holders had no say in its management, while its accumulations, with those of the Mutual Life Insurance Company and the New York Life Insurance Company, represented about all of the spare money in the United States. Mr. Hyde treated the Equitable as if it were his own, drawing upon its funds for matters which were plainly personal. He was an aesthete in mind, deeply devoted to French culture and a curious departure from the line of his hard-headed father.

The *World's* delving into insurance matters began in March, while its columns were crowded with the details of a gas trust inquiry, conducted by a young lawyer whose name had been suggested to the Chairman of the Legislative Committee, Senator Frederick C. Stephens, by Bradford Merrill, then Financial Manager of the paper. This was Charles E. Hughes, junior partner in the law firm of Carter, Hughes and Dwight, of which his father-in-law, Walter S. Carter, was the head.

Gas soon gave way to insurance. The developments in the Equitable row led the *World* to delve into the affairs of the Mutual and the New York Life. Richard A. McCurdy and his family controlled the "mutual" Mutual and John A. McCall, the New York Life. Corporations "owned by their policy holders" had been making fortunes for their masters. The annual increment was so great that none of the big three suffered any visible impairment of assets, but as the inquiry went deeper, under the lead of a very able *World* reporter, David Ferguson, it was found that the companies maintained a huge fund for corruption, employed to buy or suppress laws, with agents who kept their eyes on legislation all over the land,

*Insurance Reform — 1905-1907*

and used money lavishly to carry out the mandates of the management.

The insurance corporations had always been regarded as sacrosanct and continued to be for some time after the *World* began its revelations. They were large advertisers and above suspicion, thanks to skillful management and well-made masks. It did not seem possible that gentlemen of such austerity as their heads could be other than models of moral perfection. Quite naturally, the Mutual and New York Life took on a high attitude, the latter serving notice on the paper through its attorneys that any assault or reflection upon it would exact "responsibility" to the limit. Within a fortnight after this menace, John A. McCall had resigned, and the company was not only shown to be in the same class with the others, but that George W. Perkins, its vice-president, handled corruption funds in the common interest.

Politicians were plentifully provided for by Mr. Perkins. Insurance departments in important States were on his payroll. Eminent lawyers were carefully retained. It was an extraordinary and undreamed-of state of affairs that came to the surface under the *World's* merciless proddings.

Mr. Pulitzer, at the outset, was not much interested in the exposure, having his usual fear of office overzeal, but as the facts piled up he turned on more steam and in the end forced a climax beyond the anticipation of the editors. He was at Carlsbad through the late Spring and early Summer, and naturally did not receive information promptly. Editorials on "Equitable Corruption," written by William McM. Speer, arrested his attention. They were numbered.

The beginning of No. 4 he found "excellent." The whole "good," though too technical in spots for common understanding; also, "a few exaggerations. Thanks that there are not more." For the moment he continued doubtful; thought the "persistence of comment on corruption" might be overdone. Editorial No. 5 made him "sick" and he was sure that "hundreds and thousands of others" felt the same way. The gas "corruption" was running parallel at the time. This rather overloaded the page with corruption and politics. June 16th, Mr. Pulitzer had more fully absorbed the importance of developments in the gas matter. He wrote Cobb on that day:

> I now personally favor an experiment against the gas infamy in New York and the street railway infamy in St. Louis.
> Nothing short of revolution can mend these evils. If municipal control of the street railway system in St. Louis is not a lesser evil or the control of the Gas corporations in New York — well, let's find it out.
> I see nothing else left in the face of the latest act of the gas corporation in New York, corrupting the State Senate and preventing legislation.
> I consider the bribery of the Senators to prevent remedy and reform an infinitely greater evil morally and politically than oppression of the people by excessive charges.

The editorial page, being in junior hands, came in for daily review — a month after the offense, Mr. Pulitzer's letters dealing with dates sometimes that long away. He thought the page of June 9th "distinctly bad," because it failed to refer to any of the news of the day, being full of gas and insurance. He could have found "ten topics, at least, that would have been ten

## Insurance Reform — 1905-1907

times fresher and ten times more interesting to ten times as many people." But he next got to No. 5, on "Equitable Corruption." "Excellent, admirable, in every respect," he wrote. "Flawless, which is saying a good deal. Particularly struck by the strength coming from moderation of language and real knowledge. But again — following so long, and so very serious an article, comes immediately a dissertation on the tariff. Again in perspective, no variety or versatility. After the Equitable article should have come something lighter in touch and topics."

"The breath is not yet out of me," he went on, "dictating the above, when I hear about 'A Blow at Dingleyism,' as the leader of the next day, May 18th. It is simply terrible! I must go out of the room to draw fresh breath before reading it. It is a blow indeed, following the one of the day before. . . . I feel the heart ache when I have to read these damned things in succession. I presume the average reader is happier because he doesn't have to read them all. There are a hundred other subjects. Try to think of them. The country is not going to the devil. No country is more happy, more prosperous, more growing. If there is corruption — and I myself believe in exposing it — remember also the brighter side of life. Hold up your hand and swear that at least for one month you will not write a single word about railroad rates, free trade, tariff or any other dry as dust political matter."

Naturally, Mr. Cobb was always about six weeks ahead of criticism and it never caught up with him. So Mr. Pulitzer continued to be sorry for the poor reader during most of his stay amid the delights of Bohemia. Under instructions, Mr. Cobb had shared

## Joseph Pulitzer

editorial responsibility with John L. Heaton, but the blows all came to him. It was Mr. Pulitzer's method of reshaping men.

In the midst of the excitement Mr. Hyde sold his control of the Equitable stock to Thomas F. Ryan, who had risen to a commanding position through operations in surface railroad finance in New York, and left for lifetime exile in France. On receipt of the news Mr. Pulitzer cabled from Carlsbad:

> Groping in ignorance, I submit following ten questions, for fearless, vigorous inquiry, without exaggeration. What is this great Ryan mystery? What is the record of his benefactions, benevolencies, philanthropies? Why should he invest two and one half millions for an income of thirty-five hundred dollars, law forbidding larger dividends on Equitable stock? What is this real motive? Where and how can he secure legitimate return on his investment? Is any legitimate return possible by honest methods? If methods not honest, what is the difference between Ryan and Hyde? If honest, why is Ryan not a great benefactor to policy holders? If so, however, must not entire system be radically changed? Is any reform possible without a change of system? Can any change of man, any difference between Ryan and Hyde, work good without radical change of system? If Ryan owns majority stock, how can majority directors be bona fide? If majority directors still dummies, what's difference between dummies before and dummies now? Should not all dummies go — all, without any exception whatever? Law is law, dummies are dummies. Fraud is fraud. Majority of stock is majority of stock, whether owned by Ryan or Hyde, and majority of directors are not bona fide. Majority stock elects directors, controls management, controls property,

finances, assets, surplus, committees, President. Is Morton not a dummy himself? Indeed, are not Cleveland, O'Brien and Westinghouse, although all honorable men, still dummies of Mr. Ryan, selected by him, representing his interests as actual, positive owner of stock? If this fact truth. All dummies must go. Daily, persistently, intelligently, but briefly, without personal abuse and with conscientious conviction for public wrong and against public shame. Repeat all dummies must go, even Mr. Cleveland if he is dummy. What is the great Ryan mystery? Might make good continued headline numbered.

On June 28th, Mr. Pulitzer reached London, whence he cabled:

> During Heaton's absence (on vacation) Cobb has entire control editorial page, but I beg insist that he will personally not write one word about socialism, Bryanism, Dingleyism, the tariff, protection, question of railroad rates, political economy, or any abstract academic subject, interesting only to few, but try to force himself to select concrete current topics and events and make the page more comment and criticism on current events of deepest interest to largest number.
> I especially beg him to cultivate vein of irony, diminish very long editorials which have become chronic and to concentrate on Equitable Corruption without exaggeration, also to avoid superlatives, like: monstrous, traitor, anarchist, etc., as rather juvenile, feeble.

Sailing from England on the *Cedric*, July 8th, Mr. Pulitzer continued to review the editorial page, to dump what seemed like a cargo of criticism on Cobb when the ship reached New York. The page was "too dry, too melancholy, too much corruption." Then the leader of May 12th was three-quarters of a column long, which spoiled for him "the best thing Cobb had written." Mr. L. R. E. Paulin, a new member of the staff, had been "permitted twice within twenty-four hours," to write upon the railroad question. "I beg to ask him," observed Mr. Pulitzer, "when he goes to his home in Staten Island and returns, to look in the faces of the different people and to ask himself how many of them either read those articles, understand the subject, or who would not be much more interested in many other topics. A very abstruse argument or a very nice constitutional question is not interesting to ninety-nine of a hundred of our readers, unless, indeed, the argument came from the Chief Justice of the United States and then I am sure the majority of the people (and perhaps not all the editorial writers) would not understand it."

"Kicks" did not quite monopolize the comments. "Admirable," he wrote of a leader, "Could Paul Morton Backslide?" It was "just the light, satirical touch and vein the people sadly need." An editorial on June 10th, was "excellent"; gave him "great pleasure to read it." He forbade, in another note, the use of Latin phrases like "ultra vires" or "any other Latin or foreign language quotations."

He discovered, on reading the files, "how dreadfully slow all these State officials have been to catch on and how terribly strong and firm in trying really to defend, bolster up or hush up the Equitable business." It had been brought out that Senator Chauncey M. Depew was under a $20,000 annual "retainer" from the Equitable. "Review him," Mr. Pulitzer

## Insurance Reform — 1905-1907

instructed. "What a spectacle? A Senator of the United States! But not without giving him a chance to explain his position. I hope he may possibly set himself right or only half wrong. Extraordinary coincidence," he continued, "that so many Republican politicians had their fingers in the Equitable pie. Be careful. Only the real truth, if possible."

Later he wrote: "Apropos of Depew, I don't want to stifle the paper in its duty, don't want favoritism and am suggesting no suppression. But I don't think it necessary to kick him too hard. When a man is down we may show a little charity — especially toward an old man of seventy-two, who has some good qualities and perhaps I ought to add, who has been polite. Don't misunderstand me. I have not a word to say in criticism of the hard criticism of him. But don't be unnecessarily cruel."

He now awoke to the full importance of what the *World* had done. "Keep up the headline of Equitable Corruption," he commanded. "Count up all the editorials that have already appeared since the first one and send me the number. If they number 49 make that next one 50, or whatever it may be. We may get to 200 before we land some one in prison. Mistake to drop 'Equitable Corruption.'"

As his inveighings had caused the dropping, the editors regarded this as an important evidence of conversion and set themselves harder to their task. The paper early in the exposures had shown the great interlocking interests centered about the insurance companies. Mr. Pulitzer seized the point at this stage. "The one reform, self-evident," he wrote, "is the absolute prohibition by the State of these insurance companies going into any other business, banks, safe deposits or what not, so that directors or trustees could not really make money indirectly by being trustees of both the Equitable money and managers of said money in other companies or banks."

Mr. Perkins had become a partner in J. P. Morgan & Co., while still holding on to a $25,000 salary from the New York Life. "Why should a member of the firm of Morgan draw a salary from the savings of insurance?" asked Mr. Pulitzer. "If he earns that salary he ought to devote his whole time to the company and not to Mr. Morgan's firm. Again, is this not incompatibility, impropriety in his position as trustee of the insurance company and Morgan's financier? He ought to resign instantly. Make it brusque — just as Morgan talks. Hammer away. But briefly."

All this and much more — some ninety-nine pages were written while on the sea. When he reached New York he found things had happened fast. On July 11th, the *World* secured a full copy of evidence collected by Superintendent of Insurance Francis Hendricks but held secret that proved all that had been alleged. It showed cross-investments in shares that profited insiders, and relations with the higher powers in law and politics that were astonishing.

Located at Bar Harbor, Mr. Pulitzer now exerted his full driving power to force a complete uncovering by legislative power and reform by law. He hurled his messages at the editors in this fashion:

> Print following editorial to-morrow double-leaded under head Equitable Corruption dash the State is guilty number blank dash the State of New York is guilty paragraph the State inactive complacent acquiescent to corruption cynical towards vice indifferent

## Insurance Reform — 1905-1907

to most vital interests of the public dash the State is guilty paragraph Superintendent Hendricks represents the State and the State represents his guilt paragraph Lou Payn under whom the worst corruption flourished represented the State and the State represents his guilt paragraph Senator Depew represents the State in its highest place of honour and the State represents his guilt paragraph Elihu Root now Secretary of State at Washington whose neat brain and eminence were used and paid for as counsel by Equitable corruptionists represents the State and the State represents his guilt paragraph ex-Governor and ex-Senator Hill although no longer officially representing the State represents the Democratic party whose boss he has been for twenty years and he too at least partly shares the guilt paragraph Odell Governor of the State for four years all powerful Chairman of the Republican State Committee boss of the Republican party the one man who re-appointed Hendricks under grave suspicion of having made Chauncey M. Depew Senator in consideration of the settlement by the Equitable of his claim against the shipbuilding trust represents the State and the State represents his guilt paragraph the Legislature now assembled at Albany represents the State and by its inactivity insensibility and acquiescence becomes an accessory and the State represents its guilt paragraph following in stronger type begin last but not least indeed above all before all comes the Chief Executive the pilot of the Ship of State the man who has taken a solemn oath to see that the laws are faithfully executed and not violated whose solemn duty it is to initiate and lead in all reforms in all protests against public evils whose first duty of all should be to preserve the honor of the great State of New York the superior officer of Superintendent Hendricks the man who paralyses the legislative blocks investigation prevents exposure fights the punishment of the guilty opposes every demand for investigation and truth dash Governor Higgins represents the State and the State represents his guilt not Mr. Harriman not even Mr. Hyde or Mr. Alexander or Mr. Hendricks are now most guilty nor most entitled to the pillory but the grand trustee of the people of New York in the Governor's chair the man who shuts his eyes and ears to the voice of duty and conscience stop acknowledge. JOSEPH PULITZER.

This fiercely insistent demand for action forced Gov. Francis W. Higgins, who had most reluctantly called a special session of the State legislature, to compel the appointing of a committee of investigators, although in his quoted opinion there was "nothing to be gained by it." The men named were William W. Armstrong of Rochester; William J. Tully, James T. Rogers, Ezra P. Prentice, David J. Riordan, W. W. Wemple, Robert T. Cox and John McKeown.

Soon after their appointment, Messrs. Armstrong and Tully came to New York in search of counsel. So carefully had the great interests behind the insurance corporations taken precautions that no law firm of distinction could be found to undertake the inquiry. Despairing, the two called upon Ervin Wardman, then editor of the New York *Press*, and asked his aid. Wardman could think of no one. He reached the writer over the telephone with this remark:

"Armstrong and Tully are here. They have been all over hunting for a counsel and find that every man of any account is tied up. You are more interested in this than I am. Can you think of anybody?"

The memory of the gas inquiry, with the grasp

*Insurance Reform — 1905–1907*

on books and proceedings of its counsel, were in my mind.

"What's the matter with Charley Hughes?" I replied.

"He's in Europe."

"Well, there are cables, aren't there?"

He turned from the wire for a moment's consultation and then answered: "They will cable."

"Cable" they did and Mr. Hughes accepted. The resulting investigation was the most penetrating and revealing ever held. Republican influence of the highest order kept it from sending any one to prison, where not a few deserved to go, but the Armstrong Committee presented two bills, drawn by its counsel, which thoroughly reformed insurance practices, broke up interlocking relationships with high finance, took the corporations out of politics and protected the policy holders. The old controls were ousted from each company. Thomas F. Ryan had paid James Hazen Hyde $2,500,000 for the control of the Equitable stock — fifty-one shares of the par value of $51,000. E. H. Harriman had forced Ryan to sell him half. The elder J. P. Morgan "persuaded" Mr. Ryan to transfer the control to himself, paying back cost, plus four per cent. interest for the period it had been held. He explained before a Congressional committee in later years that he did this because he thought it would be in "better hands." He made ex-President Grover Cleveland a trustee with important functions. Some years later Mr. Morgan "mutualized" the company in fact and received back the amount of his investment from its assets.

Pleased with the result of the insurance cannonade Mr. Pulitzer had sent Mr. Cobb a substantial check.

The latter, in acknowledging the gift, rather intimated that he did not like to take tips, and could do his duty on his regular pay. Mr. Pulitzer replied:

> MY DEAR COBB: No, no, no to your letter. If there is anything you wanted to do in recognition of the little encouragement I meant to give you it is simply to remember that there s plenty more if you will please me. And you could not possibly please me more than by swearing to accept my criticism in the future without feeling hurt, even if it should seem to you very wrong. Will you remember this? Swear!
> With warmest regards, in haste, I am,
> Faithfully yours,
> J. P.

The State election was due in 1906. Mr. Hughes had won such fame as counsel for the Armstrong Committee that logic pointed to him as the best Republican candidate, one who could sweep away the system that had long prevailed, of corporate management of legislation. Mr. Pulitzer put his name to the fore and he was nominated.

His opponent on the Democratic side was William R. Hearst, named at Buffalo on September 27th, after Senator Thomas F. Grady, Chairman of the Credentials Committee, had done what he called "the dirtiest day's work in my life" at the behest of Charles F. Murphy, Boss of Tammany, in unseating delegates who were opposed to naming the publisher. Before this came about it seemed inconceivable that Hearst could be accepted by the Democrats after his course as a party wrecker, and the *World's* editorial page quoted with approval a statement made by the New York *Times:* "The notion that the Republicans may indorse him (Hearst) would be no more

## Insurance Reform — 1905-1907

fantastic than the notion that he may be indorsed by the Democrats at Buffalo."

"This," Mr. Pulitzer wired to Mr. Heaton from Bar Harbor, on August 4th, "is a great mistake and bad judgment. Should be text for an editorial making, roughly speaking, the following points, without a particle of feeling or exaggeration, philosophically."

He went on:

Mr. Hearst's chances to obtain the Democratic nomination excellent, almost probable as far as any one can see to-day. Of course, seven weeks yet before Buffalo September 25, and many things may happen, but no sign of an opposition whatever; Hearst's getting things by default; Democratic machine rotten to the core interior of State; no leader has raised his voice yet, no activity organization against him; ceaseless energy and work in his favor by his agents day and night all over State. Venality of Democratic bosses big and little; these are all in his favor, but above all the fact that corrupt and unprincipled persons like Murphy and McCarren will control at least half the membership of the convention voters should vote, free and untrammeled, in accordance with their own individual convictions, not because a ticket is labelled Democrats or Republicans. Whether Mr. Hearst is sincere or not in his professions is no more the question than whether Mr. Murphy is sincere in his alleged Democratic principles. The main question is who teaches more independence in voting, who awakens more indignation against corruption and misgovernment, who comes nearer presenting the real truth, who is more against party humbug, who against fooling the people. We sincerely hope Mr. Hearst will receive a very large vote. If Henry George could receive 65,000 votes in the then smaller New York, without Brooklyn, it is an interesting question how large a vote Mr. Hearst will receive in Greater New York, with an electorate practically three times as arge as that when Henry George ran. Give exact figures and comparison. This is a very delicate article I hope you will use the utmost discretion Improve this as much as you can. The idea is to approve his candidacy without approving his principles and character, or that of his unprincipled good work in connection with the tax franchise bill originated and pushed by the *World*. An able, independent man.

About this time a blue-law decision brought this blast to Mr. Heaton:

> For Sunday you ought to have a liberally, able, thorough article on Sunday amusements — on the beautiful, refining, elevating music shut out — the desirable amusements absolutely cut off, but the saloons open, compelling the people who work the whole week to find a substitute. Go over the whole subject of Sunday laws. They are obsolete — part of the dark ages — behind the times, against enlightenment and the progressive spirit of the age.
> 
> Particularly o in this city, which is more European and continental in sp rit than puritanical. It does not live in the twentieth century and want the laws of the sixteenth. All this is against the spirit of freedom, liberty, democracy and popular self-government.
> 
> It ought to make a popular leader. Let Heaton try.
> 
> Let him make a list of all the dead laws here and in Massachusetts and demand their enforcement simply to create a realization of the absurdity of the thing. Go back to the despotism of the sumptuary laws of Rome, or of the French Revolution, when in the name of Liberty, Fraternity and Equality they actually ordained, in the height of the Terror, that no child shculd know its father, but that all children should be educated

## Insurance Reform — 1905-1907

by the State — and eat, drink and dress and be exactly alike. A sort of Socialism as well as sumptuary. There is a great deal in the subject. Everybody will think about it.

Do not hesitate to al ude to conditions; the hypocrisy and injustice and violation of personal liberty and freedom and respect of public feeling and sentiment in the proper form of government. But do not denounce the decision of the judge, which is probably based upon the strict letter of the law, and as a law-abiding newspaper we must respect it. But I have a distinct notion that dead letter laws might be left dead. Let Speer, as he is a lawyer, go to work and dig out every single law on the statute book not executed.

Try to make this the piece de resistance; at the same time give some statistics in tabloid form, showing the population of New York. How many of the four and one half millions of people are really, in so far as race and national habit and custom are concerned, descendants of this puritan stock, and how many otherwise. This alone would make it striking. Also, and this is very important, how many laws are there that should be enforced and are entirely ignored?

I feel personally aggrieved because I like to go to the Sunday concerts at Carnegie Hall. I have no other amusement and now I am deprived of them. I feel like writing a letter to the great editor.

One of his rare letters to George S. Johns, editor of the *Post-Dispatch*, was written at this period, breathing with fighting force. It read:

August 10, 1906.

DEAR MR. JOHNS: Many thanks for your interesting letter. I dare not tell you how ignorant I am about what is going on in Missouri, but I shall try to mend.

Nothing would please me more than to see you more independent and courageous in denouncing crooks,

## Joseph Pulitzer

corruptionists, humbug and humbugs in the Democratic party. For instance, just now, I believe the Bryan craze perfectly imbecile unless the Democratic party should be really devoted to him, knowing that he *can't* be elected and as a deep devotion to principles regardless of success or, possibly, with only hope of success in the remote future, say ten or twenty years hence. That would not be war nor politics, but I could admire it as devotion to an ideal.

The lying of men like Folk, Francis, Croker, Sullivan, Murphy, that Bryan will be elected in 1908, at the very next election (and that is the reason why they and the Democratic party should be for him, because he is the only man who can be elected even against Roosevelt) — this wholesale and shameless lying against all truth and facts is a humbug which the *Post-Dispatch* should ridicule and puncture. If Bryan had a chance in 1908 his own friends ruin it by making him the candidate this year and next, with terrific odds against him. If the elections this fall go Republican, as I believe they will, they also go against the Bryan candidacy and the Bryan principles, and if he is still the candidate and next year's elections in the North show practically no change, where will he be? Can he stand such long continued tests of sincerity and character, tests of sincerity of speech, soundness of judgment and record? Would he not be infinitely better, could he keep his mouth shut during these two years until 1908, learning the importance of silence, thinking, studying, of dignity, weighing his words until the right time came?

I do not deny his talent and have admired and do admire his power as a phrase maker, orator and politician and agitator. But statesman he certainly is not and the judicial high qualifications of a chief magistrate he certainly lacks. Unsound judgment as a leader he certainly has, however a brilliant future as an agitator he may have.

These words are private and unrevised, not to be taken verbatim, but they are not strictly confidential so far as they contain any thought. I wish you would carry them out in your own way, at your own time. If you write anything on this subject, as I am terribly busy and may not see the *Post-Dispatch*, you may send me some of the editorials on this subject, but not too many, please!

I think it would be refreshing to see at least one paper not rushing with the crowd, but standing by whatever it believes to be true, against the unanimous shouting of what is still called the Democratic party.

But show no feeling, prejudice or personal dislike. I certainly have none. Nor would I hold him responsible for accepting the enthusiastic choice of his party. He cannot be expected to be more than human. But the question is why should the party be so foolish? Where are the party leaders? Where is the sagacity, wisdom, foresight, knowledge of the past, deliberation in this present hullaballoo?

Is the Democratic party not drifting to destruction, whatever there is left of it? The signs? Look at Iowa, Idaho, Tammany, Murphy, McCarren — a union with the Federation of Labor and Tammany Hall, an appeal apparently to the corrupt or ignorant or poor, of propertyless — an appeal to passion and prejudice against cold reason. And what is *the real difference* between the Republican party and the Democratic party? The war cry against corruptions and Trusts can't do Mr. Bryan any good in the face of Mr. Roosevelt's actual achievements and still greater prospects. The cry for tariff revision? But had Bryan issued that cry? I do not seem to hear it — and if it should be heard next year, the sober, moderate, intelligent people will prefer to trust Roosevelt. What is the difference between the two parties, eliminating mere exaggeration, which has characterized every opposition?

Now, I believe I have written you the longest letter you ever received from me, but as I could go on for another hour, I must stop. Summing up in a nutshell: DON'T be afraid, but be sure you are right. Don't go to the other extreme, but be exactly judicial and independent and always fair. Have nothing to do with politicians on either side. Don't ever be influenced too much by the *World's* editorials, for I am away and tired, and daily opportunities cannot be seized at a distance and every issue of the paper presents an opportunity and duty to say something courageous and true; to rise above the mediocre and conventional; to say something that will command the respect of the intelligent, the educated, the independent part of the community; to rise above fear of partisanship and fear of popular prejudice. I would rather have one article a day of this sort; and these ten or twenty lines might readily represent a whole day's hard work in the way of concentrated, intense thinking and revision, polish of style, weighing of words. I wish I had another editorial writer to help you, or still more, an editorial thinker or two. However, I know the law of limitations and will not expect too much.

In haste, with kind regards,

Faithfully yours,

J. P.

P. S. Show this to O'Neil, whose devotion to Bryan I fear.

One of the problems of the strenuous season had been the enlargement of the Pulitzer Building, long inadequate to accommodate the ever expanding energies of the *World*. Two years before, Mr. Pulitzer

## Insurance Reform — 1905–1907

had purchased from the New York Press Club the lots completing the block bounded by Park Row, Frankfort and North William Streets. He had a half-thought of moving uptown where the *Herald* had successfully migrated. The pressure from the office caused him, early in September, rather reluctantly, to order the enlargement. "I do not want a new building," he wrote the business manager. "But apparently you will not be happy until you get it. Therefore, go ahead, but make no mistakes. Remember they will haunt your children and your children's children!" He further instructed that he be asked no questions, leaving the full responsibility of a $1,500,000 construction with the office.

As a break in the strain he now took a round trip to England, remaining but a few days ashore.

The command to support Hughes for Governor came to John L. Heaton, in charge of the editorial page at the moment, from London, on September 30, 1906: "Without intemperance, with perfect accuracy, from truly independent standpoint, support Hughes as best man possible, to continue and complete his great work, regardless of party. Reprint carefully condensed pith of Democratic leaders bolting Hearst, declaring him no Democrat — Democrats relieved from party allegiance."

Mr. Pulitzer returning the first week in October, took an active interest in the election of Hughes. On the whole he was rather pleased at Mr. Hearst's continued adventuring in politics. "Treat Hearst without a particle of feeling of prejudice, if this is possible," he telegraphed Mr. Heaton from Bar Harbor on the 11th. "Concentrate on the one point previously telegraphed, that while as a matter of

## Joseph Pulitzer

conviction sincerely detest most of his professions, principles, purposes and party, the same conviction compels an expression of respect for his courage in accepting a candidacy which cannot lead to his election and must appear as devotion to his principles. If he will give vigorous articulation and organization to the deep conviction among all intelligent Democrats that the name, spirit, spell and fame of the ancient Democratic party is used by unscrupulous bosses and politicians purely for moneymaking for their own pocket all the time, see Murphy, McCarren, etc., he will render a public service whatever his motives. If he will detach from the blind followers of the Murphy machine a large body, if he will teach the voter that his first duty is to vote in accordance with his own conscience and as free man, he will render a service to the cause of independence and intelligence and show the way all if not majority and that Murphy has already seemingly made alliance with Buffalo bosses who are all for Hearst. Irony of fate, humor of situation that Hearst denounces Tammany's boss, owes his popularity to this denunciation, received at least half his vote [for Mayor of New York City] last Fall simply because the people wanted to smash Murphy and McCarren, whom Hearst with extraordinary boldness and great ability, held up to public infamy, that now Hearst is apt to receive Murphy's support and through that support, the regular nomination for Governor and not only the anti-Tammany and anti-Murphy sentiment, but also candidate of Mr. Murphy and Tammany Hall itself; point out the humor but do not deny strength such nomination would give him and the further humor, if by any stupidity of the Republicans or further irony of fate,

STEAM YACHT LIBERTY.

he should be elected and thereby become boss of Tammany, boss of the regular Democratic State machine, taking the places that both Murphy and Hill held so long, removing both McClellan and Jerome as he certainly must do if he is true to his denunciation. Nor would the removal of Jerome if he appointed a really able, honorable, fearless prosecutor, cause many tears to be shed. However, these are mere possibilities. His selection is infinitely more improbable than his nomination. All this hurriedly dictated, unrevised. Don't make it too long. Try to raise a sense of humor for Monday."

The paper supported Mr. Hughes vigorously and he was elected by a vote of 749,002 to 691,105 for Mr. Hearst. The rest of the Democratic State ticket won by modest majorities.

In 1906 Mr. Pulitzer determined to construct a steam yacht fitted for his own personal comfort. Accordingly designs were made by G. L. Watson & Sons, of Glasgow, for a steamer of 1606 tons, one of the largest private vessels ever built. The contract was given to Ramage & Ferguson, of Leith, Scotland, where she was launched on December 5, 1907, and christened "Liberty."

The vessel was 300 feet over all, beam 35 feet, 6 inches. The yacht was not designed for speed, $15\frac{1}{2}$ knots being her best showing in the trial trip. Her average cruising gait was 12 knots and she had coal capacity for 6,000 miles of steaming.

The deck plans carried a long house on the main, with dining room, music room, owner's sitting room, etc. Below, Mr. Pulitzer had a large room by himself, forward, with a gymnasium and quarters for his personal attendants. Aft were twelve staterooms for guests and secretaries. She carried a crew of forty-five men.

For once in fulfilling a heart's desire Mr. Pulitzer had no disappointment. She had been built under the eye of a favorite secretary, Mr. Arthur H. Billing, and equalled all expectations.

"I love this boat," he said. "Here I am at home and comfortable. In a house I am lost in my blindness, always fearful of falling on stairs or obstacles. Here the narrow companionways give me safe guidance and I can find my way about alone. Nothing in all my life has given me so much pleasure."

With the coming of cold weather Mr. Pulitzer betook himself to Nice, Cimiez, occupying the Villa Liserb, which Queen Victoria had occupied during her later visits to the Riviera. The estate had belonged to an Ambassador from Brazil to France, who had reversed the French spelling "Bresil" to adorn his property. Here the Winter and Spring were spent quietly. With the coming of Spring he migrated to Carlsbad.

April 10, 1907, Mr. Pulitzer's sixtieth birthday, was celebrated both in New York and St. Louis by a banquet given to sixty guests in each city, gathered from the members of the respective staffs of the *World* and *Post-Dispatch*. Mr. Pulitzer, though in Europe, was the host, and took advantage of the occasion to "retire" once more, sending an announcement to that effect for publication in the two papers. It was duly reproduced in the *Post-Dispatch*, but Mr. Frank I. Cobb, to whom it came, as editor in charge of the *World*, felt that Mr. Pulitzer was too good an asset to lose on the small excuse of three score and suppressed the message. Besides, he rather thought J. P. was getting into the Patti-Bernhardt class and retiring too often. The exclusion roused Mr. Pulitzer to vast wrath, but he did not insist on being formally eliminated. The next year when the Roosevelt-Panama storm, with which he really had nothing to do, arose he reminded Mr. Cobb with much feeling that if he had not suppressed his "retirement" he would have had a perfect alibi!

The New York *Evening Post*, then under the editorship of Rollo Ogden, had animadverted inaccurately on the *World's* share in allaying the Venezuelan excitement. Mr. Heaton wrote him a personal note of correction and sent Mr. Pulitzer a copy, which brought this response:

VILLA MILTON, CARLSBAD, May 15, 1907.

DEAR MR. HEATON: Many thanks for your clippings and more than appreciation for calling Mr. Ogden's attention to his grave blunder.

By the way, too, my impression is that I telephoned that editorial, carefully weighing every word, including the headline, and at the very hour I read Mr. Cleveland's message and kept it up with considerable fire, if not force and fury.

I do not know whether it is worth while, but if you think so, Mr. Ogden's gross and crass misstatement would give you a chance, taking that as the text and provocation to give a brief little summing of the history of the fight.

I daresay that compared to the influence of the *World* there were comparatively few people who knew what was going on in the *Post* and, incidentally, when I arrived in London a few months later, I had, to my surprise, a few Bishops and a Cardinal representing the Peace Society calling upon me and delivering a few flattering speeches for the services of the *World*.

As I remember there were bitter personal attacks in the Senate and House that recognized the effect of my fight.

However, I do not suggest this; I merely leave it to you as you really suggest this thought under the spur of the moment, having just read your letter.

Anyhow, if you do anything, treat Mr. Ogden with *exquisite* politeness, assuming that he did not intentionally mislead his readers but was probably misled himself by a singular, unaccountable prejudice against the *World*.

All this in haste — unread, unrevised, dictated in the carriage driving through the woods of Carlsbad and wishing that you are perfectly well and happy.

Sincerely yours,

J. P.

P. S. I take it for granted that that admirable editorial on McClellan's duty, giving, I believe, twelve points, was written by you. If so I really must compliment you. Try to keep up that tone and strength in just that style of courtesy and absence of violent language.

I sometimes think that even Murphy, McCarren and Grady, certainly Hearst, Roosevelt and Bryan, should be treated with exquisite politeness. Just as the critic must become harsh and severe and personal, he should abstain from intemperate and violent language.

Just in that proportion as the facts, arguments and reasons are strong, the critic should use moderation and measure in form.

Give my regards to Cobb and tell him I really have made up my mind not to criticise — at least, for a few weeks longer. Really I enjoy the editorial page most of these days.

P. S. No. 2. If you do anything in the matter of

## Insurance Reform — 1905–1907

Mr. Ogden's "grave blunder," it must *not* be an editorial. It might be done in the form of a letter or as an article; a contribution of your own.

He was much interested in Ferrero's *Greatness and Decline of Rome*, done in quite modern style and from his reading of the volumes, evolved this thought and suggestion:

Ferrero says positively that Mark Antony never made any speech at Julius Caesar's funeral, and therefore Shakespeare's story is an absolute invention, or rather he took it from Plutarch. Ferrero makes the point and proves it. He says that no speech was made at Caesar's bier. A very good literary symposium for the Sunday paper might be made. Such historians as we have, like Woodrow Wilson, Rhodes, McMaster, etc. Ask them the question, what they think about it. It destroys the universal belief.

## Chapter XIII

### ROOSEVELTISM

Early Differences With the Strenuous Statesman — The Harriman Letter — Anti-Jingo Campaign — Efforts to Coördinate the Democracy.

THE CONFLICT between the *World* and Theodore Roosevelt, which lasted as long as the latter lived, and at times reached spectacular proportions, while not always stimulated by Mr. Pulitzer owed its beginnings to him and so established an office tradition that made it easy to continue at slight provocation. Roosevelt, fresh from Harvard, was a member of the State Legislature from New York City in 1882, 1883 and 1884; in that body he showed early ability in the great art of creating excitement, which he afterwards practiced so successfully. He invested in his Dakota ranch in 1883, and subsequently gave it more time than public affairs in rebuilding a rather delicate constitution. He returned from the plains in 1886, long enough to become the Republican nominee for mayor in a three-cornered fight, the other candidates being Henry George and Abram S. Hewitt. Hewitt won with a vote of 90,552. George received 68,110, and Roosevelt 60,435 ballots. He made no great stir in the campaign, which was one of the most intense ever fought in the city, thanks to the zeal and enthusiasm of George's followers, who gave the "vested interests" a real scare.

## Rooseveltism

Rather oddly, Mr. Roosevelt does not mention this incident in his autobiography, probably because he came in third somewhat ingloriously. At any rate, the ranch engrossed his attention until President Benjamin Harrison made him a member of the National Civil Service Commission. He served here for six years, four under Harrison and two under the reëlected Cleveland, making life a burden for cabinet officers and statesmen with "friends." He was apparently lost sight of politically when the election of 1894 — a fusion fight — placed William L. Strong, a Republican merchant, in the mayor's chair. Police misrule had been a factor in Strong's success, the Lexow Committee and Dr. Charles H. Parkhurst furnishing limelight, and Mayor Strong's great problem was the reform of the force. The police board was bi-partisan and complaisant, if not corrupt. He therefore made a clean sweep of Republicans as well as Democrats, appointing for the former Theodore Roosevelt and Col. Frederick Dent Grant, son of the great general. The Democrats were Avery D. Andrews, a West Pointer who had abandoned the army, and Andrew D. Parker, a shrewd young lawyer.

The board elected Mr. Roosevelt as president and the fireworks at once began. The high officers of the force were retired one by one, such notables as Thomas F. Byrnes, the chief, and Alexander S. Williams, the most potent of the inspectors, leading the procession and preserving half pay. The *World* had been active against police corruption and felt that retiring was hardly the way to reward crookedness. It exploded, however, when Mr. Roosevelt, after appointing Peter F. Conlin, half-brother of William J. Florence, the actor, as chief, began an elaborate effort to repress liquor selling beyond the prescribed hours. This Mr. Pulitzer regarded as a waste of time in the presence of more important matters and so he assailed the move with great vigor. To his astonishment his arguments in favor of liberal interpretation of excise laws were not approved by the *World's* readers. The town largely took the side of enforcement. Inviting opinions from the public, mailbags full of letters sustaining Roosevelt were received and almost none from the other side. So victory rested on his banner, though more turmoil than reform developed in Mulberry Street.

Intervening history does not need to be recited in detail, and in Mr. Roosevelt's early days as President Mr. Pulitzer found much to praise in the continuous performance staged from the White House. His course in the great coal strike of 1902 was applauded by the *World* as an action of great moment, no one at the time perceiving that this was the beginning of a joint control between corporations and unions, that was in due season to treble coal costs to the consumers.

As affairs went on Mr. Pulitzer found that here was a child of fortune who needed a strong curb. Criticisms became the order of the day. This was resented at the White House and the President did not hesitate to try means to reach the source and temper the comments. Naturally, he did not succeed.

Ever since the flood of Argonauts in 1849 began to flow across Panama toward California, the project of cutting a canal somewhere through Central America had been rife. Enterprising Americans, under the leadership of John L. Stephens, built the railroad from Colon to the Pacific. A water route was developed by way of Lake Nicaragua. Both points enticed promoters who sought to open waterways. Finally, inspired

## Rooseveltism

by the Suez Canal, Ferdinand de Lesseps, its builder, organized a company in France to sever the Isthmus of Panama. Through bad sanitation many lives were lost in the venture, which moved considerable earth. Worse than this the operations of the corporation were so tainted with fraud that De Lesseps and his son were convicted in a French court. Work ceased and the franchise lapsed into the hands of the Republic of Colombia, through whose territory ran the right of way.

Senator Warner Miller of New York had collected considerable backing for the Nicaragua project, when Philippe Bunau-Varilla, one of De Lesseps' engineers, succeeded in enlisting the interest of William Nelson Cromwell, an able New York attorney who had shown great capacity as a salvor of wrecked corporations, and he gave the Panama project much attention. This spread over a number of years. He organized a New Panama Canal company in France to take over the assets of the old concern and labored industriously at Washington to secure Government support in clearing up the title with Colombia.

The immensity of the enterprise appealed to President Roosevelt, who set the forces of the State Department at work to secure the right of way for the United States. Secretary of State John Hay framed a treaty with Dr. Thomas Herran, the Colombian minister, under which the United States of Colombia would have received $25,000,000 for the strip needed to complete the canal. The Colombian government rejected this and after much futile negotiating, during which Cromwell had acquired control of the Panama railroad, a "revolution" was invented, managed in the main by the employees of the road and supported by the U.S.S. *Nashville*, hastily summoned from Jamaica, which prevented the Colombians from moving troops to Panama over the line. This took place on November 31, 1903. Seven days later the toy republic thus created was formally recognized at Washington, Bunau-Varilla, already at the capital, becoming the first minister. A treaty was made with Panama by which, in return for $10,000,000 and other valuable considerations, the needed canal zone was formally ceded. All this was arranged without the prior sanction of Congress or any action on the part of the people of the United States, although under a treaty dating from 1848 this country had obligated itself to protect the rights of the sister republic. As Mr. Roosevelt said in a speech made at the University of California, March 23, 1911: "I took the Isthmus, started the canal, and then left Congress, not to debate the canal, but to debate me."

To all this the *World* uttered a stern but ineffective dissent. The ruthless outrage was complete. Congress voted to pay the "French stockholders" $40,000,000 for their worthless "rights." The canal was started and in time successfully constructed. Rumors rose from time to time, indicating great profits to a syndicate of financiers grouped together by Cromwell, and there was a general feeling that something was wrong about the whole transaction. This, however, died down under the stress of success and other affairs of note.

The war between Russia and Japan, which broke out almost unwarned on February 8, 1904, deeply engaged Mr. Pulitzer's attention. It will be recalled that Russia gathered together a motley fleet, embracing almost her total tonnage, into an armada under Admiral Rojestvensky and headed it for Japan. Its first exploit was to fire into a fleet of English fishing boats on the Doggerbank, on October 22, 1904, in a panic-stricken fear that Japanese torpedo craft were operating among the anglers. This episode over and barred by international law from the use of the Suez Canal the fated fleet straggled around the Cape of Good Hope and put in for rest at Madagascar, a French possession, where by the rules of war they should have been allowed but twenty-four hours stay. Pleading disability, they lingered. The news editors lost interest in them. Not so Mr. Pulitzer. He required that the editorial page should each day keep the public mind on the fleet. As little or no word came, this task was not easy, but changes were rung on rumors and possibilities until the Russian ships, quite to the general surprise, passed at Singapore on April 15, 1905. Mr. Pulitzer then ordered it to be announced that Togo would meet them when and where he chose and annihilate them, which he did in the Straits of Tsushima on May 27, 1905.

When on September 5, 1905, the Portsmouth Treaty was signed, he sent word to John L. Heaton, in charge of the paper at the moment, to suspend comment and await his signal. It came about 4.30 in the afternoon, but was a column of copy — not about the treaty — but painting the glory of Theodore Roosevelt who, as President of the United States, had through his good offices brought it about. With his customary correctness he centred the interest where it belonged.

He had also come to accept Roosevelt as something of a darling of the gods and to admire his aggressiveness in dealing with "malefactors of great wealth" as the President has described Morgan, Hill, Harriman, *et al*, in breaking the Northern Securities merger. Indeed, so pleased was he that in March, 1907, he had written this instruction to Mr. Cobb, then officially responsible for the conduct of the editorial page:

> Support Roosevelt on main line against railway abuses, personal autocracy, downright swindle like Alton — no hypercriticism of his minor faults. His lack of dignity, inveracity are forgotten by people in the light of one or two great acts. He has subjugated Wall Street. He is right and popular — more popular than ever before for the enemies he has made. The people measure him by his enemies.
>
> There is too much nagging Roosevelt.

On the heels of this seeming submission occurred an incident that strongly substantiated his charges of corruption during the Parker campaign and made the welkin ring.

Mr. Pulitzer had complained that no one from the business office visited the shop on Sundays. I had been in the habit of staying there a good part of Saturday night struggling with the enormous Sunday run, which quite overtaxed all facilities, but agreed to drop in. On the afternoon of Sunday, March 31, 1907, I reached the news room just as Mr. C. M. Van Hamm, the managing editor, was opening his desk. "Anything new," I asked. He pulled out a drawer, took from it a couple of typewritten sheets, and said: "I don't know what you would call this. A fellow brought it in Friday and asked $150 for it. He didn't get the money, but I held the copy." The "copy" read:

> Mr. Sidney Webster,
> No. 245 East Seventeenth Street, New York.
>
> Dear Sir: I am glad to see that you are in town, and hope soon to have an opportunity of talking matters over with you.

## Rooseveltism

I had printed copies of the testimony sent you, in hopes that you would, after reading them, give me some idea of where I stand, for I confess that I feel somewhat at sea in the whole insurance matter. The trouble originated in my allowing myself to be drawn into other people's affairs, and partly from a desire to help them and at their request. I seemed to be like the fellow who got in between the man and his wife in their quarrel.

As to my political instincts to which you refer in your letter of Dec. 13, I am quite sure I have none, and my being made at all prominent in the political situation is entirely due to President Roosevelt and because of my taking an active part in the autumn of 1904 at his request, and his taking advantage of conditions then created to further his own interests. If it had been a premeditated plot it could not have been better started or carried out.

About a week before the election in the autumn of 1904, when it looked certain that the State ticket would go Democratic, and was doubtful as to Roosevelt, himself, he, the President, sent me a request to go to Washington to confer upon the political conditions in New York State. I complied and he told me he understood the campaign could not be successfully carried on without sufficient money, and asked if I would help them in raising the necessary funds, as the National Committee, under control of Chairman Cortelyou, had utterly failed of obtaining them, and there was a large amount due from them to the New York State Committee.

I explained to him that I understood the difficulty here was mainly caused by the up-State leaders being unwilling to support Depew for re-election as United States Senator; that if he, Depew, could be taken care of in some other way I thought matters could be adjusted and the different contending elements in the

[ 301 ]

party brought into close alliance again. We talked over what could be done for Depew and, finally, he agreed that if found necessary he would appoint him as Ambassador to Paris.

With full belief that he, the President, would keep this agreement I came back to New York, sent for Treasurer Bliss, who told me that I was their last hope, and that they had exhausted every other resource. In his presence I called up an intimate friend of Senator Depew, told him that it was necessary in order to carry New York State that $200,000 should be raised at once and if he would help I would subscribe $50,000. After a few words over the telephone the gentleman said he would let me know, which he did probably in three or four hours, with the result that the whole amount, including my subscription, had been raised.

The checks were given to Treasurer Bliss, who took them to Chairman Cortelyou. If there were any among them of life insurance companies, or any other like organizations, of course Cortelyou must have informed the President. I do not know who the subscribers were other than the friend of Depew, who was an individual. This amount enabled the New York State Committee to continue its work, with the result that at least 50,000 votes were turned in the City of New York alone, making a difference of 100,000 votes in the general result.

There are between 2,200 and 2,300 districts in Greater New York and in a campaign such as that the expenditure of, say, $50 in each district for campaign purposes, not including the watchers on election day, would take more than $100,000.

Some time in December, 1904, on my way from Virginia to New York I stopped and had a short talk with the President. He then told me that he did not think it necessary to appoint Depew as Ambassador to Paris, as agreed, in fact favored him for the Senate. I had not expected that he was the one (*sic*) as to what would be necessary, but he arrogated that to himself, and I, of course, could say nothing further. After that I used what influence I could to have Depew returned to the Senate, as I considered there had been an implied obligation which should be lived up to.

This is the way I was brought to the surface in the political matter, as I had never before taken any active part, and had only done what I could as any private citizen might; so you see I was brought forward by Roosevelt in an attempt to help him, at his request, the same as I was in the insurance matter by Hyde and Ryan by their request for my help; and in the case of Ryan I probably would have dropped the matter after our first interview had it not been for my desire to save Belmont from taking a position for which he could have been criticised by the public press, as he was the one Ryan desired me to influence from opposing Morton for election as chairman of the Equitable board, and Belmont afterward thanked me for taking his part, as if he had voted against Morton in view of his local traction contentions with Mr. Ryan it would have been misconstrued.

Ryan's success in all his manipulations, traction deals, tobacco combination, manipulation of the State Trust Company into the Morton Trust Company, the Shoe and Leather Bank into the Western National Bank and then again into the Bank of Commerce — thus covering up his tracks — has been done by the adroit mind of Elihu Root, and this present situation has been brought about by a combination of circumstances which has brought together the Ryan-Root-Roosevelt element.

Where do I stand?

Yours sincerely,
E. H. HARRIMAN.

## Joseph Pulitzer

It appeared that the letter had first been offered to the Brooklyn *Eagle* and rejected; then to the New York *American*, where some wise editor, knowing the state of the paper's account at the Wells-Fargo Bank, owned by Mr. Harriman, had prudently shoved it away.

Amazed after reading it, I said: "Do you mean to say you call yourself a managing editor and have allowed this to lie on your desk three days and made no use of it?"

"Well," he replied, "I thought it might be some kind of a 'plant.'"

I answered that I would assume all the responsibilities for its publication, with the result that on the morning of Tuesday, April 21st, the *World* made the letter public. Nothing printed in its columns ever made a greater sensation. Sidney Webster was a distinguished lawyer, who in his youth had been private secretary to President Franklin Pierce, and was a brother-in-law of Stuyvesant Fish. He had been long in semi-retirement, but acted as an adviser to Mr. Harriman on important matters. The recoil on President Roosevelt resulted in a backfire of abuse directed at Mr. Harriman, together with the production of correspondence with Congressman James S. Sherman, written two years after the event, in evident purpose of an alibi on Roosevelt's implied promises. This letter, however, sent by Roosevelt to Mr. Harriman on October 14, 1904, showed how plainly he had intimated the possession of a coöperative spirit:

> MY DEAR MR. HARRIMAN: A suggestion has come to me in a roundabout way that you do not think it wise to come on to see me in these closing weeks of

the campaign, but that you are reluctant to refuse, inasmuch as I have asked you. Now, my dear sir, you and I are practical men, and you are on the ground and know the conditions better than I do. If you think there is any danger of your visit to me causing trouble, or if you think there is nothing special I should be informed about, or no matter in which I could give aid, why, of course, give up the visit for the time being and then, a few weeks hence, before I write my message, I shall get you to come down to discuss certain government matters not connected with the campaign.

In short, he deftly separated $200,000 from the "malefactors of great wealth" and used it to carry New York State for himself. Harriman was not alone in contributing. It was made clear in the litigation over George J. Gould's conduct of Jay Gould's estate in 1922, that he had taken $500,000 from the family funds to help "save the country," and very oddly this confession was made at a hearing where Alton B. Parker, the defeated candidate, was present as one of the counsel.

To this huge sum from the Goulds might be added $100,000 from the Standard Oil Company, $150,000 from J. P. Morgan & Co., $75,000 from Daniel G. Reid, and $100,000 from H. C. Frick, to say nothing of minor malefactors, up to a campaign fund of an acknowledged total of $2,100,000.

Mr. Pulitzer was amazed at the editorial negligence shown in commenting on the story. To Frank I. Cobb he wrote:

> Editorial page routine of makeup and hours must be suspended in emergency. Great mistake not to have had leading editorial on the Harriman letter the

morning it appeared. Who was in charge of the page that night? Did he know the letter was to be printed? Did news department inform him? The same thing occurred regarding Root's speech on States rights.

The Harriman editorial of the following day — a day late — very, very late — has not one word about the main fact that the *World* printed it exclusively; that it revealed and exposed an infamous jobbery. Whoever wrote it should read it three times to see whether I am right.

Parker acted the perfect dolt during the whole campaign [of 1904] in pompous over-dignity and silence on this very question of campaign contributions. The *World* alone hammered and howled about them all during the campaign. Then finally Parker took it up. I think it is rather ridiculous that the *World* should ignore itself so completely. Roosevelt himself has been more truthful in giving credit. The editorial of the 4th catches the point, but three days late. Whole empires have been destroyed in less than three days. Still I am glad the *World* caught on.

It is all amazing, most amazing, considering Parker was a dead duck and Roosevelt's walk-over absolutely manifested to a certainty. The country was overwhelmingly Republican, that is, the entire north.

Is there any evidence whatsoever that the Harriman money came out of his pocket; is it not more likely it came out of the half dozen corporations he controls — like the Union Pacific or Baltimore & Ohio? I'll bet it came out of the stockholders. The editorial of April 4th, is excellent! excellent! excellent! Thanks. But what an awful scandal that the *World* is robbed of all credit by its own editors for its great exposure.

Never drop a big thing until you have gone to the bottom of it. Continuity! continuity! continuity until the subject is really finished.

## Rooseveltism

He had perhaps forgotten in the excitement of the moment that only a few days before the publication of the Harriman correspondence he had written Cobb the note indicating a disposition to regard Roosevelt favorably.

The would-be seller of the letter was Frank W. Hill, a former stenographer in the Harriman employ. He was arrested and a flurry made over him by District Attorney William Travers Jerome, but the case faded out.

Quite curiously, the moral effect upon Roosevelt was nil. Public opinion seemed to be that having trimmed a magnate the honors were his. Mr. Pulitzer's reprehension stopped at reproof of campaign corruption, and he concentrated instead on a demand that Harriman must be eliminated as a figure in American finance. "Harriman must go" furnished the text for a series of vigorous articles, at the conclusion of which Harriman remained. He was too powerfully intrenched to be dislodged. The instructions to the editors from day to day, while the crusade ran, were invigorating and worthy of repetition as samples of forceful views:

> Put utmost vigor without violence into "Harriman must go" series — say one editorial addressed to each director, stating his character, career, moral, social, religious position, pretensions, responsibilities, etc., every second or third day. Directors alone responsible. Whole country's reputation involved. Harriman vindicates Hearst and almost justifies Bryan's State ownership; certainly helps both and even worse socialistic attacks, as practical, horrible example to be pointed at railroad corruption generally. Harriman should go as railroad's worst enemy.

Later he wrote:

> Assume they [the Union Pacific directors] are all fair-minded, church-going, eminently respectable and representative citizens and then appeal to them, with the evidence before you, to really do their duty. The whole business has its roots in the dummy director idea. Men sell their names and reputations and then become absolute dummies. Tell Van Hamm to telegraph immediately for the biographical material for each man — how he rose, what he did in a public-spirited way; how he pretends, or actually is, or tries to be, good. And yet how they allow this man to be their representative, their Grand Elector, their Chosen! They are responsible, *not* Harriman.

After a short round trip to Europe Mr. Pulitzer returned to Bar Harbor in June, 1907, and became very active. On the 29th, he wrote Mr. Cobb his thoughts on journalistic ethics apropos of some editorial sputterings about Philadelphia journalism, saying:

> On principal I do not believe in pitching into other newspapers. Newspapers are always blackguarded by somebody — accused of bad motives, sensationalism, commercialism — press regarded universally as the common enemy of everybody — This is a good reason why the *World* should not join in the chorus — should not add its weight to this assault — If press has its faults it is not necessary for us to talk about them — Let others find it out — I always hope for a more high-minded standard and quite agree that there are evils — but don't think wise raise a cry against our own craft — This is apropos to attack on Philadelphia press — Intended only as future guide.

To this he added:

> The editorial page ought always to have one continuing public service feature outside of routine.

## Rooseveltism

I have forty or fifty on my notes which I hope I shall be able to present to you when you come.

His uppermost thought was the completion of the insurance clean-up. While the Hughes investigation had made Mr. Hughes governor, it stopped short of a thorough remedying of evils. Thomas F. Ryan had control of the Equitable; Otto Kelsey, the state superintendent of insurance, represented old, corrupt conditions. Mr. Pulitzer therefore began a merciless prodding of the governor, which was not destined at the moment to have any great effect, the Republican Senate refusing to permit the replacement of Kelsey by a better man. Mr. Pulitzer's attitude toward the governor, whom the *World* had done so much to elect, was stated thus in an earlier letter to Cobb, discussing the Public Service Commission measures, among the most important of the governor's initiates:

> I am simply crazy about Hughes, so vitally important do I regard his work. But I am not sure that Attorney General Jackson has not made a good point in opposing the appointment of all the Utilities Commissioners. Another Governor, like Flower, Hill, Odell or Higgins might use the very appointing power in favor of the corporations. Support Hughes with all the fire and force you possess. But be independent even about him. I would not go through thick and thin for anybody — not even myself. Your friends must be criticised when they are mistaken, like other people. It is difficult to see the truth when you are prejudiced, but try always to see the truth about friend or foe. How would a compromise do, giving the people the election of say, a majority of the board and the Governor the appointment of a minority? However, I am not sure of this: Don't be influenced by my hasty,

impulsive remarks. I only wanted to urge the general principle of making the page, really, absolutely judicial.

He now began considering some means of coördinating Democratic sentiment, looking ahead to 1908, when Roosevelt's successor would have to be chosen. To Mr. Cobb he wrote on July 1st:

> Suppose the Democrats were absolutely divided — making the walk-over of a yellow dog certain — even Cortelyou or Odell could be elected then. The death or division of the Democratic party would be the worst possible thing for the country just now. There is reason to preserve the Democratic party, however wretched and disgraceful it may be officered, platformed, and principled. It would take nine years at least before a new party could even have a chance.

This he supplemented the next day, requesting that a feature should be made on the editorial page of letters and clippings showing the difference between true democracy and false democracy. His mind was fixed upon some means for heading off the strenuous Roosevelt, whose supporters were already explaining when a third term was not a third term, through the accident of the partial first one. It chanced that following the earthquake and fire in San Francisco, Japanese boys, well grown, possessing rudimentary knowledge of English, were admitted to schools with small children, owing to shortage of seats. This was seized upon by agitators to provoke some extreme anti-Japanese legislation. This Mr. Roosevelt promptly denounced, announcing his fervid purpose to use all the power of the Government to maintain inviolate the terms of its treaty with Japan, the integrity of which was impaired by the new law.

## Rooseveltism

Following this pronouncement Eugene F. Schmitz, the rascally mayor of San Francisco, called at the White House and Mr. Roosevelt's utterances took on a tamer tone. He did not coerce California, but instead, allowed it to be intimated that he was about to send a fleet of battleships to the Pacific coast.

Mr. Pulitzer saw in the move a spectacular step toward a third term and at once began a lively campaign against jingoism. July 6, 1907, he contributed an editorial bearing the first warning. On that same day the Washington dispatches proclaimed Roosevelt's plans for sending the ships, to be commanded by Rear-Admiral Robley D. Evans, known better as "Fighting Bob." It seemed unbelievable that after his utterances in favor of sustaining the treaty with Japan he could seriously order the move. There was the usual equivocation as to the ultimate destination of the armada. On July 8th, Mr. Pulitzer ordered Cobb to make the whole editorial page —

a daring, fearless, outspoken expression against jingo agitation — Compare moderation of utterances by Japanese statesmen before and since with utterances on our side. Movement supposed to be courageous, daring; consider whether unnecessary demonstration extraordinary superiority over weaker nation is courageous or cowardly or bullying. Do people expect our course will help trade and allay the irritation behind boycott idea rather than aggravate it? Can governments control popular passion and prejudices with this subject kept up as a continuing feature? Read points of editorial telegraphed Friday; reassert and develop. Go over story of three wars made by public opinion: Franco-German War, Boer War, Spanish War. In England concert halls song: "We don't want

## Joseph Pulitzer

to fight, but by Jingo if we do, we've got the ships, we've got the men, we've got the money, too." Quote this verbatim. This carried the country away and forced savage, unjust and ruinous conflict. Tell the story how Bismarck and Moltke were in despair because their plans to make war on France seemed to fail, when Bismarck, by changing an innocent telegram, made it read like an insult to the Emperor and the nation, and by this forgery so excited Germany that war became inevitable. Show that Spain had granted to Cuba all that we demanded, but passion in Spain and here forced the hands of government. Emphasize these illustrations of danger of Jingo agitation. Consider also, is Roosevelt looking ahead as candidate for President? Will take three months to get ships ready; three months for voyage. That brings us into 1908 and time of making delegates to Presidential convention in that year with war passion in the air and Roosevelt on the bridge. Will he raise the cry "Shall we swap horses while swimming a stream?" Taft has announced we must be in Cuba for eighteen months. Will not Pacific or Japanese agitation, Cuban agitation, domestic agitation, arising from Roosevelt's motives, even if honest, create a situation which will make it impossible to nominate any one else? Force of circumstances greater than the will of any man or any thousand men. Roosevelt creating circumstances and situation to compel his nomination for third term. Try yourself to arouse public opinion among most intellectual thinking classes, Bishops, heads of universities, not the unthinking crowds nor small politicians.

So strongly did he feel on the subject that he went on to say, anent the crime of jingoism:

> I would rather be the only man in the United States to protest against shallow shouters than to echo

against conviction the general feeling of the unthinking. Give further details of jingoism causing Cuban War after Spain had virtually granted everything adding thereto horrible idiotic Boer War caused by English jingoism with its awful cost to British taxpayers to-day and generations still unborn.

The idea that battleships were to be sent to California did not win much popular support. It was therefore denied in Washington that the President had any such purpose in mind, but was thinking of sending a fleet to the Philippines. The New York *Herald* rather commended the colonel's attitude, though deprecating jingoism. The *Sun* took the same stand as the *World*. Mr. Pulitzer echoed the news in this message to Mr. Cobb on July 10th:

> To send the whole fleet to the Philippines is less idiotic than to the Pacific coast. That much may be said of Mr. Bennett's elastic genius for retreat, but still it is absurd. Roosevelt should quote from Falstaff: "Call you this backing your friends?" However, in using Mr. Bennett's double-leaded editorial try to present the thing in a sardonic, sarcastic, caustic smile-raising way. The title must remain "Crime of Jingoism." Repeat point made yesterday that the best way to encourage hoodlums in San Francisco to more violence and bloodshed against defenseless Japanese is to send all the battleships we have to that harbor, with 60,000 men to go ashore and fraternize. Also, make the point that there is not a serious statesman in Japan who has not acted with more good common sense and real moderation than any of the jingo papers, jingo speakers, naval officers and our stupid buncombe Secretary of the Navy. Incidentally, is it not a very good argument against having a third class Californian

politician who knows nothing of either navy or statesmanship at the head of the department?

It might be added parenthetically that it took six secretaries of the navy to see Mr. Roosevelt through his seven years of power.

The *Herald* rather neatly took the wind out of the *World's* sails by commenting on its heat in this fashion:

> While indorsing unreservedly the *World's* condemnation of "journalistic jingoism" the *Herald* feels constrained to differ from its able, enterprising and brilliantly successful contemporary respecting the "inexpediency" of the President's determination to send the battleship fleet to the Pacific.

This caused Mr. Pulitzer to supplement the preceding telegram with this message:

> Just saw Monday leader in *Herald* about Pacific fleet. Please reprint in double-leaded or black type, first six lines of sentences praising *World*. Treat Bennett rather more civilly.

He also mildly reproved Cobb for not making earlier use of the compliment:

> May I beg, my dear boy, that you should at least look at editorial pages of all papers morning and evening and forgive me for wondering how the very remarkable compliment to the *World's* power in the *Herald* on Monday was not reprinted in the *World* for Tuesday. Did you see and deliberately ignore the admirable talk-making line?

Mr. Roosevelt was very much in action at the moment. He had decimated the Twenty-fifth (colored) Infantry for a riot at Brownsville because the men refused to reveal the actual participants. For this he was denounced in a vigorous speech by Senator James Benson Foraker, of Ohio, who won full commendation from Mr. Pulitzer:

> Treat Foraker's speech fairly and impartially. This particularly necessary to a man whom we have so sharply, even unjustly criticised; his boldness, exceptional independence in standing out against Roosevelt with all his power and patronage deserves recognition, even if you do not agree with him. Have not the slightest doubt Roosevelt went off half-cocked in Brownsville matter, even if not influenced by Southern white vote.

To the Japanese situation and the flurry over the colored troopers Mr. Roosevelt also added a move to prohibit a merger of the great tobacco corporations centred in New York, by a Federal receivership that would deal with their interlocking relationships. To this, on July 12th, Mr. Pulitzer took violent exception, his dispatch being a general onslaught on Rooseveltism, and reading:

> Receiverships colossal. State socialism — worse than anything Bryan proposes here, Bebel in Germany, or Jaures in France — worse than anything Debs propounded. That is the utter annihilation of the judiciary as a completely non-partisan, non-political, non-administration basis of justice and turning it into a political machine. Say plainly that we do not think for a moment that Roosevelt can really wish this colossal upheaval of whole fabric of government, society, business. It is an incredible violation of all constitutional safeguards, checks and balances between the executive, judiciary and legislative; an amazing chaos with ruin for all business. More than this we do not believe for a moment that he sincerely wishes war

on Japan, or even to send the entire Atlantic squadron to San Francisco. We believe it is all politics looking for next year's nomination for the Presidency and perhaps a bigger navy, still larger appropriations for extravagant battleships, looking for effect on popular imaginations, the applause of the unthinking perhaps, and the creation of a situation that will make his nomination absolutely inevitable. We hope there is another side to Theodore Roosevelt, the side of conscientious honor, of ambition for true, lasting, final fame, and a place in history. It is to that conscience the *World* still appeals and will continue to appeal so long as there is any chance. Let him correct and reprove Secretary Metcalf and not issue the order to send a squadron half around the world to arouse mob violence in San Francisco. Point out how fairly and friendly the *World* has supported Mr. Roosevelt in his most important policies, how it abstained from criticising his many faults, exposing itself to the misapprehensions of many of its Democratic readers; how it refrained from supporting the usual shallow shouting against a third term, not believing in it or the principle. In this matter, however, it is true to its conscience and conviction of public duty — Is it mere accident or coincidence, that instead of criminally prosecuting Harriman reports say: First — at the last sitting of the Cabinet it was concluded not to proceed criminally because it would have a bad effect on Wall Street and financial conditions. Second — The Chicago report that Gov. Deneen said he would not prosecute Harriman for the infamous Chicago and Alton swindle, because President Roosevelt had told him it was inadvisable. Third — From the Interstate Commerce Commission showing that it was divided on the question of criminal prosecution largely if not entirely because it was understood Mr. Roosevelt did not wish such criminal prosecution. Lastly — From Oyster Bay, where the very able and successful attorney for the Government against Harriman, Frank B. Kellogg, was reported to have had a conference with Roosevelt with a view to overcoming his objection to criminal proceedings. Is it possible that all these coincidences have nothing whatever to do with the jingo policy against Japan to divert the public mind from interest and domestic reform?

Out of all this welter nothing came. The tobacco magnates went their way unharmed. Mr. Harriman was not prosecuted, but was tenderly treated as one "practical man" would treat another. Justice was never done the Twenty-fifth Infantry. The great white fleet serenely circled the globe and instead of bringing on a war when it reached Yokohama, ten thousand Japanese school children dressed in red, white and blue formed a vast star-spangled banner on the slope of the bluff and the Japanese statesmen, though long ignorant of the motives behind the seeming hostility of American opinion, kept peace and their heads.

It became clear during the great World War that the friction was the result of German inspiration. The German Consul-General at San Francisco acted as agent in the matter, ably supplemented by Speck Von Sternberg, then German Ambassador at Washington, who was the President's intimate at tennis and in cross country riding. The Memoirs of Von Lengerke Meyer, who was Roosevelt's Postmaster-General, furnish proof, and if more is needed Admiral Von Tirpitz, the German naval head, in his book published after the defeat of German arms, says he was consulted by Mr. Roosevelt as to the program. Wilhelm in 1907 was on the edge of war and wantonly provocative.

He desired to keep America and Japan busy. Hence the German activity here in the matter.

Thus for more than a decade we were kept at seeming odds with the island empire.

On July 19th, Mr. Pulitzer instructed the *World's* editors to close the incident after "first pointing out that Roosevelt has played with fire" and further had "made a grave mistake, deserving loss of public confidence" after "indulging in bluff" that "must have aroused lowest and vilest passions and prejudices among ignorant people."

Mr. Pulitzer endeavored from time to time to get further action against Harriman, but in vain. The magnate had declined to answer questions put to him by the Interstate Commerce Commission. Mr. Pulitzer was indignant at what he called an "impudent refusal" and offered "a pair of boots" for "the cleanest, simplest, briefest condensed statement of what the Chicago and Alton swindle really was," but hampered effort by the condition that it must be so plain that "a child of ten" could understand it. He wanted this put into a Harriman editorial and gave the editors a couple of days to make it "perfectly perfect," as he put it.

Out of the Roosevelt naval venture Mr. Pulitzer evolved an idea which he thought might lure Bryan away from Populism by taking up the question of Imperialism, head off the imperious president and restore some semblance of democracy in American politics. As a preliminary Mr. Bryan was invited to express through the *World* his view as to "what is a Democrat." The Commoner cannily declined on the ground that he had all he could do "at present," so the effort to bring him nearer to Thomas Jefferson failed. A request that he explain the celebrated Initiative and Referendum brought no better response. He refused to be snared.

Late in July, 1907, it became clear that Mr. Roosevelt did not care to risk a fight for a third continuous term but had selected William H. Taft, his Secretary of War, to take the next turn at the wheel. The *World* editorially denounced this procedure, but Mr. Pulitzer dissented. July 28th, he wired from Bar Harbor:

> Attack on Roosevelt for preferring Taft and trying to secure his nomination preposterous. Jefferson selected Madison, Madison selected Monroe, Jackson nominated Van Buren as his successor. What more natural than Roosevelt should feel anxiety and ambition to have his work finished in his own spirit as far as possible? Taft unquestionably very able, upright, independent, honorable, with most valuable experience in Cuba, Philippines and Panama as Judge, Governor, Secretary of War; splendid lawyer, administrator; moderate, modest, judicial in spirit. He would make a more statesmanlike, just, law-respecting chief magistrate than Roosevelt, though lacking latter's amazing initiative in everything. However many and manifest Roosevelt's faults, instead of charging him with Mexicanizing the Government as Republican papers do, his selection and active support of Taft is entitled to credit because it is practical evidence of his sincerity not to desire and seek the nomination himself.

He also strongly opposed the taking of Hughes from the governorship of New York to become a presidential candidate, as more needed where he was. "The State of New York," he observed, "regardless of party, would suffer a great loss by his elevation."

The decision of Judge Kenesaw Mountain Landis,

## Joseph Pulitzer

of the United States Supreme Court, fining the Standard Oil Company $29,000,000 for its violation of the anti-trust law evoked great enthusiasm on the part of Mr. Pulitzer. He telegraphed from Bar Harbor on August 5th:

> Treat Landis's great decision as a great event. Will do more to restore respect for law and courts among discontented and all the people, and to prevent violations by corporations and trusts than all Bryan's speeches a thousand times over. All discontent touches loss of faith in courts. Point out that the size of fine which astounds public is small compared with earnings for period covered by indictment, say two hundred million. Uphold soundness of reasoning by which Judge shows that fine on the smallest basis would have been a license and an encouragement to continue particularly good. Incidentally show that indictment was under the despised Elkins law, and that it is a terrible slap at Bryan in his offensive attitude toward United States under cry of Government by Injunction. He wanted United States Judges elected by the people. Could such a decision ever come from a judge nominated by some primary governed by boss of the Tammany type?

Further reading of the Landis' decision stimulated Mr. Pulitzer to observe on August 7th:

> The greatest breeder of discontent and socialism among the masses of the poor is not only lack of confidence in the justice of the law, but popular belief that the law is one thing for the rich and quite another thing for the poor, and after all justice and faith in justice is the quintessence of all government. Just in proportion as the administration of Justice is reliable or unreliable in that proportion is government good or

bad. This is the greatest value of Judge Landis' sentence, besides giving terrible warning to other corporations to stop ignoring laws. They will certainly stop now. Incidentally this decision of Landis' is really a terrible blow at past Administrations, which did not enforce the law, which allowed every corporation in the land to assume that the Elkins' law was a dead letter and to treat it with contempt. It is the greatest decision since the Sherman anti-trust law was passed. That is twenty years ago. Neither Cleveland, McKinley, nor any of their Departments of Justice having carried out the anti-trust laws, but led corporations and trusts to believe that the Sherman anti-trust law was a dead letter: treating it as Mr. Cleveland's Attorney-General Olney openly did against a hundred protests of the *World*, which always insisted it was constitutional. Can you really blame the corporations that have no souls or men of the Harriman-Rockefeller type, if they felt that the Government was in sympathy with them, winked at their ignoring the laws. In fact, clearly indicating that these laws were not to be enforced or as both Cleveland, Olney, McKinley, yes, yes, yes. Even McKinley by more than silent acquiescence, inertia, indicated that these laws were not to be enforced. If Roosevelt had never done anything else and if he had committed a hundred times more mistakes and if he were one hundred times more impulsive, changeable, unpresidential in dignity, more inaccurate, loud and vociferating in manner and speech, appealing always rather to the unthinking and their prejudices and passions than to reason (Damned long sentence; please forgive) if he had nothing else except to start the great machinery of the Government and the most powerful force and majesty of the law in the direction of prosecuting these great offenders despite their huge campaign tributes, he would be entitled to

## Joseph Pulitzer

the greatest credit for the greatest service to the nation. This one initiative impulse and persevering instinct must be held as offsetting a hundred wrong impulses of a minor character. Please forgive prolixity. Have no time to be brief.

Beautiful as this seemed the Standard Oil Company never paid its $29,000,000 fine. "Dissolved," each of its parts became richer and stronger than the original whole, and lived to more than double the cost of their products to the public.

## Chapter XIV

## THE LAST CAMPAIGN

The Map of Bryanism. — William Howard Taft against William Jennings Bryan. — A Move to Preserve Democracy. — Some Crisp Correspondence.

MR. PULITZER usually entered upon a presidential campaign with extraordinary zest. That of 1908 was destined to be his last. Looking toward the next year, in November, 1907, he wrote Cobb:

> Try to have a sense of humor. You used to give some glimpse of it until lately. I am no doubt responsible. Semi-seriously and semi-satirically take up both Roosevelt's and Bryan's program of new legislation concerning capital, credit, banks, currency, railroads, trusts and of course, general business. Assume that both were President of the United States (on the Swiss plan) and enumerate the various laws they propose and see what would be left of the country.

The "Roosevelt panic" had run its course and perhaps more than any other factor led to his determination to avoid renomination. He had made George B. Cortelyou his secretary of the treasury, to Mr. Pulitzer's great wrath. "Is Mr. Cortelyou the man for the present emergency?" he asked. "And was it not a great mistake to place him where he is simply because he was a clever wire-puller and knew the political ropes, when the country needs a student, a scholar, a statesman? All the more so because Mr. Roosevelt had no head for business, finance or law, himself. I want you (Cobb) to go through every secretary of the treasury of note from the beginning of the Government, from Hamilton up to Shaw, who, whatever you may think of some of his eccentricities, is a man of decided intellect; was a banker, student scholar, thinker before he became Governor of Iowa. Would the country not breathe easier if it had a John Sherman, for instance, or Chase, at the treasury?"

He recurred again to the anti-third-term theory in outlining an editorial: "Nothing in it but sentiment," he observed, which was going rather far for him. Ordinarily he treated sentiment and temperament with respect. "Fifteen million people," he went on, "must vote upon any man's ambition or election and they can be trusted as a rule far more than any supposed tradition, when the methods of the Presidential electoral system still practiced are a most radical departure and reversion from the intent of the Fathers as to how a President should not be elected by the masses. He certainly should not be nominated in the way we do nominate by machine methods and in howling conventions, but on the contrary be elected by Electors specially chosen for their superior coolness and eminence, and actually forbidden to meet together, but be compelled, as intended, to vote in forty-six separate departments segregated at the time, with the understanding that they could not know what the other States would do. Of course, circumstances might make it exceedingly bad for a President to use his patronage in forcing a nomination. On the other hand supposing we were in the midst of a war, would you swap horses then and rob the people of the privi-

## The Last Campaign

lege of voting as they see fit? I repeat, I want the truth and the whole truth, but I do not like to run with the crowd and clamor."

In early December Mr. Roosevelt made officially clear his determination not to stand for renomination. Mr. Pulitzer commented, on the 13th: "One very significant, remarkable sign is the great satisfaction, relief and utmost enthusiasm with which Roosevelt's declaration is accepted by his own party. Hardly anything he ever said received such unanimous approval as this announced retirement from the field. Make this brief, if you please, simply a statement of fact, but a little ironical, yet serious, as a queer sign of popularity. If really so wonderfully popular, there should be grief and lamentation — at least regret. But not even his most ardent officeholders and organs failed to approve of the act."

"The main point," he urged, "is to knock Taft's critics on the head because he is to be Roosevelt's successor. . . . The need of the country after this amazing initiative and shake-up given by Roosevelt is a comparatively calm and judicial chief-magistrate; that is, a man who will let the Government govern and not govern the Government entirely in his own personality. There is no doubt we now have a personal Government."

He appended a little personal note to Cobb:

> Private gossip, private belief, private conviction even, can never be permitted to be the basis of editorial action influencing cold, responsible and presumably provable and conscious type and print. I am more and more alarmed by the way you talk about public persons in private and perhaps allow this talk to influence your action, which should be judicious, calm,

as well as conscientious — instead of personal and passionate.

With Mr. Roosevelt out of the way and the certainty that Mr. Taft would receive the Republican nomination, Mr. Pulitzer had continued to adjure Bryan. He got up a striking Map of Bryanism, which was often reprinted, showing what it had done toward diminuting Democracy. This was published a number of times

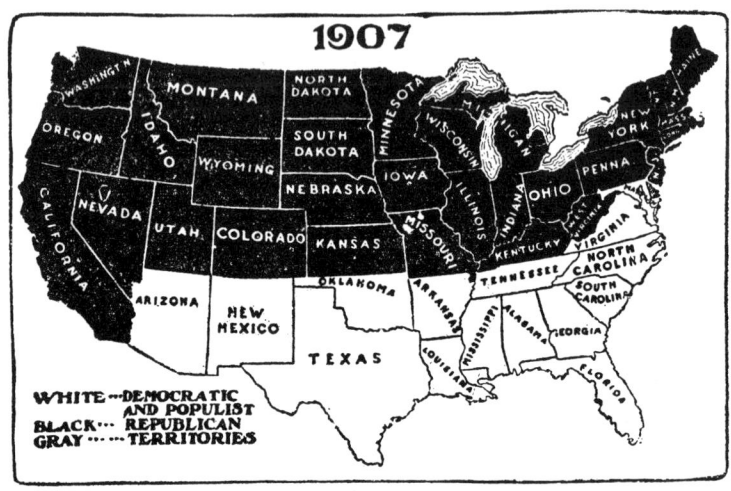

The Map of Bryanism

in the paper, enhanced by plenty of peppery text. In February, 1908, the most forceful of the comments, together with a series of progressive cartographs, illustrating the political rake's progress and final extirpation of Democracy in the North and West were printed in a pamphlet. Its title read: "The Map of Bryanism. Twelve Years of Demagogy and Defeat. An Appeal to Independent Democratic Thought, by The New York *World*."

Mr. Pulitzer also attempted to stir up interest in the

## The Last Campaign

candidacy of other men, striving, if possible, to raise up someone who could defeat Bryan. As a slight tribute to the latter's fancy for 16 to 1, he suggested the names of sixteen Democrats of prominence who ought to be considered at a really Democratic convention, where unpledged delegates might work their will, saying in a letter to Cobb in late November, 1907:

> If there is a new thought — a new tone that you could bear in mind that I should like, it is the sense of the ridiculous — a sense of the utterly preposterous — a sense of the comic (if I may use synonyms) as applied to the Democratic politicians and thinkers if they nominate Bryan. I can hardly blame Bryan, considering what you know personally, if the fools are going to give him the nomination, but why should the politicians be such asses? I think you had better turn it straight against the thinkers. I have a headache and must not talk. As a P. S. consider a subhead of "16 to 1" without a solitary word of elucidation. Say sixteen names that might be considered. There is Fuller, White and Peckham, whose father was an illustrious judge. There is Gray, there is Woodrow Wilson, there is Douglas, of Mass., who was elected Governor at the very hour when Roosevelt swept the State. A shoemaker. There is Tom Johnson, if a Socialist is wanted. There is John Johnson, a blacksmith, who could not carry his State in a Presidential year, son of a washerwoman — a good man. We need washwomen and blacksmiths. There is Folk, Governor of Missouri and a Southern man who prosecuted the thieves. There is Governor Higgins, of Rhode Island. There is Gaynor, if the party wants a radical Socialist of the most pronounced type. There is Francis. I don't believe in him, but he is an ex-

Governor. There is Governor Hoke Smith. All Democrats. Now pick out four from the South. I give you that inestimable privilege. There is Culberson, Daniel of Virginia and Bacon of Georgia.

Now these are sixteen Democrats who might be considered. Another point is that the Alabama people have already started the right thing. Every Democrat should have a free and unlimited deliberative convention, unpledged, uninstructed and unrestricted to select the best man at the time they meet. Now don't put this list of sixteen as if we were committed to support any of them. There are many that I would not support.

The sixteen were duly presented to the Democracy but without avail. Continuing his effort to head off Bryan he wrote Cobb further:

I wish you would, at your earliest pleasure and leisure, jam and crowd and condense into not exceeding 500 words all the points, arguments, reasons that can be suggested in favor of Woodrow Wilson as a Southern candidate. He was born in the South. His wife was born in the South. What better candidate could they present who would have a better chance to carry New York and New Jersey than anybody I can think of now — now. He is a statesman and a scholar and a man of very extraordinary ability, etc. Still I say suggest him in connection with Gray and Johnson and not as our permanent candidate to whom we are permanently committed. Make it as strong as you can. Read the *Times* article on Sunday and on Wednesday, November 24th and 27th. I believe you suggested Wilson's name to me yourself, although I had thought of him. Headline should be "A SOUTHERN CANDIDATE." The headline alone would attract attention. There is no hurry but I should not be surprised if some other paper did not steal your thunder.

## The Last Campaign

That Wilson was chosen four years later adds interest to this instruction, and shows again the remarkable prescience of the writer in picking men.

He was greatly interested in the success of Charles E. Hughes as Governor, and on the same date wrote this comment upon a speech made by Bourke Cockran, the "silver tongued" orator of Tammany, which had assailed certain men of wealth and the State's executive:

See *Times* report of Bourke Cockran's speech. Clever but exaggerated, misleading, demagogic. Ever since the world existed; ever since there is any history of Greece or what not, appeals against the rich and the wealthy are made to the poor and not to wealth. Ever since the earth began and as long as the earth will last, inequalities and injustices from general human imperfection have existed and will exist. Under no system of government, under no spirit of liberty, Republican or Democratic or what not, can perfect perfection be expected.

The first duty of any honest man in politics is to appeal to truth and reason and intelligence, not to ignorance, prejudice and passion. Bourke Cockran knows perfectly well that while the power of these men he names is great, it is only financial, and not political, but on the contrary there is not one of them who could be elected to Congress or the Legislature from the very fact that they are financial financiers, which makes them odious. He knows perfectly well that Hughes is the greatest Governor this State has had in his time, etc. I have no time to be brief and wish you would treat this man sarcastically, as I really have admired him at one time and was instrumental in sending him to Congress the first time. (This is private.) I paid his expenses. But hold him up to ridicule. He ought to be ashamed to talk such stuff. The Republic is safe despite its wealth; safer than it was for years, although quite in need of progress and reform by men like Hughes, rather than Cockran.

Mr. Pulitzer also favored Cobb with a lovely paragraph of praise, referring to an editorial which pleased him: "By Acclamation! Your article clever — very clever. Thanks! Thanks particularly for brevity. Brevity is really beauty. I presume if you had written it day before it would have been three times as long. Take a drink!"

The Parker experiment of 1904, permitted by Mr. Bryan, had turned out so badly as to warrant the Commoner in taking the field again. This he determined to do. No candidate arose to defeat him in the convention held at Denver, Col., July 7, 1908, and he carried off the nomination with John W. Kern, of Indiana, as his running mate. The Republicans had already named William Howard Taft, secretary of war in the Roosevelt Cabinet, and Congressman James S. Sherman, of New York, as their candidates. While Taft had no such potentiality as Roosevelt Mr. Pulitzer was certain that Bryan could not beat him. Yet he felt it time to make a stand on behalf of opposition. Bryan's nomination, he observed in a note to the editors, was "a remarkable tribute to a remarkable man." So succinct are the lines of thought that follow in his chart for editorial guidance in the campaign, that they are given herewith:

> Bryan is as dead as a door nail. A vote for Bryan is not a practical living vote, but a protest; a protest against the tendencies of the party in power; a check and rebuke to stop these tendencies; an exceedingly important rebuke and check if the vote is large enough

## The Last Campaign

to keep the party in power after election on the anxious seat. Without such emphatic popular protest the successful party, instead of being checked and restrained, would be encouraged to carry these tendencies further than ever. A strong protest would also mean a strong opposition party, while the absence of such a protest would mean an impotent opposition without vitality or effect. Another point apropos of this is the sympathetic side. If the party is dying why kick it? Is it not better to stand by a dying party than a dangerous, demoralized party? Again, the paper has supported but one anti-Democratic candidate in twenty-five years, and that one most reluctantly. Bryan is not one-hundredth, not one-thuusandth part as dangerous or bad to-day as he was in 1896.

Again looking ahead, always looking ahead beyond November, Bryan absolutely beaten, new lines drawn, new men coming to the front, new ideas — the *World* will have ten times more influence, if it does not now antagonize the Democratic party too bitterly, or in fact, at all bitterly. Whereas if the *World* does antagonize the party it will always rankle through the minds of millions, and the charge will always be made that the *World* was after all indirectly supporting Taft, without any special necessity, all the more unjustifiable because the election was a foregone conclusion. You cannot possibly escape the charge of having supported Taft and the entire Taft administration and party, if during the campaign, you attack Bryan. Call it independence, if you please, and be it independence in truth, the inevitable effect of attacking one man is to support the other. Democrats would consider it support of Taft even if you never said a single word in his favor and, in effect, it would be. You need make no argument in favor of Taft; the effect is the same if you attack Bryan. Take the case of '96, when every-

## Joseph Pulitzer

body either gave credit to the *World*, or abused it for supporting McKinley. I believe the editorial page did not directly support him. I tried to be very careful on this point. It simply fought the principle of free silver and sixteen to one; argued against it and showed its fallacy, but the effect was the same. However, my memory is bad. The page still exists, somebody should look it up.

Again there are two sides, two sides, I repeat, as well as two parties. Now whilst the *World* will never belong to the Democratic party, and never did, as a matter of fact I am astonished in looking over the anniversary number to see that thirty years ago the *Post-Dispatch* salutatory carefully guards that point and deliberately declares its independence of party and speaks of truly Democratic ideas, etc. But there is no question that while we don't belong to the party as such we have always stood on the Democratic side and our honest sympathy and affiliations, not allegiance, are with that side. On that side we will remain for the next twenty-five years. Even if the party were to die, on that side we will still remain.

Apropos of Seymour's idea that the *Post-Dispatch* should be rather more Democratic than the *World*, as Missouri is a hotbed of Bryanism, my view is that it should be more independent than the *World*, more fearless; that its editor should have distinctly more discretion to act on his own individual judgment in departing from the *World*, but not of course, on any fundamental or cardinal policy — that is, where supreme principle is involved the two papers cannot make themselves ridiculous by differing. But apart from these necessarily limited cardinal principles, the freedom of the *Post-Dispatch* should be greater to disagree and to discuss, for one reason, because I do not read the paper and do not consider myself one-tenth as much

## The Last Campaign

interested in or responsible for it as for the editorial page of the *World*. I don't believe the people in St. Louis, or in Missouri will think I have very much to do with that page.

Facts! facts! facts! are events, news happenings, actualities changing from day to day. Nothing can be dictated in the way of a fixed policy when the events of the very next day may create astonishment, sensation, contradiction — a totally different situation. Whatever I say is subject to this great law of the unexpected, the great unknown, and freedom to tell the truth. Of course, it is not necessary to comment on every single event editorially. It is necessary to print the truth in the news columns: to print all events and happenings of public interest impartially, but it is almost impossible and certainly unnecessary, to comment on everything and anything. That is left to the discretion of the editorial writer, and that discretion is in itself an enormous power — that is, the power of silence about events and phases of the campaign he may not deem it necessary to comment upon.

I shall not have seen a single line of any paper for a month when I arrive; know nothing of news, editorials, drift; that is, have no facts, and yet I shall put down on paper frankly, the political course the paper ought to pursue, not only now, but until November 3d — that is, for over four months. It is rather a difficult problem, rather dangerous, as I don't know the facts. However, I will try. Opposition to the party in power, and a strong opposition, is just as essential as government itself, and the proper balance between the different coördinate branches of the Government. An Administration without opposition, a party government without adequate check, has an unlimited license to indulge in every form of extravagance without being subject to parliamentary criticism and review. A vote for Bryan would unquestionably be a protest against Republicanism, Rooseveltism, centralization, amazing extravagance and expenditures, Philippinism, militarism, etc. A vote for Bryan would unquestionably be a vote to check the party in power and its extravagant tendencies.

The country has gone crazy under Roosevelt's leadership, in extravagance for the war idea. All my life I have been opposed to that so-called militarism. I may be crazy in thinking the country crazy, but the fact remains that we have increased our war expenditures over one hundred millions a year; I believe quadrupled them, without in my judgment, any ground whatsoever. We need no greater navies or armies now than thirty years ago, because we have doubled our population and quadrupled our resources, thereby quadrupling our strength for national defense. Any man who pretends to see danger from Europe or Japan is either an ignoramus or a Jingo demagogue. The logic of jingoism, Rooseveltism, seems to be that the greater we are in population and strength the more afraid we must be of foreign attack and war. That is, the stronger we grow the weaker we are. On this question alone, if I could only separate it from other entangled issues and the prejudices of the past, I would unquestionably support Bryan with enthusiasm.

Another point which struck me in favor of Bryan was either in a speech or editorial sent in which he really expresses himself against the principles of Socialism as the levelling of individuals down, when of course, Democracy ought to level them up. I don't say these were his words, but what he said was frank, clear and unequivocal. If he will maintain that position he certainly cannot be denied credit for improvement and reform. In '96 he certainly appealed

## The Last Campaign

to the Socialistic idea. "Down With the Rich" of course, is not only Bryan's chief strength, but it has been either a cry or a feeling ever since there has been any political record. Principles, principles, support principles; ideas, — ideas rather than men or men in proportion as they represent right principles. Take the good and leave the bad.

A republic governed by one party is unthinkable. There must be at least two great parties and such are the elements of the Democratic faith that the continued existence of that organization or one representing its original principles is a necessity to the republic. The Democratic party is the only party that is as old as the republic. It is the only American political party which from the beginning has been truly national in its scope. When the Democratic party was rent asunder at Charleston in 1860, the Union itself was shattered.

There are wrongs to redress. There is a persistent demand for wide reforms in many directions. Under Republican rule, corporate abuses have become manifest. But the first practical issue that must be faced and met squarely is that of dislocated business and industry. Our people must have bread and they must have employment. They do not crave agitation. They need prosperity, peace, bread.

So far as the *World* is concerned the service which it may render the Democratic party in this campaign will depend upon Mr. Bryan himself. It will be great or small, according as Mr. Bryan himself shall show or shall fail to show, a true and worthy appreciation of his own great responsibility and opportunity. The *World* is opposed to Rooseveltism. Its views are unaltered and unalterable. It is opposed to every phase of populism and socialism, it believes in true Democratic ideas as the hope of the republic and of mankind. Where that flag flies the *World* will ever be found at the very front of the battle.

With the result of the campaign predetermined in his mind Mr. Pulitzer did not greatly concern himself about its conduct. He found comfort in the fact that both party platforms reprehended the use of money in elections, and considered the manifestation "a wonderful reform" expressing the belief that the contest would be freer from corruption than any held in a half-century before, "wrought without statute or law and against the reluctance and refusal of both Congress and President" to do anything to stop it. He added: "While Roosevelt sent a few perfunctory words in his message, Congressmen knew privately that he was not sincere and that the words were only wrung from him for sake of public opinion." He thought on July 18th, that "in all modesty the *World* is entitled to some credit, for it had stoutly and steadfastly fought at least twenty years for the reform."

George R. Sheldon, treasurer of the Republican National Committee, had announced his purpose to give full publicity to all campaign contributions. While Mr. Pulitzer thought the *World* should have a little recognition for its share, the chief credit belonged, he said, to the Democratic platform, which "Compelled Taft to compel Sheldon" to make the declaration. This reacted on the Democratic Committee, with what he was sure would be a further reflex from the Republican body.

"Every honest Republican, every honest Democrat, every honest American," he wrote, "regardless of party and regardless of the result of election has already reason to congratulate himself upon this great moral victory over campaign boodle, which will do more to restore confidence in justice and fair elections among discontented socialists than one hundred speeches by Roosevelt, or any law passed under his whip."

Despite the several "declarations" he observed that "the *World* and the press generally will have to continue very sharp vigilance and watchfulness as the eyes and ears and tongue of the nation to prevent campaign committee bosses from evading the spirit of the law."

On the same day he suggested to Cobb, anent William R. Hearst's activities: "Treat Hearst and his statement either with silent respect, or, if you can possibly control your feelings, with respect without silence. Anyhow encourage him. He is doing a marvellous piece of work; actually organizing a new party all over the Union on nothing."

To keep things active without the paper being too much involved he urged the extension of an invitation "to people regardless of previous condition of servitude, party, sex or color to express their opinion about presidential preferences, whether Republican, Democratic, Independence League (Hearst's), Socialist, Populist, Prohibitionist or Labor Party. But except single taxers, because they are too verbose."

The aversion to single-taxers was not so much criticism as it seems. He was rather afraid of their talent as propagandists. In cautioning Cobb on another date, not to print too many Bryan letters without proper antidotes, he observed: "Never in my life did I receive so many letters, persistent, plausible and almost convincing as from the single-taxers more than twenty years ago. One might have thought everybody was a single-taxer, judging by the letters received at the *World* Office."

## Joseph Pulitzer

A day or two later he adopted the *World's* earlier view and ordered a cartoon showing Taft's subserviency to Roosevelt: "He is Roosevelt's man and Roosevelt his boss — something never before known by a presidential nominee." This he followed on July 23d, with a terse command:

> Make leader to-morrow brief, but double-leaded, on Taft's melancholy submission to Roosevelt. His open Declaration of Dependence will cost him thousands of votes among the most intelligent thinking citizens, disgusted with Roosevelt, who regard the question of his moral courage and absolute independence to act upon his own conscience rather than Roosevelt's wishes as the critical test. Quote from the official Republican *Tribune* Taft's open excuse; certainly an indiscretion, making his pilgrimage to the shrine all the more humiliating. This in a kindly spirit — sorrow, not anger — and not retracting anything about Taft's admirable character and qualities.

He devoted the following day to defining a demagogue in reply to a question propounded by himself, basing it upon a very warm eulogy passed by President Roosevelt on the enlisted men of the Navy, whom he set a peg higher than their officers. Mr. Pulitzer sardonically suggested scrapping Annapolis, as such details as the scientific knowledge there acquired "would never mitigate the noble rage of the President's enthusiasm for the enlisted men who at any time can outvote the officers one hundred to one." As to Mr. Taft, he observed rather sharply: "He has already demonstrated he is not a politician. He ought to shut up. Campaign may prove a surprise. Remember, Rum, Romanism and Rebellion!"

Turning his attention to the Democrats he urged:

## The Last Campaign

Make it red hot for Ryan (Thomas F.) — red hot, I repeat. More so even than Hearst has done. The Democratic party must purge itself, . . . though it is only just to say that there is not another like him in the whole Democracy from Texas to Maine, from New York to California.

Since writing his first chart for the campaign he had become unsettled by Taft's impolitic utterances. "Never say Bryan will be defeated," he wrote on July 28th, "any more than that he will be elected. In other words, be careful to abstain on these points throughout the entire campaign." He wanted an editorial setting forth the difference between the Democratic masses and the "organization," saying in support of the suggestion:

> The masses, perfectly honest and sincere, vote for an idea, a sentiment, a tradition, a habit, a spirit — something in their bones. They do not really vote for the bosses, but bosses unquestionably own the party so far as nominations are concerned, through controlling the convention or machine, just like a monarchy. The strength of the king is not in the person who happens to be king, but in the idea of kingship, inherited by the people for centuries and centuries, sucked in with mother's milk. To illustrate: Conners and Murphy have absolute control of the machine and the nomination of candidates in New York State. Six or seven hundred thousand voters, despising them, will nevertheless vote the Democratic ticket, because they have been brought up that way. Yet probably five hundred thousand of these same Democrats would vote to send Conners and Murphy into exile, if not a more confined place, if that question could be submitted to an entirely separate poll.

## Joseph Pulitzer

"Where," he asked in continuing his comments, "are the real last remains of Democratic intellect in New York: Shepard, ex-Judge Herrick, Osborne, Gaynor, ex-Governor Hill? Have they come out for Bryan? No doubt they will later, but so far they are silent and show no enthusiasm."

Coming from a newspaper man it reads oddly to have Mr. Pulitzer say, apropos of "Taft's indiscretions," that "he talks too much to reporters." The English movement in favor of old age pensions was up for the moment. Mr. Pulitzer thought the spirit of socialism was growing under cover. He wished an editorial written to draw "a cardinal, fundamental line between Socialism and true Democracy — two entirely different things."

Bored by a campaign in which he was elected to spend most of his time on the fence, Mr. Pulitzer arranged to go abroad to remain until Fall. Mr. Bryan had just made a rather sound speech and it was editorially commended, with the result that the Commoner sent Mr. Pulitzer this note:

DEAR MR. PULITZER: In view of your Sunday editorial on Imperialism I send you my Indianapolis speech. I agree with you that it is the best I ever delivered. Appreciating the more friendly tone of the paper,

I am, Yours truly,
WILLIAM J. BRYAN.

This Mr. Pulitzer forwarded to Mr. Cobb with the following comment:

August 10th

DEAR COBB: I send you a copy of a letter from our friend Bryan, quite unexpected of course. It is a sign of forgiveness which might amuse you.

## The Last Campaign

I am sailing in a few hours; will not see you but hope you will send me a little summary of your powerful thoughts on the political situation, care of Tuohy, London, so that I can get it upon my arrival about September 1st.

You can send him also at cable press rates, just about August 31, giving the very latest points since writing your letter. My opinion is unchanged. It is exactly what it was a year ago, and when I spoke to you. The paper can't possibly be independent and honest if it supports Taft, considering its lifelong principles and Taft's identification with Rooseveltism.

Yet I would avoid and shun like poison any partisan tone, anything done from a partisan or party standpoint. However, if you don't understand me now nothing I could write would make much difference.

I think that Bryan's speech is really very, very careful and anxious to please those who hitherto opposed him. It is a far better statement than I thought he could make and in tone and temper infinitely superior to any of Mr. Roosevelt's state papers.

Still no final committal till I say so specifically. Say — wait for another thirty days.

Final editorial instructions came in the following form:

1. Don't commit the paper for Bryan unless you hear from me.
2. Don't hamper the paper's freedom for the next forty days to do anything after that.
3. Don't cease vigorous opposition to Rooseveltism in all phases; ditto Republicanism whenever wrong.
4. Don't say an unnecessary unkind word about Taft. Treat him fairly. Not a word of untruth under any circumstances against him or Bryan; or anybody else, not even Hearst.

5. Don't hesitate to criticise Taft politically as Roosevelt's proxy or dummy until he disproves it.

6. Don't defend Bryan on any charge made against him which you know to be founded.

7. Don't hesitate at all proper times to repeat that his platform is a great improvement over '96 and 1900 especially on (a) jingoism and Roosevelt's war fake spirit (b) Philippinism (c) Publicity Plank (d) Tariff Reform (e) Retrenchment in National Expenses. Bryan coming to it rather than the *World* going to them.

8. Don't comment on everything Bryan says. Don't be afraid to ignore his speeches and talk. Don't forget that you are not compelled to write and express an opinion on anything; that *silence, silence, silence* is peculiarly wise at times.

9. Don't, whatever happens, ever say that Bryan will or should be elected or that he is even fit and qualified.

10. Don't forget that I will give you several hats after the election if you can observe these rules, especially the last, No. 9.

All this subject to change, perhaps tomorrow, if the news and facts should change.

September found Mr. Pulitzer in Wiesbaden, where he took some lively interest in the Governor of New York State. He was pleased at the renomination of Hughes and wanted Roosevelt to receive credit for permitting it. The President had been hostile to the governor and was expected to prevent his being accorded a second term. Lieut.-Gov. Robert L. Chanler was named by the Democrats. The *World* supported Hughes as one who should stay in office and finish his work, adding a few demands, such as the completion of insurance reform and the reduction

## The Last Campaign

of taxation, to his tasks. The rest of the Democratic State ticket was favored.

From Wiesbaden, on October 2d, Mr. Pulitzer ordered some smashing broadsides against Republican corruption, together with one on William Nelson Cromwell, asking, "What is he doing in the Republican campaign? Who is he? What great devotion to public purity and public morality has he contributed? Examine his record, especially his Panama record and his relations with corporations and trusts. Is it true he gave $50,000 to the campaign fund? If so, why?"

The editors were also told not to neglect George R. Sheldon, the Republican campaign treasurer, and to make "one of the broadsides on Mr. Harriman's letter to Webster" repeating "Roosevelt's entire defense," adding: "If not a single scrap of evidence existed in the whole world except Roosevelt's own letter [to Sherman] of defense, he ought to be rebuked and, if a candidate, defeated."

To these adjurations he appended a confidential P. S.:

> One thought — but a single thought — to remember, repeat and use whenever applicable till election and perhaps after it: — The Republican party only means to defeat the Democratic, but the Hearst, Debs, Watson parties mean to destroy it and to build upon its ruins a new party and therefore the extraordinary spectacle of Bryan's former supporters and warm adherents, becoming the most vindictive, malicious enemies he now has — far more unscrupulous personally than any Republican leader.
>
> From the same motive, the same audacity and amazing vindictiveness of Hearst, Debs and Watson extend to include the Democratic party, because not

defeat, but destruction is desired. Question: Would it be best for the country if the Democratic party were destroyed by a new party, led by Hearst and Debs? Would it not be *infinitely worse* however many faults the Democratic party may have? Is there any question that if the Democratic party were really destroyed as they hope, the new party would be a Socialistic party largely composed of labor union and workingmen — the discontented, the poor, unemployed, etc.? In other words, the question is between plutocracy and Democracy *now*, but if the Democratic party were destroyed it would be distinctly and unquestionably between the Republican party or a Socialist or Social-Democrat party.

Now the one word has run away with me but I hope you may see the point why, without any partisan feeling whatever, and with full knowledge of the defects of the present Democratic party any independent thinker must prefer it infinitely to the danger of a new party under Hearst, Debs or Watson. Develop this really by picking out some characteristic planks.

This is only a stray thought written but unrevised and unread in the automobile.

Mr. Pulitzer rejoined the yacht in October and was at Southampton on the 9th. He planned a return voyage by way of Bermuda, aiming to reach the island about election day. Before sailing he sent Mr. Cobb a few observations:

See whether you cannot give the extract from the Constitution in the fewest possible words, double-leaded, under the headline "Take Care!" with exclamation and quotation marks "What the Governor of New York has sworn to do, etc., etc., from the Constitution of the State of New York." This is very roughly dictated indeed, and my headache is worse than usual.

## The Last Campaign

But you ought to see the point and keep that standing double-leaded and "Take Care" in black type until the election. That is, unless Hughes makes some satisfactory assurances on this point. I specially beg to warn against the appearance of hounding an official. I am in favor of giving him time and his own method of action, but there is a difference between persistence and over-zealous hounding.

Apropos of Hughes, I have read his Brooklyn speech in full in the *Eagle* of the 27th — a whole page — and I find it dreadfully dull, pedantic, bureaucratic, unpromising.

I hope he will say better things and do better things than promised in this speech. Anyway, don't say an unnecessary or unkind thing against Chanler. It looks to me like '88 *possibly* when the Democrats elected a Governor and the Republicans a President.

DON'T FAIL TO SHOW WHEREVER POSSIBLE, *that is, honestly possible, and only when honestly possible, the utmost Democratic sympathy both before and after election should I not be home, which of course, does not mean puffery for anybody, including Bryan.*

In great haste. Roughly dictated and unrevised just before sailing from Southampton.

A final word was forwarded on October 19th. It read:

About the last thought before going to sea:

If I should not turn up after election don't deprive me of the pleasure of drawing my own morals and conclusions as to the lesson of the election, causes and effect. There will be enough on the face of things for you to talk about until you hear from me — it is not necessary for you to commit yourself to anything except the obvious on the very first day unless the result should be overwhelming.

But one thing I insist upon most particularly whatever the result:

## Joseph Pulitzer

> *The paper after election must be Democratic in tone, temper, sympathy and principles,* indeed it required no brains to see that the logic of events and circumstances make the *World the* great Democratic paper of the country and the only one in New York City. This, of course, does *not* impair in the least its freedom and independence.
>
> I need hardly say that as long as I live I shall be far more anxious to make it independent and *non-partisan* than Democratic, if these qualities must be separated, but they can be united and you must remember it as a permanent principle.

In mid-ocean this plan of making Bermuda was changed and the *Liberty* steered for New York, arriving in time to lay down a program for the day-after election leader. He wrote Cobb:

> I do not suggest a single thing for tomorrow except reserve and caution until the fullest returns are finally in, but without interfering in the least with your own freedom and fully recognizing my ignorance, not having had a word for a month, the thought seems obvious if Taft is elected that this was due to the weakness of Mr. Bryan rather than his own strength. His election or Bryan's defeat becomes more significant when it is remembered how vulnerable Taft was. Here are just a few of the undercurrents against him. You can of course add ten more if you feel like it.
> 1. Hard times generally.
> 2. Working men out of employment.
> 3. Business men complaining, dissatisfied.
> 4. Increased cost of living, simultaneously.
> 5. Unparalleled disaffection of labor organizations.
> 6. Double disaffection of both Prohibitionist and anti-Prohibitionists in Western states like Ohio and Indiana.

## The Last Campaign

7. Gross blunders in the Chicago platform.

8. Popular objection to Roosevelt's bossism — the use of 300,000 office holders. The enormous power and prestige of the Presidency managing campaign and reducing Taft to secondary shadow or proxy.

9. Insidious use of religious prejudice and bigotry against Taft's liberal and advanced belief.

If the Democrats elect any Governors where Bryan runs behind the ticket generally, it is clear *that the party is stronger than Bryan* and Bryan weaker than the party, and that his nomination was a grave blunder as the *World* predicted a hundred times. Say this.

Lastly and Firstly, of course, you will say whatever can be said in appreciation of Taft emphatically pledging the support of the *World* wherever he shows that judicial, magisterial, independent spirit in administering law and government according to reason and justice, which the country peculiarly needs in the successor of Rough-riderism. If the figures of the returns are suitably applicable to warrant it, reprint the best parts from that long editorial which appeared the day after Taft's nomination under the same headline "President Taft; the Reign of Terror Over." If you do this do not fail to print the headline across two columns as before, giving the date in black type, June 2d, or whatever it was and you might have a little editorial referring to it. A very little one under the head of "Was the World not Prophetic?" All this is respectfully submitted with the repeated injunction that it is only submitted subject to your free will in accordance with the figures.

This is dictated exactly at seventeen minutes before three P.M., before a single poll has been counted, but after a very thick headache, and the Lord only knows what surprises the figures may contain.

**Please** remember the latest figures that will come in

## Joseph Pulitzer

about midnight when you are writing at ten or even earlier. I wish you would put in the editorial summing up results the exact time you write, to guard against the inevitable contradiction in the news columns, which, of course, go to press several hours later. You might explain that I have never yet known the contradiction to fail between figures and the editorial page. Now please remember you are absolutely free, at least tonight, to express your own opinion with daring and boldness grafted upon caution and the latest figures.

I honestly declare that no prior conclusion, prejudice or idea is to be pronounced or woven out of the figures. I honestly declare that I want you to say nothing that your conscience, carefully examined, does not approve as really true. Impartiality, entire dismissal of prejudice on personal dislike alone can discover the real truth. I know this is difficult, especially to a gentleman of your ardent temperament, but I pay you the compliment of supposing that you at least try. I pay you another compliment, which possibly I may regret, as I have not read your damned page for over a month, and that is that you have labored under very trying circumstances, which I appreciate.

P. S. I hope you are well, fresh, bright and self-satisfied and happy at the end of this wretched trial and triumph, but I am going to bed at ten o'clock sharp to the second, and I wish you would tell me at just fifteen minutes before, what you have carefully thought out as your opinion at that time based upon the latest figures with a little summary of the results and with special consideration of Hughes. Is he elected? I hope so *indeed*, and of course you will treat him kindly.

Just as the great Napoleon went to bed and slept on the night of the *coup d'etat* that was to make him Emperor, so Mr. Pulitzer duly retired at 10 P.M. on

## The Last Campaign

election night, refusing to await the returns. "What is the use," he said, "of sitting up for a foregone conclusion?"

The contest having concluded to his satisfaction Mr. Pulitzer now turned with zeal to the resuscitation of the Democracy. As he wrote Cobb:

> Is it not time to say plainly, boldly, if you please, boldly I repeat, and yet very simply after you have done Bryan justice, etc., if not at the same time, what the motive of the *World* was in supporting the Democratic party and Democratic principles and the Democratic future and the grave, great need of an opposition. That it never supported Bryan personally; that it never advised its readers to vote for him personally, or that he was qualified; that it never even said that he was fit to be President or should be elected; although it did say and does say now that the platform was infinitely better than the first two platforms and that it does give him credit for improving it and that certainly we did wish the Democratic party to be saved from destruction.
>
> But above all, dear boy, don't fail in treating Bryan in the most generous spirit consistent with facts and truth when quoting the *Times* and the Hearst business. That is not fair. It is overdone and underdone, — that is, below the belt and we say this who certainly have said a great deal, and don't forget to make the editorial encouraging to the Democrats. Every Democrat ought to feel as I honestly feel, not pretendingly, that the chances of a Democratic President for four years or eight years hence are infinitely stronger than they have been for the last sixteen years. Make every Democrat happy tomorrow and yet make every independent man feel that is so, that that is true.
>
> Let them feel the *World* is pretty fair about Bryan in

coming to his defense when he is down, and, generally speaking, I do not want to be on the winning side. When he was up it was different, but now that he is down and besides being the truth, I believe it will be good policy. Anything is good policy that shows that the paper is really perfectly fair, independent and personally unprejudiced, however hot its political vigor.

His parting verdict on Mr. Bryan was:

He . . . will remain an important factor and force on the Democratic side although he never can, never will be elected President. He is an agitator, not an administrator. So far he has only been of great service to the Republican party, having done more to keep it in power than a thousand Republican speakers. Let us hope he will realize the final verdict of the people, drop the Presidential bee and devote himself to real Democratic ideas.

Without retracting anything the *World* has said about Roosevelt "as Chief Executive and Chief Magistrate, for which he is utterly unfitted, . . . however inconsistent it may seem" Mr. Pulitzer desired to secure that gentleman's future. "We think," he went on, "he ought to go to the Senate and it is the best thing the* Republican party can do. Of course, we do this outside the Republican breastworks. If we could elect an Independent Democrat we would, but as no Independent Democrat can be elected we think it the best thing for the State that Roosevelt should become Senator. An ex-President of the United States ought to have a liberal pension of $25,000 a year, and a seat in the Senate. . . . It is a perfectly logical conclusion that they should step

## The Last Campaign

into the Senate to keep them out of business, away from the necessity, or indeed any excuse, for money making and prevent such a disgrace as Grant's going into a Wall Street firm that turned out to be a terrible fraud and also the shame of Mr. Cleveland becoming an employee of Ryan and accepting one of Ryan's sinecures. An ex-President should be above temptation."

It had just been announced that after retiring Mr. Roosevelt would become "contributing editor" to Dr. Lyman Abbott's *Outlook*. Of this Mr. Pulitzer took further occasion to comment:

> As an instance, apropos of Presidential pensions, with all respect for journalism, whose noble ideas we appreciate far more than Mr. Roosevelt, the plan would prevent the purchase for cash of an ex-President of the United States by any newspaper for advertising purposes — a mere réclame — before the returns are really completed; practically the very day after election, before the President is out of office; indeed, four months before he actually leaves the White House is already used as an advertisement all over the world, just like a new and attractive liver pill or skin soap.

With this parting adjuration he put to sea, having in mind a considerable cruise to the West Indies. The *Liberty* reached Havana. Then some restless instinct caused her owner to turn North, putting into Charleston, S. C., in course, where he was to encounter a new and exciting episode in the continuing contest with Rooseveltism.

CHAPTER XV

THE PANAMA PROSECUTION

President Roosevelt's efforts to send the Owner of the "World" to Prison for Libelling the United Sates. — Liberty of the Press Vindicated in the Courts.

VARIOUS Panamanians who had not felt themselves sufficiently recompensed for their share in enriching William Nelson Cromwell and his associates when Roosevelt "took the canal" came to New York from time to time to press their claims for more. On October 2, 1908, William McM. Speer, a member of the editorial staff, heard through an acquaintance that one of the groups was in town hunting largesse and suggested to George Carteret, then city editor, that a story might be had if the men were located. He assigned Allen Sangree, an extra able man, who had done good work, to hunt up the buccaneers. Sangree failed to find them, but in stumbling around roused William Nelson Cromwell's office staff. He got no story at all, so reported and the assignment was crossed off the schedule. That night about ten o'clock Jonas M. Whitley, a former *World* man, who had the run of the office but was then working under Roger L. Farnham, also an ex-*World* man, in charge of Mr. Cromwell's publicity forces, came in and demanded of Caleb M. Van Hamm, the managing editor, what the *World* meant by getting after "his boss" without giving him a look-in. Van Hamm did not even know the tip had

## The Panama Prosecution

been given and exhausted, but being very astute, he observed: "Dear, dear, Jonas, sorry to hear that. Tell us all about it." Jonas being thus bidden told his tale — all new to Van Hamm, — who invited him to come back in an hour and he would show him the copy, which he intimated the reporter would probably have ready by that time. Whitley went out and Van Hamm, calling in his own stenographer, dictated to him the precise tale Whitley had told him. On the latter's return he was given the copy to revise. Briefly, the tale as written by Van Hamm from Whitley's lips was that William J. Curtis, of Mr. Cromwell's office, had called upon District Attorney William Travers Jerome to take action against some persons who were trying to blackmail the lawyer through certain allegations concerning the sale of the canal. These were that Cromwell, backed by a syndicate, had paid but $3,500,000 for the securities involved and had received $40,000,000 from the United States. In the course of the story Charles P. Taft and Douglas Robinson, brother-in-law of President Roosevelt, were mentioned as alleged participators. Whitley read the copy over, changed "C. P. Taft" to "H. W. Taft," then changed it back again to "C. P." He next asked permission to read the copy over the telephone to Mr. Cromwell, who had just returned from the opera — it was then near midnight. This was given. Cromwell made no corrections, but added a statement on his own behalf, all of which was duly printed the next morning with pictures of Cromwell, C. P. Taft and Robinson. It was treated entirely as if an effort was being made by Vice to assail Virtue.

This was all very pretty, but it was not the story Speer had heard. He was indignant at the clumsy way his tip had been handled and so expressed himself to Van Hamm. The latter fooled with the case for a few days and dropped it without further revelations. That a deep and unrevealed secret lay behind the rumors and gossip Speer was certain. It rankled in his admirable newspaper mind that there could be such a falldown in a properly conducted office. This slumbering indignation was soon to bear extraordinary fruit.

The *World* made no editorial mention of the matter and it seemed to have dropped wholly by the wayside. In forcing Taft's nomination, the President had used his powers to shut out the Vice-President, Charles W. Fairbanks, from the succession. Fairbanks came from Indianapolis, where the *News* enjoyed a masterful monopoly. To the outside it was the property of Delavan Smith, but in fact — and this was not known until after his death, June 4, 1918 — it belonged to Mr. Fairbanks. During the campaign it had refused to support Mr. Taft.

On November 2, 1908, the day before election, the *News* printed an editorial attacking the Panama Canal transaction and expressing a strong desire to know who got the $40,000,000 paid by the United States for the wreckage of the De Lesseps enterprise. Mr. Taft carried the State of Indiana the next day by 10,731 votes over Bryan, but the Republicans lost the Governor, the United States Senator and all but three of the fifteen Congressmen. The editorial read:

> The campaign is over, and the people will have to vote tomorrow without any official knowledge concerning the Panama Canal deal. It has been charged that the United States bought from American citizens for $40,000,000 property that cost those citizens only

THE AUTHOR, MR. PULITZER AND JOSEPH PULITZER JR. ON THE LIBERTY.

## The Panama Prosecution

$12,000,000. Mr. Taft was Secretary of War at the time the negotiation was closed. There is no doubt that the Government paid $40,000,000 for the property. But who got the money? We are not to know. The administration and Mr. Taft do not think it right that the people should know. The President's brother-in-law is involved in the scandal, but he has nothing to say. The candidate's brother has been charged with being a member of the syndicate. He has, it is true, denied it. But he refuses to appeal to the evidence, all of which is in the possession of the administration, and wholly inaccessible to outsiders. For weeks this scandal has been before the people. The records are in Washington, and they are public records. But the people are not to see them — till after election, if then.

On the heels of this William Dudley Foulke, an adopted Indianan who had made the reform of the Civil Service his specialty, and had an infinite capacity for excavating excitement, wrote the President a rather pertinent letter, enclosing the editorial, in the course of which he remarked: "If the statements of the *News* are true our people ought to know it; if not true, they ought to have some just means of estimating what credit should be given in other matters to a journal which disseminates falsehoods."

Foulke and Mr. Roosevelt had been fellow members on the Civil Service Commision and very friendly. It is not stretching the imagination much to believe that this letter was invited. The slur at the end of the paragraph makes this fairly clear. It was written on November 9th, but its recipient did not reply until December 1st. His letter was given publicity by Foulke, through the Associated Press, a convenient instrument much used by the colonel, on December 7th.

## Joseph Pulitzer

I was ordered to join the *Liberty* at Charleston with Joseph Pulitzer, Jr. We made the trip by train and went on board the boat on the morning of December 7th, taking a copy of that day's Charleston *News and Courier*, in the first column of the first page of which was the Roosevelt letter to Foulke.

Naturally the outburst excited comment. Besides spanking Delavan Smith, the President paid his respects to William M. Laffan, of the New York *Sun*, and to enterprising newspapers generally. He did not mention the *World*. Accompanying the letter was an interview with Mr. Smith, in which he said: "The President's comments on the Panama editorial are based on statements made by a prominent New York newspaper, not the New York *Sun*, which the Indianapolis *News* printed at the same time with many other papers, giving full credit to the source from which they obtained it."

When this was read to Mr. Pulitzer he asked: "What New York paper does Smith mean?"

"The *World*," I answered.

"I knew d——d well it must be," he replied. "If there is any trouble you fellows are sure to be in it."

With his singular intuition he was at once filled with forebodings, but not until we reached New York did he know how gorgeously the paper had risen to the occasion. Mr. Speer, with his wrath uncooled and thoroughly conversant with the real facts in the case, had written a leader, published December 8th, assailing with merciless particularity the accuracy of Mr. Roosevelt's assertions to Foulke. As it embraced comprehensively all the differences developed it is herewith reproduced in full:

## The Panama Prosecution

### THE PANAMA SCANDAL — LET CONGRESS INVESTIGATE

In view of President Roosevelt's deliberate misstatements of fact in his scandalous personal attack upon Mr. Delavan Smith, editor of the Indianapolis *News*, the *World* calls upon the Congress of the United States to make immediately a full and impartial investigation of the entire Panama Canal scandal.

The investigation of 1906 by the Senate Committee on Interoceanic Canals was blocked by the refusal of William Nelson Cromwell to answer the most pertinent questions of Senator Morgan, of Alabama. Since that time nothing has been done because after Senator Morgan's death there was no successor to carry out his great work of revealing the truth about Panama corruption.

The Indianapolis *News* said in the editorial for which Mr. Roosevelt assails Mr. Smith:

"It has been charged that the United States bought from American citizens for $40,000,000 property that cost those citizens only $12,000,000. There is no doubt that the Government paid $40,000,000 for the poperty. But who got the money?"

President Roosevelt's reply to this most proper question is for the most part a string of abusive and defamatory epithets. But he also makes the following statements as truthful information to the American people:

"The United States did not pay a cent of the $40,000,000 to any American citizen.

"The Government paid this $40,000,000 direct to the French Government, getting the receipt of the liquidator appointed by the French Government to receive the same.

## Joseph Pulitzer

"The United States Government has not the slightest knowledge as to the particular individuals among whom the French Government distributed the same.

"So far as I know there was no syndicate: There certainly was no syndicate in the United States that to my knowledge had any dealings with the Government directly, or indirectly."

To the best of the *World's* knowledge and belief, each and all of these statements made by Mr. Roosevelt and quoted above are untrue, and Mr. Roosevelt must have known they were untrue when he made them.

### WHO GOT THE MONEY?

As to the detailed distribution of the Panama loot only one man knows it all. And that man is William Nelson Cromwell. The two men who were most in Mr. Cromwell's confidence are Theodore Roosevelt, President of the United States, and Elihu Root, former Secretary of War and now Secretary of State. It was they who aided Mr. Cromwell in consummating the Panama revolution, arranged the terms of the purchase of the Panama Canal, made the agreement to pay $40,000,000 for the canal properties, and an additional $10,000,000 for a manufactured Panama republic, every penny of both of which sums was paid by check on the United States Treasury — not to the French Government, as Mr. Roosevelt says, but to J. P. Morgan & Co.

The natural query of the Indianapolis *News* as to "who got the money" was based on the *World's* historical summary of Mr. Cromwell's connection with the Panama Canal. The inquiry was originally the *World's*, and the *World* accepts Mr. Roosevelt's challenge. If Congress could have all the documents in the case, as Mr. Roosevelt says, let Congress make

## The Panama Prosecution

a complete investigation of the Panama Canal affair, and in particular of William Nelson Cromwell's relations with the French company, with Panama and with the Government of the United States. Let Congress officially answer this question: "Who got the money?"

The old French company organized by Ferdinand de Lesseps in 1879 failed in 1889, years before Mr. Cromwell's relations with President Roosevelt began. As Mr. Cromwell testified before the Senate committee on February 26, 1906, "we never had any connection with the so-called De Lesseps company. Neither did the United States Government conduct negotiations with the old French Panama Canal Company."

### CROMWELL'S CONTRACT

What Mr. Cromwell did represent was the new Panama Canal Company, the American Panama Canal Company and the $5,000,000 syndicate which he formed to finance the new companies. After Mr. Cromwell had testified "I do not recall any contract" Senator Morgan produced a contract reading (Panama Canal Hearing, Vol. II, page 1146):

"Mr. William Nelson Cromwell is exclusively empowered, under the formal agreement with the Board of Directors of the Compagnie Nouvelle du Canal de Panama (New Panama Canal Company of France), to effect with an American syndicate the Americanization of the Panama Canal Company on the following basis."

The basis on which Mr. Cromwell was "exclusively empowered" in this contract was that an American Panama Canal Company with a capitalization of $60,000,000 preferred and $45,000,000 common should be organized to take over the Panama Canal concessions and of other property belonging to the new

French Panama Canal Company, which had bought the same from the old De Lesseps company. This company was incorporated in New Jersey with dummy directors. There was also incorporated in New Jersey, with dummy directors, the Interoceanic Canal Company.

Senator Morgan unearthed a copy of the $5,000,000 syndicate agreement, which provided that the subscribers should contract with William Nelson Cromwell to pay $5,000,000 in cash and to take their several allotments in the enterprise.

Five million dollars was more than ample to buy the majority of the old Panama stock. As the *World* said on October 25:

"Mr. Cromwell applied to the Canal situation methods of American high finance by which a syndicate takes over the property of a bankrupt concern, then creates a holding company and a recapitalization, keeping the majority control in a syndicate trusteeship."

Following that, to quote from Mr. Cromwell's testimony, "in May, 1904, I, representing the new Panama Canal, and Judges Day and Russell, representing Attorney General Knox, consummated" the transfer and sale to the United States.

Mr. Roosevelt says, "The Government paid this $40,000,000 direct to the French Government."

Mr. Cromwell testified that "the United States paid the money to J. P. Morgan & Co."

Mr. Roosevelt says, "The French Government distributed the same."

Mr. Cromwell testified as to how he distributed it.

Mr. Roosevelt talks of "getting the receipt of the liquidator appointed by the French Government to receive the same."

Mr. Cromwell testified: "Of the $40,000,000 paid

## The Panama Prosecution

by the United States Government $25,000,000 was paid to the liquidator of the old Panama Canal Company under and in pursuance of an agreement entered into between the liquidator and the new company. . . . Of the balance of $15,000,000 paid to the new Panama Canal Company, $12,000,000 have already been distributed among its stockholders, and the remainder is now being held, awaiting final distribution and payment."

What follows is further eloquent testimony taken by the Senate committee:

Senator Taliaferro — There is $3,000,000?

Mr. Cromwell — Three million. Yes, sir.

Senator Taliaferro — Who holds this money?

Mr. Cromwell — The new Panama Canal Company in its treasury.

And yet Mr. Roosevelt says that "the United States Government has not the slightest knowledge" as to the distribution of the $40,000,000 and that "this was the business of the French Government."

As to Mr. Roosevelt's statement that "there was no syndicate," he could have read the "syndicate subscription agreement" on page 1150, Vol. II, of the testimony before the Committee on Interoceanic Canals — if he had cared for the truth.

### HOW THE REVOLUTION WAS MANUFACTURED

That the United States Government was not dealing with "the French Government," or "the liquidator appointed by the French Government," or with Colombia, or with Panama, or with any one else except William Nelson Cromwell and his associates, is made still more plain by the description of Senor J. Gabriel Duque as to the Panama revolution and as to the manner in which Mr. Cromwell got $10,000,000 from the United States Treasury. Senor Duque said:

"Mr. Cromwell made the revolution. He offered to make me President of the new republic and to see me through if I would raise a small force of men and declare a secession from Colombia. He made promises that we should have the help of his Government. . . . It was accomplished by a liberal use of money. We bought this general and that one, paying $3,000 to $4,000 per general. The Colombian officers were all paid off and the Colombian general, who was sent to stop the revolution, was also paid off."

Then Mr. Cromwell, having been elected by the Panama Republic as general counsel, and he and J. Pierpont Morgan having been appointed a "fiscal commission," negotiated with President Roosevelt, by which the United States paid $10,000,000 more to "the fiscal commission" for Mr. Cromwell's Panama Republic. Of this money three quarters is still in the control of "the fiscal commission."

Who did the United States pay $10,000,000 for a bankrupt property whose control could undoubtedly have been bought in the open market for less than $4,000,000?

Who were the new Panama Canal Company?

Who bought up the obligations of the old Panama Canal Company for a few cents on the dollar?

Among whom was divided the $15,000,000 paid to the new Panama Canal Company?

Whether Douglas Robinson, who is Mr. Roosevelt's brother-in-law, or any of Mr. Taft's brothers associated himself with Mr. Cromwell in Panama exploitation or shared in these profits is incidental to the main issue of letting in the light.

Whether they did or not, whether all the profits went into William Nelson Cromwell's hands, or whatever became of them, the fact that Theodore Roosevelt

## The Panama Prosecution

as President of the United States issues a public statement about such an important matter full of flagrant untruths, reeking with misstatements, challenging line by line the testimony of his associate Cromwell and the official record, makes it imperative that full publicity come at once through the authority and by the action of Congress.

By the time the *Liberty* made port the mischief had been well done. The editorial made an enormous sensation in and out of the White House. Soon rumors came that the President intended to take drastic action against Mr. Pulitzer and the *World*, holding the former responsible, which of course, he was not in a personal sense. On December 15th, Mr. Roosevelt favored Congress with a special message on the subject, harking back, not to the Speer editorial, which had burned through, but to the Van Hamm-Whitley story of October 3d. In the course of a long statement that denied what the *World* had printed as allegations made by men who were attempting to blackmail Mr. Cromwell, upon the authority of the latter's own representative, who gave the names of Taft, Robinson, *et al.*, he observed:

These stories were first brought to my attention as published in a paper in Indianapolis, called the *News*, edited by Mr. Delavan Smith. The stories were scurrilous and libelous in character and false in every essential particular. Mr. Smith shelters himself behind the excuse that he merely accepted the statements which had appeared in a paper published in New York, the *World*, owned by Mr. Joseph Pulitzer. It is idle to say that the known character of Mr. Pulitzer and his newspaper are such that the statements in that paper will be believed by nobody; unfortunately, thousands of persons are ill informed in this respect and believe the statements they see in print, even though they appear in a newspaper published by Mr. Pulitzer. . . .

Now, these stories as a matter of fact need no investigation whatever. No shadow of proof has been, or can be, produced in behalf of any of them. They consist simply of a string of infamous libels. In form they are in part libels upon individuals, upon Mr. Taft and Mr. Robinson, for instance. But they are in fact wholly, and in form partly, a libel upon the United States Government. I do not believe we should concern ourselves with these particular individuals who wrote the lying and libelous editorials, articles from correspondents, or articles in news columns. The real offender is Mr. Joseph Pulitzer, editor and proprietor of the *World*. While the criminal offense of which Mr. Pulitzer has been guilty is in form a libel upon individuals, the great injury done is in blackening the good name of the American people. It should not be left to a private citizen to sue Mr. Pulitzer for libel. He should be prosecuted for that by the governmental authorities. In point of encouragement of iniquity, in point of infamy or wrongdoing, there is nothing to choose between a public servant who betrays his trust, a public servant who is guilty of blackmail, or theft, or financial dishonesty of any kind, and a man guilty as Mr. Joseph Pulitzer has been guilty in this instance. It is therefore a high national duty to bring to justice this vilifier of American people, this man who wantonly and wickedly and without one shadow of justification seeks to blacken the character of reputable private citizens and to convict the Government of his own country in the eyes of the civilized world of wrongdoing, of the basest and foulest kind, when he has not one shadow of justification of any sort or description for

## The Panama Prosecution

the charge he has made. The Attorney General has under consideration the form in which the proceedings against Mr. Pulitzer shall be brought.

In the course of his statement to Congress Mr. Roosevelt remarked further:

> The accounts and records of this liquidation (of Canal stock), which was concluded in June last are on deposit with the Credit Lyonnais of Paris, as a proper custodian of the same, appointed upon such liquidation. Recently, a request was made by a private invididual to inspect the records of these payments but answer was made by the custodians that they saw no proper reason for granting such request by a stranger, and, inasmuch as there is not the slightest ground for suspicion of any bad faith in the transaction, it hardly seems worth while to make the request: But if the Congress desires, I have no doubt that on the request of our Ambassador in Paris the Lists of individuals will be shown him.

It chanced that Mr. L. R. E. Paulin, of the *World's* editorial staff, was enjoying a vacation in England. He had family connections in France and knew Gallic ways and speech. Seizing the above declaration Mr. Pulitzer instructed Mr. Paulin to proceed at once to Paris and "dig twelve hours a day" into the Panama matter, with "who really got the money" in his mind and to trace possible benefits to an American syndicate, giving attention generally to the American aspects of the case. He crossed the channel at once and began to dig but failed to get below the surface. Most of the De Lesseps directors were dead; the survivors out of reach. Maurice Bo, head of the Credit Lyonnais, refused to become interested. Mr.

Roosevelt's assertion was repeated to him but he remained unmoved. "Roosevelt no longer counts," he observed. "A new President has come in."

The new President had "come" but was not yet in. Under the French law all the papers in liquidations or receiverships are sealed when the transactions are closed and deposited with the Chamberlain of Seals for the Department of the Seine. Here they remain twenty years, available for reference should any evidence of fraud arise. But they cannot be used to create this evidence. At the end of the double decade they are destroyed. No access was ever given to these documents and they have never been made public in any form. The French have perfected the art of preserving mysteries. Who has ever identified "The Man in the Iron Mask?"

That Mr. Roosevelt was set in his purpose events soon proved. The prosecution was foremost in his mind. In 1924, sundry letters of Captain Archie Butt, his military aide, were made public, and in one of these, written in January, 1909, he details a White House luncheon at which George R. Sheldon, then Treasurer of the Republican National Committee, was present, together with the President's brother-in-law, Douglas Robinson, and his wife, Mr. Roosevelt's sister. Robinson was one of the "libelled" in the Panama tale. "They discussed the Panama libel suit," records Butt, "and both the President and Mr. Robinson think they will put Pulitzer in prison for criminal libel."

Yet no one around the *World* office believed that Roosevelt was considering serious action. Mr. Pulitzer was much disturbed, however, knowing the psychology of the rough rider in the White House.

## The Panama Prosecution

He took up the question of a lawyer for the defense and sounded former Gov. Frank S. Black as to taking a retainer. Black hated Roosevelt from the ground up, though he had made the nominating speech in the Chicago Republican Committee of 1904. He considered the matter with interest, but as nothing developed for the moment, no arrangement was made.

Tired of waiting for developments in a New York winter, Mr. Pulitzer sailed again for the West Indies, this time getting as far away as Havana. In the meantime Charles J. Bonaparte, Attorney General of the United States, had really been busy. About one o'clock on the afternoon of February 17, 1909, John M. Bowers, who was counsel for the *World* and for Mr. Pulitzer personally, as well as his trustee, came to the office much excited laden with inside knowledge that Mr. Pulitzer and the *World* were to be indicted for criminal libel. He was insistent and went on to say that as counsel for Douglas Robinson, Mr. Roosevelt's brother-in-law, in many large real estate matters, he would not be able to defend Mr. Pulitzer or the paper, but had determined, in his capacity as trustee, to retain De Lancey Nicoll. There was no question as to Mr. Nicoll's great talents, but his legal relationships were not the kind that made him agreeable either to the paper or Mr. Pulitzer. However, Mr. Bowers stood upon his "duty" as trustee and left to carry out his purpose. About 2:30 the early edition of the *Evening Mail* came in with the reports that indictments had been ordered.

Soon the full news became known. Joseph Pulitzer, Caleb M. Van Hamm, managing editor, Robert Hunt Lyman, night editor, and the Press Publishing Company, publisher of the *World*, were accused of criminally libelling Theodore Roosevelt, J. Pierpont Morgan, Charles P. Taft, Douglas Robinson, Elihu Root and William Nelson Cromwell. Delavan Smith and Charles R. Williams of the Indianapolis *News* were indicted on seven counts at the same time. The *World* group were favored on five. All the indictments were filed with Judge Gould of District Criminal Court No. 1, who ordered a summons issued for the Press Publishing Company and bench warrants for the others.

The indictments were drawn up under a clause in the local laws enacted by Congress that had been lifted from the statutes of Charles II, passed in 1662, providing a tight muzzle for the press. Of course this could not be made to apply outside of a Federal district. President Grant used it once in an effort to hale Charles A. Dana, of the *Sun*, to Washington and failed superbly in the attempt. This fact did not greatly soothe Mr. Pulitzer, especially as private reports came to his ears that Mr. Roosevelt had said he was "after old Pulitzer" and that, criminal libel being a jail offense, he expected to land him in one of these democratic institutions. Mr. Pulitzer felt the President's powers were great enough to overawe courts and juries and that he had the will to do it.

The *Liberty* flitted in and out of New York harbor in the icy winter, putting in at Charleston now and then to get the news, always in the nervous anticipation that a United States marshal might be sitting on the dock. Mr. Pulitzer even took pains to find out which kind of jail might be made use of in his case. In the course of these winter voyages Capt. A. E. Caws, the splendid skipper of the *Liberty*, caught a cold that ended in pneumonia and his death in a New York hos-

## The Panama Prosecution

pital. He was a native of the Isle of Wight and a master mariner.

Mr. Pulitzer himself was taken ill at the same time — more from vexation than cold. He was indignant at the action of Bowers in retaining Nicoll and retired him both as counsel and trustee. Bowers was glad to part company under the circumstances. No attempt was made to capture Mr. Pulitzer on the high seas, but during this period District Attorney William Travers Jerome endeavored to inject himself into the case through an ingenious suggestion, urged by Mr. Nicoll, that he compliment Mr. Pulitzer with a local indictment, on which he could be decently bailed and relieve him from fear of kidnapping by the strenuous Roosevelt.

Mr. Pulitzer had sensed something of the sort long in advance of its occurrence. Writing to Cobb as early as December 23, 1908, he observed:

> My opinion is that if anything comes out of this Roosevelt Panama matter it will be through Jerome. If they should go for me personally through Jerome it will be necessary to show Jerome's animus. I don't think I would be silent then. Show how the machinery of justice is prostituted. For years we have asked Roosevelt to send somebody to jail; so he begins on the editors of the *World*. We pitched into Jerome because he did not do anything about wealthy lawbreakers; now he turns against the *World*. Say frankly that neither he nor Roosevelt can muzzle the *World*, nor anybody. But make it dignified. Illustrate how justice is perverted for personal ends. In this connection will Cobb kindly make a personal statement over his own signature asserting that he knows Mr. Pulitzer wants to take the responsibility for whatever the paper has done; that Mr. Pulitzer is deeply interested in politics; that Mr.

## Joseph Pulitzer

Pulitzer was out of the country when the Panama articles were printed; that he never saw these articles or had any communication about them; that he was in Charleston on his yacht when the editorial broadside appeared; that he knew nothing about that; that Roosevelt knew that Mr. Pulitzer knew nothing about it; that Cobb, who is well acquainted with Roosevelt personally and has no personal feeling whatever against him, published this article in the public interest as chief editor of the *World;* that Mr. Roosevelt is assailing Mr. Pulitzer merely to gratify his resentment against the paper for its long criticism of his jingoism, his centralization, and his cowboy policies.

When the Jerome proffer came along it was duly dealt with in double leads. Coincidentally, feeling that no move could be made under the Washington indictments unless the defendants would volunteer to appear, Mr. Roosevelt set the machinery of the United States District Attorney for Southern New York in motion. Henry L. Stimson held the office. He put the Grand Jury at work, on a Government complaint to the effect that twenty-nine copies of the *World* containing the article of October 3d had been circulated on the Government reservation at West Point and in the New York Federal Building — the last being free copies sent by request to postal inspectors on duty to detect specious advertising. Stuart McNamara, of Bonaparte's office, took part in the inquisition. No testimony was deduced showing any complicity on the part of Mr. Pulitzer and he was not indicted in New York, but the paper and Mr. Van Hamm were, on March 4, 1909, under a statute invented by Judge Isaac Story in 1825 and perfected July 7, 1898, during the war with Spain, entitled:

## The Panama Prosecution

"An act to Protect the Harbor Defense from Malicious injury, and for other purposes." To such a basis for prosecution Mr. Pulitzer took vigorous exception. He felt, as he expressed it in a memorandum to Mr. Cobb, that all of the President's power through his appointment of Judges and District Attorneys, had not sufficed "to send one 'malefactor of great wealth' to jail," but was being used to "stifle the only Democratic newspaper in New York City" for its criticism of his administration — in short, for *lèse-majesté*, after the fashion in Germany, where he added "hundreds of editors are always locked up." In referring to the message to Congress he observed that "Roosevelt's only authority for sending a message to Congress is to give information on the state of the Union. Is the *World* or Joseph Pulitzer the State or the Union?" He asked further: "What would the Democratic party do if we were shut up?"

"Is there a single human being," he observed, "who believes that such a $40,000,000 job could go through Congress in such a sudden and extraordinary manner against the Nicaragua and other interests without somebody making money out of it besides Cromwell?"

He caused a series of sarcastic editorials to be written on *Lèse-Majesté* under the following instruction:

> *Lèse-majesté* seems worse in America than Europe. There you have it limited to the sacred person of the ruler, representing God, crowned by God and oiled with the sacred oil. It is not extended to his brother-in-law or the relations of the ruler. In America Roosevelt is developing *lèse-majesté* to the extent of protecting his brother-in-law (by the way, an estimable and admirable gentleman). To terrifying and bulldozing

the House of Representatives and the Senate, abusing and blackguarding judges, he now adds threatening the Press and freedom of speech. What is the matter? Treat the thing ironically, sarcastically and yet in a serious vein. He is drunk with success, drunk with power, drunk with popularity — perhaps because of Bryan's work in destroying opposition. Please try to make fun of it. Of course I am referring to the Jerome-Stimson criminal prosecution idea.

The question is: Who got the money?

As to the proposed prosecution he commented in detail:

This is a case of political persecution for printing opinions about the President. The Panama business is a mere pretext. That is proven by Cromwell's attitude — by the way he treated it in the campaign and in his last statement; by the absolute contempt with which Charley Taft dismissed it; the joke that it was to Robinson until Roosevelt pitched into him and compelled him to notice it. And Roosevelt did not do anything until the *World* printed a certain editorial charging him with inveracity — an editorial, perhaps too strong, let us frankly admit — still, is it not cowardly for a trustee for the nation to use the whole machinery of Government for revenge? He does not say that he has been libelled by the charge of inveracity. The paper may be really guilty on these points. He may be perfectly right even to bring a charge of libel and send the whole staff to the galleys, but he does not say so. He is usurping power from private, personal feeling. Bringing his brother-in-law in is mere hypocrisy. If Robinson had been libelled he ought to have come out in October, November or December.

Make a list of names and places of Government forts, islands, possessions, reservations absolutely belonging to the United States, like Fort Slocum, Governors

## The Panama Prosecution

Island, West Point, Annapolis, Hawaii, Porto Rico. I presume there are thousands. If this precedent is established because a paper is "published" in Fortress Monroe, Governors Island, Sandy Hook, or wherever the United States own property, it would hold. It would apply to Yellowstone Park or to the twelve hundred islands in the Philippines, compelling editors to go to these places, if need be, and defend themselves. The mere threat of such a thing would stop any liberty of the press. If this precedent is established we shall have to go to the Yellowstone, or suspend publication and have a Government organ take our place. There would be no newspapers or editors. The papers would die of inanition. Editors would become nomads and take to the road. Make up a map in the news columns, indicating the number of these possessions, but don't be too funny; give the two sides of the globe. Make this the feature to-morrow, with perfect good humor. In your editorial you must be serious and brave, and you must appeal to every serious man; you can't do that if you crack jokes, but it is possible to combine seriousness and a mock vein of severity. This is a new kink, now that we have governments everywhere.

The Administration placed an extraordinary number of secret agents upon the *World's* trail; its mail was opened in the postoffice; the portfolios of its messengers between New York and Washington were examined and the Pulitzer Building itself filled with spies. Anent this Mr. Pulitzer wrote:

> Don't forget to call attention to all the secrecy and also the remarkable fact that they have had detectives examining every mail bag, but they have not subpœnaed a single editor or manager who might know, or who could really tell something, or who might have

committed the offense and is ready to testify. Also, don't forget to prove very clearly that we did not charge anything of the kind that Roosevelt charges we charged and that Jerome now re-echoes. That in itself is worth stating. We printed current gossip without any criminal intent. We did not impugn Roosevelt or any member of the Government. It is a scarecrow that Roosevelt has erected for personal revenge; it might as well be punctured once for all. His message openly avowed his malevolent, vindictive spirit. This is called a square deal!

Take up that Stimson letter to-day. He says there can be prosecutions in a hundred places. It is the most outrageous theory ever advanced. They have never subpœnaed an editor, but gone after a man who was not in the country. Point out the enormous power of the State in presenting indictments, not for a libel against eighty million people, but against a brother-in-law; and now this man Jerome, whom we wanted removed, is in a highly moral state of indignation.

In a note written March 8, 1909, Mr. Pulitzer remarks succinctly:

If there is any single lesson taught by this Roosevelt business it is first, the wonderful vitality and, I think, the extraordinary intelligence of the people who listen and even perhaps shout at demagogic appeals, and yet go to the polls without acting upon them. There is another lesson, it is that Roosevelt should have made all his speeches and yet the people did not vote for the labor candidate, or the Socialist candidate, or the Hearst candidate. They did not seem to be influenced, but voted for the man of common sense. The one vote of thanks that Roosevelt deserves, is that he has given a test of Republican institutions.

Another lesson I want to impress upon you all is

that we shall not increase the power of the Executive any further; if this is to be a government of the people, for the people, by the people, it is a crime to put into the hands of a President such powers as no Monarch, or King, or Emperor ever possessed. He has too much power already, and if there is anything further to be said on that subject, it is that Congress is largely responsible for it. We must have an independent Congress, just as much as an independent President. Congress has given this man too much power. I would rather have corruption than the power of one man. Congress is responsible. I want you to express this; I feel that my opinions ought to be expressed.

More than Congress, however, the Democrats are responsible. Roosevelt did not do so badly the first three years after he was elected. Why was his head so terribly turned? Because Bryan gave him the support of the opposition. It was the opposition in Congress that compelled the party to take it up as a matter of tactics. So Bryan is more responsible for making Roosevelt lose his head than anybody else. This I would say, the first time I had a chance — but without abusing Bryan.

With the passing of Roosevelt from power Mr. Pulitzer felt that he had danced attendance on contingencies long enough. As noted, he had spent most of the winter on the yacht, voyaging up and down the coast awaiting eventualities. Convinced that future proceedings would be orderly and wearying of the alarms and annoyance, he came to a sudden determination to depart for Europe. In mid-March the *Liberty* put into Hampton Roads, where Harold S. Pollard, chief of the secretarial staff, was sent ashore to give the office some last words on the telephone from the Hotel Chamberlain, at Old Point Comfort. The length of the conversation alarmed the operator, who frequently interrupted our talk to make sure that the speaker knew he was on the road to bankruptcy; to be assured each time that he was quite aware of it. The cost of the conversation totalled $104!

This occurred in the evening. Orders were given to "loaf" off Norfolk. At breakfast the next morning Mr. Pulitzer asked Captain Hiram Dixon who had replaced Caws, which way the yacht was heading.

"Due east, sir," was the response.

"If we keep on 'due east,'" queried Mr. Pulitzer, "where will we fetch up?"

"Lisbon, sir."

"Keep on, due east."

To the consternation of all on board the command went into immediate effect and the *Liberty* continued on what proved to be the most disagreeable voyage in her history — and she steamed during her career some 130,000 miles! Off the Capes a terrible gale befell, followed by a long period of heavy swells, in which she once executed a roll of 45 degrees. To add to the general misery Mr. Pulitzer was taken ill with a bronchial affection, the nature of which the ship's young physician, Dr. O. E. Wrench, could not fathom. When all were exhausted the *Liberty* made port at Lisbon, where Dr. Frank P. Kinnicut was summoned from Pau. He at once pronounced the disease whooping cough! This juvenile ailment is very dangerous in the case of adults and no doubt was responsible for the weakening of the patient's heart, with its fatal after-consequences. As if this were not enough, a new "secretary" came on board at Lisbon, Mr. William Romaine Paterson, a charming and accomplished Scotchman. He celebrated his arrival

## The Panama Prosecution

by coming down with smallpox, which he had picked up during a stay en route, at Madrid. He was landed at Gibraltar, where a few weeks in the lazaretto accomplished a cure. The yacht, after a thorough fumigation and general vaccination, which included its owner, was allowed to proceed and reached Marseilles, whence Mr. Pulitzer journeyed to Aix-les-Bains and disposed of his cough.

Mr. Cromwell had expected to be made Attorney General under the Taft administration, but George W. Wickersham, a distinguished New York lawyer, received the appointment. He continued the case with vigor, while the *World* and Mr. Nicoll showed equal energy in preparing for trial. The latter procured letters rogatory by court order for the taking of testimony in Paris and Panama. Henry A. Wise had succeeded Henry L. Stimson as United States District Attorney. He, together with Deputy-Attorney General Stuart McNamara, went abroad to be present at such examinations as the *World's* counsel might enforce, Mr. John D. Lindsay, of Mr. Nicoll's firm, representing the paper in France. The *World* had to pay the bills for both parties to the suit. The Paris office of Coudert Brothers were formal counsel. Presumably by diplomatic action some access was now to be had to the records sealed up in the Credit Lyonnais. It all came to nothing, however. No information whatever was obtained that would shed light on Mr. Pulitzer's vital query: "Who got the money?"

Two reporters, Earl Harding and Henry N. Hall (later London *Times* correspondent in Paris) did some remarkable sleuthing in Bogota and Panama. Nor was the Government less active on its side. Secret Service agents trailed our men; Harding was once waylaid in Colombia in the belief that he carried certain documents of value — which he did not. They had already been sequestrated. Lines were developed in Panama that brought out abundantly the fact that Cromwell and Roosevelt had coöperated closely. A volume could be written about the contest of wits and effort, but it is out of place here.

Before the Washington case against Mr. Pulitzer, Mr. Lyman and Mr. Van Hamm could be reached, that against Delavan Smith and Charles R. Williams was dismissed by Federal Judge Albert Barnes Anderson, sitting in Indianapolis. While it was pending United States District Attorney Joseph H. Kealing had resigned rather than represent the Government. "I am not in accord with the Government" he wrote, in retiring, "in its attempt to put a strained construction on the law; to drag these defendants from their homes to the seat of the Government, to be tried and punished, while there is good and sufficient law in this jurisdiction in the State court. I believe the principle involved is dangerous, striking at the very foundation of our form of government."

Judge Anderson in his opinion, discussing the indictments said:

> It was well stated by a former President of the United States that it is the duty of a newspaper to print the news and tell the truth about it. It is the duty of a public newspaper, such as is owned and conducted by these defendants, to tell the people, its subscribers, its readers, the facts that it may find out about public questions, or matters of public interest; it is its duty and its right to draw inferences from the facts known — draw them for the people.
>
> Here was a great public question. There are many

## The Panama Prosecution

very peculiar circumstances about the history of this Panama Canal or Panama Canal business. I do not wish to be understood as reflecting upon anybody, in office or out, in connection with this matter, except such persons as I may name in that way. The circumstances surrounding the revolution in Panama were unusual and peculiar. The people were interested in the construction of a canal; it was a matter of great public concern; it was much discussed. A large portion of the people favored the Nicaragua route. They investigated and reported in favor of the Nicaragua route. Shortly afterward — I do not recall just how soon afterward — they changed to the Panama route. Up to the time of that change, as I gathered from the evidence, the lowest sum that had been suggested at which the property of the Panama Canal Company could be procured was something over $100,000,000. Then, rather suddenly; it became known that it could be procured for $40,000,000. There were a number of people who thought there was something not just exactly right about that transaction, and I will say for myself that I have a curiosity to know what the real truth was.

Thereupon a committee of the United States Senate was appointed to investigate these matters — about the only way the matter could be investigated. The committee met. As stated in these articles, the man who knew all about it — I think that is the proper way to speak of Mr. Cromwell — who knew all about it, was called before the committee. Mr. Cromwell upon certain questions being put to him, more or less pertinent, stood upon his privilege as an attorney and refused to answer.... Mr. Cromwell stood upon his privilege whenever questions were asked the answers to which would or might reflect upon him and his associates. But whenever a question was asked which gave him an opportunity to say something in their behalf he ostentatiously thanked the examiner for the question and proceeded to answer. To my mind that gave just ground for suspicion. I am suspicious about it now. . . . The question is: Did these defendants under the circumstances act honestly in the discharge of this duty, of which I have spoken and which the law recognizes, or were they prompted by a desire to injure the person who is affected by their acts? If it were necessary to decide this case upon the question of privilege, the lack of malice, I would hesitate quite a while before I would conclude that it was my duty to send these people to Washington for trial.

But that is not all. This indictment charges these defendants with the commission of a crime in the District of Columbia. The Sixth Amendment to the Constitution of the United States provides: In all criminal prosecutions the accused shall enjoy the right to a speedy and public trial by an impartial jury of the State or district wherein the crime shall have been committed, which district shall have been previously ascertained by law. . . .

To my mind that man has read the history of our institutions to little purpose who does not look with grave apprehension upon the possibility of the success of a proceeding such as this. If the history of liberty means anything — if constitutional guarantees are worth anything — this proceeding must fail. If the prosecuting authorities have the authority to select the tribunal; if there be more than one tribunal to select from; if the Government has the power and can drag citizens from distant States to the capital of the nation, there to be tried, then, as Judge Cooley says, this is a strange result of a revolution where one of the grievances complained of was the assertion of the right to send parties abroad for trial.

## The Panama Prosecution

There was much doubt in the *World* office as to the best course of procedure. Mr. Nicoll was strongly inclined to meet the charges, though created in the accidental manner already disclosed. He believed that much of the evidence gathered could be made effective in court and would convince a jury. On the other hand, the issue of the freedom of the press was far more vital than exposing profiteers. Mr. Pulitzer endorsed this view. "I think it is an act of public service," he wrote, "an act of special value to the entire press of the United States that these test questions should be adjudicated without any compromise whatsoever. I am opposed, not only to any compromise, but to any delay or dilatory tactics. I want the paper to get out of the clutches of the lawyers even far more than of the courts." Accordingly, the right of the Government to bring such a suit was challenged. The case was called before Judge Charles M. Hough in the District Court of Southern New York, on January 25, 1910, when Mr. Nicoll moved the quashing of the indictment, on the following grounds:

1. The Court has no jurisdiction in this case. There is no statute of the United States authorizing this prosecution.
2. The Act of 1898 does not apply to the case as disclosed by the evidence.
3. If the Act of 1898 is construed as to cover the acts shown by the evidence it is unconstitutional.
4. The offense, if any, was committed wholly within the jurisdiction of the State of New York, and was punishable there.
5. The defendant, being a corporation, is incapable of committing the offense charged in the indictment.

## Joseph Pulitzer

District Attorney Wise endeavored to construe the act protecting reservations as a Federal libel law. The Court accepted Mr. Nicoll's view. In quashing the indictment Judge Hough said:

> The court is relieved of much embarrassment by the form of one of the motions made. The jurisdiction of this court is peremptorily challenged by the motion to quash. Other motions have been made which will not be considered. But inasmuch as a decision under a motion to quash is now speedily reviewable by the highest court, I shall dispose of the case under that motion. . . . It seems to me that there is a plain distinction between that jurisdiction which grows out of the necessary exercise of national powers and that which is based on the physical ownership of areas of land. The first basis or foundation of jurisdiction is governmental and fundamentally governmental. The existence and exercise of that species of jurisdiction is vital to the National Government but territorial jurisdiction is merely a convenience. It is frequently a very great convenience, but it is no more than that.
>
> The criminal statutes passed in the exercise of Congressional authority have always, as far as they have come under my observation, seemed to me to view offenses and offenders from one or two standpoints. The prescribed act is made an offense or crime because it either lessens the authority or attacks the sovereign, or interferes with the operation of or injures the property of the United States, or else it is an offense against general municipal law which happens to be committed upon a place within the exclusive jurisdiction of the nation. Now, it may be, it has in the past been thought that under some circumstances the crime of libel might be considered to impair the authority and interfere with the efficiency of the Government of the United States, but so far as I know or am informed by counsel,

## The Panama Prosecution

this thought has not found expression in any national statute now in force. Therefore in this court the crime charged in this indictment is to be regarded only as an offense against the United States, if it is an offense against the law of New York, which happened to be committed upon national land physically within the Southern District of New York. . . . The question is this: The libellous matter here complained of was printed and published in the county of New York. Therefore the State court sitting in that county has jurisdiction. It was also published in the county of Orange; therefore the State court sitting in that county has jurisdiction. But it was also published in the West Point reservation, which is both in the County of Orange and in the Southern District of New York, and therefore this court has jurisdiction. To the proposition that this can be true I am unwilling to yield assent until instructed by higher authority. . . .

I am of the opinion that the construction of this act claimed by the prosecution is opposed to the spirit and tenor of legislation for many years on the subject of national territorial jurisdiction. It is a novelty, and the burden of upholding a novelty is upon him who alleges it. . . . It is therefore ordered that a judgment of this Court be entered quashing the indictment herein, because upon the construction of the statute, hereinbefore stated, the indictment is not authorized by the statutes on which it rests.

The Government filed a writ of error and this appeal was heard by the United States Supreme Court October 24, 1910, Justices Harlan, White, Day, Holmes, McKenna, Lurton and Hughes sitting. A unanimous decision in the *World's* favor was handed down January 3, 1911, written by Chief Justice White, in which he said:

## Joseph Pulitzer

I have the opinion of the court in the case of the United States *vs.* The Press Publishing Company. Two propositions are, the Court holds, clearly established:

First, That adequate means were afforded for punishing the circulation of a libel on a United States reservation by the State law and in the State courts without the necessity of resorting to the courts of the United States for redress:

Second, That resort could not be had to the courts of the United States to punish the act of publishing a newspaper libel by circulating a copy of the newspaper on the reservation upon the theory such publication was an independent offense, separate and distinct from the primary printing and publication of the libellous article within the State of New York, without disregarding the law of that State and frustrating the plain purpose of such law, which was that there should be but a single prosecution and conviction.

These propositions being true, it follows in the light of the construction given to the act of 1898 that the lower court was right in quashing the indictment as not authorized by that act. No other conclusion was possible, the Supreme Court holds, as the court below could not have sustained the indictment without giving to the statute a meaning directly conflicting with the construction affixed to it by the Supreme Court. In other words, the Court could not have upheld the indictment without deciding that, because the statute provided that acts when committed on United States reservations, which were not expressly made criminal by the law of the United States, might be prosecuted and published in accordance with the State law, therefore, a prosecution was authorized which was inconsistent with that law and in disregard thereof.

*The Panama Prosecution*

On motion of the Attorney General the Washington indictment against Mr. Pulitzer and the others was dismissed March 31, 1911. So the case ended without the real facts ever becoming known. The Canal has since vindicated itself as a commercial enterprise, Colombia has been paid by vote of Congress, the $25,000,000 she refused at the beginning, and grass grows over the episode — one of the most vivid in all the history of newspapers.

Costly and vexatious as it was the Panama conflict gave the *World* a prominence that no other occasion ever supplied and placed it definitely out of comparison with the Hearst newspapers. Here at least was something they could not imitate or follow!

## Chapter XVI

### LAST YEARS — 1909–1911

The Gaynor Campaign — Stay at Berlin — Taft's Administration — Forcing the Market Basket Special Session — Death at Charleston, S. C.

OVER–VEXED by the Panama prosecution and the whooping cough, Mr. Pulitzer did not return to America during 1909. He visited Carlsbad in the Spring and cruised in Summer to the North, taking in the fjords of Norway and the Scandinavian capitals. This concluded he spent a short season at Aix-les-Bains, where he began to take an interest in the New York City Mayoralty campaign, which resulted in the choice of William J. Gaynor.

"Urge vigorously Gaynor's nomination by Democrats," he cabled Cobb from Aix-les-Bains on September 10th. "Admitting his defects he is an able man; nobody's pocket judge. Urge nomination of equally strong Fusion candidate, mentioning President (Nicholas Murray) Butler type, insuring good Mayor, whoever wins. This is true independence. After both candidates are nominated and their qualities examined, will decide which to support. Meanwhile, use great power, opportunity, duty, to influence highest character in both nominations."

Following this message Mr. Pulitzer began a stay in Berlin, taking an apartment at No. 23 In den Zelten, near the Tiergarten. The particularity that had

## Last Years — 1909-1911

to be exercised in making his quarters satisfactory is shown in this copy of the requirements laid down for the landlord:

Mr. Pulitzer's bedroom: Heavy, plate glass windows, glass of the thickest available quality to be added to the already existing double windows throughout. Furthermore, everything is to be done to render the windows as silent as possible. The furniture shall include a heavy carpet, necessary small rugs, and at least one heavy arm chair of the style already suggested. Electric bells to be fitted to ring in the valet room. The two windows and the two doors, are to be hung with curtains of the heaviest, most sound deadening quality.

Bathroom: The existing sunken bath is to be carefully covered over in the safest possible manner. A new selected bathtub to be installed, completely fitted with hot and cold water, the present brass railings to be taken away, sharp edges in construction to be carefully avoided and the whole to be carried out with the direction and approval of Mr. Pulitzer's agent. The furnishings should include extra large toilet table with all conveniences, and heavy rug on the floor.

Breakfast Room: The furnishing should include the heavy carpet, rugs, writing table, chaise longue, two heavy arm chairs, and several small tables.

Dining Room: The furnishings should include heavy carpet and besides the usual dining room furniture including at least ten chairs, two or three bookcases.

Drawing Room: The furnishing should be that usual and adequate for a parlor.

Hall: The furnishing of the hall must include a long, particularly heavy strip of carpet and heavy portieres, half way down, as already indicated by Mr. Pulitzer.

General: All the rooms are to be fully and adequately equipped with electric chandeliers or fixtures, including at least five reading lamps to be placed as later directed.

Doors and windows, hinges, locks, etc., throughout the apartment are to be rendered by careful adjustment and oiling as noiseless as possible.

The bed linen, table linen, silver, porcelain, glass, etc., must be in quality and quantity satisfactory and adequate for a household of at least twelve persons.

This Berlin visit was a particularly happy one, Mr. Pulitzer was in the best of spirits, dined frequently at public resorts, attended the opera and concerts and saw many friends. He was in pleasant humor as this note to Cobb shows:

No. 23 In den Zelten,
BERLIN, Sept. 25,'09.

DEAR COBB:

Thanks very much for your letter about books. I wish you would always let me know what you are reading, because I find it almost impossible to get anyone to suggest new books to me, although it is the first question I ask.

That book, Stimson's "American Constitution," please buy at my expense for Ralph. He needs it more than I do.

All good wishes and kind regards to Mrs. Cobb.

Yours sincerely,
JOSEPH PULITZER.

The enjoyable stay was interrupted by a shock, when on October 3, 1909, his brother Albert committed suicide in Vienna, where he had been for some time a resident, ending a period of suffering from mental disease in this fashion.

From Berlin Mr. Pulitzer followed the local campaign closely. Gaynor, an interesting and aggressive personality, was much courted by Independents for the Fusion nomination. He kept the several elements in the dark as to his purpose, even when one body filed a petition naming him as their nominee, The *World's* urgings, and the desire to corner Senator Patrick Henry McCarren, boss of Brooklyn, led Charles F. Murphy, leader of Tammany Hall, to name Gaynor, to the dismay of William R. Hearst, who had been one of the Judge's strongest backers for the Fusion nomination. Gaynor accepted. Indignant at what he regarded as a betrayal, Mr. Hearst caused himself to be nominated for the office, while the Republicans, hoping for victory over divided forces, named Otto Bannard. Mr. Pulitzer would have preferred to support a Fusion candidate, but the situation as developed left him nothing to do but back Gaynor. Cobb had recommended a "passive non-committal, sitting-on-the-fence attitude." This did not appeal to Mr. Pulitzer. "The page ought to have a vigorous policy, and more than policy, it ought to have conscience, convictions, forbidding the fence," was his view.

This policy he soon developed, supporting Gaynor for Mayor, and Charles S. Whitman, Republican, for District Attorney. He wanted "an ideal District Attorney" who would resemble "young Tilden, Cleveland," and the like. His motive for supporting Gaynor as outlined to Cobb was his belief that the Judge would build up an independent local Democracy that would overturn Charles F. Murphy and "seriously cripple Tammany Hall." The paper was to say frankly, however, "when necessary," that Judge Gaynor "has serious faults for which we have criticised him in the past and for which we shall probably have to criticise him in future."

## Joseph Pulitzer

The Judge's course, while successful as a political move, bred a bitter contest, and developed an amusing incident. To Mr. Pulitzer, in Berlin, Mr. Brisbane, as chief polemist for Mr. Hearst, cabled this message on October 13th: "Should be glad to contribute two columns a day over my signature to *Evening World* during campaign if acceptable. Thought you might like to give our side. If you accept proposition I shall write no other signed articles except for *World*."

This Mr. Pulitzer repeated to me with the comment: "Might make good feature, but you alone must decide and let him know." I promptly decided to accept the offer and so advised Mr. Pulitzer. "Be careful in announcement," he replied, "to avoid editorial identification with Brisbane's views. Might be good idea to have another column representing Tammany's views answering Brisbane, and another column representing Republican views as equal chance for all."

The *Evening World's* columns were accordingly thrown open. As a little stimulus to interest we caused a twenty-four sheet poster to be placarded over the city, with a six-foot portrait of Brisbane as its chief ornament, announcing his daily efforts. He attacked Gaynor with such virulence that the Judge sued the *World* for libel, a proceeding without precedent, in view of its stout support of his candidacy. There was consternation in the office as to the best course to pursue. Some were for instant repudiation of the candidate, but Mr. Cobb very amiably met the crisis with this admirable editorial:

> Judge Gaynor's libel suit against the *World* for the publication in its evening edition of one of Mr. Brisbane's entertaining articles in behalf of Mr. Hearst,

MISS EDITH PULITZER, MR. PULITZER AND H. S. POLLARD AT MONTE CARLO.

is to be accepted as further proof of the Democratic candidate's militant independence.

If Judge Gaynor, in the midst of the campaign, brings suit against the *World*, which is his chief newspaper supporter, we have high hope that as Mayor he would be equally courageous in starting litigation in the public interest. That kind of a man could bring all the tax dodgers to time, collect the franchise taxes that the corporations have evaded for years and compel the traction companies to fulfill their contract obligations. That is what we want a Mayor to do.

New York needs a Mayor who is not afraid to start lawsuits against anything or anybody, and who will not be swerved by personal considerations of any sort.

The Judge was not soothed, and the *World* had considerable difficulty after his election in getting the case off the calendar. He won by a vote of 250,378 to 177,304 for Hearst and 154,187 for Bannard.

The Berlin sojourn ended October 23d, when Mr. Pulitzer rejoined the yacht for a cruise to the Greek islands, whence he returned to Cap Martin, taking quarters in the Villa Arethusa, where he had for neighbor, among others of distinction, Eugenie, late Empress of the French.

The *Liberty* lay conveniently in the snug harbor at Mentone and was in frequent use for short cruises, one in particular made early in December taking in the Ligurian Islands of Corsica, Monte Cristo and Elba, where a brief stay was made visiting the short-lived kingdom of Napoleon.

The winter of 1909–1910 was spent in this fashion at Cap Martin. His eyesight had now become almost, if not totally, eclipsed. One evening the rare moon of the Mediterranean rose with special splendor and Mr. H. S. Pollard of his secretarial staff, was so moved with its glory that he led Mr. Pulitzer to the bow of the *Liberty* on which they chanced to be cruising and invited his attention to the wondrous orb, placing him so he could look in the right direction. He strained his eyes for some moments, then said sadly: "It's no use, my dear boy, I cannot even get a glimmer of its light."

He had hitherto kept a strong electric lamp placed where it would throw its beams upon his plate at meal times, but now gave it up as he was no longer conscious of light.

He was also certain that his hard worked heart was running down. Riding on the Corniche Road the automobile engine stalled while I was in his company. Mr. Pollard left in search of a relief machine at the little village of Roquebronne near which we were becalmed. Mr. Pulitzer took the delay philosophically.

"You see how quiet I am," he remarked. "Real troubles never bother me. It's only the small annoyances that upset me."

He then asked where we were. I told him: "On the height above Cap Martin looking across to Monaco."

"When you write a book, as I hope you will, describe it, so I can have it read to me. You know I was here thirty-five years ago for the first time and the sight is always with me. Though I have lived here much since, I have never seen it." (The book was duly written and the scene described. It greatly pleased him.) "We will not have many more rows," he resumed. I interrupted to hope that pleasure was not going to be denied us.

## Last Years — 1909–1911

"No, I am serious," he said. "I am not going to live long. I have had warnings. Beside I am no longer equal to thinking or deciding. You will have to get along without me more and more from now on and see less and less of me."

Yet he seemed particularly well. The problem of building a new structure for the *Post-Dispatch* was under consideration, and his portfolio bulged with correspondence and matters under consideration.

He never visited India, but often thought of doing so. In a late cruise the *Liberty* lay off Port Said at the entrance to the Suez Canal, with no special port in view. "Why not India?" someone suggested. Mr. Pulitzer was favorable, but feared it would be hot in the Red Sea. A joker in the party observed that it might pay to test the temperature by sending the launch on a short run in the Canal. Mr. Pulitzer took the tip seriously and sent several secretaries on the expedition. They found it extremely warm. On this report he decided not to visit the Hindoos that morning and was delighted at the success of the experiment.

As Ponce de Leon sought the Fountain of Youth, Mr. Pulitzer was forever seeking the fountain of health. Consulting doctors became a passion with him. The most distinguished practitioners in Europe passed in review, taking fees and leaving no cures behind. The entourage came to believe that seeing doctors was more of a pastime than a hope, especially after the distinguished Carl H. Von Noorden, who journeyed from Vienna to Wiesbaden, was turned away with the excuse that his prospective patient was "too ill" to see him!

A sample note to a distinguished member of the faculty, written from the Hotel Quisisana, Wiesbaden,

*Joseph Pulitzer*

September 8, 1910, shows his manner of approaching a medico:

> Frankly I should be very glad to know if it would be possible for you to see me alone — without the fatiguing formality of a consultation. You may understand that with a doctor in the morning and another massage doctor in the afternoon, I should particularly like to avoid the added unnecessary irritation of having several doctors in the room at once.
> Can you not see me quite independently?

The search for the attendant doctor was always on, even with a satisfactory man in the entourage. He always wanted a better, or the certainty that another could be had if the incumbent should weary of his job, as was not infrequently the case. This letter to the late James M. Tuohy, the *World's* London correspondent, written from the Villa Arethusa, Cap Martin, March 9, 1910, by Mr. Pulitzer's secretary, Norman G. Thwaites, shows the system:

> MY DEAR MR. TUOHY: Mr. Pulitzer asks me to write to you at once that it may catch you before you start on your holiday. He has been ill in bed for two weeks with severe bronchial cold, reviving his old whooping cough and is now amazingly weak and sleepless. As soon as he is able to be moved, he is planning a month's trip on the yacht, probably into the East and the Red Sea.
> The point is this: Utterly disregarding all qualifications heretofore specified as to agreeability, conversation, knowledge of history, editorial ability, etc., can you set in immediate motion a search for a first-rate, practical physician who would be willing to go off immediately for a month on the yacht? Mr. Pulitzer underlines three times the point that *you can drop all*

## Last Years — 1909-1911

*former requirements as to personal qualifications* concentrating on experienced, reliable, first-class professional ability. The man need not be a specialist so long as he is able to study and diagnose Mr. Pulitzer's peculiar history and condition of nervousness, insomnia and recently recurring complications of whooping cough.

You can also dismiss the idea of permanency. Mr. Pulitzer's present plan is to leave here about the 15th of March, and to be gone till about the first of May, calling very probably at Constantinople, Athens, Egypt and the Red Sea. The man will have nothing to do except to enjoy himself, and apart from his study of Mr. Pulitzer's case, it ought to be an exceedingly pleasant trip for any one.

NEEDLESS TO SAY THE MAN MUST BE SEA SICK PROOF!!

Mr. Pulitzer says emphatically he does not wish this matter to interfere with your holiday, or to spoil it. It must not interfere with that.

You will see that it is quite different from anything he has asked for before in that it distinctly eliminates the point of intellectual companionship, and asks merely for a first-rate doctor. Mr. Pulitzer says he may stutter, or be a hunchback, but, of course, not preferably so. This ought to make the search much easier. Mr. Pulitzer has really been very ill and ought not to go off without a serious-minded, capable physician in whom he and Mrs. Pulitzer can have some confidence. I am sure you can understand why the present author-physician fails to inspire that feeling.

Hoping that someone may be found as soon as possible as it is entirely desirable that Mr. Pulitzer should get away at once, and with best wishes to yourself,

Yours sincerely,
NORMAN G. THWAITES.

## Joseph Pulitzer

Next to finding a physician the search for a lawyer who could draw up a perfect will was in mind. An instruction written by Mr. H. S. Pollard to William R. Hereford, then the *World's* Paris correspondent, gives an outline of what was wanted:

> DEAR HEREFORD: Mr. Pulitzer directs me to ask you to please make it your business to find out exhaustively, in the most direct manner, who is the *one* best lawyer in Paris, among or apart from the four you mentioned, bearing carefully in mind the following points:
>
> (1) Experience and skill in the drawing of legal documents is the prime essential — not success in the trial of a case, or in talking to a jury.
>
> (2) Familiarity with American law is needed — not necessarily French law at all.
>
> (3) Having carefully reached your conclusions as to the best man, give fully specific reasons why he is by age, aptitude, ability, training, best capable of managing a documentary rather than a court case, remembering that the record of cases actually tried or managed by him is more important than influential friendships.
>
> (4) Please be very minute but also discreet in your inquiries and make your report on your final choice of one man as full and detailed as to age, character, specific experience, and above all American experience, as possible.
>
> Please also continue on the lookout for American lawyers arriving in Europe, particularly William B. Hornblower, of New York.

Although far away, he followed Mr. Taft's administration with interest, having in mind the certainty that Roosevelt would try to succeed him for a third term. His views were briskly expressed in a letter

## Last Years — 1909-1911

to Horatio W. Seymour, of the editorial staff, written on January 20th:

Here are some *suggestions about Taft:*

1. No fire, no rhetoric, no sacrifice of truth or accuracy, inevitable in the anxiety to make a phrase or show brilliant rhetorical style. *Moderation,* reasonableness in every word whether criticising or praising. *No partisanship,* no feeling between the lines, that whatever is said is inspired by hope of turning the opposition to the party in power. Get, if truth justifies, all the hope possible to the opposition to carry the elections this fall, but with a big *IF,* in one word always moderation, impartiality, real truth and independence.

2. Criticise fairly Taft's leaning towards extreme protectionists, unfortunate, surprising and inconsistent with his record before election and general character.

3. Yet *Do not write one line about tariff.*
   a. Because it is an extremely dull subject, academic.
   b. Because it is a peculiarly dangerous subject to any gentleman like yourself who has been extreme in that respect all his life.
   c. Because, while I am opposed to monopoly protection, or extreme protection, and *decidedly* in favor of lower tariff, I believe in general principles of protection as Jefferson, Washington, Cleveland and everyone did, including Tilden, and even Wilson, and cannot shut my eyes to the fact that France and Germany have flourished wonderfully under protection and that the *United States owe their amazing prosperity largely to protection in spite of its corrupt influence.* I don't ask you to express these opinions. I wish every editor to write only what he conscientiously believes, and if he

disagrees with the policy of the paper to remain simply silent. *But I do ask you to be silent* when you don't agree with me.

4. Criticise his itch for travel as lowering the dignity of the Presidency, cheapening as it were his personality for mere curiosity-mongers, lessening his influence with Congress and the respect due Congress, who know all his views before they assemble, when they are absolutely entitled to receive his opinions afresh.

5. Criticise his talk about war. Absurd, shows ignorance about European conditions, where they are crazy watching each other, afraid of each other and crazy to have the friendship of U.S.A. This applies to general jingoism, militarism about U.S. being compelled to take part in European politics, &c., &c. My ideas about militarism ought to be known and ought not to be forgotten, but I cannot dictate a column on this subject alone.

6. *Praise* his policy for economy and retrenchment. Make this your *paramount*, most conspicuous, continuing, cumulative feature. It is worth more than twenty hypercritical efforts. It is the first time since Roosevelt's advent that the word economy has ever been heard in any state paper or message. Support him in this, *warmly* and *strongly*, showing the amazing increase in our expenditures of Government, most of them for war or preparation for war without any excuse. One reason for this amazing increase is undoubtedly the protectionist desire to compel the need of large revenue and higher tariffs. One reason for the increase in cost of living is just such amazing increase of expenditures causing deficits and new taxes and excusing high tariffs. Nothing more important in national legislation.

7. Incidentally, his second term will depend, next to Democratic imbecility, almost entirely on the pros-

## Last Years — 1909-1911

perity of the country and the success of the tariff and the cost of living.

8. Support Taft strongly in his scheme for a Court of Commerce, *opposing* him strongly in his scheme of Federal licenses for all corporations; if for no other reason, because the one-man power at White House is too alarming already, and to subject all the railroads practically to his whim, would give him more power and compel the railroads to go into politics and even justify them as a matter of self-interest. But there are other reasons, Constitutional and practical.

9. Apropos of sugar and tobacco frauds. If Congress has not ordered an investigation of the sugar frauds, take about two weeks to dig up all the facts in a resume, all that has been printed before, most condensed and pointed, as a broadside and appeal to Congress for Light and Truth, to force an investigation. Simply facts, not one single over-statement or exaggeration.

10. If you want Roosevelt nominated the best possible policy for you is of course, to tear Taft to pieces. That is, if I allow you, which I don't.

11. If you think that Taft is not radical enough I respectfully disagree with you. Not only respectfully, but *vigorously, uncompromisingly.*

12. Taft is quite radical enough. I think *too radical*, in advocating Roosevelt's policies. One instance is enough, and that is his advocacy of the old military cries of Roosevelt that we must have a bigger army and a bigger part in European politics. Quite preposterous.

There had been a long period of anti-Japanese agitation, decorated with war scares, when Mr. Pulitzer decided to send someone to Japan and secure first hand information concerning that country's attitude toward the United States. He first broached the idea to Mr. Cobb, in these terms:

*Joseph Pulitzer*

April 2, 1910.

DEAR COBB:

I have just re-read your recent political predictions and I do not consider you crazy at all. On the contrary, I agree with you — have felt as you write for some time and talked in the same spirit to Pollard a hundred times, so that Pollard made the not altogether unfounded remark: "You seem to want to make another Democratic President."

There is just one little thing I do not agree with you and that is, whether the Democrats can carry the Legislature to elect a United States Senator. It is possible, of course, but it would require an enormous sweep — a majority of 50,000 for the Democratic Governor would not insure a Democratic majority in the Legislature under the present apportionment.

Now will you think *me* crazy if I have a suggestion to make? No, don't call it a suggestion, as I wish you to be absolutely free and you may be foolish enough not to appreciate the idea; besides, I want to be free too, considering something might happen. What would you think of a trip to Japan during July and August at my expense? Primarily, for broadening, widening your general horizon, but also to enable you to study the country with a special view to the insane feeling manufactured about the possibility of war. Perhaps I should add, lest you consider me too selfish that, thirdly, I fully expect that you will have a great deal of pleasure from the trip.

Or, all the same to me, what do you think of spending July and August in Europe next year, incidentally studying the war craze in America — the folly of supposing there is any power in Europe would dream of war with America.

In any case on the first of this September I want you back fresh and re-inspired.

Faithfully yours,
J. P.

## Last Years — 1909-1911

P.S. I have given Seitz an alternative hint, so you had better show him this and see his note lest you deem me guilty of double-dealing, although it is strictly a double hint. If you should jump at the idea you must cable me and immediately proceed to gather letters of introduction. Fairbanks, possibly even Taft, would do good. Fairbanks I am sure of and the Japanese Minister of course, too.

In a P. S. of April 26th, he further adds:

Apropos of the Japan idea, do not think of asking any letter or favor from either Taft or Knox, implied in letters of introduction. I don't know whether I wrote this in your letter or Seitz's, so you had better tell Seitz at the same time. We cannot afford to accept any favors from the powers that be.

Cobb declined the mission and I was accordingly given the opportunity, the considerable results of which appeared in the *World* over the signature of the leaders of Japanese thought and progress, effectively tempering the situation until German pre-war propaganda revived the friction.

Having counselled moderation, Mr. Pulitzer grew incensed at the paper's patience with President Taft. He had, about the time of the latter's inauguration in 1909, advised that he be let alone for a year. Other journals followed suit. The President was stunned at the outburst that came with 1910. Mr. Pulitzer asked that the President receive praise for appointing Gov. Charles E. Hughes to a seat on the United States Supreme Court bench, "though a great loss to the State," but on the critical side he wrote, April 5th:

I have never known the *World* to come so near to being muzzled, afraid of saying anything about Taft, or his weaknesses, or his administration, as during the past six months or so up to my Palermo cable. If there is anything under the sun that I hate, and that I believe the *World* was never guilty of before, it is trimming or sitting on the fence or failure to do its duty about men in the highest places. Now Taft has the very highest place in the country, and has made a lot of mistakes perfectly obvious to everybody, and yet the *World* remained silent — studiously silent. Please — Why? — Frankly! And don't think that my desire to treat Taft with *sympathy* and *fairness* has changed for a moment. Taft as a tariff reformer is one thing. Taft as the defender of the extreme protectionists is another character. Why not praise Taft for retrenchment and economy, as I suggested in my letter of January 20th?

Now do ignore, without hesitation, some of my suggestions coming from far, far away with complete ignorance of conditions on the spot, or when the conditions are entirely changed by time, or if you have any other strong reason I cannot possess. I do not wish to kill initiative, courage, discretion in the gentleman who is in charge of the page.

The *Liberty* put in at Athens in April and from the American Minister Mr. Pulitzer received a few copies of the *World* that gave him food for criticism and suggestion. It was on this visit that he gave way to an emotion not often manifest during his long affliction. It had been planned that all hands, including himself, should go ashore and inspect the Acropolis. At the last moment he refused to go, and remaining alone with his faithful personal attendant, J. E. Dunningham, he gave way to tears.

Writing from Athens to Cobb he reprehended "the hundreds of examples of Executive interference and

## Last Years — 1909-1911

control, and outrageous encroachment upon parliamentary independence and the freedom of Congress" which began in the Roosevelt era and continued under Taft. "We are driving," he continued, "steadily toward one-man power, practically Democratic despotism or attempt at the control of party, House and Senate by one man. If that man were an angel from Heaven I should object, because it is certainly a bad principle, inimical to the country's future and opposed to the cardinal principles of the Constitution and its careful intent to avoid just such one-power by the independence of each of the coördinate branches of the Government. This same principle could be applied to Albany. Very much as I admire Hughes, I still think the politicians were perfectly right in ignoring and rebuking Root's dictatorial interference. Indeed, I have a better opinion of these Republican politicians, simply because of the courage and independence shown."

Mr. Taft came into conflict with Congress and showed temper. Mr. Pulitzer cabled Cobb on May 17th, "Advice to Taft: Bismarck said 'Revenge is a delicacy that should be taken cold.' Repeat this thrice. Support insurgents warmly, criticising Rotund (Taft) for folly and partisanship. He should conciliate."

Mr. Roosevelt was turning his return from Africa into a triumphal tour as the guest of Kings. "As much silence as possible for Roosevelt during his holiday glorifications," Mr. Pulitzer urged on the editors. "There is time enough afterwards."

"Please find clipping enclosed," he wrote Cobb on May 20th, appending a paragraph from the Topeka *Capital*. "Admirably put. Please reprint it with reflections of your own. Poor Taft! Every time he opens his mouth he puts his foot in it. Also, every time he puts his foot into a Pullman car."

The Spring ending, he spent a short season at Aixles-Bains and returned to America on the Cedric June 19, 1910. The *Liberty* had preceded him across the sea, took him on board at quarantine, and for a few days loafed comfortably off Greenwich, Conn. From this point he continued his interest in the Japanese agitation, writing Cobb on June 27th:

> Immediately send for that Japanese man, Adachi Kinosuke, who wrote the letter appearing on *World* page March 20, and ask him to prepare two or three articles like the one printed.
>
> He can't do better than that one, I must say, but let him try. Make it half a dozen articles while we are about it. Give him a month if necessary to prepare them. Then print the series simply to enlighten and educate the people and the Press, as to the preposterous nonsense in the so-called danger of war. Reprint the first article as a beginning. And do exactly what I tell you when I ask you to reprint anything. I notice you did not quote from the Massachusetts Constitution that Gaynor quoted.

The Summer was pleasantly divided between Chatwold and short cruises on the *Liberty* up and down the coast. He kept a close eye on events, but was not very active, sending in an occasional critique to the office. "It is the irony of fate," he wrote on July 6th, "that Taft should make it impossible for himself to hold the Chief Justiceship and have to appoint a man for life. No doubt that is really his ambition; in fact, he admitted it publicly that he would rather be on the Supreme bench, and if Justice Fuller had

MR. PULITZER AND RALPH PULITZER
ON FIFTH AVENUE.

## Last Years — 1909-1911

lived three years longer, Taft himself would have had this great office during the remainder of his life."

That Mr. Taft finally came to fill the "great office" is an interesting aftermath to this far-away thought.

Mr. Pulitzer was always annoyed when editors failed to make instant comment on the news, as for example this word to Cobb on August 7th: "I read some days ago what Gaynor said on the subject of the Mayoralty of New York being a bigger office than that of Governor. How many days is today's editorial behind the news?"

In view of the prominence with which the name of "Jake" Hamon, of Oklahoma, figured in the oil scandals of 1924, this note is interesting, written also on August 7th: "Representative McGuire, of Oklahoma, lives in the same rooms as Lobbyist Hamon and McMurray who wanted legislation. Who is Hamon? Note this lobbyist was Chairman of the Oklahoma Republican Campaign Committee and a member of the Republican National Committee." He had in mind linking Vice-President Sherman up with Hamon as a factor in campaign corruption.

Preparing to sail for Europe early in September, he handed Mr. Cobb a few directions for exercise during his absence, viz.:

> Watch Roosevelt in connection with Governorship and Senatorship. Republicans may nominate him for Governor with intention of making him Senator. When he was elected Senator that would make the machine Lieutenant Governor the Governor, and give the bosses exactly what they wanted. Roosevelt could play that game beautifully and is capable of playing it.
>
> Have a strong endorsement of Woodrow Wilson as Democratic candidate for Governor. Force his nomi-

nation. Great thing for party, not only in New Jersey, but all over the country. Encourage this ex-Chief Justice [Baldwin] in Connecticut. Help the Democrats everywhere, especially in Ohio, but support insurgents like Bristow, Cummins and Dolliver warmly, and insurgent movement in States where Democrats have no chance. Be fair with Beveridge, but don't go so far in his behalf. He is a rampant jingo, although I admire his courage.

Keep to the idea that Taft will reorganize the Supreme Court, and appoint more judges than any other President since Washington. It will be a Taft court and he can make the appointments the most important work of his administration. Its decisions will have a tremendous history-making effect.

As to the editorial page in general:

It lacks persistence and continuing force. Instead of striking once it should strike a dozen times; hammer its ideas into the people's heads. It lacks the red thread of continuous policy, which should run through it like a Wagnerian motif. Just as in the coming campaign, for example, all the issues and principles, including tariff, Aldrich, Rooseveltism, extravagance, etc., can be grouped around the words "Turn on the Light." Make that the bloody angle of the campaign.

I want the *World's* Democratic sympathies plain and unmistakable, while retaining full measure of honest independence. The *World* should be more powerful than the President. He is fettered by partisanship and politics and has only a four-years term. The paper goes on year after year and is absolutely free to tell the truth and perform every service that should be performed in the public interest. You have the utmost liberty and freedom, only do not slop over and do not be inaccurate. Be fair. If Roosevelt, for example, should come out in favor of a great reform

## Last Years — 1909–1911

like tariff revision, I'd praise him for that one thing and support him on that one thing, without altering a word of criticism as to his follies. Don't be content with making the best editorial page in town, because there is no other editorial page, and when you have made the best you are taking only a small part of your opportunity. Remember — vigor, persistence and continuing force and lead, lead, lead, do not wait to follow. Make the other papers follow.

Mr. Pulitzer seldom wrote to individuals outside of the *World* office, hence personal letters are rare. He was moved to write Mayor William J. Gaynor, after he had been shot on the deck of his ship August 9, 1910, just as he was about to sail for Europe, in these appreciative terms:

MAYOR WILLIAM J. GAYNOR,
HOBOKEN, NEW JERSEY.
SAINT MARY'S HOSPITAL.

Before sailing I must congratulate you most heartily upon your narrow escape and excellent prospect of complete recovery. If I have not expressed my sentiments before it was because I was ill. The news of the dastardly attempt upon your life caused me the same sickness of heart as when the news of the assassinations of Lincoln, Garfield and McKinley reached me. I regarded it as a special calamity to the City of New York; a threatened loss to the Republic, the cause of Reform, and the great masses of democracy who yearn for a leader.

JOSEPH PULITZER.

The *Liberty* dropped down from Bar Harbor to Greenwich, Conn., and after a few days sailed directly for Europe. Mr. Pulitzer made Wiesbaden his stopping place for the early Fall, going thence to Cap

Martin, where the *Liberty* awaited him for the usual course of Winter cruising.

On the last cruise to Corsica, Col. Henry Watterson was a guest and went ashore at Ajaccio to visit the birthplace of Napoleon. He remained some time and returned to the *Liberty*, overcome with emotion and the vintage. Throwing himself upon Mr. Pulitzer's bosom he burst into tears and began to sob out a mournful monologue on the misfortunes of the Emperor:

"O, Joe," he wailed (being one of the elect few, Thomas Davidson and Charles H. Taylor the others, who could call Mr. Pulitzer "Joe"), "I've seen it all — his cradle, the room where he was born, the streets on which he walked, the school where he learned his letters, the... the... and O, Joe, it all came over me. Paris, Vienna, Victory, Waterloo! O, Joe, what does it all mean?"

Mr. Pulitzer was almost drowned under the briny flood that flowed from the Colonel's eyes and very much embarrassed by the damp endearment before the bystanders daintily disentangled Watterson and led him to his room.

Mr. Pulitzer's last strenuous editorial effort was to stimulate President Taft into calling an extra session of Congress in 1911, to deal with tariff iniquities in the interest of reduced living costs. He began the agitation in January, 1911, to forestall a delay until December following, which, with the six months' time allowed for passing legislation, meant a delay of eighteen months in fulfilling the popular mandate for a reduction. He ordered the preparation of a questionnaire to be sent by mail and telegraph "to all the foremost Democrats, Independents and Insurgents, of the land — shunning nobodies"; to all

## Last Years — 1909-1911

Governors, Senators, new members of the House, editors, college presidents, bishops, clergymen, labor leaders, boards of trade, chambers of commerce and one hundred Mayors of biggest cities, on the following lines:

> Do you favor calling a special session of the new Congress in March to reform the tariff and lower the cost of living, thus responding as promptly as possible to the popular verdict of last November elections? Or do you believe that Mr. Taft is justified in disobeying the will of the people expressed in those elections for tariff reform, lower duties and decreased cost of living, by refusing an extra session and postponing tariff reduction till the first regular session of the new Congress, which will not meet for a year; whose work could not be completed before the summer of 1912, a year and a half after election in the midst of the party passions of a Presidential campaign?

The session followed with considerable results in the way of tariff relief.

February 20th, he sent Cobb these "reminders" from aboard ship:

> 1. Knox's foreign policy — foreign, indeed —, acting as agent to Morgan, Kuhn-Loeb and other financiers.
> 2. Review crime every month unpunished, undiscovered. Main point not simply to revel in reprinting crime but in urging police, and law, ministers of justice to do their duty.
> 3. Gaynor wrong on personal taxes, even if present law bad or defective, unenforced. Remedy lies in stronger law and stricter enforcement. Taxing real estate alone is actually increasing the cost of living and adding to the weight upon the poor and middle classes, all, in fact, except the rich, who can stand it.

4. Cost of living to the bottom. Somebody should travel in Europe and see how American wives compare with European wives in economy and extravagance. It would make a very interesting series if the right woman (it ought to be a woman) could be found. The Greeley Smith girl is the only one I can think of. Incidentally, it would be a very nice trip for the person who is sent and she might do some other things besides. But actual details and comparisons, illustrations from actual observation. How the wife of the laborer, the $2 and $3 a day man, the clerk, the bookkeeper or even the average man with a competency, as well as the wealthy man's wife, compare in America and in Europe. Archbishop Ireland and James J. Hill say that American women are extravagant and that naturally has much to do with the cost of living. It is true. Everybody knows it and yet no paper seems to have the courage to admit it. It is a good feature and a nice trip for somebody who will work.

Woman suffrage. Analyze, argue against it without fear, but satirically, sardonically, perhaps humorously. Don't be afraid; idol worship has been abandoned for some thousands of years. Women worship might at least be subjected to truth. That would make a devilish good and entertaining analysis.

The *Liberty* and her owner returned for a Summer at Bar Harbor and a renewed season of coastwise cruising. He made several trips to New York and back in the yacht. Nothing of importance developed and the Summer was tranquil, though he spent much time considering the recasting of his will, with the help of William B. Hornblower.

Looking toward 1912, he kept Woodrow Wilson, then Governor of New Jersey, in his mind, writing to Mr. Heaton on July 4th:

## Last Years — 1909-1911

I would like very much anything Woodrow Wilson has said on Standard Oil, Tobacco and Union Pacific-Southern Pacific decisions. Should prefer essence to verbosity. Ditto Bryan's opinions in essence on the same subjects. Ditto reciprocity by both gentlemen. But brevity, brevity!

Clark B. Firestone, a new writer, had joined the editorial staff. Mr. Pulitzer on seeing him for the first (and last) time, found him reserved and unresponsive. He spoke rather sharply about this lack of responsiveness, but on further examination of his work, wrote in quick repentance:

August 30, 1911.

*Private.*

MY DEAR COBB:

Please expunge my foolish and unjust remark about Firestone not having read anything or whatever I said. I find, on the contrary, that he has read some very good books, although also some queer ones. Still I wish he could have read more. Nevertheless, whatever my remark, I consider it unjust and you must not mention it to him or anybody.

In great haste,
J. P.

He decided to make the *World* independent in its paper supply and in early October authorized the purchase of the De Grasse Company's mills at Pyrites, New York.

October 2d, he sent Cobb what was to be his final message. It read:

Oct. 2, 1911.

NOTES FOR MR. COBB:

I wish you would gather courage and really dismiss any possible fear in treating Taft's Waterloo speech.

## Joseph Pulitzer

It is a splendid opportunity to bring out some of the talk and thought I gave you on the yacht. Apropos of this great Trust problem and the clamor against corporations, capital and the money power. I approve *almost*[1] every word Taft uttered — every word, I repeat a second time — all that part which referred to the treatment of trusts by the Government, but most especially those parts appealing to moderation and against class prejudice and class hatred, for peace and prosperity. I wish you could take a whole day and think of nothing else, reading that part of his speech and quoting from it, analysing it; re-writing much of it thoughtfully and approvingly, but treating it as a very courageous, sensible, sound, serious and patriotic declaration. What he says about the necessity of free *competition* I would reprint verbatim, in the first place, before you dwell on the necessity of harmony and unity and the removal of buncombe and prejudice and passion created by demagogues for personal party and political interest. I wish you would make this notable article if it takes two columns, praising Taft, and not spoiling things in this article at least by harping *too* heavily upon sending Morgan or somebody to jail. Yet to avoid mistake you ought to have somewhere at the end (perhaps the very end), a reaffirmation and reassertion of our shibboleth that half a dozen men, nay, one man (say Mr. Morgan) or Swift or Armour, particularly the Beef Trust fellows, in prison for twenty-four hours, would do more to help the law and make it respected than all the monopolies dissolved and a hundred prosecutions by Mr. Wickersham may start for the galleries or partisan capital, as many people

---

[1] "*Almost*" means that I personally dislike the weight and emphasis given to stockholders, investors; my interest is in the general prosperity, the general welfare; the general good; the interest of all the people as a whole, not of the small class of investors or stockholders. I hate those illusions — that particular standpoint.

believe. It would save further prosecutions. A telegram sent you last Sunday a week ago on this point was not well treated. Read it over again. The spirit behind, and of the words themselves, was missed altogether. I repeat. The power of example. The power of example! The whole code of criminal procedure is based upon two ideas: First the power of example to *deter* repetition of crime, but not punishment. Punishment is the instrument. A means to an end. The second is intent. Read that telegram over again. There is a chance for a very neat bit of serious, ironical and sarcastic writing. That is, not that Mr. Morgan is behind the bars, but that the public welfare would be more affected by the example of his being in jail for twenty-four hours, than by one thousand speeches by the most illustrious demagogues in the land, including Wickersham, Bryan and Roosevelt. But the Morgan idea is an example, not expectation; a hypothetical illustration, not an illusion.

I object strongly to editorial "Ill-Advised Strike" (Friday), because totally unnecessary. The story is three thousand miles away, the facts unknown and partially stated, yet showing sympathy with investors, the Stock Exchange, stockholders against the "people," which I don't want.

Saturday editorial, same subject, even more unwise and unnecessary. Stop it! When the strikers do something wrong, requiring comment, it will be time enough, but so far they have done nothing. Why this extraordinary interest in a thing so far away? What is the cause to sympathize with the stockholders, etc.? Generally speaking my sympathies are with the people, and with the strikers even in a just cause. But it is not necessary to show such interest nor such treatment. We are not the Evening *Post*, nor a commercial paper.

*Joseph Pulitzer*

During the last eighteen years of his life Mr. Pulitzer visited the *World* office but three times. The first was a morning call en route from Lakewood, when he walked around the block to take in the dimensions the Pulitzer Building would assume, when property in the rear running to North William Street should be built upon, as then projected. The second followed the opening of the Subway, when he took an experimental ride in that admirable institution. The third was soon after the opening of the enlarged Pulitzer Building, in the Summer of 1908. He had been told the columns in the corridor were to be round. His hands found them square. He was much annoyed. The reason for the change was that when the old partition walls were razed, the uprights were found out of line. This was remedied by boxing them in, but they would not synchronize rounded.

As previously stated, he never visited St. Louis after 1889. For one reason, he had always associated with men much older than himself. These were gone. For another, on two visits he had narrow escapes in the several fires that destroyed the Planters, and Southern Hotels. He did not think it a very safe place for a blind man.

The *Liberty* sailed from New York for the last time under her owner's flag, October 18, 1911. Mr. Pulitzer's health had not been good, and he contemplated a leisurely cruise to the Southward. The ship's company included his youngest son, Herbert, then sixteen years old, and tutor, Miss Elizabeth Keelan; Friedrich Mann, Mr. Pulitzer's German reader; J. E. Dunningham, his personal attendant; Norman G. Thwaites, his secretary; Harold S. Pollard and James Barnes, the naval writer.

## Last Years — 1909–1911

Dr. G. W. Hosmer had retired, and the yacht's surgeon, Dr. Guthman, was new. On the second day out illness kept Mr. Pulitzer in bed, and it was decided to put into Charleston, S. C., for abler medical attendance. Here Dr. Robert Wilson was called. He diagnosed the case as one of indigestion. Veronal was administered to relieve pain. The patient did not rally and Mrs. Pulitzer was summoned from New York.

On the morning of Sunday, October 29th, Mr. Pulitzer roused a little. No one suspected that a crisis was near. The routine went on as usual. Mann was summoned in mid-forenoon for an hour of German, and found him drowsy but seemingly attentive to a chapter from the *Life of Louis XI*. It was the reader's custom to watch his auditor and when sleep seemed near, to lower his tone. Sometimes he would fail to note the near approach of slumber; then Mr. Pulitzer would command a lessening of sound, so "Leise, ganz leise, ganz leise" — "Softly, quite softly" — fell naturally from his lips. These were his last words. Mrs. Pulitzer had arrived at the moment and replaced Mann by the bedside. At 1:40 the end came, and he who all his life had ridden upon the storm, left it as gently as the dying of the wind.

## Chapter XVII

### METHODS

Instructions to Editors — Developing News — Sample Days — His points of View — Accuracy and Character insistence.

THE driving impulse, which was Mr. Pulitzer's foremost characteristic, while much in evidence, was at times quiescent, mercifully so, for the office. Surrounded by stenographers and readers he could fulminate without other limit than the hours of the day. He was insistent on close reading of his rivals and of the exchanges, a relic, perhaps, of the day when the news flood rose to lesser heights and when the "developing" of an overlooked item meant a real "beat" for the columns of the *Post-Dispatch* or the *World*. A letter written to Charles M. Lincoln, then managing editor of the *World*, is a good example of his system:

July 30, 1910.

*Memo. on How to Read the Papers.*

How to read the papers, how, in fact, to think when taking part in the news machine. Concentrate your brain upon these objectives:

1st. What is original, distinctive, dramatic, romantic, thrilling, unique, curious, quaint, humorous, odd, apt to be talked about, without shocking good taste or lowering the general tone, good tone, and above all without impairing the confidence of the people in the truth of the stories or the character of the paper for reliability and scrupulous cleanness.

*Methods*

2nd. What is the one distinctive feature, crusade, public service or big exclusive? No pa[per can] be great, in my opinion, if it depends simply up[on a] hand-to-mouth idea, news coming in anyhow. [A] big distinctive feature every day at least. One stinking feature each issue should contain, prepared before, not left to chance.

3rd. Generally speaking, always remember the difference between a paper made for the million, for the masses, and a paper made for the classes. In using the word masses I do not exclude anybody. I should make a paper that the judges of the Supreme Court of the United States would read with enjoyment, everybody, but I would not make a paper that only the judges of the Supreme Court and their class would read. I would make this paper without lowering the tone in the slightest degree.

4th. Accuracy, accuracy, accuracy. Also terseness, intelligent, not stupid, condensation. No picture or illustration unless it is first class both in idea and execution.

Please ask yourself whether in such papers as the Philadelphia *Press*, the New York *Herald* or New York *Times*, you had popular papers of large circulation or rather high-priced class papers; whether as Sunday editor a man may not have gotten out of the news current, news feeling; whether concentration upon Sunday features and pictures can be without deflection of the quick, hair trigger action of news impulses, news instincts and news features and news beats; whether after years of Sunday deflection, where a man has whole weeks, if not months, to do things in full pages for subjects it is not difficult to readjust the brain and ideas and work with the best news initiative and intuitive news judgment such as the *World* wants.

## Joseph Pulitzer

This is roughly dictated in the automobile and should be continued. When you come to serious, heavy matter, towards which you have a manifest bent, please exercise your faculty by putting upon the headlines, however roughly, merely guessing, the percentage of *World* readers apt to read things on corruption, graft, politics, legal dissertation, flabby interviews with nobodies.

His criticisms were delightfully pungent, as these samples from the constant showers that fell on Mr. Lincoln will show:

SOUTHAMPTON, Oct. 14, 1910.

*Memo. for Mr. Lincoln.*

The man who wrote the enclosed story on "Why Tennessee will Elect a Republican Governor" certainly ought to be discharged and the copy reader and the man who passed it. Who is Hooper? Banker, cow puncher, astronomer, or what? The story does not say, except that he was an orphan found in the streets. Somebody ought to be ashamed of himself.

Apropos of the sketch of Stimson in the paper of Sunday, October 2d, what is ordinary height? Would it not have been just as easy to have said "The man is five feet six, or seven, or eight?" Just ask any number of men "What is ordinary height?" and see whether you can get two men to agree.

Again, "A sizeable nose!" Who edited that copy? Who was the reporter? Who was the editor in charge? Is this the result of over twenty-seven years of teaching the importance of personal description on special occasions like this? I want to know every man who had anything to do with this description. And this is already two days after the event. I really do hope that if I have any influence, this story of a "sizeable nose" and "ordinary height" will be pasted up as a warning example.

## Methods

Again, "His hands do not hide themselves because of nervousness." Who said they did? Did anybody make that charge? All this appeared on the Sunday following the Wednesday on which Stimson was nominated. Pretty bad workmanship and an example of what I have called one hundred times bad English, loose writing, careless editorship. Style, diction, care are essential.

Apropos of the destruction by explosion of the Los Angeles *Times*, what is the matter with twenty people killed? The story is put on the thirteenth page of the Main News section. I wonder it was not put on the eighty-seventh page. Has there been any story like this for years? Did it not happen on Saturday morning? That would be four o'clock New York time. Kindly explain. It was worth first page position, more than that it was a dreadful story. The P–D printed it Saturday afternoon and a hundred times better. Whose fault? Whose judgment?

S. Y. *Liberty*, November 10, 1910.

*Memo. for Mr. Lincoln.*

When exactly did M—— go on his vacation and when did he return? Why did he stay away so long? Is his health bad or is his another case of wife or what? When I was a City Editor and ambitious, I should have considered myself deeply wounded, if sent off in a highly interesting, important campaign like the present one with special opportunities for distinction.

On October 27, page 5, the headline says "Shepard for Senate Boomed by Osborne," yet not a word that Osborne is reported as saying confirms this headline. Most important speeches terribly butchered. The political copy-reading and editing and reporting strangely bad, needing radical reform patiently, perseveringly. As a sign and sample, see reports of Shepard's and Osborne's speeches on the 26th and 27th October.

## Joseph Pulitzer

If the editors were often spanked, they were frequently praised, as this kindly word to Mr. Lincoln, following the caustic criticisms will show:

Cap Martin, Nov. 11, 1910.

I want to thank you for your notes during the summer and your effective efforts. You certainly cannot complain about my having interfered or being disagreeable. I am in a very appreciative mood, although disappointed about Curate. If you don't know the word, ask Seitz. It is either a dreadful word or a very fortunate one. You should always have it on your mind.

"Curate" was cipher for "circulation," something never out of Mr. Pulitzer's mind. Coming back to criticism, he wrote apropos of a supposition that the United States was about to annex the Republic of Panama: "Please check your far-away, speculative tendencies like Panama waste. Concentrate your brain on local, immediate features. One man at Panama was bad and two absurd. Of course, mistakes must be made by gentlemen whose blood is warm and impulsive, but don't you think if anything were contemplated about Panama's annexation, Panama is the last place in the world where you could find out about it and Washington the first? Now go ahead and let Panama go to the devil and all far-away, speculative conjectures. Concentrate on the six or seven million people in Greater New York and its easily accessible region. Forgive me. Hope you are well and happy. Ditto Madam and the babies."

Of the Canal itself he wrote: "It is a great work — the greatest of the century in construction and we cannot afford (we less than anybody else) to be regarded as out of sympathy or having aversion or antipathy to the work itself. I am enthusiastic. It

## Methods

is a great thing for the Republic and the Nation, and the charge that it will cost $500,000,000, instead of $375,000,000 is, so far, without foundation."

Here follows a further lesson in journalism:

VILLA CYNTHIA,<br>Dec. 24, 1910.

DEAR LINCOLN:

The most mysterious defect, if not disgrace, of the news columns is the wretched reporting of any public dinners or banquets or meetings or speeches. This mystery I beg you to explain. It is not new. It was very bad last year, but it is just as bad today. I dare not read the paper. If any big meeting takes place, I am sure to be made sick by reading of it. Please take this more seriously than former rapid criticism to others. Go over the reports of campaign meetings, etc., and see yourself how bad these reports are, compared with other papers, and still worse, compared with what common sense alone would require, leaving my own wishes out of the question.

Now the first thing a man wants to know in reading a report of a banquet, like that of the Democratic Merchants Association, where Dix spoke and Murphy and Cady Herrick and Huppuch and Parker, in fact the whole gang of the Democratic notables, the first thing a man wants to know is: "Who were there?" I have expressed this at least one hundred times and yet — look at that report and explain how it is there are so few speakers named. Yet there were five hundred politicians present — everybody in fact. There was Herrick sitting next to Murphy. A little picture! It is a disgrace, but not your fault, perhaps. But it is time for you to pay attention to this, if you want me to read my own paper. I could give you fifty other instances within an hour or two. If a man makes a speech, why not describe him? What he looks like? A little description would give life and color.

## Joseph Pulitzer

I have a frightful headache while dictating this and will not revise it, but wish you would go over the papers of October and November. And this is not the only instance. There have been worse mistakes and stupidities than this. But this happens to be the last paper I have read and it has been the last straw to break the poor blind camel's back.

P. S. Apropos of description, instruct the reporter to always mention the weight of his hero, the color of his eyes and hair, the exact shape of his head and forehead, etc.

To palliate this came on Christmas Day: "Lincoln, New York. Sincere wishes for a pleasant Christmas, Happy New Year, a better paper and much better reporting."

He never ceased to urge exact personal description. Writing later to Lincoln he said: "Please impress on the men who write our interviews with prominent men the importance of giving a striking, vivid pen sketch of the subject; also a vivid picture of his domestic environment, his wife, his children, his animal pets, etc. Those are the things that will bring him more clearly home to the average reader than would his most imposing thoughts, purposes, or statements. Incidentally, this element of vivid description is badly neglected on the paper, and should be specially inculcated and encouraged in many other kinds of stories besides interviews."

When the figures of the 1910 census came drifting along he was anxious to have published a striking article on America's growth, on which he wrote:

It is my intention to submit this most romantic and unparalleled of stories of the change in America, the continuing growth of power, wealth, as well as popu-

## Methods

lation to the foremost statesmen, thinkers and publicists and especially statisticians of Europe for their opinions, reflections and ideas. I don't want to ask too plainly what they think of the danger of European invasion, but I think the simple question, "What do they think of this amazing growth continuing, and the future growth of America"? should bring out a number of very remarkable views, comments, opinions, statements, speculations, peculiarly readable to Americans.

P. S. The foregoing is in very bad form, as I dictated it hurriedly and am too lazy to revise. I have struck. I will not revise the D — d thing. Better do it for me.

When the basic article and question were in form Mr. Cobb was instructed to write "A polite circular letter, very carefully compressed, composed, a literary masterpiece, introducing the question of the census and send it not only to statesmen and Prime Ministers, Secretaries of War and of the Navy, statisticians and publicists, editors of all serious magazines and periodicals and really great newspapers, authors and thinkers, but also to all royalties — yes, to the crowned heads, if your letter puts the request upon the basis of the cordial good wishes of America and an expression of good will. Try to send this letter to at least 100 notables, including college presidents, deans of the universities, a few dozen Bishops, and Cardinals. Include in your list the foremost generals and commanders in chief in England, Germany and France: Lord Roberts, Kitchener, Wolseley, perhaps Gaedke."

Writing again suggestively to Mr. Lincoln on February 2, 1911, he said:

> Apropos of enclosed clipping from the London *Times* showing that there were 185 homicides in New York

during 1910, this would make a good magazine feature if properly worked up. Pick out the most interesting cases. What were these homicides? Who committed them? What was the motive? Give a table of motives, of social rank, of age, of nationality, etc. But give the facts more reliably, more strikingly than would the magazines. This is one of those big stories that the monthly magazines would print. But don't print it from the standpoint of mere sensationalism, but rather from the moral point of view. It should be a thoughtful article with a great moral to it. Compare the figure with Paris, and with London, and with other great European cities. Allude also to the administration of justice and the methods of dealing with murder cases in the different countries, with statistics of indictments, convictions, executions and failure to punish or to solve murder mysteries.

To stimulate better matter in the Sunday paper, on February 3, 1911, he authorized the spending of

say $250 per article, or even $500, if worth it. Nor is it necessary that a $250 or $500 article should require a whole page. That is secondary. A subject might be most striking and yet fill but one column. . . . Try hard to get General Sickles to write reminiscences for the *World*. It ought to make a splendid series with pictures. Of course, you know perfectly well what a life he has led. Murdered Key. He was a Tammany man half a century ago. It would make a real history of Tammany, of the war, of Washington for the past sixty years.

Apropos of that editorial section, which ought to contain all these big stories, try old Bigelow (John). Of course he would be much more dull, and he has already written his reminiscences, but interviewed by a very clever writer, a lot of pictures and the charm of

## Methods

the first person singular conversational talk would make a good series. . . . New York of fifty, sixty, or even seventy years ago in the case of Bigelow would make a good series, quaint, curious, odd. What a change! What a wonder! The thought grows on me. Make up a list of a dozen old people conspicuous in name, of position, intelligent, with memory. Include Frank Work, father of Mrs. Burke-Roche, who is now ninety-two years old. Take a year for all these if necessary. Don't spoil it by dashing it off like the usual slap-dash article.

Here is another thing you might try and that is a Jules Verne, or semi-Jules Verne actual description of the water of the river, East, West and North, under which people travel. (The New Hudson and subway tunnels were in his mind.) What does the water look like? What does it contain? Are there any fish? What is the condition of the soil of the bed of the river? Anything developing this most wonderful thought and appealing to the importance of everybody; but one fact should be absolute and that is the number of people going in all the tunnels under water every single day and every single night. These should be official figures. Was there ever anything more imaginative?

He had no secret service and the editor was always told who his critic was. H. W. Seymour had written in a report that the paper was not well condensed and there was "an almost complete absence of bright and clever writing." To this Mr. Pulitzer rose in a letter to Mr. Lincoln: "I need hardly tell you that I think the paper is getting worse in workmanship, lack of striking ideas, and overloaded with politics, verbose, conjecture, speculative and in crying need of intelligent condensation. This for the 447th time.

If you took all the serious business, class material, whether politics or business, or otherwise, and condensed it one half, yes one half, you would still have employed much more than enough — much more. Try it. I hope you will not ascribe all this to Mr. Seymour's extract, as it has been on my mind, long, long ago, and I beg of you not to let Seymour know of your receiving this criticism. That would choke him off forever."

"I think", he wrote, on March 8, 1911, "it would be a good idea, an interesting feature, to give a full list of all the partners of J. P. Morgan & Co., with a little personal description of each, a little condensed history of their rise to prominence; their education, college, antecedents, how they grew; how the departments are run; the system; the machine, also what young Jack Morgan does, the specific work of each partner — their age; individual wealth of each. But no exaggeration, for God's sake. There is hardly a statement about any man's wealth that is not exaggerated and every reporter ought to be knocked on the head and told that he does not improve his work or do the office any good by exaggeration.

"And apropos of this, the story of the house of Morgan & Co. would be one of those magazine stories that McClure would print. To it might be added a chapter on the Philadelphia branch of the firm, the Morgan Drexels of which Stotesbury is the head. Who are the partners there? Are there any Drexels still in the firm? Also, the London house and the partners there. All this came to me apropos of the story about Davidson in the Sunday *World* of the 18th December. Now an interesting feature of this story would be to go back about thirty years, since

## Methods

J. P. Morgan's father died, and show how many members of the firm have retired and how constantly they have been changed. There were Bacon, Fabbri and now Perkins. How much trouble Morgan has to find partners. There is Charles Steele in New York. There was Burns who died in London. Morgan has had bad luck in his partners either dying or making a fortune so quickly that they retire. He is always hunting for partners. If you only take a little time and care, you could make a good magazine story, but don't slap-dash, slam-wang it. I am not proud of it, but I have taken trouble to suggest it as a sign or sample of the stories that the magazines would print without any hesitation. It would make just the kind of story people are interested in, that is, J. P. Morgan & Co. as a government, a machine, an organization, just like Tammany is a machine — Morgan the boss, but with all these partners. Of course, give the pictures of all the partners in a group.

"There was a story the other day of a woman drawing a pension for four husbands who were veterans of the Revolutionary war. It sounds incredible, but is just possible. But verify it. What evidence is there that they were veterans, that they were born at such and such a place, at such and such a time?"

The outbreak of the Boer war and the flood of news events made him particularly active during the latter part of 1899 and early in 1900. Determined to get close to the workers he devised a plan of sending a letter in form, which was to be passed around to each person involved, to be signed and kept on file, so that he could later check up and see how much attention was paid to his wishes. October 30, 1899, pleased with the progress of the *Evening World,* he wrote from Bar Harbor where he lingered late:

> Mr. Pulitzer greatly appreciating the energy and industry of the "good fellows" on the Evening *World* requests that Mr. Coates, Mr. Duneka and Mr. Chapin arrange to take Saturdays off in series: that is to say that each Saturday some one of them shall take the full day off. This to continue until further notice, or in the event of some emegency which will require a full house.
>
> Have special arrangement made instantly but economically with General Miles to review twice a week situation in Transvaal from military standpoint, explaining all tactical strategic points, movements, unintelligible to the lay mind, the significance of things which even when they appear are spoilt by haste, superficiality, stupidity of reports and correspondents. That is Miles to be Editor of our War News. Let Clarke give Miles my personal compliments, but if he declines try get Merritt or other first class military name.

A very brilliant young lady, Lavinia Hart, had an interview with Croker in the paper on the date noted. It roused Mr. Pulitzer's ire. Here is his hot comment:

> Lavinia Hart very clever, but if her Croker story had been a thousand times as good I should resent it. My wishes are to be respected just as Mr. Bennett's are on the *Herald* or Mr. Dana's are on the *Sun.* I will not put up with any disregard.
>
> Apropos of the Transvaal War and the real causes, not the pretext, a few stories can be written attracting great attention and involving real universal, popular interest, and giving knowledge and information, all suggested by the two words "Kaffir Shares."
>
> I do not myself know what this phrase means, but I suppose it means a great story as to what the Diamond

## Methods

mines really are, their origin, history, development, value, and that romance connected with the De Beers mines and the gold mines now producing one-third of the total output of gold in the world.

I am sure there are half a dozen extremely interesting stories, real romances, not fakes, romances based on facts that would not have been believed twenty or thirty years ago.

The De Beers Consolidated Diamond Mine, the gold mines, the British South African Company — who are connected with these, who have made their future out of them, who has become the Monte Cristos?

I ask again whether the report that Carnegie was selling out and receiving one hundred millions from a company as reported last Spring has been carried out. If this has been done, it would make a good story; and if the report can be shown to be untrue, it would also be a good story.

Carnegie might be got again as he has not been heard of for some time; not by cable but by mail, to review the Filipino situation or the industrial situation or anything.

Here follow some further reflections:

The sporting should be grouped together most effectively, contiguously, compactly. The same idea mentioned above with respect to other matters of having experts on each branch should be systematized for all sports. In the case of each of the 40 different branches, whether it be fishing or golf or cycling or rowing, the foremost expert should regularly contribute to the World and one ought to be in every Sunday issue.

Offer three Xmas prizes to the copy readers who will do the best work in intelligent condensation. I don't say the most condensation, I don't say the best condensation, but I say the most *intelligent* condensation. It can be carried too far, can be done to death, killing the very essence of the story.

Offer four more prizes to the best reporters, who do the best writing as to good English:

   *a.* style as to clear statement of facts.
   *b.* style as to humor.
   *c.* style as to picturesque description, i.e., conveying an actual picture.
   *d.* best description (pen sketch) of a face, a figure, character, minute and analytical — per portrait painter.

Offer three Xmas prizes for the best headlines, best not in sensationalism, but in graphic description and summary, saying much in a nutshell, attracting attention without repelling belief and good taste.

Organize ahead, think ahead of getting signed statements of editors all over the United States, also editors of New York papers, the big papers, men with names like Whitelaw Reid, Paul Dana, Horace White, Laffan, Miller of the Times, Henry Loomis Nelson of Harper's Weekly, and editors of the foremost influential religious press, the idea being that the Forum above all should deserve its name, be a real editorial Forum not merely of the New York *World* but of the thought, mind and brains of the whole country.

Try to arrange a topic which should be not only of the widest possible general interest, but most timely: e.g., Get up at the very first a symposium on the question "Do you favor a national divorce law? If not, why not? If yes, why yes? Please state your reasons succinctly."

Above all, try to have one — and as a rule not more than one although no rule is inflexible — but one very strong religious name every Sunday, practically modelled on the Hepworth idea in the *Herald,* but modify-

## Methods

ing, improving and variegating it and not having the same pen, same style, same tone, but something fresh and new from some great religious teacher every Sunday. Organize this ahead by making arrangements with say at least a dozen of the best writers.

Go over the files of the A.P., take some clippings showing with what care and unanimity the A.P. either did not send out anything about our striking Transvaal cables or if they did grudgingly send a few lines, they ignored the *World*, which is tantamount to stealing.

State the facts without epithets or adjectives in a very clear letter to Melville Stone. Ask whether it is fair and whether he will not as a matter of justice communicate with his agent in New York about honest dealing, sharply protesting in my name, but letting the facts speak chiefly.

Somebody ought to make a regular investigation and report upon what appears to be systematic and intentional suppression of the *World*, by the Associated Press, not only in New York, but in Washington and Boston. The name of the *World* has not appeared in the Bangor or Boston papers in anything sent out by the A.P. though at least twenty times things have been taken from the *World*. This was particularly noticeable in the splendid cable despatches that we received from the Transvaal and the Petition, all of which were mentioned with the name of the *World* carefully eliminated.

The phrase "a page" is not to be taken literally. It is rather a figurative expression for a good story. If put in one column, I would prefer it, but if the meat, marrow and substance should run to over a page, I would not hesitate to give it that much. The office needs the greatest possible warning and strongest injunction against the tendency to give up a whole page to any one thing.

## Joseph Pulitzer

Mr. William H. Merrill must write an editorial, a tribute to Godkin's ability, all the more so because the man never failed in fifteen years to abuse the *World*, and no doubt hated me. I think the profession has lost the ablest mind since the death of Greeley. It is a great loss to the independent thought of the press.

A compliment on the picture of the Custom House. The very thing I had on my pad.

I recall a statement that five per cent of the entire population of Kansas City is suing for divorce. A splendid subject. It should be *deepened* dramatically, till covered and exhausted. Advocate national divorce law.

Apropos of the point I sent down yesterday on Gorki, use the letter in today's paper by Gaylord Wilshire, as a sort of text or peg to hang it on and refer to the different standards in different countries in Europe. Also George Eliot, living with Lewes as husband and wife without being married. George Sand's living with everybody. Byron living not with his wife but Countess Guiccioli, and with everybody else's wife and so many other genii. Goethe has housekeepers; Voltaire the Marquise du Chatelet.

Even Gambetta, the greatest political genius produced in France since Talleyrand and Thiers, although unfortunately his early death deprived him of his reputation — lived with a mistress.

The article could be made very interesting by these historical illustrations, but don't be cocksure, rather pick up the thoughts and suggest them rather than clubbing it into the heads of the readers. Suggest rather than make bold assertions.

Among the clippings on the editorial page are five from the Philadelphia *Bulletin*. This is rather excessive. I should have left at least two of them out, unless the *Bulletin* is paying heavy advertising rates.

## *Methods*

December 5th:

I think both the bigamy story on Saturday (outside column, first page) and the Beecher story, same place Monday may be good, but the four column head bad anyhow. It distinctly tends to lower the tone of the paper and to revive the idea of sensationalism, the giving of the foremost place and extraordinary headlines to what is, after all, a salacious story and not an important or serious matter.

I think it tends towards the other extreme — sensationalism — and although the wisdom of placing such stories in the most important column is a question, there is no question about the four column headline being *bad*.

For Sunday, December 31st, I want Fontaine, or somebody, to write a perfectly accurate, honest, review of the chief incidents in Wall Street during the year. Give concrete examples of gain or loss. Who made money, who lost it. There is more than a week to do this in accurately, digging out facts to illustrate the vague nebulosity of vast gains and losses by giving *concrete examples and persons*. Detail and describe as many cases as can be found. It is just as interesting to know who lost, as who won, and particularly the losses of small speculators on margins in the bucket shops.

Who wrote that asinine story on page 3 in Friday's *World* Dec. 6 about the Hungarian banquet? Why allow a reporter to be used by a faction?

It so happens that Baron Hengelmuller is a friend of mine and stays in my house. Even if he were not you ought not allow somebody to make use of the paper in this way. I want you to read this story. Is this a fair report or chronicle without bias or prejudice? Is it a real mirror of events?

Someone should see Baron Hengelmuller and present

the apology of the paper for the blunder and give the Baron the chance to set it right and correct the matter. Let him tell the Baron that Mr. Pulitzer never read the story until today.

The project for buying the Danish West Indies which cropped up from time to time, and was eventually carried out twenty years later, came to life at the beginning of 1900. Mr. Pulitzer thus viewed it on January 5th of that year:

> Granted the erroneous premise, I think the purchase of St. Thomas perfectly logical and on that basis should approve of it. It would be interesting to carry this thought out to the logical extreme and take up all the West Indies. Review all other foreign possessions in the West Indies. A beautiful vista anyhow, and interesting as a bit of imagination.

A sample criticism of a news feature came from him to the Managing Editor on the same day:

> The story "How Standard Oil manages a Bank" is exaggerated, sensational and objectionable because inaccurate in one single point, although excellent otherwise. The capital is assumed to be ONE MILLION when it has been decided to raise it to TEN MILLION. How much more effective it would have been to have given the truth; that the capital stock is really TEN MILLION and raised to that sum only NOW just because of such enormous dividends. Accuracy! Accuracy!! Accuracy!!! More effective.

## Chapter XVIII

### BENEFACTIONS

*The School of Journalism at Columbia University — Scholarships — Gifts to Barnard College — Bequests to Art, Music, the Drama and Literature — The Plaza Fountain.*

IN FOUNDING the School of Journalism at Columbia University, Mr. Pulitzer was moved by an impulse to educate newspaper writers and editors up to a standard of ideals. He had long had the project in mind. In the Winter of 1903, journeying to Jekyl Island, he took me along as far as Washington. As the train left Jersey City, Dr. G. W. Hosmer, chief secretary, handed me the outline of the scheme to read over and be prepared for an opinion when called upon. I was isolated in a stateroom and read the document. Before it was well digested, Mr. Pulitzer appeared, having groped his way down the car corridor. Without asking for my view, he observed by way of opening: "You don't think much of it."

"I do not," I said.

"Well, what shall I do?" he asked. "I want to do something."

"Endow the *World*," I replied. "Make it foolproof."

"I am going to do something for it," he replied, "in giving it a new building."

There was some further talk, all quite inconclusive. The plan underwent much modification. The authorities at Columbia were inclined to look rather doubtfully upon the proposition. Mr. Pulitzer himself had some fears as to how the suggestion would be received, coming as it did from the head and front of journalistic aggressiveness. He expected severe criticism and was quite overwhelmed at the cordial greeting that met the announcement. Of course, there were carpers. These he answered in the *North American Review* for May, 1904, replying, as he remarked introductorily, to "criticisms and misgivings, many honest, some shallow, some based on misunderstandings, but the most representing only prejudice and ignorance." He added: "If my comment . . . shall seem to be diffuse and perhaps repetitious, my apology is that — alas! I am compelled to write by voice, not pen, and to revise proofs by ear, not eye — a somewhat difficult task."

"Some of my critics," he continued, "have called my scheme 'visionary.' If it be so I can at least plead that it is a vision I have cherished long, thought upon deeply and followed persistently. Twelve years ago I submitted the idea to President Low of Columbia, but it was not accepted by the trustees. I have ever since continued to perfect and organize the scheme in my mind, and now it is adopted. In examining the criticisms and misgivings I have been anxious only to find the truth. I admit that the difficulties are many, but after weighing them all impartially I am more firmly convinced than ever of the ultimate success of the idea. Before the century closes schools of journalism will be generally accepted as a feature of specialized higher education, like schools of law or of medicine."

This prophecy came quite true. Few colleges

*Benefactions*

of consequence in America are now without their departments of journalism.*

The first contention he met was that a newspaper man must be born; he could not be made. This he dismissed with scorn. "Perhaps," he said, "the critics can name some great editor, born full-winged like Mercury, the messenger of the gods? I know none. The only position that occurs to me which a man in our Republic can successfully fill by the simple fact of birth, is that of an idiot. Is there any other position for which a man does not demand and receive training — training at home, training in schools and colleges, training by master craftsmen, or training

* Journalism is now taught in special schools or in special classes at the following institutions:

*At State Universities* — Arkansas, California, Colorado, Florida, Illinois, Indiana, Iowa, Kansas, Kentucky, Louisiana, Michigan, Minnesota, Missouri, Maine, Montana, Nebraska, North Carolina, Ohio, Oklahoma, Oregon, South Carolina, South Dakota, Texas, Utah, Virginia, Washington, West Virginia, Wisconsin.

*At State Colleges and Schools* — Colorado Agricultural College, Delaware College, Fort Hays (Kansas) Normal School, Georgia Technical School of Commerce, Indiana State Normal School, Iowa State College, Kansas State Agricultural College, Kansas State Normal School, Massachusetts Agricultural College, Missouri State Normal College, Nebraska State Normal School, North Dakota Agricultural College, Oklahoma Agricultural and Mechanical College, Pennsylvania State College, Purdue University, South Dakota State College, Wisconsin State Normal School.

*At Endowed Colleges and Universities* — Austin College, Beaver College, Beloit College, Billings Polytechnic Institute, Boston University, Bucknell College, Buena Vista College, Carleton College, Colby College, College of Emporia, Columbia University, De Pauw University, Emmanuel Missionary College, Goucher College, Howard College, Kansas City Polytechnic Institute, Knox College, Lawrence College, Lehigh University, Leland Stanford Junior University, Marietta College, Marquette University, McKendree College, Miami University, Morningside College, Mount Union College, Municipal University of Akron, New York University, Pomona College, Ripon College, St. Xavier College, Toledo University, Trinity College, Tulane University, University of Chicago, University of Denver, University of Notre Dame, University of Pittsburgh, University of Southern California, Vassar College, Western Reserve University.

through bitter experience — through the burns that make the child dread the fire, through blunders costly to the aspirant? . . . I seem to remember that Lincoln, whose academy was a borrowed book read by the light of a pine knot on the hearth, studied Euclid in Congress when near forty. But would it not have been better if the work had been done at fourteen? . . . Shakespeare's best play, Hamlet, was not his first, but his nineteenth, written after growth and maturity, after hard work, the experience, the exercise of faculties and the accumulation of knowledge gained by writing eighteen plays. As Shakespeare was a 'born' genius, why did he not write Hamlet first?"

He argued further that the brain, like Sandow's muscles, had to be developed by hard work, though admitting that in every field natural aptitude was the key to success. "When the experiment was tried of turning Whistler into a disciplined soldier," he went on in illustrating his assertion, "even West Point had to lay down its arms. Your sawmill may have all modern improvements, but it will not make a pine board out of a basswood log. No college can create a good lawyer without a legal mind to work on, nor make a successful doctor of a young man whom nature designed to sell tape. Talleyrand took holy orders, but they did not turn him into a holy man."

Sometimes in the course of his contention Mr. Pulitzer almost proved the other fellow's point, a defect that comes from breadth of view when matched in argument. Using a military analogy he went on: "The brilliant general is simply a man who has learned to apply skilfully the natural laws of force, and has

## Benefactions

the nerve to act on his knowledge. Hannibal, the greatest of all in my opinion, is called a typical example of native military genius. But can we forget that he was the son and pupil of Hamilcar, the ablest soldier of his generation, born in the camp, never outside of military atmosphere, sworn in earliest boyhood to war and hatred of Rome and endowed by his father with all the military knowledge that the experience of antiquity could give. He was educated. In his father he had a military college to himself. Can we think of Napoleon without remembering that he had the best military education of his time at Brienne, and that he was always an eager student of the great campaigns of history? Frederick the Great lost his head in his first battle. It took him years to learn his trade and finally to surpass his instructors. There is not a cadet at any military school who is not expected as a necessary part of his professional preparation to study every important battle on record — to learn how it was fought, what mistakes were committed on each side and how it was won?

"Every issue of a newspaper represents a battle — a battle for excellence. When the editor reads it and compares it with its rivals he knows that he has scored a victory or suffered a defeat. Might not a study of the most notable of these battles of the press be as useful to the student of journalism as is the study of military battles to the student of war?"

Of the need of "born" news instinct, he observed: "Certainly. But however great a gift, if news instinct as born were turned loose in any newspaper office in New York without the control of sound judgment bred by considerable experience and training, the results would be much more pleasing to the lawyer than to the editor. One of the chief difficulties of journalism is to keep the news instinct from running rampant over the restraints of accuracy and conscience."

At an historic moment in the career of the *World* he had caused great placards reading

> ACCURACY
> TERSENESS
> ACCURACY

to be posted in its editorial rooms; he was forever insisting on these points. Compelled to be diffuse in expressing himself, as noted, he wished no such excuse for others. As he said in continuing his homily: "If a 'nose for news' is born in the cradle, does not the instinct, like other great qualities, need development by teaching, by training, by practical object lessons illustrating the good and the bad, the Right, the Wrong, the popular and the unpopular, the things that succeed and the things that do not — not the things only that make circulation for to-day, but the things that make character and influence public confidence?"

This last was a perpetual study which carried insistence to all his executives. "Why did the circulation go up?" he once asked me during an unexplained rise in the number of readers. I did not know. "Find out," he ordered. "It is just as important to know why circulation goes up as why it goes down." This also applied to fluctuations in advertising. On one occasion during the Russo-Japan War the "Want" advertising moved upward.

## Benefactions

"Why?" he asked. I said I did not know unless it was due to "The virtue of the Emperor," a phrase that had come from Japan anent the cause of victories.

"What virtue?" he asked sharply. "What Emperor?"

The joke was lost. To his mind the question was, as indeed it needed to be, one of basic importance. Turning again to his critics he observed:

> They object that moral courage cannot be taught. Very true. I admit that it is the hardest thing in the world to teach. But may we not be encouraged by the reflection that physical courage is taught? It is not to be supposed that every young man who enters West Point or Annapolis, Brienne, St. Cyr or Sandhurst is a born hero. Yet the student at any of these schools is so drilled, hammered and braced in the direction of courage that by the time he graduates it is morally certain that when he takes his men under fire for the first time he will not flinch. Pride and the spirit of emulation can make masses of men do what even a hero would not venture to do alone. Is it likely that Napoleon himself would have charged in solitary grandeur across the bridge at Lodi if there had been no one to see him do it? Or would Pickett's brigade at Gettysburg have gone forward to destruction if every man in it had not been lifted out of himself by the feeling that he and his comrades were all doing a heroic thing together — a thing in which he simply could not do less than the rest?
> 
> If such things can be done for physical courage, why not for moral courage? If the mind can be taught to expose the body fearlessly to wounds and death, cannot the soul be taught to cling to its convictions against temptation, prejudice, obloquy and persecution? Moral courage is developed by experience and by teaching.

## Joseph Pulitzer

Every successful exercise of it makes the next easier. The editor is often confronted by an apparent dilemma — either to yield to a popular passion that he feels to be wrong or to risk the consequences of unpopularity. Adherence to convictions can and should be taught by precept and example as not only high principle but sound policy. Might not a hundred concrete examples of inflexible devotion to the right serve as a moral tonic to the student?

Answering the point that much that it was proposed to teach in his school was already taught in colleges, he agreed. But, he thought, they were overtaught for the purpose he had in mind. Things in professions were specialized, even in newspapers. "The object of the College of Journalism," he commented, "will be to dig through this general scheme intended to cover every possible career of work in life, every profession, to select and concentrate only upon the things the journalist wants and not to waste time upon things he does not want."

Yet he had a broad perspective: "Historians like McMaster, (Woodrow) Wilson and Rhodes; college presidents like Eliot, Hadley and Angell; judges like Fuller, Brewer and Gray — could help the work with lectures and suggestions. It is nothing new for a justice of the Supreme Court to lecture in college. Justice Story did it at Harvard, Justice Field did it at the University of California, Justices Harlan and Brewer do it now at the Columbian University at Washington. Even ex-Presidents have not thought such work belittling. Harrison lectured at Stanford and Cleveland at Princeton."

He remarked in conclusion: "Our Republic and its press will rise or fall together. An able, disinterested, public-spirited press, with trained intelligence to know the right and courage to do it, can preserve that public virtue without which popular government is a sham and a mockery. A cynical, mercenary, demagogic, corrupt press will produce in time a people as base as itself. The power to mould the future of the Republic will be in the hands of the journalists of future generations. This is why I urge my colleagues to aid this important experiment. Upon their generous aid and co-operation the ultimate success of the project must depend."

That he had made no provision for a course in business training for newspaper men caused some comment. Mr. Pulitzer answered this in his *North American Review* article, saying:

> That a newspaper, however great as a public institution and a public teacher, must also be a business is not to be denied, but there is nothing exceptional in this. Elements of business, of economy, of income and outgo, are in the government of the city, the State, the nation, in art, in every school, in every college, in every university, indeed, in every church. But a bishop, even though he receives pay for his work, is not regarded as a business man; nor is a great artist, though he charge the highest possible price for his paintings and die as rich as Meissonier or Rubens. Many distinguished lawyers, such as Mr. Tilden — one of the greatest — were shrewd business men, able probably to outwit the majority of publishers, yet they were rightly considered members of an intellectual profession.
>
> George Washington had extraordinary business capacity. By intelligent economy, method, sound judgment and the closest attention to details he accumulated the greatest American fortune of his time. Yet

## Joseph Pulitzer

when he was called to serve the country in the field he did it without a salary. At Mount Vernon he was a business man; in history he is a soldier, a statesman and the father of his country.

To sum up, the banker or broker, the baker or the candlestick maker is in business — in trade. But the artist, the statesman, the thinker, the writer — all who are in touch with the public taste and mind, whose thoughts reach beyond their own livelihood to some public interest — are in professions.

He truly believed that a properly edited, high-principled paper needed little business attention beyond bookkeeping. Speaking of his own early success he once said: "I had no business manager. I was my own business manager. I had no circulation department." It need not be inferred from this and the previous quotations that he was negligent of business; far from it, but he knew brains, not "business management," made the paper. In later years he was at times relentless in prodding the business office as this note, dated January 4, 1909, shows:

> Apropos of advertising. It is never too late. I want Mr. Seitz to understand that he has got to hustle for more advertising. He thinks we have it all, but we have not. We want special enterprise, more steam, new energy. Now, I want him to spend $10,000 at least, but most judiciously and carefully, not wastefully, in booming the paper and our advertising record: That we have the biggest circulation in the city of New York and are the biggest advertising medium.

It will be seen that Mr. Pulitzer desired to inculcate Knowledge, Judgment and Character through the operations of his school. The proposition was submitted to President Nicholas Murray Butler of

SCHOOL OF JOURNALISM

*Benefactions*

Columbia University, and to Dr. Charles W. Eliot, President of Harvard College, in the Spring of 1903, but without revealing the identity of the principal, Dr. G. W. Hosmer, Mr. Pulitzer's chief secretary, acting as intermediary. President Butler had been sounded in the previous September. He laid it before the Columbia University Committee on Education, March 27, 1903, and presented it to the trustees on April 6th. Mr. Pulitzer had previously caused Dr. Hosmer to write a cogent pamphlet setting forth the needs of such a school, for the information of doubters. Armed with this the doctor made a trip to Cambridge to present it in person to Dr. Eliot, but found him absent. He left the pamphlet and his address. Dr. Eliot responded warily.

Meanwhile the trustees of Columbia concluded to accept the responsibility. On June 23, 1903, Mr. Bradford Merrill, then Financial Manager of the *World*, was instructed to deliver to their hands a formal agreement, dated back to April 10th, in long distance celebration of Mr. Pulitzer's fifty-sixth birthday. It read:

> THIS AGREEMENT, made the tenth day of April, 1903, between JOSEPH PULITZER, of the City of New York, hereinafter referred to as "the Donor," party of the first part, and THE TRUSTEES OF COLUMBIA COLLEGE IN THE CITY OF NEW YORK, hereinafter referred to as "Columbia University," or "The University," party of the second part:
>
> WHEREAS, the Donor desires to establish and endow a School of Journalism in Columbia University, and at the time of the execution of these presents has given two hundred thousand dollars, and has agreed and by these presents doth agree to give to the Uni-

## Joseph Pulitzer

versity upon or before June 1, 1904, the sum of eight hundred thousand dollars, to be used as hereinafter provided; and upon the following conditions agrees also to give the additional sum of one million ($1,000,000) dollars on or before the end of the third year of the actual operation of the School of Journalism:

1. That the Donor shall be satisfied that for three years the School has been and then is in successful operation.

2. That one-half of the income of this second million shall be applied to prizes or scholarships for the encouragement of public service, public morals, American Literature, and the advancement of education, to be awarded in accordance with a plan to be agreed upon by the Donor and the University on or before the expiration of such three years.

3. That so much of both the first million and the second million dollars as the University shall actually receive under this agreement shall be deemed to be in ademption and diminution of any legacy or devise that the Donor may have given to the University for any of the purposes named herein by a Will executed prior to this agreement:

AND WHEREAS, the University is to provide a suitable site upon land owned or to be acquired by the University for a building for the accommodation of a School of Journalism, and out of the moneys received under this agreement is to undertake to erect and maintain thereon the said building and also to maintain and conduct the said School of Journalism, and after receiving the second million to make the said awards:

Now, THIS AGREEMENT WITNESSETH, that, in consideration of the premises and of the performance of the agreements herein contained, the University and the Donor mutually have agreed and by these presents do agree, as follows:

## Benefactions

*First:* The University will apply Five Hundred Thousand (500,000) Dollars of the said first sum of One Million Dollars to the erection upon the land now owned, or hereafter to be acquired, at Morningside Heights, of a building suitable for the accommodation of a School of Journalism, including provisions for heating, lighting and ventilating, and equipment, with all the mechanical and technical apparatus and plant for the demonstration of the physical and mechanical part of the instruction. This building shall bear the name of the Donor after his death, and shall have erected within it a tablet inscribed to the "Memory of My Daughter Lucille."

*Second:* The University will hold the residue of said sum of one million dollars and also the additional sum of one million dollars when received as an Endowment Fund, to be known as the "JOSEPH PULITZER FUND," and will use the income thereof (except the income from one-half of the second million as before stated) for all current expenses, to the care and maintenance of the building, to the payment of the salaries of such officers as may be required to give instruction in the technical and other subjects essential to the training of a journalist, and to the payment of the matriculation fees of students taking a course in journalism.

*Third:* The University will establish a School of Journalism, which will furnish technical and professional instruction in journalism, and will maintain the school in such a liberal spirit as to make its advantages available to the largest number of students consistent with the highest degree of educational efficiency. The plan of organization and course of study in the School shall be prescribed by the University, but in the making of this plan the University shall be influenced by the advice and conclusions of an Advisory Board, composed of the foremost journalists and editors possessing expert knowledge on the subject. The members of the Board shall be appointed by the University upon the nomination of the Donor, excepting the President of the University who shall be ex-officio a member, and the Board shall have a continuing advisory relation to the School for a period of not less than twenty years. The course and plan so adopted may be modified from time to time by the University as experience and changing conditions may render necessary or desirable as tending to increase the usefulness of the School.

*Fourth:* Candidates for admission to the course in journalism shall be admitted after an examination and inquiry into their general intelligence, moral character, and fitness for the work of the course, and without any requirement of previous collegiate courses, and shall receive an appropriate academic attestation in the form of a certificate or diploma upon satisfactorily passing their final examinations in the Course in Journalism.

Mr. Merrill received at the same time a lengthy communication from Mr. Pulitzer under Dr. Hosmer's hand, filled with the details of his desire, reading:

June 23, 1903.

DEAR MR. MERRILL:

Mr. Pulitzer wishes you to attend to some details touching the delivery to the authorities of Columbia University of certain documents sent herewith. Please consider that what is written here is mainly memoranda, as Mr. Pulitzer has been unable to revise it. He believes the thoughts are clear enough, and where they are not, he prefers you should anyhow use your judgment.

*First.* You will be very careful before delivering the check and agreement, in comparing the latter with the one Columbia is to execute; and seeing that all legal forms are complied with. If necessary you can

*Benefactions*

consult a lawyer; but be perfectly satisfied that the agreements are identical.

*Second.* This contract was drawn early in April, when it was thought the school would be opened in 1904; (see Dr. Butler's memo herewith); which now seems most unlikely.

Although the contract makes the full sum of one million dollars due in June, 1904, Mr. Pulitzer has signed it in that shape to avoid further delay, but the dates were based upon a presumed progress that cannot be realized. He therefore wishes it to be distinctly understood that the dates of payment shall not be technically insisted upon if the building cannot be finished, nor the school opened until 1905, but that payments are to be made upon the basis of the understanding with Dr. Butler, whose written memorandum upon the subject is sent with this. Anyway, Mr. Pulitzer will pay the half million upon the construction of the building as required and the remainder when the building is completed.

He likes to feel that he can do it in this way. That was the spirit of the understanding; and it seems to him illogically inconvenient that they should have the whole amount when the building is only begun and not finished.

If it be possible legally to make after the signature an interlineation covering this point, Mr. Pulitzer would prefer it; but you need not insist upon it. He would undoubtedly have done this if he had been at home, but the desire to finish the subject induced him to sign as it stands.

*Third.* Please pay the utmost attention to the announcement of the scheme, or first publication. Mr. Pulitzer attaches great importance to first impressions; and is particularly desirous that on this occasion the first impression shall be favorable.

He wishes you scrupulously to avoid conveying the impression that the school is the *World's* scheme; or that the *World* is to run it; or will have anything to do with it. The endowment once made it is out of his hands.

*Fourth.* He desires that the name of the *World* shall not be identified with it in the *World* itself. His intention is that the University shall stand forward conspicuously in the case and act independently. He has put the responsibility in the hands of the University and the Advisory Board.

*Fifth.* The following is verbatim as dictated by Mr. Pulitzer.

Read, however, the part of the agreement referring to the Advisory Board. It is particularly important, and has given me a great deal of worry for over a year. See personally Mr. Whitelaw Reid, St. Clair McKelway and Emory Smith, immediately; before the execution of the agreement. Explain the situation and urge them in my name to accept the first three places on the Advisory Board. I shall consider it a favor, as I am convinced the success will depend upon their professional skill and talent, which the college cannot possibly possess. So great is my anxiety to enlist the sympathy and support of these three gentlemen that if they were to decline I should very seriously consider the fact as a reason to drop the whole scheme for the present, or during my life; having trouble enough and not needing any outside the *World* office to be occupied.

If these gentlemen have sympathy with the project, and are ready to accept the position, not nominally, but really, I shall be glad to consider their suggestions in filling the other positions on the Advisory Board with gentlemen whom they may name. I may add that you will probably be one of them. My mind would

## Benefactions

be to select the other gentlemen absolutely without regard to any personal consideration, making the sole test capacity and interest in the scheme; enthusiastic interest, if possible, for the first year or two and until the machine is set up; at all events actively.

While my will providing for the second million, as well as the first, requires a Board of nine members (in addition to the president of the University, member ex officio) the agreement, you will see, does not mention any number.

If the three gentlemen named accept, with yourself (or somebody for the *World*) and President Butler, this will make five; and five more are to be named. I have thought about these names for a year, and am yet at a loss.

I shall be very glad if neither you nor the three gentlemen named will be influenced by my own judgment beyond their own opinions of the merits of those named below.

I have thought of Mr. Miller of the *Times* and of Mr. Norris, one or the other, not both; Mr. Chester Lord, or Mitchell of the *Sun;* and Mr. Reick of the *Herald*, asking of course, the consent of Mr. Bennett. Also Mr. Taylor in Boston, as one practical man of business, shrewd and successful; because such a man should be there. Three should be chosen at once, in order that there should be a quorum in or near town. As soon as you and the two agree cable the names, and I will nominate them. The other two could be selected at leisure; but if in looking over the possibilities you have the names ready I will nominate them also.

After securing a quorum near town, I have thought the other places might go to the West. I have considered Mr. Noyes, Mr. Patterson and Mr. Lawson of Chicago, possibly Johns of St. Louis, both because I don't like to ignore St. Louis and I know no one else. I have also thought of Mr. Bowles of the Springfield *Republican*.

Upon further reflection as this is read to me I have decided that one of the places shall be tendered to either Colonel Taylor of the Boston *Globe* or to Samuel Bowles of the Springfield *Republican*, unless the quartette first named, of which you are one, have better names to offer, which I hope they may have.

Also that the *Evening Post* shall be considered for one position. I know no one there personally. They have abused me constantly for twenty years. Yet I will appoint Mr. Oswald Villard, or Rollo Ogden, or even Mr. [Hammond] Lamont; any one of the three whom the gentlemen named may favor; or who will be really interested in and helpful to the scheme. My idea is to raise the character of the profession to a higher level.

*Sixth.* Before verbally explaining the subject to Messrs. McKelway, Reid, Smith and Taylor, hand to each one a copy of the article in proof (referred to below) and one also to each of the other gentlemen you may consider for the additional places. It explains the subject and will save you time.

*Seventh.* Prepare carefully a statement of the facts for the Associated Press and for Reuter. Reuter's people should be told that every newspaper in the world will be interested in this project and Mr. Pulitzer would rather have a dozen lines in Reuter's report than pages elsewhere. You can pay Reuter's tolls if they desire.

*Eighth.* See Dr. Butler personally about the official announcement. This should be made by him, or in his name; but you should assist him and perhaps may write the statement yourself.

*Ninth.* Of course, the private details etc. of the con-

INNER COURT, SCHOOL OF JOURNALISM BUILDING

tract should not be published. It is private — strictly; except of course, so much as must necessarily be communicated to the public and the Advisory Board. They for instance should know about the scheme of prizes as they will have (under my will) complete control of that subject. The facts are enough, that the thing is settled; that a building for half a million will be promptly begun and that the endowment is on a basis of $2,000,000.

The part about the prizes must not be mentioned in the public announcement, as that relates to the future. Mr. Pulitzer wishes not to divert attention from the main foundation.

*Tenth.* Mr. Pulitzer does not wish the *World* to get a beat out of this story. All the papers should have it at the same time; although he sympathizes with the natural office passion for beats.

*Eleventh.* Herewith you will find the proof of an article, written last year as a statement of reasons in favor of the establishment of this school. The type is perhaps still standing in the *World* office. Mr. Seitz knows. Mr. Pulitzer wishes to have this article printed in a neat and attractive pamphlet, and to have such a number made as will suffice to send a copy to every important paper in the United States; and to all important periodicals, especially those devoted to education.

Perhaps this should be done through the University, but the point does not seem material.

Very truly,
GEORGE W. HOSMER.

While the agreement was under consideration at Columbia Mr. Pulitzer had departed for Europe, where he spent the Summer, instead of at Bar Harbor. Whitelaw Reid and St. Clair McKelway accepted as members of the Advisory Board. On July 20,

1903, the University trustees formally approved the arrangement.

Mr. Merrill had assented to delay in announcing the Advisory Board, but assumed that the foundation would be made public at once and advised Dr. Butler, that "Mr. Pulitzer expected the endowment would be announced by the University as soon as the agreement was ratified, leaving the selection of the Advisory Board until later." To this Dr. Butler replied:

July 22, 1903.

MY DEAR MR. MERRILL:

I thank you for yours of the 21st and inclosures, which I am very glad to have. My own judgment is confirmed by a conversation with two or three of our trustees, that the attitude of a certain portion of the newspaper press of the country is likely to be antagonistic, or at least cynical, toward the proposal to establish a School of Journalism, but that, by careful management of the form and careful calculation of the time of the first announcement, it will be possible to prevent this attitude from finding expression in large degree. My own feeling is that if we can delay an announcement until we have something more to say than merely that a School of Journalism is contemplated, it will forward the end which both Mr. Pulitzer and the University have in view. I shall give the matter very careful consideration, however, in view of your letter, and shall ask the opinion of Mr. Reid and Mr. McKelway about it when we all meet this afternoon.

Cordially yours,
NICHOLAS MURRAY BUTLER.

A summary of the correspondence sent to Mr. Pulitzer at Etretat on July 24th brought this reply: "Postpone publication. Tell Butler Board can be enlarged to fifteen if good men discoverable. Of

*Benefactions*

course, you will be beaten on news item costing $2,000,000."

This last fear of a "leak" was quite reasonable. There was no leakage, however, but a crisis now developed over the Advisory Board. Mr. Pulitzer wished to endow the School with distinction as well as money, and went at the problem painstakingly, in an endeavor to acquire educators and journalists in proper proportions and of the right calibre. He decided to meet the postponement of the announcement with a delay in completing the Board until his return, then planned for October. Mr. Merrill was instructed to sound out Dr. Charles W. Eliot, Andrew D. White, of Cornell, Victor F. Lawson, of the Chicago *Daily News*, Gen. Charles H. Taylor, of the Boston *Globe*, Samuel Bowles, of the Springfield (Mass.) *Republican* and Oswald Garrison Villard, of the *Evening Post*, who with the others already agreed upon would make a body sufficient to act, the remainder to await his return. There followed some canvassing of names backwards and forwards under the sea, then on July 30th, Mr. Pulitzer, having become restive under the fear that news of his great project might get out in such a way as to spoil the desired effect, cabled to Mr. Merrill:

*First.* After another week urge early publication; desirable because dull summer days; best to stir up, start mind of nation, discussion, new question, nothing else diverting.

*Second.* Would give anything to have Eliot accept. Worth twenty editors. Sure you could get him if you would only trust to your own ingenuity and present subject in proper form and spirit. Reid, McKelway and Butler should make request.

*Third.* Mistake in your letter saying I forbade any other publication in the *World* than the one given by Columbia to all papers; quite the contrary — *World*, without depriving other papers of news, should develop the main point into most intelligent, carefully thought out great feature; educating public up to an understanding of the idea. If that great feature not already long ago prepared surprising, considering notice you had. *World* must treat endowment as it would if made by Smith or Jones. Should develop popular thought, opinions of cultivated people, raise discussion, dissipate doubts, indicate possible consequences, continuing feature several days without slopping over.

*Fourth.* Mr. Bennett declines by private correspondence urgent request. Reick therefore eliminated.

Mr. William C. Reick was then in general charge of the New York *Herald*, though enjoying only the title of City Editor. Mr. Bennett did not share Mr. Pulitzer's liberal view of activities outside of the office on the part of gentlemen in his employ. Possibly, too, he did not care to adorn the tail of the kite.

President Butler declined to join in the commandeering of President Eliot and Andrew D. White. He did not feel that these eminent rivals in the educational field should exercise any authority at Columbia and voiced his view in a letter addressed to Mr. Merrill to this effect:

Rye Beach, N. H.<br>Aug. 7, 1903.

My dear Mr. Merrill:

Your telegram was received last night, and your letter of the 6th is here this morning.

Mr. Andrew D. White is a personal friend of mine and I esteem him highly, but I do not care to have him upon the Advisory Board. He is completely identified, academically, with Yale and Cornell and bears no relations to journalism that would justify his appointment. There are also reasons, lying back in the past, why he would not be persona grata to some of our trustees.

I should prefer Mr. Eliot's indorsement to take the form of a personal interview with him after the announcement is public. He will undoubtedly support the plan heartily.

Such a supplementary statement as you suggest ought not, I am sure, to be made until the Advisory Board has met and formally agreed upon it. To issue it at the same time with an official announcement will give the impression of "protesting too much." The scheme is good in itself and will go on its own merits.

I hope that Mr. Pulitzer will consent to nominate the full board as we agreed upon it, namely, Messrs. Bishop, Lamont, Lawson, Lord, Miller, Stone, Taylor and Williams, in addition to Hay, Reick, McKelway and yourself. As Mr. Pine explained to you, we should be greatly embarrassed if Messrs. Bishop, Lamont and Miller were not included. I am sorry that Mr. Reick cannot serve and suppose that in view of our uncertainty regarding Mr. Cabaniss, he ought not to be named at present. The South is so sensitive, however, that I wish one of their men might be on the first list. Have you inquired further concerning Hemphill?

I hope that Mr. Pulitzer will consent to nominate these men, as I am confident that such a course is best for the new School and best for the University as a whole.

Cordially yours,
NICHOLAS MURRAY BUTLER.

President Butler's attitude was cabled to Mr. Pulitzer at San Moritz. Back came the reply on August 11th: "Understand jealousy. Telegraph Butler my insistence. Unalterable. Final."

## Joseph Pulitzer

President Butler answered that he would withhold announcement until the following week, when he would be in New York City, for further conference, and followed his telegram with a letter in which he again emphasized his judgment that it would be unwise to appoint high officers of other universities, not themselves journalists, upon the Advisory Board of the new School. "Therefore," he added, "I shall not myself attempt to anticipate any action that the trustees of the University may wish to take, and ask that Mr. Pulitzer submit formally all of his nominations for the Advisory Board as provided in the agreement between himself and Columbia University, for action by the trustees at their next stated meeting, which falls on the first Monday in October. Naturally, no announcement of the completion of the Advisory Board can be made until that time. Inasmuch, however, as the number of persons who have knowledge of this gift and its purpose is constantly increasing, and there is manifest danger of the matter becoming public in an unauthorized and harmful way, I will make an official announcement to the press for release on the morning of Monday, August 17th, mentioning the fact that there will be an Advisory Board, but leaving its composition to be determined by Mr. Pulitzer and the trustees of the University as the Agreement provides."

Mr. Pulitzer declined to await President Butler's date and ordered the announcement to be published on Friday, August 14th. "Follow instructions with backbone," he cabled Mr. Merrill. "Print names. Say Eliot, White, Reid, McKelway, Lawson, Taylor are part of the Advisories selected by donor, who has undoubted right under agreement. Others Octo-

## Benefactions

ber. If White not heard from say he is expected to accept. All others agreed to act. Interview every trustee of Columbia; also, if possible, ablest Judges; Cleveland, Roosevelt. Remind Seth Low same proposition made him in 1892. Wire Butler publication Friday inevitable. Can telegraph any statement if he likes. You using discretion whether to publish."

Mr. Merrill had, however, assented to Mr. Butler's suggestion for delay. This provoked Mr. Pulitzer to great wrath. He relieved him of everything concerning the affair except publishing the news, and forbade his attending any conference with President Butler, instructing him further to telegraph the latter that he, Mr. Pulitzer, was indignant and wished to know whether or not the former would "respect the spirit of the agreement and the founder's unselfish wishes or return foundation." He added that he neither desired nor feared a row and included Dr. Butler on the Advisory Board ex officio. White he regarded as immaterial, but he did not wish Dr. Eliot to get away.

The order to print on the 14th having become without effect, Mr. Pulitzer cabled again on the 15th to publish the announcement on Sunday, the 16th. President Butler was so notified and Columbia furnished an official statement covering the receipt of the gift. The *World's* story gave the names of the Advisory Board, as far as it had been completed by the acceptance of seven nominees, including Dr. Butler ex officio. These were Whitelaw Reid of the *Tribune;* St. Clair McKelway, editor of the Brooklyn *Eagle;* Dr. Charles W. Eliot, President of Harvard University; Andrew D. White, President of Cornell University; Victor F. Lawson of the Chicago *Daily News;*

*Joseph Pulitzer*

Samuel Bowles of the Springfield *Republican*, and Gen. Charles H. Taylor of the Boston *Globe*.

The announcement was received with surprising cordiality. Neither the misgivings of President Butler, nor Mr. Pulitzer's doubts, were realized. The New York papers were unanimous in loud praise and a wave of approbation came from the country at large. Indeed, everybody seemed pleased, except Mr. Pulitzer. The fact that President Butler had not flatly admitted his full right to name the Advisory Board enabled the donor to continue his indignation. He cabled me on the 17th, knowing that the publication had been made.

> Further cables about Butler forbidden. Everything must await my return. Inform Butler verbatim unless he really welcomes greatest advisors, Eliot, White, my confidence in him and trust committed to his charge lost. I will stop promptly and assume sense of honor, pride, trustees will return endowment allowing transfer where advisors, gift and giver more appreciated. Hope he realized his responsibility. Again: All disagreeable cables forbidden.

He also asked for the file of newspapers covering the week. Communication was thus summarily cut off and as the acclaim had been so loud, I did not deliver Mr. Pulitzer's ultimatum.

The bales of clippings sent to Switzerland soothed Mr. Pulitzer's anger, though he later took me to task for not delivering his ultimatum. My reply was that I did not want to spoil all the applause. He returned in season, and feeling that the bother of organizing the School and selecting the Board would be too great to bear, decided to postpone further action during his lifetime. He deposited the balance

## Benefactions

of the first million with Columbia, which in turn paid him the income until his death, after which the second million also became available.

It had not at the moment, perhaps, occurred to either Mr. Pulitzer or President Butler that the *World* had become an established institution beyond the realm of controversy with an undisputed position in American journalism.

The cornerstone of the School structure was laid July 2, 1912, by Mrs. Joseph Pulitzer on a site at Broadway and One Hundred and Sixteenth Street. The School opened September 30th, but did not occupy the building until the next college year, entering its quarters on September 13th. The Advisory Board as first constituted numbered twelve, viz.: John Langdon Heaton of the *World;* George S. Johns, editor of the St. Louis *Post-Dispatch;* President Nicholas Murray Butler of Columbia University; Samuel Bowles of the Springfield *Republican;* Victor Fremont Lawson of the Chicago *Daily News;* Dr. St. Clair McKelway of the Brooklyn *Daily Eagle;* Charles Ransom Miller of the New York *Times;* Edward Page Mitchell of the New York *Sun;* Whitelaw Reid of the New York *Tribune;* Melville Elijah Stone of the Associated Press; Gen. Charles H. Taylor of the Boston *Globe*, and Samuel Calvin Wells of the Philadelphia *Press*. Mr. Reid died December 15, 1912, and Mr. Ralph Pulitzer, President of the Press Publishing Company, was later added to the list.

Thanks to the suggestion of Dr. St. Clair McKelway, Dr. Talcott Williams, then of the Philadelphia *Press*, became Director, March 10, 1912, and the School started auspiciously under journalistic, rather than academic, auspices, as at first seemed likely.

## Joseph Pulitzer

The balance of the faculty included: Associate Director, Prof. John W. Cunliffe; Frederick P. Keppel, Dean of Columbia College; William P. Trent, Professor of English Literature; Henry R. Seager, Professor of Political Economy; James T. Shotwell, Professor of History; Ashley H. Thorndike, Professor of English, and Charles A. Beard, Associate Professor of Politics.

To these selections from the University staff Robert E. McAlarney from the *Tribune*, and Franklin Matthews from the *Sun*, were added as instructors in practical journalism.

Besides establishing the School of Journalism at Columbia, Mr. Pulitzer in his will provided a series of prizes in the interest of letters, the drama, music and good newspaper work, to wit:

1. For the most disinterested and meritorious public service rendered by any American newspaper during the year — $500 gold medal.

2. For the best example of a reporter's work during the year; the test being strict accuracy, terseness, the accomplishment of some public good, commanding public attention and respect — $1,000.

3. For the American novel published during the year which shall best present the wholesome atmosphere of American life, and the highest standard of American manners and manhood — $1,000.

4. For the best book of the year upon the history of the United States — $2,000.

5. For the best American biography, teaching patriotic and unselfish service to the people illustrated by an eminent example — $1,000.

6. For the best cartoon published during the year — $500.

*Benefactions*

7. For the best book of verse published during the year — $1,000.

Three travelling scholarships of $1,500 each were established for the graduates of the School of Journalism who passed their examinations with the highest honor, to enable each of them to spend a year in Europe for the study of social, moral and political conditions and the character and principles of the European press.

An annual scholarship of $1,500 was also established for the student of music in America who may be deemed most promising to continue study in Europe; also another annual scholarship of $1,500, under the same conditions, to be awarded by the National Academy of Design for the most promising and deserving art student. The awards are under the control of the University authorities.

In his will Mr. Pulitzer testified his lasting admiration for Thomas Jefferson, by setting aside $25,000 "that a statue of that great statesman may at last adorn some public place in New York, the foremost Democratic city of the New Republic." The commission was given to William Ordway Partridge and the statue stands within the inner court of the School of Journalism.

The sum of $50,000 was left for the purpose of erecting a fountain "at some suitable place in Central Park, or preferably at or near the Plaza entrance at Fifty-ninth Street, and to be as far as practicable like those in the Place de la Concorde, Paris." The Plaza site was selected and designs for its reconstruction and the building of the fountain were made a matter of competition in January, 1913. The jury, consisting of Paul P. Cret of the University of Pennsylvania, Whitney Warren, George B. Post, Charles A. Platt

## Joseph Pulitzer

and Herbert Adams, selected the plans of Carrere & Hastings as most in accord with Mr. Pulitzer's wishes. The fountain occupies the square on Fifth Avenue between Fifty-eighth and Fifty-ninth Streets.

A permanent fund of $500,000, to be known as the "Joseph Pulitzer Bequest," was established for the Philharmonic Society of New York, concerning which he remarked in his will:

"I direct that the income from such fund shall be applied and used to perfect the present orchestra and to place it on a more independent basis and to increase the number of concerts to be given in the City of New York, which additional concerts I hope will not have too severely classical programs and to be open to the public at reduced rates and to recognize my favorite composers: Beethoven, Wagner and Liszt." Subsequently, by a codicil, Mr. Pulitzer increased this amount to $919,416.33, making the entire legacy contingent on that Society becoming within three years after his death a membership corporation under the Laws of New York, representing the general public with a membership of not less than 1,000 paying dues.

The bequest to the Philharmonic was the natural result of his liking for good music. He had helped it before by subscription and a substantial donation. Pending the bequest he had asked the office to look it up, in these terms:

April 19, 1911.

I want a report on the Philharmonic Society, not as it is superficially, nominally, and apparently, but *really* who runs it; who are the actual members; what are the dues; how many members actually pay these dues; what is the system — not what is on the letter

*Benefactions*

heads, but the real thing; are any meetings held — annual, monthly, or otherwise — by the members; how many attend; is Carnegie still the president; if not, who is?

Give all officers or so-called directors or anybody really elected by members and taking part in the management or showing capacity, outside of Mrs. Sheldon and some other ladies, who, I suspect, in fact believe, are running the whole show.

I want this very, very brief, but reliable; from the inside, not outside; and in a spirit of close scepticism and scrutiny as to whether the society is not a mere shell. I want to know who really runs it.

The Metropolitan Museum of Art received a bequest of $500,000, subsequently increased to $919,416.33, the income of which is devoted to the purchase of works of art.

Mr. Pulitzer's interest in education, and his desire to open opportunities for young men to advance themselves, had a practical manifestation in 1891, when, on the 21st of May, he provided twelve annual stipends of $250 each to sustain deserving New York City schoolboys as students at the College of the City of New York, to cover a period of five years. In June, 1893, this plan was replaced by an arrangement with the Horace Mann High School and Columbia College, whereby free tuition was annually provided for ten boys, three years in the school and four in the college, plus the yearly stipend of $250 each for their maintenance. The later opening of public high schools in New York led to the dropping of the Horace Mann scholarships, and to the selection of beneficiaries by competition from their graduates. Ten stipends each year and as many free scholarships — forty in all — are

*Joseph Pulitzer*

maintained, the latter by the donation to Columbia University of $100,000. The $250 stipends were paid direct during Mr. Pulitzer's lifetime. His will set aside a fund of $250,000 for their support.

Something like four hundred young men have received a higher education under this arrangement, chiefly at Columbia, but in some instances at Harvard, Princeton, Cornell, Brown, Dickinson, Amherst, Fordham, Williams and other institutions. Only in Columbia is free tuition furnished, but the stipend can be combined with local scholarships in other colleges. In all, Mr. Pulitzer expended considerably more than half a million dollars upon this ideal. Many of the men thus aided have become eminent as college professors, chemists, lawyers, engineers, journalists and men of affairs. The scholarships rank among the most useful of their type in the country.

Mr. Pulitzer's charities were liberal and in the main, secret. Men in his employ were aided by the office under a blanket instruction. In 1886, he endowed a bed on behalf of the New York Press Club, in Roosevelt Hospital, with $5,000, and in 1893 added a second, with a like contribution.

His gross estate, as set down in final appraisal before the Surrogate of New York County, was $18,645,249.09, excluding the value of Chatwold, at Bar Harbor, Maine, and his cottages at Jekyl Island, Georgia.

## DESCENDANTS OF JOSEPH PULITZER

| Children | Grandchildren |
|---|---|
| RALPH PULITZER, born June 11, 1879. Married Frederica Vanderbilt Webb. | Ralph Pulitzer, Jr., born Aug. 28, 1908. Seward Webb Pulitzer, born Oct. 5, 1911. |
| LUCILLE IRMA PULITZER, born Sept. 30, 1880. Died Dec. 31, 1897. | |
| KATHERINE ETHEL PULITZER, born June 30, 1882. Died May 9, 1884. | |
| JOSEPH PULITZER, JR., born March 21, 1885. Married Elinor Wickham. | Joseph Pulitzer, 3d, born May 13, 1913. Kate Davis Pulitzer, born Oct. 13, 1916. Eleanor Wickham Pulitzer, born March 31, 1922. |
| EDITH PULITZER, born, June 19, 1886. Married William Scoville Moore. | Clement Clark Moore, born Jan. 28, 1914. Adrian Pulitzer Moore, born Aug. 8, 1917. William Worthington Moore, born Aug. 4, 1920. Richard Wraxall Moore, born July 29, 1921. David Moore, born June 10, 1923. |
| CONSTANCE PULITZER, born, Dec. 13, 1888. Married William Gray Elmslie. | Cynthia Edith Elmslie, born July 1, 1914. Vivian Elmslie, born May 24, 1924. |
| HERBERT PULITZER, born Nov. 20, 1895. | |

# INDEX

## A

Abbett, Gov. Leon, 182.
Abbott, Dr. Lyman, 351.
Able, Barton, 98.
Adams, Col. A. W., 45.
Adams, Capt. F. C., 45.
Adams, Herbert, 464.
*Advertiser*, Morning, 184, 190, 211.
Aix-les-Bains, 377, 404.
Alexander, A. W., 98.
Alexander, John W., 267.
Alexandria, Va., 46.
Allen, Thomas, 106.
Allen, Gov. William, 105.
Allenton, 64.
Allison, W. H., 99.
*American*, New York, 304.
*Amerika*, St. Louis, 106.
Amherst College, 466.
Anderson, Judge A. B., 378.
Anderson, John, 118.
Andrew, A. D., 295.
Angell, J. B., 442.
Anthony, Mark, 293.
Antioch, 46.
*Anzeiger*, St. Louis, Mo., 106.
Arnold, Sir Edwin, 192.
Arsenal Island, 54.
Arthur, Chester A., 106, 113.
Associated Press, 120, 122, 123, 355, 431, 452, 461.
Associated Press, Western, 103.
Astor House, 9, 183.
Astor, John Jacob, 112.
Athens, 402.
Atlantic and Pacific R. R., 54.
Augustine, Capt. Edward, 64, 65, 66, 67, 68.
Austrian Army, 42.

## B

Bacheller, Irving, 2.
Baldwin, Simeon E., 406.
Barclay, D. R., 99.
Bar Harbor, 2, 28, 37, 39, 193, 196, 197, 247, 250, 252, 254, 261, 276, 281, 308, 320, 466.
Barnes, James, 6, 414.

Barney, Charles T., 169.
Bartholdi, Auguste, 155.
Beard, Chas. A., 462.
Beaver, Gov. James A., 182.
Beaverdam Flat, 46.
Bebel, Herr, 315.
Bedloe's Island, 155.
Beecher, Henry Ward, 123, **124**, 168.
Belgrade, 41.
Belmont, August, 117.
Benecke, Louis, 61.
Bennett, James Gordon, 8, 22, 130, 145, 146, 153, 180, 181, 182, 197, 214, 451, 456.
Benton Barracks, 51.
Beveridge, A. J., 406.
Billing, Arthur H., 6, 19, 20, 250, 290.
Bismarck, 207, 228, 403.
Black, Frank S., 367.
Blair, Frank P., 98.
Blau, Max, 42.
Bliss, C. N., 302.
Blythe, Samuel G., 252.
Bo, Maurice, 365.
Boer War, 250, 311, 313.
Bonaparte, Charles J., 367.
Boston, 42.
Bouchard, Dr., 171.
Bowers, John M., 151, 367, 369.
Bowles, Samuel, 452, 455.
Boyd, Capt. W. H., 44.
Brachvogel, Udo, 53, 57.
Brewer, Justice, 442.
Brisbane, Albert, 230.
Brisbane, Arthur, 24, 25, 209, 229, 230, 231, 242.
Bristow, B. H., 406.
British Guiana, 201.
Broadhead, Col. James O., 109, 111.
Brockmeyer, Lt. Gov. H. C., 57.
Brooklyn Bridge, 140, 142, 144, 230.
Brown, John, 46.
Brown-Sequard, 171.
Brownsville, 314, 315.
Brown University, 466.
Bryan, William J., 9, 32, 226, 227, 232, 233, 234, 249, 250, 251, 259, 284, 285, 315, 320, 323, 326, 327, 330, 331, 332, 334, 337, 339, 340, 341, 342, 343, 345, 346, 347, 349, 350, 375.

[ 469 ]

# Index

Buckland, Frank, 246.
Budapest, 40, 41.
Bulkley, Gov. Morgan G., 182.
*Bulletin*, Philadelphia, 115, 116, 432.
Bunau-Varilla, Phillipe, 297.
Burton, Pomeroy, 9, 23, 238.
Bush, G. Charles, 235, 236.
Butes, Alfred, 5, 6, 7, 234.
Butler, Benj. F., 147, 236.
Butler, Nicholas Murray, 444, 445, 451, 452, 454, 455, 456, 457, 458, 459, 460, 461.
Butler, Richard, 155.
Butt, Capt. Archie, 366.
Byrnes, Thomas F., 295.
Byron, Lord, 432.

## C

Cabaniss, H. H., 457.
Cady, C. C., 67.
Caesar, Julius, 293.
California, 296.
California University, 442.
Cambridge, 445.
Cameron, Simon, 4, 5, 116.
Cap Martin, 15, 37, 38, 228, 229.
Carleton, Henry Guy, 162.
Carpathian Mountains, 40.
Carpet Baggers, 82.
Carrere & Hastings, 464.
Carroll, Howard, 186.
Carroll, John F., 245.
Carter, Walter S., 268.
Carvalho, S. S., 9, 165, 190, 192, 193, 194, 199, 212, 213, 214, 217.
Cavender, John S., 98.
Caws, Capt. A. E., 368, 376.
Cemetery Ridge, 8.
Central Park, 463.
Cervera's Fleet, 240.
Chamberlain, John, 152.
Chamberlain, Joseph, 207.
Chamberlin, E. O., 193.
Chamber of Commerce, N. Y., 206.
Chandler, Zach., 73, 118.
Chanler, Robert L., 342, 345.
Charcot, Dr., 171.
Chase, Salmon P., 324.
Chatwold, 13, 14, 19, 24, 200, 242, 466.
Chew, Rev. J. H., 95.
Childs, George W., 132, 140, 172.
Choteau, Pierre, 112.
City Hall Park, 43, 49, 150.
Clarke, Sir Andrew, 171.
Clarke, Dumont, 36, 209.
Clarke, James W., 246, 428.
Clarke, Gen. John E., 90.

Cleveland Convention, 98.
Cleveland, Grover, 144, 147, 148, 149, 150, 159, 169, 170, 195, 200, 201, 202, 204, 211, 225, 442.
Clopton, William H., 110, 111.
Coal and Iron Police, 180.
Coates, Foster, 242, 428.
Cobb, Frank I., 30, 36, 256, 258, 259, 265, 266, 270, 271, 273, 274, 279, 280, 290, 300, 305, 308, 309, 310, 324, 325, 330, 344, 346, 349, 399, 400, 401, 409, 410, 411, 423.
Coburn, Richard T., 98.
Cockerill, Col. John A., 18, 26, 104, 109, 110, 111, 112, 113, 142, 143, 144, 160, 161, 166, 167, 170, 174, 183, 184, 185, 186, 190.
Cockerill, Col. Joseph R., 104, 105, 110.
Cockran, W. Bourke, 151, 329.
Colcord, Joseph P., 70.
Cole, Victor T., 110.
College, City of New York, 465.
Colombia, U. S. of, 385.
Columbia College, 238, 445, 453, 454, 456, 458, 459, 461, 462, 465, 466.
Columbia College Library, 37.
*Columbia*, Yacht, 249.
*Commerce, Journal of*, 119, 120, 121.
*Commercial Advertiser*, 164.
Commune, Paris, 8.
Conlin, Peter F., 295.
Conner, Washington E., 127.
Constitution, Frigate, 236.
Cook, Theodore A., 7.
Cooley, Judge, 380.
Coplestone, J. H., 134.
Cornell University, 459, 466.
*Corsair*, Yacht, 37.
Cortelyou, George B., 263, 264, 323.
Coudert Bros., 377.
County Court, St. Louis, 63.
Cox, Gen. J. D., 73.
Cox, Robert T., 278.
Crane, Stephen, 241.
Crawford, T. C., 152.
Creelman, James, 197.
Credit Lyonnais, 365.
Cret, Paul P., 463.
Crickmore, H. G., 134.
Crinkle, Nym, 134.
Croker, Richard, 247, 284.
Cromwell, William Nelson, 297, 298, 343, 352, 353, 357, 358, 359, 360, 361, 362, 363, 368, 371, 377, 379.
Crowell, Luther C., 153, 154.
Csnad County, 40.
Cuddy, Col. William, 98.
Cummings, Alexander, 115, 116, 117.

[ 470 ]

## Index

Cummings, Amos J., 164.
Cummins, A. B., 406.
Cundy, Capt. W. H., 119.
Cunliffe, Prof. John W., 462.
Cunningham, A. B., 108.
Curtis, William J., 353.
Curtiss, Glenn, 16.
Custer, Gen. G. A., 45.

### D

Daenzer, Carl, 57.
Daly, Marcus, 226.
Dana, Charles A., 89, 130, 147, 160, 173.
Dana, Paul, 430.
Daniels, Josephus, 262.
Danish West Indies, 432, 434.
Danube River, 55.
Davidson, Prof. Thomas, 8, 33, 56, 408, 426.
Davies, Randall, 6.
Davis, Charles B., 76.
Davis, Mrs. Jefferson, 162, 242.
Davis, Miss Kate, 90, 91, 92, 93.
Davis, Varina Annie, 242.
Davis, Col. William L., 170, 173, 177, 183.
Davis, William W., 90.
Day, Justice, 383.
Dayton, 427.
Debs, Eugene V., 196.
Delane, John Thaddeus, 3.
Delaware, Lackawanna & Western R. R., 36.
De Lesseps, Ferdinand, 297, 365.
*Democrat*, Missouri, 62, 66, 67, 69, 98, 99.
Deneen, Governor, 315.
Depew, Chauncey M., 172, 274, 275, 277, 302, 303.
Deutsche-Gesellschaft, 54, 57.
De Wecker, Dr., 171.
Dewey, Admiral George, 249.
Dickinson University, 466.
Dillon, John A., 184, 191, 192, 233, 235, 254.
*Dispatch*, St. Louis, 11, 97, 99, 101, 104, 182.
District of Columbia, 380.
Dix, Gen. John A., 119, 121.
Dixon, Capt. Hiram, 376.
Dolliver, J. P., 406.
Dougherty, Daniel, 172, 182.
Douglass, J. D., 186.
Driscoll, Frederick, 191.
Duke, J. B., 186.
Duneka, Frederick A., 5, 428.
Dunningham, J. E., 402, 414.

### E

Eads, Col. J. B., 77, 112.
*Eagle*, Brooklyn Daily, 25, 74, 122, 125, 182, 304, 345, 459, 461.
Eakins, Joseph J., 230.
East St. Louis, 50.
Edwards, John N., 99.
Eggleston, Edward, 231.
Eggleston, George Cary, 192, 243, 244, 251.
Electoral Commission, 89.
Eliot, Charles W., 442, 445, 455, 457, 458, 459, 460, 461.
Eliot, George, 432.
Elm Park, 45.
Elysian Fields, 159.
*Empire*, Dayton, 105.
England, 201.
England, Isaac W., 89.
Engleman, Dr. George, 57.
English, William H., 106.
*Enquirer*, Cincinnati, 105, 106, 210.
Epiphany, Church of, 95.
Equitable Insurance Co., 267, 268, 271, 272, 274, 275, 279.
Evans, Rear-Admiral Robley D., 311.
Evarts, William M., 155.
Ewell, Gen. Robert S., 46.
*Examiner*, San Francisco, 210, 212.

### F

Fairbanks, Charles W., 354, 401.
Farnham, Roger L., 352.
Fayel, William, 60.
Fearing, Charles B., 166.
Fellows, Col. John R., 165.
Ferrero, G., 293.
Field, Eugene, 97, 147.
Field, Justice, 442.
Field, Roswell Martin, 97.
Filley, O. D., 98.
Firestone, Clark B., 411.
Fish, Stuyvesant, 303.
Fishback, George W., 74, 98, 99.
Fisse, John H., 72.
Fitzgerald, Frank T., 182.
Florence, W. J., 295.
Flower, Roswell P., 309.
Fogg, Josiah, 98.
Folger, Charles J., 113, 148.
Folk, Joseph W., 262, 263, 284, 327.
Fontaine, S. S., 433.
Foraker, James B., 315.
Fordham University, 466.
Foreign Legion, 42.
Foy, Peter L., 98.
France, 95, 96.

# Index

Francis, David R., 194, 234, 284.
Frederick the Great, 5, 439.
Frederick William, King, 5.
Fremont, Gen. John C., 98.
French's Hotel, 49, 168, 169.
Frick, H. C., 305.
Fuller, Justice, M. W., 442.

## G

Gambetta, 432.
Gasconade River, 55.
Gaynor, William J., 244, 245, 327, 340, 386, 389, 390, 391, 404, 405, 407, 409.
*Gazette*, Baltimore, 105.
Gentry, William, 79, 80.
George, Henry, 237.
George, Jr., Henry, 237.
Gerard, James W., 151.
Germany, 95, 96.
Gibbons, Cardinal, 206.
Gibson, Charles, 104.
Gladstone, William E., 205.
*Globe*, Boston, 152, 172, 182, 452, 455, 460, 461.
*Globe-Democrat*, St. Louis, 99, 101, 104.
*Globe*, St. Louis, 78.
Glover, John M., 110.
Goddard, Morrill, 211, 212, 229.
Goethe, 4, 432.
*Golden Rule*, The, 231.
Goldkin, E. L., 432.
Gorki, 432.
Gould, George J., 131, 305.
Gould, Jay, 113, 114, 126, 129, 130, 131, 148, 167.
Grady, Thomas F., 280, 292.
Grant, Col. F. D., 295.
Grant, Hugh J., 151, 197.
Grant, Lt. Gen. U. S., 72, 74, 81.
Grantham, Samuel A., 63.
Grasse, 15.
Gray, Justice, 442.
Great Britain, 20, 201, 203, 204, 206, 222, 238.
Greaves, E. Tracy, 164.
Greeley, Horace, 3, 72, 73, 74, 117, 118.
Greeley-Smith, Nixola, 410.
Greene, Gen. George S., 8.
Gribayédoff, V., 162.
Grosvenor, William S., 78.
Grozier, E. A., 152, 187.
Gruelle, Wallace, 65, 67.
Guiccioli, Countess, 432.

## H

Hadley, A. T., 442.
Hafiz, 34.
Halstead, Murat, 75, 103, 182.

Hamburg, 42.
Hamilton, Alexander, 324.
Hammond, C. M., 2.
Hamon, "Jake," 405.
Hancock, E. C., 135, 142.
Hancock, Gen. W. S., 106.
Hanna, Marcus A., 225.
Harden, E. W., 239, 240.
Hardin, Charles M., 78.
Harlan, Justice, 383, 442.
Harmsworth, Alfred C., 238.
Harriman, E. H., 299, 303, 304, 305, 306, 307, 308, 316, 317, 318, 321, 343.
Harrison, Benjamin, 169, 170, 442.
Hart, Josh, 131.
Hart, Lavinia, 428.
Hart's Island, 43, 47.
Harvard College, 442, 459, 466.
Harvey, Col. George B. M., 9, 182, 192, 193.
Hastings, Hugh, 184.
Hay, John, 297, 457.
Hayes, Rutherford B., 87, 125.
Hearn, Lafcadio, 26.
Hearst, William R., 9, 210, 211, 212, 214, 215, 217, 231, 241, 259, 280, 281, 287, 288, 289, 307, 337, 339, 343, 344, 385, 389, 390.
Heaton, John Langdon, 251, 273, 281, 282, 287, 291, 299, 461.
Hemphill, Major J. C., 457.
Henderson, John B., 82.
Hendricks, Francis, 276, 277.
Hengenmuller, Baron, 433.
*Herald*, Boston, 151, 152, 231.
*Herald*, New York, 22, 113, 119, 124, 125, 129, 130, 145, 146, 160, 164, 167, 180, 182, 185, 197, 230, 313, 314, 451, 456.
Herran, Dr. Thomas, 297.
Herrick, D-Cady, 259, 264, 340, 421.
Hewitt, Abram S., 138.
Higgins, Francis W., 264, 309.
Hill, Britton A., 71.
Hill, Gov. David B., 165, 169, 170, 172, 182.
Hinton, Major Richard J., 46.
Hitt, R. R., 204.
Hoar, E. R., 73.
Hobart, Garret A., 225, 251.
Hoboken, 159.
Hodnett, John Pope, 108.
Hoffman, Charles A., 107.
Hoe, R. M., 153.
Holmes, Justice, 383.
Homer, 31.
Homestead, Pa., 189, 190.
Hopkins, Mark, 184, 185.
Hornblower, W. B., 396, 410.

## Index

Hosmer, Dr. George W., ix, x, xi, 7, 8, 9, 19, 30, 31, 435, 445, 448, 453.
Hough, Judge Charles M., 381, 382.
Houser, Daniel M., 76, 99.
Howard, John Tasker, 123, 124.
Howard, Jr., Joseph, 122, 123, 124, 163, 164.
Howe, John, 98.
Hughes, Charles E., 268, 279, 281, 289, 309, 329, 345, 348.
Huntington, C. P., 184, 185.
Huppuch, W. A., 421.
Hurd, Frank, 200.
Hurlbert, William H., 125, 126, 128, 133, 134, 135.
Hutchins, Stillson, 99.
Hyde, James Hazen, 267, 268, 272.
Hyde, Col. W. B., 107.
Hyde, William, 99.

### I

Ingraham, Chief Justice, 18.
Ireland, Alleyne, 6.
Irving, Henry, 27, 28.
*Isere*, Transport, 158.
Ittner, Anthony, 69, 70.

### J

Jackson, Attorney-General, 309.
Japan, 61, 63, 65, 66, 67, 69, 70, 74, 82, 103, 207, 441.
Jaures, M., 315.
Jefferson City, 61.
Jefferson, Thomas, 319, 463.
Jekyl Island, 19, 37, 198, 199, 435, 466.
Jellett, Mrs. Morgan, 252.
Jerome, William Travers, 307, 353, 356, 369, 370, 374.
Johannisberger, 19.
Johns, George S., 233, 262, 283, 451, 461.
Johnson, Charles Philip, 53, 71, 97, 98.
Jones, Col. Charles H., 193, 195, 196, 198, 199, 207, 208, 227, 233.
Jones, George W., 130, 200.
Jones & Sibley, 54.
*Journal*, N. Y. Morning, 113, 130, 146, 210, 211, 212, 213, 214, 215, 229, 231.
Judson, Fredk. N., 208, 234.
Jump, Charles, 78.
Junot, 18.

### K

*Katerina*, Yacht, 187.
Kearny, Gen. Philip, 44.
Kealing, Joseph H., 378.

Keenan's Cafe, 143.
Keene, James R., 138.
Kellogg, Frank B., 317.
Kelly, John, 112, 130, 184.
Kelly, Col. R. M., 160.
Kelly, W. J., 231, 232.
Kelsey, Otto, 309.
Kenealy, Alexander, 229.
Keppel, Fredk. P., 462.
Keppler, Joseph, 2, 57, 92.
Kern, John W., 330.
King, Lt. Wm. Nephew, 18.
Kingsbury, A. B., 161.
Kinnicut, Dr. F. P., 377.
Kinosuke, Adachi, 404.
Knapp, Chas. W., 234.
Knapp, Dr. Herman, 166.
Knollys, Sir Francis, 205.
Kolbenheyer, Dr. Frederich, 57, 104.
Kruger, President, 249.

### L

Laffan, William M., 173, 356, 430.
Lake Shore, 36.
Lakewood, 22, 208.
Lamboldt, Dr., 171.
Lamont, Hammond, 452.
Landis, Judge K. M., 318, 320.
*Lanterne, Die*, 100.
Lawson, Victor F., 451, 458, 459, 461.
Leach, Oscar E., 225.
*Ledger*, Dayton, 105.
*Ledger*, Public, 140.
Ledlie, George H., 5, 184.
Lee, Gen. Robert E., 46.
Lehman, F. W., 208.
Leisler, Jacob, 168, 169.
Leland, Charles Godfrey, 116, 125.
Lewes, G. H., 432.
Lewis, Charles B., 163.
Lexow Committee, 295.
Lexow, Rudolph, 87.
Liberty Mills, 46.
*Liberty*, Yacht, 14, 15, 24, 37, 289, 346, 351, 356, 363, 375, 391, 402, 404, 407, 408, 410, 414.
Lincoln, Abraham, 8, 44, 45.
Lincoln Cavalry, 43, 48.
Lincoln, Chas. M., 416, 418, 419, 420, 422, 423, 425.
Lindell, Hotel, 75.
Lindsay, John D., 377.
Lipton, Sir Thomas, 249.
Livingston, Mrs. Louise, 193.
Lockerman, Covert, 168.
Lockerman, Elsie, 168.
Logan, Gen. John A., 47, 232.
Logan, Mrs. John A., 232.

## Index

London, 15, 42.
Longstreet, Gen. James, 8.
Lord, Chester S., 160, 451, 457.
Low, Seth, 37, 237, 254, 459.
Luks, George B., 232.
Lurton, Justice, 383.
Lyman, Robt. Hunt, 230, 367, 378.

### M

MacColl, D. S., 7.
Macdona, H. D., 6, 200.
Macmonnies, Fredk., 176.
Mako, 40, 41.
*Mail & Express*, 164.
Mallison, Frank W., 122, 124.
Mann, Friedrich, 6, 24, 414.
Mann High School, Horace, 465.
Marble, Manton, 118, 119, 121, 123, 124, 125, 127, 160.
Maria Theresa, 43.
Maros River, 40.
Marseilles, 15.
Matthews, Franklin, 462.
Maximilian, Archduke, 42.
McAlarney, Robert E., 462.
McAllister, Ward, 163.
McCall, John A., 268, 269.
McCalla, Capt. B. H., 18.
McCarren, Patrick H., 285, 288, 389.
McClellan, George B., 292.
McClure, S. S., 426.
McCullagh, J. B., 76, 104, 105.
McCullough, John, 27, 92.
McCurdy, Richard A., 268.
McDougall, Walt, 162, 194.
McDowell, Dr. Joseph N., 54.
McGuffin, J. B., 108, 110, 142, 145, 163.
McHenry, E. B., 98.
McHenry, William H., 98.
McKee, William, 76, 77, 98.
McKelway, St. Clair, 25, 74, 124, 131, 182, 450, 452, 453, 454, 455, 457, 458, 459, 462.
McKenna, Justice, 383.
McKeown, John, 278.
McKim, Mead & White, 13, 253.
McKinley, William, 225, 226, 237, 238.
McLane, Dr. J. W., 166, 179.
McLean, Dr. J. H., 111.
McLean, John R., 210, 211.
McLean, William L., 116.
McMaster, John B., 293, 442.
McNamara, Stuart, 370, 377.
McReynolds, Col. A. T., 44, 45.
Meissonier, 443.
Memphis, 52.
Mentone, 228.
Mercantile Library, 53, 56.

*Mercury*, Sunday, 211.
Merrill, Charles J., 166.
Merrill, W. Bradford, 216, 230, 236, 445, 448, 454, 455, 456, 458, 459.
Merrill, William H., 161, 166, 182, 186, 191, 192, 193, 240, 243, 246, 256, 257, 258, 264, 265, 266, 432.
Metcalf, Secretary, 316.
Metropolitan Museum of Art, 12, 465.
Metz, Katy, 162.
Meyer, Dr., 171.
Meyer, Von Lengerke, 317.
Milborne, Jacob, 169.
Miles, Gen. Nelson A., 428.
Miles, W. A., 242.
Miller, Chas. R., 430, 451, 457, 461.
Miller, Warner, 170, 182.
Mills, Roger Q., 182.
*Mirror*, London, 229.
Missouri, 52, 73, 74, 79, 83, 85, 103.
Missouri Constitutional Convention, 82.
Mitchell, E. P., 451, 461.
Mitchell, Dr. S. Weir, 178.
Moffett, Samuel E., 257, 258, 260.
Moltke, General, 312.
Monaco, 12, 228.
Monaco, Prince of, 9, 12.
Monroe Doctrine, 201, 203.
Monte Carlo, 12.
Montgomery, Elizabeth, 252.
Moray Lodge, 200, 218.
Morgan, E. D., 187.
Morgan, J. Pierpont, 37, 299, 362, 368, 409, 413, 427.
Morgan & Co., J. P., 208, 276, 305, 358, 360, 426.
Morgan, Jr., J. P., 426.
Morse, C. W., 245.
Morton, Paul, 273, 274.
Mosby's Guerrillas, 46.
Motley, John L., 73.
Munsey, Frank A., 184.
Murphy, Charles F., 245, 280, 284, 285, 288, 289, 292, 389, 421.
Murray, U. S. Marshal, 122.
Murray, W. H. H., 321.
Mutual Life Insurance Co., 268, 269.

### N

Naples, 177.
Napoleon, 1, 13, 42, 186, 266, 348, 439, 441.
Narragansett Pier, 242.
National Academy of Design, 463.
Nazro, Lt. A. P., 188.
Nelson, Henry Loomis, 430.
New Bedford, 49.

[ 474 ]

# Index

Newell, Robert H., 118.
New England Society, 9.
New Jersey Central R. R., 36.
New Rochelle, 43.
New York City, 37, 42, 49, 112, 113, 114, 115, 117, 118, 119, 125, 166, 167, 180, 181, 196, 200, 458.
New York Life Insurance Co., 268, 269, 276.
*News*, Indianapolis, 354, 357.
*News*, N. Y. Daily, 112, 113, 164.
Nicaragua, 296, 297, 379.
Nicaragua, Lake, 296.
Nice, 15.
Nicoll, DeLancey, 29, 165, 181, 367, 369, 377.
Noah, Major M. M., 77.
Norfolk, 377.
Norris, John, 9, 191, 193, 197, 198, 451.
*North American Review*, 436, 443.
Northcliffe, Lord, 5, 6, 7, 238.
Noyes, F. B., 451.
Nye, Bill, 163.

## O

O'Brien, Morgan J., 35, 273.
Odell, B. B., 245, 277, 309, 310.
O'Donnell, John R., 142.
Odyssey, 31.
Ogden, Rollo, 291, 292, 293, 452.
Olney, Richard, 201, 321.
Osborne, William Church, 340.
Outcault, R. F., 231.

## P

Paderewski, 12.
Pagenstecher, Albrecht, 171.
Pagenstecher, Dr. Herman, 171.
Palmer, Charles M., 211.
Panama, 10, 27, 296.
Panama Canal, 379, 420.
Panama Canal Company, 379.
Paris, 42.
Parker, Alton B., 259, 260, 261, 263, 264, 305, 306, 330.
Parker, Andrew D., 295.
Parkhurst, Rev. Charles H., 295.
Partridge, William O., 463.
Paterson, William R., 6, 376.
Patrick, William, 53, 56.
Patterson, J. M., 451.
Pattison, Gov. R. E., 182.
Paulin, L. R. E., 274, 365.
Payn, Louis F., 277.
Peckham, James, 98.
Perkins, George W., 269, 276, 427.
Philharmonic Society, N. Y., 12, 464.

Phillips, David Graham, 5, 243, 246, 247, 248, 254.
Pierce, Franklin, 304.
Pinkertons, 189.
Platt, Chas. A., 463.
Platt, Thomas C., 225, 237, 244, 251, 254.
Plutarch, 293.
Pollard, Harold S., 6, 15, 375, 392, 400.
Ponsomby, Claude, 171, 177.
Ponsomby, Sir Henry, 171.
Port Arthur, 197.
Porter, Robert P., 211.
Post, George B., 175, 463.
*Post*, N. Y. Evening, 150, 151, 196, 197, 199, 200, 226, 227, 234, 235, 283, 285, 290, 291, 452, 455.
*Post*, St. Louis, 11, 101, 104.
*Post*, Washington, 105.
*Post-Dispatch*, 11, 101, 102, 106, 107, 108, 109, 110, 131, 163, 461.
Potter, Clarkson N., 151.
Potter, Henry C., 205, 206.
Prentice, Ezra P., 278.
*Press*, New York, 211.
Press Club, N. Y., 166, 287, 466.
Press Publishing Co., 384, 461.
Pretorious, Dr. Emil, 54, 56, 57, 58, 59, 76.
Priest, Rev. William, 83.
Princeton University, 466.
*Puck*, 3, 92.
Pulitzer, Albert, 17, 40, 41, 113, 130, 210, 388.
Pulitzer Building, 49, 181, 210, 286, 373.
Pulitzer, Constance, 252, 467.
Pulitzer, Edith, 252, 467.
Pulitzer, Herbert, 252, 467.
Pulitzer, Irma, 40.
Pulitzer, Joseph, ix, x, xi, xiii, xiv, 1, 2, 3, 5, 7, 8, 9, 10, 11, 14, 15, 16, 17, 18, 19, 20, 21, 22, 24, 26, 27, 28, 29, 30, 31, 32, 33, 34, 35, 36, 37, 38, 39, 40, 41, 42, 43, 47, 48, 56, 58, 61, 62, 65, 66, 67, 68, 69, 70, 71, 72, 73, 74, 75, 77, 78, 79, 80, 82, 83, 84, 85, 87, 88, 89, 92, 97, 99, 100, 101, 102, 103, 104, 105, 106, 107, 108, 109, 110, 112, 113, 114, 115, 129, 130, 131, 132, 133, 134, 135, 136, 137, 138, 140, 141, 142, 143, 144, 145, 146, 148, 149, 150, 151, 152, 153, 154, 155, 158, 159, 160, 161, 162, 163, 164, 165, 166, 167, 168, 169, 170, 171, 172, 173, 175, 177, 179, 180, 181, 182, 183, 184, 185, 186, 187, 188, 189, 190, 191, 192, 193, 194, 195, 196, 197, 198, 199, 200, 202, 207, 208, 209, 212, 213, 214, 215, 216, 217, 218, 225, 226, 227, 228, 229, 230, 231, 232, 233, 234, 235,

## Index

236, 240, 241, 242, 243, 244, 245, 246, 247, 248, 249, 250, 251, 252, 253, 254, 255, 256, 257, 258, 259, 260, 261, 262, 263, 264, 265, 266, 269, 270, 271, 272, 273, 274, 275, 276, 278, 279, 280, 281, 286, 287, 289, 290, 291, 296, 299, 300, 305, 307, 308, 309, 311, 313, 314, 315, 318, 319, 320, 323, 325, 326, 330, 336, 338, 340, 342, 343, 344, 348, 349, 350, 356, 363, 365, 366, 367, 368, 369, 370, 371, 373, 375, 376, 377, 378, 381, 385, 386, 387, 388, 389, 390, 391, 392, 393, 394, 395, 396, 399, 401, 402, 403, 405, 407, 408, 411, 414, 415, 416, 420, 425, 428, 432, 434, 435, 436, 438, 443, 444, 445, 447, 448, 449, 450, 452, 453, 454, 455, 456, 457, 458, 459, 460, 461, 462, 463, 464, 465, 466.
Pulitzer, Mrs. Joseph, 39, 107, 130, 232, 252, 395, 415, 461.
Pulitzer, Jr., Joseph, 171, 356.
Pulitzer, Lucille Irma, 236, 447.
Pulitzer, Louise Berger, 40.
Pulitzer, Louis, 40.
Pulitzer, Philip, 40, 41.
Pulitzer, Ralph, 109, 218, 257, 258, 259, 388, 461.

### R

Rainsford, Dr. W. S., 19.
Ramsey, Capt., 44.
Ralph, Julian, 179.
Rapp, J. D., 67, 68.
Raymond, Henry J., 117.
*Recorder*, New York, 184, 186, 213, 227.
Red Sea, 393, 394.
Reed, James, 107.
Reick, William C., 45, 451, 456, 457.
Reid, Daniel G., 305.
Reid, Whitelaw, 130, 430, 450, 452, 453, 455, 458, 459, 461.
Reiner, Mathias, 41.
Remount, Camp, 43.
*Republican*, Missouri, 80, 97, 106.
*Republican*, Springfield, 151, 452, 455, 460, 461.
Rhodes, James Ford, 293, 442.
Richardson, Stephen J., 146.
Ridley & Sons, Edward, 146.
Riordan, David J., 278.
Roach, Mrs. Burke, 425.
Roach, John, 139.
Robinson, Gov. George D., 152.
Rockefeller, William, 235.
Rodin, 38.
Rogers, James T., 278.
*Romola*, Yacht, 187.
Roosevelt Hospital, 466.

Roosevelt, Theodore, 244, 245, 251, 253, 259, 261, 264, 267, 285, 286, 292, 294, 295, 296, 297, 298, 299, 300, 301, 304, 306, 307, 311, 312, 313, 314, 315, 316, 317, 318, 319, 323, 325, 326, 330, 334, 336, 338, 341, 342, 347, 350, 351, 352, 355, 356, 357, 358, 360, 361, 363, 365, 366, 367, 368, 369, 370, 371, 372, 374, 375, 378, 398, 399, 403, 405, 406, 413.
Root, Elihu, 247, 303, 358.
Rosebery, Lord, 206.
Rothschild, Lord, 37.
Rubens, 442, 443.
Russell, Chas. Edward, 216, 229.
Russo-Turkish War, 105.
Ryan, Thomas F., 162, 193, 273, 279, 303, 309, 339, 351.

### S

Saalburg, C. W., 232.
Sailor's Creek, 46.
St. Louis, 50, 51, 52, 76, 77, 85, 86, 102, 106, 107, 194, 198, 199, 208, 452.
St. Louis County, 64.
St. Louis High School, 56.
St. Louis Lottery Co., 103.
St. Louis & San Francisco R. R., 55.
St. Moritz, 457.
St. Thomas, 138.
Sampson, Admiral W. T., 240.
*Sans Peur*, Yacht, 187.
Sargent, John S., 11.
Schell, Augustus, 118.
Schleswig-Holstein, 42.
Schmidt's Hotel, 65, 66, 67, 68, 69, 70.
Schmitz, Eugene F., 311.
Schomburgk, Richard H., 201.
School of Journalism, 255, 435, 442, 455, 458, 460, 461.
Schurz, Carl, 43, 44, 54, 57, 58, 59, 61, 73, 75, 88.
Schuyler, Montgomery, 134.
Schwarzmann, Adolph, 92.
Schweninger, Dr. Ernest, 228.
*Scion of Temperance*, 105.
Scott, Col. Thomas A., 125, 126.
Scovel, Sylvester, 241.
Scripps-McRae League, 196.
Seager, Henry R., 462.
Seitz, Don C., 9, 20, 401, 420, 444, 453.
Seventy-first Regiment, 241.
Sewall, Arthur, 226.
Seward, W. H., 72, 119.
Seymour and Blair, 124.
Seymour, Horatio W., 30, 332, 397, 442.
Shafer, Ira, 162.

[ 476 ]

## Index

Shafter, Gen. W. R., 241.
Shakespeare, William, 28, 438.
*Shamrock*, Yacht, 249.
Sharp, Jacob, 161.
Shaw, J. Angus, 9.
Shaw, Leslie M., 324.
Sheldon, George R., 336, 343, 366.
Sheldon, Mrs. George R., 465.
Shepard, Edward M., 254, 419.
Sheridan, Gen. Philip H., 45, 46.
Sherman, John, 324.
Sherman, Gen. William T., 110.
Shotwell, James T., 462.
Singerley, William M., 191.
Slayback, Col. Alonzo W., 109, 110, 111.
Smith, Ballard, 5, 160, 161, 183, 188, 190, 191.
Smith, Chas. Emory, 230, 450, 452.
Smith, Delevan, 354, 357, 363, 378.
Smith, Hoke, 328.
Solden, Prof. Louis, 57.
Speck, Chas., 72.
Speed, John Gilmer, 134.
Speer, Wm. McM., 18, 269, 352, 353, 354, 356, 363.
*Staats-Zeitung*, St. Louis, 76, 100.
Standard Oil Co., 305, 320, 322, 434.
Stanley, Henry M., 59.
Stannard, Lt. Gov. E. O., 71.
*Star*, New York, 112, 113, 130.
Starin, John H., 186.
*Star-Sayings*, St. Louis, 96.
Stedman, Edmund Clarence, 118.
Steele, Chas., 427.
Steigers, Wm. C., 108, 163, 199, 233.
Stephens, Fredk. C., 268.
Stephens, John L., 296.
Sternberg, Speck von, 317.
Stevens, Thaddeus, 73, 118.
Stewart, Eugene, 107.
Stillson, Jerome B., 134.
Stimson, Henry L., 370, 377.
Stires, Rev. E. M., 19.
Stone, Gen. Chas. P., 158.
Stone, Melville E., 431, 457, 461.
Stone, William Joel, 208.
Story, Justice Isaac, 370, 442.
Stotesbury, E. T., 426.
Straight, Willard D., 29.
Strauss' Lumber Yard, 54.
Strong, Wm. L., 197.
Suez Canal, 297, 393.
Sullivan, Danl. W., 187.
*Sun*, Evening, 89, 95, 125, 160, 164, 190, 313, 462.
*Sun*, New York, 113, 129, 130, 147, 153, 169, 173.
Supreme Court, U. S., 383, 384.
Sutton, W. H., 122.

### T

Tadpoles, 78, 79.
Taft, Chas. P., 353, 372.
Taft, H. W., 353.
Taft, Wm. H., 32, 150, 319, 325, 326, 330, 331, 336, 339, 341, 342, 346, 347, 354, 355, 377, 396, 397, 399, 402, 403, 404, 405, 406, 408, 411, 412.
Talleyrand, 432.
Taylor, Gen. Chas. H., 140, 152, 163, 172, 182, 408, 451, 452, 455, 457, 458, 460, 461.
Taylor, Danl. G., 71.
*Telegram*, N. Y. Evening, 164, 181.
Tennant, John H., 195, 208, 249.
Terry, John H., 62.
Theiss, River, 41.
Thiers, 432.
Thomas, E. B., 98.
Thorndike, Ashley H., 462.
Thwaites, Norman G., 6, 15, 394, 395.
Tiffany, 10.
Tilden, Saml. J., 87, 89, 125, 443.
*Times*, New York, 113, 122, 125, 127, 130, 145, 175, 186, 280, 329, 451, 461.
Tirpitz, Admiral von, 317.
Togo, Admiral, 299.
Tracy, Gen. B. F., 237.
Tree, Beerbohm, 28.
Trent, Wm. P., 462.
*Tribune*, New York, 113, 120, 122, 125, 130, 175, 461, 462.
*Truth*, 130.
Tully, Wm. J., 278.
Tuohy, James M., 5, 394.
Turner, George W., 163, 174, 179, 183, 184, 186, 187.
Turner Hall, 62.
Tuthill, Lt., 119.
Twain, Mark, 257.
Tweed, Wm. M., 85.
Twenty-fifth Infantry, 314.
Tyler, C. W., 33.
Typographical Union No. 6, 142, 143.

### U

*Union*, St. Louis, 97, 98.
United States, 65, 431, 462.
University of Pennsylvania, 463.

### V

Vallendingham, C. L., 105.
Vanderbilt, W. H., 140.
Van Hamm, C. M., 9, 23, 300, 308, 352, 353, 354, 363, 367, 370, 378.
Van Wyck, Augustus, 245.

## Index

Van Wyck, Robt. B., 237, 245.
Van Zile, Edward S., 161.
Vaughn, Cardinal, 218.
Venezuela, 201, 238.
Verne, Jules, 425.
Victoria, Queen, 142.
Villa Cynthia, 38.
Villard, Oswald Garrison, 452, 455.
Von Noorden, Dr. Carl H., 393.

### W

Wade, Benj. F., 73, 118.
Wakefield, Alanson B., 102, 103.
Wales, Prince of, 205.
Ward, Artemus, 173.
Wardman, Ervin, 278.
Warren, Whitney, 463.
Washington, Booker T., 260.
Washington, George, 443.
Watson & Sons, G. L., 289.
Watterson, Henry, 160, 408.
Waynesborough, 46.
Webb, Gen. James Watson, 117.
Webster, Daniel, 9.
Webster, Sydney, 300, 304.
Weill, Joseph, 107.
Welge, Theodore, 65, 72.
Wells-Fargo Bank, 304.
Wells, Saml. Calvin, 461.
Wemple, W. N., 278.
Western Union, 37.
Westinghouse, George, 273.
*Westliche Post*, 51, 58, 60, 61, 63, 64, 65, 66, 67, 68, 74, 75.
Wetmore, Elizabeth Bisland, 26.
Wheeler, A. C., 134.
Whibley, Chas., 7.
Whistler, J. A. McNeill, 7, 438.
White, Andrew D., 455, 456, 458, 459, 460.
White, Chief Justice, 383.
White, Florence D., 9, 199, 233.
White, Horace, 430.
White Star Line, 13.
Whitley, Jonas, 352, 353.
Whitman, Chas. S., 389.
Whitney, Dorothy, 29.
Whitney, Wm. C., 29, 138, 151, 162, 172, 188, 193.
Wiggins Ferry, 50.
Williams, Alexander S., 295.
Williams, Chas. R., 368, 378.

Williams, Major Geo. F., 146.
Williams, Saml. M., 6, 31, 256.
Williams, Dr. Talcott, 457, 461, 466.
William II, 207, 317.
Wilson, Woodrow, 293, 327, 328, 405, 410, 442.
Wilshire, Gaylord, 432.
Winchester, Battle of, 45.
Winton, Gen. Francis de, 5.
Wise, Henry A., 377, 382.
Woerner, Judge J. G., 57.
Wolcott & Hume, 99.
Wood, Fernando, 118.
Woods, Judge, 208.
Work, Frank, 425.
*World*, The, xi, xiii, xiv, 2, 3, 4, 11, 12, 16, 17, 18, 22, 25, 27, 28, 30, 31, 32, 33, 34, 35, 37, 114, 115, 118, 119, 120, 121, 123, 125, 126, 127, 129, 130, 131, 132, 133, 134, 136, 137, 139, 140, 141, 142, 143, 144, 145, 146, 147, 148, 149, 150, 151, 152, 153, 154, 156, 157, 158, 159, 160, 161, 162, 163, 164, 165, 168, 171, 172, 173, 177, 178, 179, 180, 181, 182, 183, 184, 185, 186, 187, 188, 189, 190, 191, 192, 193, 194, 195, 197, 198, 200, 202, 203, 205, 206, 207, 208, 210, 211, 212, 213, 214, 215, 216, 217, 220, 224, 226, 229, 230, 231, 232, 233, 234, 237, 239, 240, 241, 242, 245, 247, 249, 251, 253, 255, 259, 264, 267, 268, 269, 276, 282, 286, 290, 291, 292, 294, 295, 296, 298, 304, 306, 308, 309, 313, 314, 318, 319, 321, 326, 331, 332, 335, 336, 337, 338, 346, 347, 349, 350, 352, 356, 357, 358, 360, 363, 364, 365, 366, 367, 368, 369, 370, 371, 372, 373, 377, 381, 383, 385, 389, 390, 391, 394, 396, 401, 402, 407, 411, 414, 416, 418, 430, 431, 435, 440, 445, 450, 451, 453, 456, 459, 461.
*World*, Evening, 16, 164, 165, 168, 190, 428.
World Building and Loan Association, 159.
Worthington, Catherine Louise, 90.
Wrench, Dr. O. E., 377.
Wyndham, Chas., 27.

### Y

Yaeger, H. C., 72.
York, Duke of, 205.